Deke McClelland's

Look & Learn™ Photoshop®

version **6**

Deke McClelland

with additional content by
Amy Thomas Buscaglia
& Daniel McClelland

A Type & Graphics Book

IDG BOOKS WORLDWIDE

IDG Books Worldwide, Inc.
An International Data Group Company

Foster City, CA ✦ Chicago, IL ✦ Indianapolis, IN ✦ New York, NY

Deke McClelland's
Look & Learn™ Photoshop® 6

Published by
IDG Books Worldwide, Inc.
An International Data Group Company
919 E. Hillsdale Blvd., Suite 400
Foster City, CA 94404
www.idgbooks.com (IDG Books Worldwide Web site)

ISBN: 0-7645-3508-0

Library of Congress Catalog Card No.: 00-109637

Printed in the United States of America

10 9 8 7 6 5 4 3 2 1

1O/QW/RR/QQ/NY

Distributed in the United States by IDG Books Worldwide, Inc.

Distributed by CDG Books Canada Inc. for Canada; by Transworld Publishers Limited in the United Kingdom; by IDG Norge Books for
Norway; by IDG Sweden Books for Sweden; by IDG Books Australia Publishing Corporation Pty. Ltd. for Australia and New Zealand; by
TransQuest Publishers Pte Ltd. for Singapore, Malaysia, Thailand, Indonesia, and Hong Kong; by Gotop Information Inc. for Taiwan; by
ICG Muse, Inc. for Japan; by Intersoft for South Africa; by Eyrolles for France; by International Thomson Publishing for Germany, Austria,
and Switzerland; by Distribuidora Cuspide for Argentina; by LR International for Brazil; by Galileo Libros for Chile; by Ediciones ZETA
S.C.R. Ltda. for Peru; by WS Computer Publishing Corporation, Inc., for the Philippines; by Contemporanea de Ediciones for Venezuela;
by Express Computer Distributors for the Caribbean and West Indies; by Micronesia Media Distributor, Inc. for Micronesia; by Chips
Computadoras S.A. de C.V. for Mexico; by Editorial Norma de Panama S.A. for Panama; by American Bookshops for Finland.

For general information on IDG Books Worldwide's books in the U.S., please call our Consumer Customer Service department at
800-762-2974. For reseller information, including discounts and premium sales, please call our Reseller Customer Service department
at 800-434-3422.

For information on where to purchase IDG Books Worldwide's books outside the U.S., please contact our International Sales department
at 317-572-3993 or fax 317-572-4002.

For consumer information on foreign language translations, please contact our Customer Service department at 800-434-3422, fax
317-572-4002, or e-mail rights@idgbooks.com.

For information on licensing foreign or domestic rights, please phone +1-650-653-7098.

For sales inquiries and special prices for bulk quantities, please contact our Order Services department at 800-434-3422 or write to
the address above.

For information on using IDG Books Worldwide's books in the classroom or for ordering examination copies, please contact our
Educational Sales department at 800-434-2086 or fax 317-572-4005.

For press review copies, author interviews, or other publicity information, please contact our Public Relations department at
650-653-7000 or fax 650-653-7500.

For authorization to photocopy items for corporate, personal, or educational use, please contact Copyright Clearance Center, 222
Rosewood Drive, Danvers, MA 01923, or fax 978-750-4470.

About The Author

Fifteen years ago, Deke McClelland oversaw the implementation of the first personal computer-based production department in Boulder, Colorado. He later served as artistic director for one of the earliest all-digital service bureaus in the United States. He wrote his first book, *Desktop Publishing Type & Graphics*, specifically to educate his clients.

These days, Deke is the author of more than 50 books published in 25 different languages with 3 million copies in print. Among these is the award-winning *Photoshop Bible* series, published by IDG Books Worldwide. Now in their eighth year, the *Bibles* have sold more copies than any other guides on computer graphics.

In 1989, Deke won the Benjamin Franklin Award for Best Computer Book. Since then, he has received honors from the Society for Technical Communication (once in 1994 and twice in 1999), the American Society of Business Press Editors (1995), the Western Publications Association (1999), and the Computer Press Association (1990, 1992, 1994, 1995, 1997, and twice in 1999). In 1999, Book Bytes named Deke its Author of the Year.

Other best-selling titles include *Photoshop For Dummies*, *Photoshop Studio Secrets*, and *Web Design Studio Secrets* (all IDG Books), as well as *Real World Illustrator* and *Real World Digital Photography* (both Peachpit Press). He also serves as host to the video training series *Total Photoshop*, *Total InDesign*, and *Total Illustrator* (all Total Training). He is a long-time contributing editor for *Macworld* magazine.

Deke lives in Boulder County with his family, enchanting Elle and magnificent Max.

Production Credits

Series designer: Deke McClelland
Project editor: Amy Thomas Buscaglia
Acquisitions editor: Michael Roney
Technical editor: Ted Padova
Copy editor: Susan Pink
Indexer: Sharon Hilgenberg

Additional Content

Chapters 12, 15, & 17: Amy Thomas Buscaglia
Chapters 16, 18, & 19: Daniel McClelland
Index art & layout: Barbara Obermeier

Stock images courtesy of Corbis Royalty-Free Collection.

Original images captured with an Olympus C-3030 Zoom digital camera & a Umax PowerLook 3000 flatbed scanner.

Page design and composition in Adobe InDesign.

ABOUT IDG BOOKS WORLDWIDE

Welcome to the world of IDG Books Worldwide.

IDG Books Worldwide, Inc., is a subsidiary of International Data Group, the world's largest publisher of computer-related information and the leading global provider of information services on information technology. IDG was founded more than 30 years ago by Patrick J. McGovern and now employs more than 9,000 people worldwide. IDG publishes more than 290 computer publications in over 75 countries. More than 90 million people read one or more IDG publications each month.

Launched in 1990, IDG Books Worldwide is today the #1 publisher of best-selling computer books in the United States. We are proud to have received eight awards from the Computer Press Association in recognition of editorial excellence and three from Computer Currents' First Annual Readers' Choice Awards. Our best-selling ...*For Dummies*® series has more than 50 million copies in print with translations in 31 languages. IDG Books Worldwide, through a joint venture with IDG's Hi-Tech Beijing, became the first U.S. publisher to publish a computer book in the People's Republic of China. In record time, IDG Books Worldwide has become the first choice for millions of readers around the world who want to learn how to better manage their businesses.

Our mission is simple: Every one of our books is designed to bring extra value and skill-building instructions to the reader. Our books are written by experts who understand and care about our readers. The knowledge base of our editorial staff comes from years of experience in publishing, education, and journalism — experience we use to produce books to carry us into the new millennium. In short, we care about books, so we attract the best people. We devote special attention to details such as audience, interior design, use of icons, and illustrations. And because we use an efficient process of authoring, editing, and desktop publishing our books electronically, we can spend more time ensuring superior content and less time on the technicalities of making books.

You can count on our commitment to deliver high-quality books at competitive prices on topics you want to read about. At IDG Books Worldwide, we continue in the IDG tradition of delivering quality for more than 30 years. You'll find no better book on a subject than one from IDG Books Worldwide.

John Kilcullen
Chairman and CEO
IDG Books Worldwide, Inc.

Eighth Annual
Computer Press
Awards ≥1992

Ninth Annual
Computer Press
Awards ≥1993

Tenth Annual
Computer Press
Awards ≥1994

Eleventh Annual
Computer Press
Awards ≥1995

IDG is the world's leading IT media, research and exposition company. Founded in 1964, IDG had 1997 revenues of $2.05 billion and has more than 9,000 employees worldwide. IDG offers the widest range of media options that reach IT buyers in 75 countries representing 95% of worldwide IT spending. IDG's diverse product and services portfolio spans six key areas including print publishing, online publishing, expositions and conferences, market research, education and training, and global marketing services. More than 90 million people read one or more of IDG's 290 magazines and newspapers, including IDG's leading global brands — Computerworld, PC World, Network World, Macworld and the Channel World family of publications. IDG Books Worldwide is one of the fastest-growing computer book publishers in the world, with more than 700 titles in 36 languages. The "...For Dummies®" series alone has more than 50 million copies in print. IDG offers online users the largest network of technology-specific Web sites around the world through IDG.net (http://www.idg.net), which comprises more than 225 targeted Web sites in 55 countries worldwide. International Data Corporation (IDC) is the world's largest provider of information technology data, analysis and consulting, with research centers in over 41 countries and more than 400 research analysts worldwide. IDG World Expo is a leading producer of more than 168 globally branded conferences and expositions in 35 countries including E3 (Electronic Entertainment Expo), Macworld Expo, ComNet, Windows World Expo, ICE (Internet Commerce Expo), Agenda, DEMO, and Spotlight. IDG's training subsidiary, ExecuTrain, is the world's largest computer training company, with more than 230 locations worldwide and 785 training courses. IDG Marketing Services helps industry-leading IT companies build international brand recognition by developing global integrated marketing programs via IDG's print, online and exposition products worldwide. Further information about the company can be found at www.idg.com.

1/26/00

Look & Learn™

There are lots of ways to teach **computing** and **electronic design**. Books, videos, online courses, live seminars—I've done (and continue to do) them all. But while each method appeals to a specific learning style, none works so well as the inevitable training device of the future: a syringe to the brain. One day, you'll plunk down **$19.99** at your local InfoMart and receive a cylinder of pure knowledge. Poke it in, push the plunger, and **zap!** You've upgraded your head.

Sadly, I got a **C** in chemistry. (One experiment in particular caught on fire, but that's another story.) So I'm hardly qualified to invent the **information elixir**. But it got me thinking. How can I accomplish the next best thing?

The answer is a book. A **highly visual book** that conveys information «FAST» by showing it. A relatively short book «CONCISE» that you can absorb in a few sittings. A book that remains affordable by **maximizing** «EFFICIENT» page space. A book that page after page «COMPLETE» teaches the **most reliable techniques** in the business, and does so as **instantaneously** as humanly possible. A «LOOK & LEARN» book where you **look** at a page and, without delay, **learn** precisely what you need to know.

Fast   concise   efficient   complete.

These are the watchwords for **Look & Learn**, a new series of computer training guides designed for the visual mind.

How does it work? For starters, every word on every page relates to a graphic. This means **features and steps appear in context**, so you can see how they work. It also permits you to hone in on the stuff you're most keen to learn. See an option, read the explanation, and you're ready to get back to work.

To speed your learning, dictionary-like **thumbtabs** show you where chapters start and stop. Each chapter gets a **unique icon**, so you know where you are in a flash. Contents @ A Glance (**page vii**) uses the thumbtabs to show you where to go.

Tips and insights 🅣🅘🅟 are **clearly labeled** and highlighted. Commands, options, and other literal software text appear in bold type. **Color-coded callouts** reference related information within a discussion. And when I decide to refer you to another section, I tell you the **exact page number** to go to. (Shouldn't every book?)

Finally, when you're in a hurry to find information about a specific topic, turn to Look It Up & Learn (**page 289**), the only index that uses both words and pictures to point you toward the answers you need most.

Throw in **step-by-step tutorials**; succinct, no-nonsense writing; and unflinching discussions of even the most complex topics, and you have what I consider to be the best training value on the market. I hope you'll agree with me that no reference provides so much, so quickly, and so clearly as **Look & Learn**.

Contents
@ A Glance

Detailed Contents *with* steps

Detailed Contents with steps

⑥ Apply Color & Gradients   79

Learn everything you need to know about defining colors and applying them to an image.

⑦ Paint & Retouch   91

Use Photoshop's paint and edit tools to add brushstrokes and fix defects in an image.

⑧ Create & Modify Layers   103

So long as an element resides on its own layer, you can edit it independently of the rest of the image.

⑨ Define Channels & Masks   115

Use alpha channels, quick masks, and layer masks to define highly accurate selection outlines.

⑩ Blend & Stylize Layers   135

Learn how to blend layers as well as apply drop shadows, glows, and beveled edges.

Detailed Contents *with* steps

⑪ Draw Vector Shapes 157

Draw editable shapes and clipping path outlines that output at the full resolution of your printer.

⑫ Create & Edit Type 169

Photoshop's type capabilities are perfect for creating logos, headlines, and Web text.

⑬ Adjust & Correct Colors 183

Learn how to change the colors in an image to make them appear more like those in real life.

⑭ Apply Filters & Effects 213

Use Photoshop's exhaustive collection of filters to enhance an image and create special effects.

Detailed Contents *with* steps

Get To Know Photoshop

Sections @ A Glance

This chapter offers a basic but essential introduction to Photoshop 6.0. Not only will it help you and Photoshop become more familiar with each other, you'll also need this information to make sense of future chapters.

Welcome to Version 6 of **Adobe Photoshop**. Photoshop is an *image editor*, which means it lets you modify photographs and scanned artwork. And I'm not talking about just *any* image editor either. Photoshop is the most popular and arguably the most powerful image editor on the market.

If you're new to Photoshop or trying to get up to speed with Version 6, this chapter provides an introductory tour of the program. You'll learn how to work in Photoshop's on-screen environment, called the *interface*. You'll also learn how to use your mouse, make Photoshop run better, and get help.

Some of Photoshop's features are different on a **PC** running **Microsoft Windows** than they are on an **Apple Macintosh** computer. But don't worry, I'll say "under Windows" or "on a Mac" so you can identify these differences at a glance.

The Photoshop Desktop, Windows

A *toolbox*
B *menu bar*
C *application title bar*
D *image window title bar*
E *options bar*
G *foreground image*
H *background image*
I *minimize*
J *maximize*
K *close*

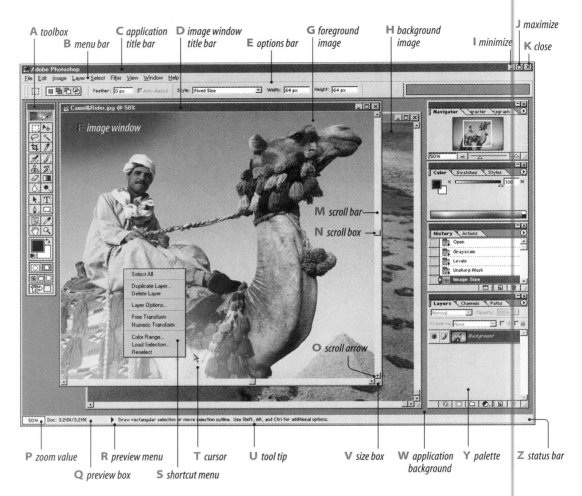

F *image window*

M *scroll bar*
N *scroll box*
O *scroll arrow*

P *zoom value*
Q *preview box*
R *preview menu*
S *shortcut menu*
T *cursor*
U *tool tip*
V *size box*
W *application background*
Y *palette*
Z *status bar*

A toolbox

The toolbox contains *tools* that you can use in the image window (F). To select a tool, click its icon in the toolbox. To find out how to use a tool, consult the tool tip (U).

B menu bar

Click on a name in the menu bar to display a list, or *menu*, containing a series of *commands*. Choose a command by clicking on it. A command followed by three dots—such as **New...** or **Open...**—displays a window of options called a *dialog box*. Otherwise, the command works right away.

C application title bar (Windows)

On the PC, the name of an application appears at the top of its window. Click this *title bar* to make Photoshop the active application. Drag the title bar to move Photoshop so you can see a program or window behind it. If Photoshop is really in your way, hide it by clicking the minimize button (I).

D image window title bar

Each open image is topped by a title bar that lists the name of the saved version of the image. If you've never saved the image and you didn't name the image when creating it, the name reads **Untitled**.

The Photoshop Desktop, Macintosh

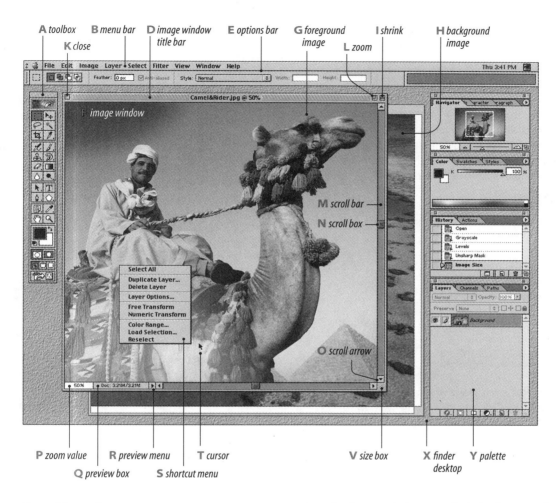

A toolbox   B menu bar   D image window title bar   E options bar   G foreground image   I shrink   H background image   L zoom   K close

F image window

M scroll bar
N scroll box

Select All

Duplicate Layer...
Delete Layer

Layer Options...

Free Transform
Numeric Transform

Color Range...
Load Selection...
Reselect

O scroll arrow

P zoom value   R preview menu   T cursor   V size box   X finder desktop   Y palette
Q preview box   S shortcut menu

E options bar

New to Photoshop 6, the options bar contains settings that you can use to modify the behavior of the active tool. If the options bar is hidden, press the **enter** (Win) or **return** (Mac) key to display it.

F image window

Each open image appears inside a frame, or *window*. This allows you to open several images at a time.

G foreground image

You can open several images in Photoshop, but you can edit just one image at a time. Click on the title

bar of an image window to make it the *foreground image*. Then you can edit it.

> *tip* To cycle an image to the foreground, press **ctrl+tab** (Win) or **control-tab** (Mac). On the Mac, move a window without bringing it to the foreground by pressing **command** and dragging it.

H background image

All other image windows are *background images*. You can view background images, but you can't edit them. To edit an image, you have to click on its title bar and make it the foreground image.

I minimize (Win)/shrink (Mac)

If you use Windows, click the *minimize button* in the application title bar (C) to hide the Photoshop application window. An **Adobe Photoshop** button appears in the Windows taskbar. Click it to redisplay Photoshop.

You can also click the minimize button in the image window title bar (D) to hide a single image. The hidden image shrinks down to a small title bar. To redisplay the image, click the title bar to display a menu, and then choose **Restore**.

Or click the *restore button*, which is the first of the three buttons on the right side of the title bar.

On the Mac, each image window title bar (D) includes a *shrink icon*. Click it to collapse the window so only the title bar remains visible. Click the shrink icon again to redisplay the image.

J maximize (Windows)

Under Windows, click the *maximize button* in the application title bar (C) to fill the screen with the Photoshop application window. This is useful when you want to hide all open programs and focus exclusively on Photoshop.

> *tip* You can also click the maximize button in the image window title bar (D) to expand an image to fill the entire Photoshop application window.

K close

Click the *close button* in the image window title bar (D) to close an open image. If you've changed the image since it was last saved, Photoshop asks you whether you want to save the changes.

> *tip* Under Windows, click the close button in the application title bar (C) to exit Photoshop. The program will ask you to save all open images that have been modified since they were last saved.

L zoom (Macintosh)

On the Mac, click the *zoom icon* in the image window title bar (D) to fit the image window so it snugly surrounds the boundaries of the image. The only purpose of this feature is to keep things nice and tidy on screen. If you're feeling fastidious, knock yourself out.

M scroll bar

Every image window includes two *scroll bars*, one vertical and one horizontal. Click inside the scroll bar to pan the image inside the image window and reveal hidden details. Click above the scroll box (N) in the vertical scroll bar to pan up, click below the scroll box to scroll down. For more on scrolling, read Scroll Bars & Hand Tool on page 38 of Chapter 3.

N scroll box

Drag the *scroll box* to pan the image inside the image window. For example, drag the scroll box in the horizontal scroll bar to the right to pan the image to the right inside the image window.

O scroll arrow

Click a scroll arrow to pan the view of the image very slightly. Alternatively, you can press **shift-page up** or **shift-page down**, as I explain in Page Up & Page Down on page 38 of Chapter 3.

P zoom value

Change the size at which the image appears on screen by entering a new value in the *zoom value box* and pressing the **enter** (Win) or **return** (Mac) key. Use the **up arrow** (↑) or **down arrow** (↓) key to nudge the value higher or lower.

Q preview box

The preview box lists the size of the image in memory. You can also click in the preview box to see how the image will fit on the page when printed. For more information, read Image Preview & Status Bar on page 15.

R preview menu

Click the arrowhead to the right of the preview box (Q) to display a list of options. Choose an option to change the information displayed in the preview box. See Image Preview & Status Bar on page 15 for more information.

S shortcut menu

Under Windows, click with the right mouse button to bring up a *shortcut menu* of options that pertain to the active tool. If your Macintosh mouse doesn't have a right mouse button—as most do not—then press the **control** key and click. The shortcut menu is often said to be *context sensitive* because its commands change to suit what you're doing. For more information, read The Shortcut Menu on page 14.

T cursor

The *cursor* moves on screen to track the movement of your mouse. The appearance of the cursor changes to reflect the active tool or operation. To learn more, read Mouse & Cursor on pages 6 and 7.

U tool tip

Under Windows, the Photoshop status bar (Z) offers a brief explanation of how to use the active tool. Whether you use Windows or a Mac, you can see the name of a tool and its keyboard shortcut by hovering the cursor over the tool icon.

V size box

Drag the lower-right corner of the image window to change the size of the window.

W application background (Win)

The Windows version of Photoshop includes a flat-colored *application background* that hides programs running behind it. Double-click the application background to open an image stored on disk.

X finder desktop (Macintosh)

On the Mac, there is no application background, so you may be able to see other programs running behind Photoshop. If this becomes distracting, choose **Hide Others** from the **Application** menu at the far right side of the menu bar.

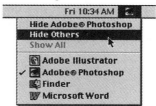

> *tip* The background behind Photoshop is the *Finder desktop*. If you click this background, the Mac transfers you from Photoshop to the Finder. Press the **option** key and click the Finder desktop to hide Photoshop.

Y palette

A *palette* is a floating window of options that can remain visible on screen regardless of what you're doing. Move a palette by dragging the horizontal title bar at the top of the palette. Each palette contains multiple *panels*. Switch between panels by clicking on the *tabs* below the title bar. For more information, read Palettes & Panels on page 17.

Z status bar (Windows)

Under Windows, the status bar contains the zoom value (P), preview box and menu (Q and R), and tool tip (U). If you can't find the status bar, display it by choosing **Show Status Bar** from the **Window** menu.

On the Mac, the zoom value (P), preview box (Q), and preview menu (R) appear at the bottom of each image window. So a status bar is unnecessary.

Mouse & Cursor

The mouse is the digital artist's best friend. It's your primary means for selecting elements, moving them, painting brushstrokes, and otherwise modifying the appearance of an image. A mouse doesn't have to be a palm-sized plastic block either. It can be any *pointing device*, whether a trackpad, a trackball, a pressure-sensitive tablet—anything that's capable of grabbing and manipulating what you see on your monitor.

The cursor (sometimes called the *pointer*) is the mouse's on-screen doppelganger. It moves as your mouse moves. The cursor also shows you what kind of operation is occurring. Photoshop provides hundreds of different kinds of cursors. Some of the most representative appear at right.

	A arrow			I light source	
	B marquee			J touch	
	C add marquee			K hold	
	D move			L type	
	E cut			M eyedropper	
	F clone			N precise	
	G brush			O hand	
	H art history			P wait	

A arrow

The arrow cursor is the most common cursor in Photoshop. It appears when you move the cursor over the menu bar, toolbox, scroll bar, or some other interface element. By default, the Windows cursor is white; the Macintosh arrow cursor is solid black.

B marquee

By default, the rectangular marquee is active the first time you start Photoshop. When you use this tool in the image window, the cursor appears as a cross.

C add marquee

This is how the marquee cursor looks when you press the **shift** key. The tiny plus sign (+) next to the cross indicates that the next selection you draw will be added to the existing selection. Meanwhile, a minus sign (–) indicates that the selection will be subtracted; an **x** shows that Photoshop will maintain the intersection of two selections. All demonstrate how Photoshop communicates operations via the cursor.

D move

When you see this cursor, you can drag to move one or more layers. The cursor appears when the move tool is active. It also appears if you press the **ctrl** (Win) or **command** (Mac) key when using any other tool.

E cut

Position the move tool cursor over a selection to see an arrowhead with a tiny pair of scissors. This tells you that dragging will *cut* the selection, which means to move the selected pixels and leave a hole filled with the background color.

F clone

Press the **alt** (Win) or **option** (Mac) key when moving a selection or layer to create a copy. Copying an image element without using the **Copy** command or replacing the contents of the Clipboard is called *cloning*.

G brush

When using a paint or edit tool, Photoshop shows you a cursor in the shape of the active brush in the **Brushes** palette. This helps you predict the outcome of brushstrokes and free-form edits.

H art history

You can change the appearance of all paint and edit cursors by choosing **Edit ➡ Preferences ➡ Display & Cursors**. Then select **Standard** from the **Painting Cursors** options to make the cursor match the tool. This identifies which tool is selected (in this case, the art history brush), but makes it more difficult to anticipate the effects of your edits.

I light source

Photoshop offers a handful of cursors that appear exclusively inside specific dialog boxes. This particular cursor lets you add a light source inside the **Lighting Effects** dialog box (which you access by choosing **Filter➥Render➥Lighting Effects**).

J touch

Other cursors are specific to palettes. Move the cursor over an item in the **Layers**, **Channels**, **Paths**, **History**, or **Actions** palette to see a hand with a raised index finger. Click to select the item in the palette.

K hold

Often, a cursor changes when you drag. For example, dragging with the touch cursor produces this hold cursor. As soon as you release the mouse button, the touch cursor returns.

L type

Select the type tool to see the familiar *I-beam cursor* found in word processors and other text editors. The difference is that in Photoshop, clicking with the type tool creates a new layer. You can also drag with the cursor to highlight text that you want to edit.

M eyedropper

This common cursor appears both when you select the eyedropper tool and when you move the cursor outside of a color adjustment dialog box.

N precise

Press the **caps lock** key to turn on the *precise cursors*. Depending on the active tool, the precise cursor appears as either a crosshair or, in this case, a target. This helps you to better identify the *hot spot* of the cursor, which is the point at which the click occurs.

O hand

Press and hold the **spacebar** to access the hand tool. Then drag to scroll the image inside the window. For complete information on scrolling, read Scroll Bars & Hand Tool on page 38 of Chapter 3.

P wait

When performing a complex operation, Photoshop asks you to wait. By default, the Windows cursor changes to an hourglass, and the Macintosh cursor becomes a watch. Your choices are to wait for the operation to complete or switch to another program and let Photoshop finish up in the background.

Common Mouse Operations

You know how to use your mouse, but you may not know the names for what you're doing. To make sure you and I are speaking the same language, here's a brief glossary of mouse operations:

Click

Click by pressing and releasing the mouse button in rapid succession. If your mouse offers two or more buttons, click the left one.

Right-click

All PCs and some Macs include mice with multiple buttons. To *right-click* is to press and release the right mouse button, which displays a handy shortcut menu of commands relevant to the active tool or operation.

Key-click

Some operations require you to press a key and click the left mouse button. For example, *ctrl-click* means to press and hold the **ctrl** key and click.

Mouse down

Some tricks require you to hold down the left mouse button for an extended period of time. For example, *mouse down* on an icon in the toolbox to display a flyout menu of alternative tools.

Move

To *move* the mouse is to move it without pressing any button.

Hover

To *hover* the cursor is to move it to a specific location and leave it there for a moment. For example, hover the cursor over a tool icon to see the name of the tool.

Drag

Drag the mouse by pressing the left mouse button, moving the mouse, and then releasing the button. Drag the mouse to move a selection or layer, or to reposition an item in a palette.

The Toolbox

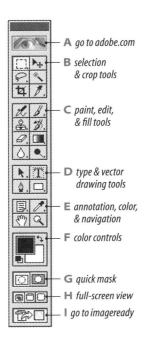

- **A** *go to adobe.com*
- **B** *selection & crop tools*
- **C** *paint, edit, & fill tools*
- **D** *type & vector drawing tools*
- **E** *annotation, color, & navigation*
- **F** *color controls*
- **G** *quick mask*
- **H** *full-screen view*
- **I** *go to imageready*

The Photoshop toolbox contains *tools* and *buttons*. When you click a tool, you select that tool. You can then use the tool to edit the foreground image. The paintbrush tool paints colored lines, the type tool creates independent layers of text, and so on. On the other hand, when you click a button, an operation occurs immediately, much as if you had chosen a command. Photoshop's tools are clustered in the central portion of the toolbox (B, C, D, and E). The buttons appear at the top (A) and the bottom (F, G, H, and I) of the toolbox.

A go to adobe.com

Click the eye icon to display the Adobe Online screen, which offers you access to a wide variety of training and support options from Adobe's Web site, including full lessons from my video series, **Total Photoshop** from Total Training (*www.totaltraining.com*). If you're connected to the Internet, click the **Refresh** button to get started.

B selection & crop tools

The first cluster of six tools lets you select the specific portion of an image that you want to edit, as discussed in Chapter 5, Make Selections. If you look closely, you'll see that several of these tools feature tiny right-pointing arrowheads. Click and hold on a tool icon with an arrowhead to display a *flyout menu* of alternative tool choices.

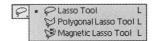

> *tip* To cycle through each of the tools in the flyout menu, press the **alt** (Win) or **option** (Mac) key and click the tool icon.

C paint, edit, & fill tools

The second cluster of tools lets you edit a photograph by painting inside the image window. You can even clone portions of an image to cover up flaws and imperfections. See Chapter 7, Paint & Retouch, for complete information.

D type & vector drawing tools

Photoshop 6 lets you add high-resolution, vector-based artwork to your images. It's like having a little bit of Illustrator built into Photoshop. To find out more, consult Chapter 11, Draw Vector Shapes, and Chapter 12, Create & Edit Type.

E annotation, color, & navigation

The final group of tools is a bit of a hodgepodge. The first lets you add notes and sounds to your image, as discussed in Chapter 4, Personalize Photoshop. The second, the eyedropper, lifts a color from the image so you can apply the color elsewhere (see Chapter 6, Apply Color & Gradients). The last two tools let you move around the image window to get a better view, as documented in Chapter 3, Open, Navigate, Save.

F color controls

The color controls comprise four icons, all devoted to the relatively modest task of adjusting the foreground and background colors. Click an icon to select or change a color. For the full story, see Eyedroppers & Color Controls on pages 81 and 82 of Chapter 6.

G quick mask

Click the right-hand button to enter the quick mask mode, which lets you draw precise selections, as explained in Chapter 9, Define Channels & Masks. To exit the quick mask mode, click the left-hand button.

H full-screen view

These buttons let you fill the screen with the foreground image. The first button shows the image in a normal window, the second fills the screen, and the third hides the menu bar and sets the image against a black background.

tip The F key cycles between the three window modes. Press F once for the full-screen view, again to hide the menu bars, and a third time to return to the standard image window. To hide or show the menu bar in either of the full-screen modes, press shift-F.

tip Whether you click a button or press the F key, Photoshop changes the foreground window only. To change *all* open images to a view, press the shift key and click the desired button. Then press ctrl+tab (Win) or control-tab (Mac) to advance one-by-one through a slide show of images.

I go to imageready

Click this button to switch from Photoshop to its companion Web graphics program, ImageReady. If ImageReady isn't already running, clicking this button starts it up. To return to Photoshop, click the similar button at the bottom of the ImageReady toolbox.

tip One more tip: To hide the toolbox and all palettes, press the tab key. This can be especially useful when working in one of the full-screen modes. Press tab again to bring the toolbox back.

The Options Bar

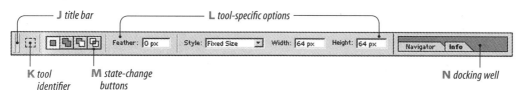

J title bar   L tool-specific options

K tool identifier   M state-change buttons   N docking well

Photoshop 6 replaces the familiar **Options** palette with the horizontal options bar. Situated immediately below the menu bar, the options bar lets you modify the behavior of the selected tool. It's convenient, mobile, and constantly available.

J title bar

By default, the options bar is fixed to the top of the screen. However, you can move it by dragging the title bar. Drag the title bar to the top or bottom of the screen to fix the options bar in place so the docking well (N) is visible.

K tool identifier

Click to see two commands that reset the options to their defaults.

L tool-specific options

The specific options offered by the options bar vary depending on the active tool.

M state-change buttons

The options in the options bar are like those in any palette. The exception is the *state-change button*, which looks something like a tool but is actually an icon that changes the way the active tool works.

N docking well

Drag a palette tab into the docking well on the far right side of the options bar to drop the palette into safe hiding. See Palettes & Panels on page 17 for complete information on docking.

tip When you press tab to hide the toolbox, you hide the options bar as well. To display the options bar, press enter (Win) or return (Mac). Handily, this also activates the first option in the options bar.

Menus & Commands

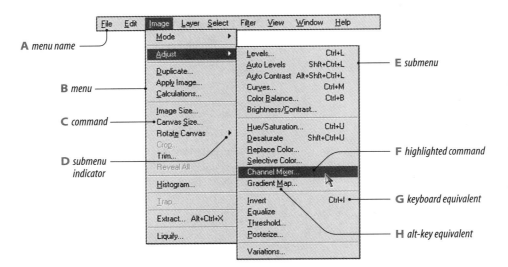

A *menu name*

B *menu*

C *command*

D *submenu indicator*

E *submenu*

F *highlighted command*

G *keyboard equivalent*

H *alt-key equivalent*

Photoshop's extensive network of menus and commands permits you to open and close images, correct the colors and focus of a photograph, and even change the way Photoshop behaves. In the next two pages, I explain how menus and commands work. I also introduce you to Photoshop's menu bar so you can better predict where you are most likely to find a desired feature.

A menu name

Every menu has a name, starting with **File** and ending with **Help**. The name identifies the contents of the menu. For example, the name **Image** tells you that the **Image** menu (L) contains commands that you can use to adjust the general appearance of the image.

B menu

Click a menu name to display a menu. Folks sometimes call this a *drop-down list* because it drops down from the menu bar, but plain old *menu* is simpler, don't you think?

C command

The command is the actual nut of the menu, the thing that the menu is all about. Because it's so important, any reference to a command in this book is formatted in bold, as in **Canvas Size** or **Trim**.

D submenu indicator

An arrowhead to the right of a command name tells you that choosing the command brings up a *submenu* of additional commands.

E submenu

A submenu is nothing more than a menu that happens to be buried (or *nested*) inside another menu. Frankly, submenus are a pain in the neck—they make the process of hunting down a command that much more difficult. I try to make the trail to a command as clear as possible using the ➥ symbol. For example, if I ask you to choose **Image➥Adjust➥Curves**, click the **Image** menu, then click the **Adjust** command, and finally click the **Curves** command.

F highlighted command

As you move your cursor over the menu, the command name under the cursor *highlights*. Click on a highlighted command name to *choose* it.

G keyboard equivalent

Many commands have *keyboard equivalents*, also called *shortcuts*. A keyboard equivalent is a combination of keys that you can press instead of choosing the command manually. For example, the shortcut for the **Curves** command is **ctrl+M** (Win) or command-M

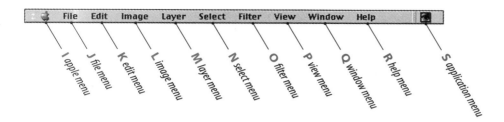

(Mac). Under Windows, press and hold the **ctrl** key and then press M; on the Mac, press and hold **command** (the key with the cloverleaf symbol) and **M**.

H alt-key equivalent (Windows)
Under Windows, you can access still more commands by pressing the **alt** key along with the underlined letter in the menu name. For example, press **alt+F** to bring up the **File** menu. Then press the underlined key—with or without **alt**—to choose a command. This means to choose **File**➞**Automate**➞**Batch**, you press **alt+F**, then **U**, then **B**.

> *tip* Once a menu is displayed, you can use the arrow keys to move through the menus. Press → to open a submenu; press ← to close it. Press enter to choose a highlighted command.

I apple menu (Macintosh)
The **Apple** menu appears only on the Mac. The first two commands provide information about Photoshop and its programmers. Under Windows, you find these same commands in the **Help** menu.

J file menu (alt+F, Windows)
The commands in this menu let you open, save, print, and otherwise modify the image file on disk.

K edit menu (alt+E, Windows)
The **Edit** menu lets you copy, paste, and transform portions of an image. You can also set preferences, as explained in Chapter 4, Personalize Photoshop.

L image menu (alt+I, Windows)
From color space to resolution to orientation, the commands in the **Image** menu let you make whole-sale changes to the foreground image.

M layer menu (alt+L, Windows)
Use these commands to create and modify layers. Many of these commands are duplicated—and more conveniently located—in the **Layers** palette.

N select menu (alt+S, Windows)
The **Select** menu lets you edit and save selection outlines created with the selection tools. For more information, read Chapter 5, Make Selections.

O filter menu (alt+T, Windows)
As explained in Chapter 14, Apply Filters & Effects, the commands in the **Filter** menu can sharpen the focus of a photograph, smooth away scanning artifacts, add water-like ripples, and much more.

P view menu (alt+V, Windows)
These commands change the way the image looks on screen. They have no effect on how the image looks on the Web or how it prints.

Q window menu (alt+W, Windows)
Use these commands to display palettes or bring an open image to the foreground. Under Windows, you can close all open images by choosing **Close All**.

R help menu (alt+H, Windows)
As explained in Get Help on page 18, the **Help** menu provides access to Photoshop's on-screen documentation, a real comfort for those times when you're confused about a specific command or option.

S application menu (Macintosh)
On the Mac, the far right-hand menu lists all programs (also known as *applications*) that are running at any given moment. Choose **Hide Others** to focus exclusively on Photoshop.

Keyboard Shortcuts, Windows

You might not expect a graphics program to be particularly reliant on the keyboard. But like most Adobe products, Photoshop buries all kinds of tips and tricks into the keys. The program assumes you have both hands in action, one on the mouse and the other on the keyboard. A few shortcuts are sufficiently complicated that you have to devote both hands to the task.

Not all keyboard shortcuts are essential. Many, in fact, are so obscure that there's no reason on Earth to memorize them. For a list of what I consider to be the most practical shortcuts, refer to Chapter 19, Essential Shortcuts. In the meantime, here's an introduction to your keyboard and the overarching logic behind the shortcuts inside Photoshop.

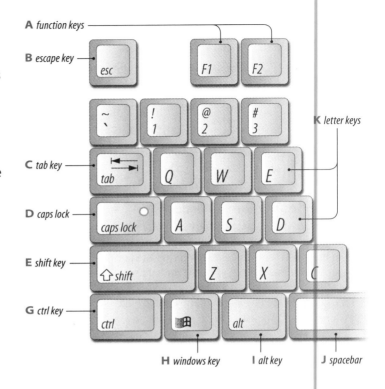

A *function keys*
B *escape key*
C *tab key*
D *caps lock*
E *shift key*
G *ctrl key*
K *letter keys*
H *windows key*
I *alt key*
J *spacebar*

A function keys

By default, function keys are assigned to a mixed variety of operations. For example, press **F1** to display the on-screen help. **F6** through **F9** display key palettes; **F12** reverts the foreground image to the way it looked when last saved. There's not much rhyme or reason to these shortcuts, which is why you can create your own function-key shortcuts using the **Actions** palette, as discussed in Chapter 16, Play & Record Actions.

B escape key

Press the **escape** key to cancel an operation. It's typically an alternative to clicking the **Cancel** button in a dialog box or window, but you can also use **escape** to cancel a long operation that's taking too much time to complete. Some dialog boxes let you press **alt+escape** (Win) or **option-escape** (Mac) to revert all settings to their defaults, a pleasant alternative to cancelling out and starting over again.

C tab key

The **tab** key is amazingly eclectic. You can use it to advance from one option to another inside a palette or dialog box. You can also press **alt+tab** (Win) or **command-tab** (Mac) to cycle through active applications. But the best use for **tab** is to hide and restore Photoshop's toolbox and palettes. Note that if ever this shortcut doesn't work, it's because an option in a palette is active. Press **enter** (Win) or **return** (Mac) and try pressing **tab** again.

D caps lock

Press the **caps lock** key to get the precise cursors, as explained on page 7 of Mouse & Cursor.

E shift key

The shift key is used to distinguish between related shortcuts. For example, on the PC, **ctrl+S** saves an image; **ctrl+shift+S** saves it under a different name.

Keyboard Shortcuts, Macintosh

F control key (Mac)

The Mac **control** key (sometimes abbreviated **ctrl**) is a lesser modifier. Its main function: **control**-click to display the shortcut menu.

Most PCs go a step further by providing a **shortcut menu** key on the right side of the keyboard. Press the key and up pops the menu—no need to click.

shortcut menu key

G ctrl key (Win)/ command key (Mac)

On the PC, all menu commands that offer shortcuts include **ctrl** in their keystrokes. The equivalent on the Mac is the aptly named **command** key, identified by the Apple logo and cloverleaf symbol.

H windows key (Windows)

If I had to choose a key to gouge out of the PC keyboard, it would be the **windows** key. Pressing it interrupts all activity in Photoshop and brings up the **Start** menu. Because it's located between **ctrl** and **alt**, you spend a lot of time accidentally hitting it. Its best function: press **windows**+M to hide Photoshop and all other applications and switch to the desktop.

I alt key (Win)/option key (Mac)

On the Mac, there's a popular saying that goes, "When in doubt, press the **option** key." On the PC, substitute, "Press **alt**." Either way, the main purpose of the key is to force the display of a dialog box. For example, **command-F** applies the most recently used filter, **command-option-F** brings up the dialog box for that filter. But you can just as easily bypass a dialog box. **Option**-click or **alt**-click a trash can in Photoshop to skip the warning. Other uses are clon-

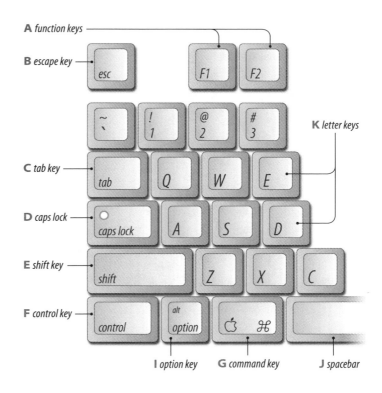

A *function keys*
B *escape key*
C *tab key*
D *caps lock*
E *shift key*
F *control key*
K *letter keys*
I *option key*   G *command key*   J *spacebar*

ing, drawing a straight-sided selection, and accessing the eyedropper. When in doubt, press that key.

J spacebar

In Photoshop, the **spacebar** implies navigation. Press the **spacebar** to temporarily access the hand tool. Press **ctrl+spacebar** (Win) or **command-spacebar** (Mac) and click to magnify the image. To learn more, read Scroll Bars & Hand Tool and Zoom In, Zoom Out, Zoom Tool on pages 38 and 39 of Chapter 3.

K letter keys

Unless a text layer is active, pressing a letter key selects a tool. Press **A** to get the arrow, **B** for the paintbrush, **C** for the crop tool, and so on. To switch between tools in a flyout menu, press **shift** along with the letter. Or remove **shift** from the picture by choosing **Edit➡Preferences➡General** and selecting the **Use Shift Key For Tool Switch** check box. Then you can press the letter key by itself to switch tools.

The Shortcut Menu

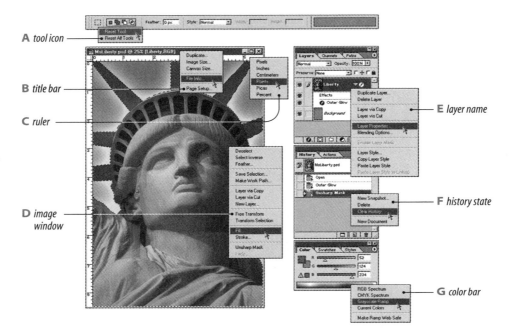

A *tool icon*

B *title bar*

C *ruler*

D *image window*

E *layer name*

F *history state*

G *color bar*

Every program claims to offer context-sensitive shortcut menus, but very few follow through on this promise with as much vigor as Photoshop. The program is literally teeming with shortcuts. It's safe to say, if you can't find a command or you don't want to go hunting for it in the standard menu bar, then right-click (or **control**-click on the Mac) and it may well spring into view. Here are a few examples of places you can right-click.

A tool icon

Right-click the tool icon in the options bar to view a small shortcut menu with two commands. You can either reset the active tool to its default settings or reset all tools.

B title bar (Windows)

Under Windows, you can right-click the image window title bar to access **Image Size** and **Canvas Size**. As discussed in Chapter 2, Understand The Image, both commands are exceedingly useful, yet neither is blessed with a keyboard equivalent.

C ruler

Right-click the horizontal or vertical ruler to change the unit of measurement used throughout Photoshop. To display the ruler, press **ctrl+R** (Win) or **command-R** (Mac).

D image window

Right-clicking in the image window displays an extensive shortcut menu that varies according to the active tool and the state of the image.

E layer name

Right-click a layer name in the **Layers** palette to duplicate, delete, or edit the active layer. You can right-click in the **Channels** and **Paths** palettes as well.

F history state

If Photoshop behaves sluggishly, right-click a state in the **History** palette and choose **Clear History**.

G color bar

Right-click the bar at the bottom of the **Color** palette to change the model used to define colors.

Image Preview & Status Bar

Some of Photoshop's most clandestine controls are frequently some of its most important. Cases in point: Along the bottom of the screen on the PC, and in the bottom-left corner of the image window on the Mac, you'll find a wealth of highly special-ized options devoted to the task of measuring the size and composition of an image. You can check how your image will print, scope out the resolution, and see how efficiently Photoshop is running. Though easily overlooked, I consider these options essential tools for main-taining a predictable working environment.

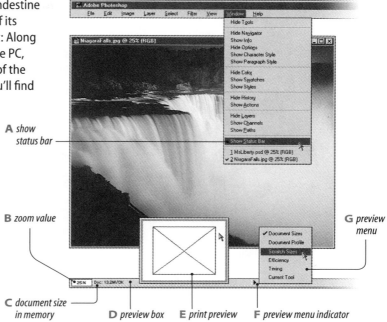

A *show status bar*

B *zoom value*

C *document size in memory*

D *preview box*   **E** *print preview*   **F** *preview menu indicator*

G *preview menu*

A show status bar (Windows)
On the PC, choose **Window➞Show Status Bar** to dis-play the status bar along the bottom of the screen. Although the Mac version of Photoshop lacks a status bar, it offers the very same options.

B zoom value
Enter a new zoom value to magnify the image on screen. Interestingly enough, this is the only editable item in the status bar.

C document size in memory
By default, the preview box (D) sports two numbers divided by a slash. The first number tells the size of the image in memory, uncompressed and without layers. The second number tells the size of the layers. If there are no layers, the number reads **0K**—that's *zero kilobytes,* incidentally, not *okay.*

D preview box
Click and hold the mouse button on the preview box to display the print preview (E).

E print preview
The box with an inset X shows the size at which the image will print. To change the print size, choose **File➞Print Options**, as explained in The Print Options Command on pages 252 and 253 of Chapter 17.

> *tip* Press **alt** (Win) or **option** (Mac) and click on the preview box to display the numerical size and resolution of the image.

F preview menu indicator
Click the triangle to display the preview menu (G), which changes the numbers in the preview box (D).

G preview menu
In addition to **Document Sizes** (C), you can preview the color profile (Color Settings, pages 58 and 59), the size of the scratch disk (Preferences, Scratch Disks & Memory, page 55), and how efficiently Photoshop is running. The **Timing** option shows how much time it takes to complete an operation; **Current Tool** tells you which tool is selected.

Dialog Boxes

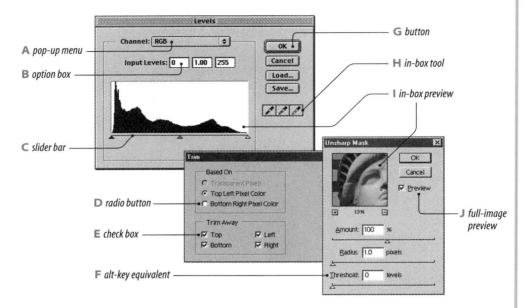

A *pop-up menu*

B *option box*

C *slider bar*

G *button*

H *in-box tool*

I *in-box preview*

D *radio button*

E *check box*

F *alt-key equivalent*

J *full-image preview*

The *dialog box* is Photoshop's way of soliciting more information so it knows how to apply a command. The program's idea of a dialog is a bit dense, so here are the kinds of questions you can expect.

A pop-up menu
If an item has arrowheads to the right of it, you can click it to display a *pop-up menu* of options.

B option box
An *option box* contains an editable number or text. Press **tab** to advance from one option box to the next; press **shift-tab** to move backward.

> *tip* Press ↑ or ↓ to raise or lower a numerical value by 1 or 0.1, depending on the option. Add **shift** to raise or lower by ten times the increment.

C slider bar
Move a triangle along the horizontal *slider bar* to adjust a numerical value in a neighboring option box.

D radio button
Radio buttons are multiple-choice questions. You can select one answer, but no more.

E check box
A *check box* is similar to a radio button, but you can select several or even none.

F alt-key equivalent (Windows)
On the PC, you can activate an option by pressing **alt** and the underlined character in the option's name.

G button
Click a button to exit the dialog box or open yet another dialog box. Press **return** or **enter** for **OK**; press **esc** for **Cancel**.

H in-box tool
Some dialog boxes offer tools that you can use in the image window, even while the dialog box is open.

I in-box preview
Some dialog boxes preview effects using thumbnail images; others use complex graphs. Once you know how to read them, both kinds of previews are useful.

J full-image preview
Whenever you see a **Preview** check box, turn it on to take in the full effect inside the image window.

Palettes & Panels

A *palette* is a dialog box that you can leave on screen as you work on an image. Most of Photoshop's palettes can be set to 208 pixels wide so that they form a perfect column on the right side of the screen, permitting you a large, uninterrupted area for the image window. The exceptions are the toolbox and options bar, discussed in The Toolbox on pages 8 and 9.

Display a palette by choosing a command from the **Window** menu or by pressing a function key—F6 for the **Color** palette, F7 for **Layers**, F8 for **Info**, and F9 for **Actions**.

> *tip* Press **tab** to hide or show all palettes as well as the status bar. Press **shift-tab** to hide or show all palettes *except* the toolbox, options bar, and status bar.

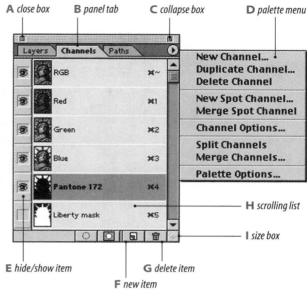

A *close box*   B *panel tab*   C *collapse box*   D *palette menu*

H *scrolling list*

I *size box*

E *hide/show item*   G *delete item*

F *new item*

A close box
Click the close box to close the palette. On the PC, the close box appears as an X on the right side of the palette.

B panel tab
By default, each palette contains multiple *panels*. To switch from one panel to another, click a wedge-shaped *tab*.

> *tip* To relocate a panel to another palette, drag its tab and drop it into the receiving palette. Drop the tab along the top or bottom of the palette to *dock* two palettes into vertical alignment. Or just drop the tab into space to start a new palette. Last, drop the tab into the options bar's docking well to stow the panel. To view a stowed palette, click its tab.

C collapse box
Click the collapse box to reduce the palette to its smallest size. Alternatively, you can double-click a panel tab. To restore the palette, click the collapse box again.

D palette menu
Click the triangle-in-a-circle to display a menu of commands related to the palette.

E hide/show item
Where an eyeball exists, click it to hide the item next to it. Press **alt** (Win) or **option** (Mac) and click an eyeball to hide all items *except* the one you click.

F new item
Where available, the tiny page button permits you to create a new item in the palette.

G delete item
Click the trash can to delete the selected item in the palette. An alert message will ask you to confirm.

H scrolling list
When a palette holds a long list of items, you can peruse up and down the list using the scroll bar.

I size box
Drag the size box to change the height and width of a palette. Bear in mind that you can always return the palette to its 208-pixel width by dragging the size box up and to the left.

Get Help

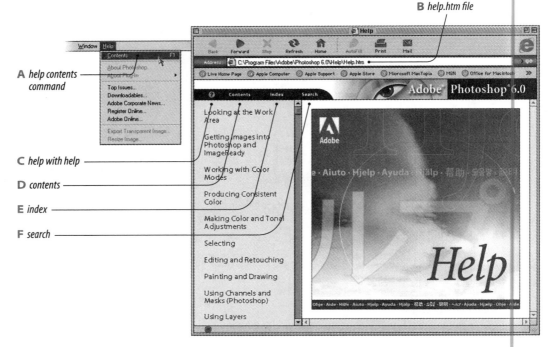

A *help contents command*

B *help.htm file*

C *help with help*

D *contents*

E *index*

F *search*

Hopefully, this book provides you with 99 percent of the information you need. But every so often, you may stumble on a question I neglect to answer. In that case, you can consult Photoshop's **Help** menu, which offers access to tricks and tips that you can reference on screen. The help document is actually a collection of HTML files on your hard disk. This permits Adobe to update old information from its Web site. It is not absolutely necessary to be connected to the Internet. But I recommend that you start up Internet Explorer or Netscape Navigator so Photoshop can easily locate your browser.

A help contents command

Choose **Help➥Contents** (Win) or **Help➥Help Contents** (Mac) to open the help file inside your browser. On the PC, press F1. On the Mac, press **help**.

B help.htm file

Photoshop is working from a file on your hard drive called **help.htm**. If for some reason you can't get the **Contents** command to work, try searching for

help.htm on your hard drive and opening it directly inside your Web browser.

C help with help

Once the **help.htm** page loads, you're in business. If you're unclear about what's going on, click the **?** to get help on using Adobe's online help.

D contents

The **Contents** button takes you back to the same page you started at after choosing the **Contents** command inside Photoshop. Select from the list of contents in the scrolling list.

E index

Click this button to select a topic alphabetically. This helps when you're not sure what you're looking for.

F search

The **Search** button is most likely your best bet. Click it to display an option box. Enter the words you want to find and press **enter** (Win) or **return** (Mac). Then click the link that looks most promising.

Understand The Image

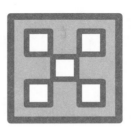

Photoshop lets you edit photographs and scanned artwork, known generically as *images*. Technically, an image is a file that consists of tiny squares of color called *pixels*. Each pixel may be colored with any one of 16,777,216 hues and shades. Take all that color variety, pack in a million or so pixels, and you have what looks for all the world like a *continuous-tone photograph*, in which one color blends seamlessly with the next.

This chapter looks at how Photoshop works with pixels and images. I explain how to increase or decrease the number of pixels, rotate a crooked scan, crop away extra background, and specify an ideal print resolution. These are core questions that plague some Photoshop users years after they start using the program. I want you to understand the image before you go any farther.

Rulers & Units

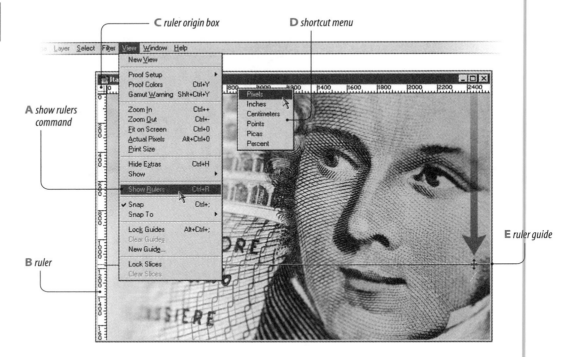

C ruler origin box

D shortcut menu

A show rulers command

B ruler

E ruler guide

Gaining control over an image is initially an experiment in measurements. How tall is the image? How wide? What will it look like when printed? How big will it appear on the Web? If you're a creative type, these technical (not to mention boring) details can be a nuisance. But once you get up to speed with Photoshop's horizontal and vertical rulers and the various units of measure, you'll be able to gauge the size of an image without even thinking.

A show rulers command

Choose **View➞Show Rulers** or press **ctrl+R** (Win) or **command-R** (Mac) to display rulers along the top and left edges of the image window. These rulers do not print—they are merely used for reference.

B ruler

A vertical ruler runs along the left side of the image window; the horizontal ruler runs along the top. In each case, all measurements appear in the active unit of measure, in this case, pixels.

C ruler origin box

By default, all ruler measurements are made from the upper-left corner of the image, a point known as the *ruler origin*. To change the location of the ruler origin, drag from the ruler origin box, located at the intersection of the horizontal and vertical rulers.

> *tip* To restore the ruler origin to the upper-left corner of the image, double-click inside the ruler origin box.

D shortcut menu

To change the unit of measure used by the rulers—and elsewhere throughout Photoshop—right-click (Win) or **control**-click (Mac) on either the horizontal or vertical ruler, and then choose an option from the shortcut menu. **Pica** is a unit equal to ⅙ inch; **Point** means 1/12 pica. Choose **Percent** to make measurements relative to the height or width of the image. When in doubt, choose **Pixels**, which is the only unit that is not based on another setting in the software.

Double-click a ruler to display the **Units & Rulers** panel of the **Preferences** dialog box. If you're feeling fastidious, you can change how many points are in an inch using the **Point/Pica Size** options. More practical are the **Column Size** options. If you plan on placing your image into a QuarkXPress or InDesign document, specify the width of the columns and the spaces between columns (gutters) in that document. Then set the width of the image to exactly fit one or more columns using **Image→Image Size,** as explained in The Image Size Command on page 23.

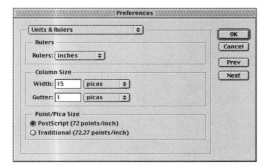

E ruler guide

Drag from the horizontal or vertical ruler to create a *ruler guide* to which you can align selections and layers inside Photoshop.

> ***tip*** Press **alt** (Win) or **option** (Mac) when creating a new guide to make a horizontal guide vertical or vice versa. To move a guide, press **ctrl** (Win) or **command** (Mac) and drag it. Delete a guide by moving it back to its ruler; ctrl- or command-double-click a guide to change its color.

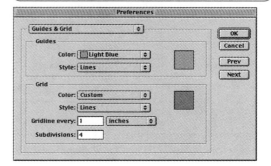

The Info Palette

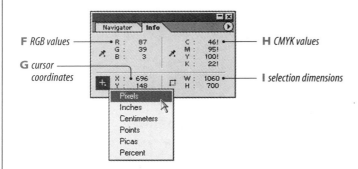

In addition to using the rulers, you can measure elements inside the image window using the **Info** palette. To display the **Info** palette, press F8 or choose **Window→ Show Info.** On a PC, you can also press alt+W, then F.

F RGB values

These values show the RGB (red, green, blue) recipe for the color of the pixel under the cursor. For more information on RGB colors, read RGB Versus CMYK on page 82 of Chapter 6.

G cursor coordinates

These values tell the coordinate location of the cursor, as measured from the ruler origin.

> ***tip*** Click the cross to display a menu of units that affect both the **Info** palette and the rulers.

H CMYK values

This is the CMYK recipe for the pixel under the cursor. An exclamation point indicates that the color exceeds the CMYK gamut. Again, see RGB Versus CMYK on page 82 for complete details.

I selection dimensions

These are the dimensions of the selected area inside the image.

The Image Size Command

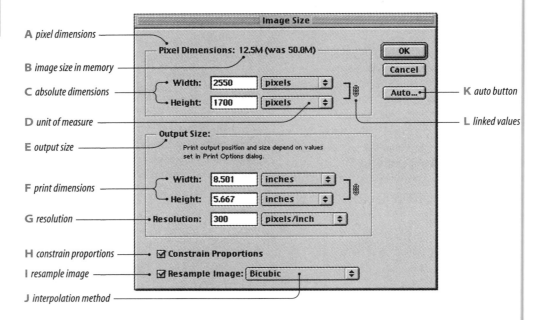

A *pixel dimensions*

B *image size in memory*

C *absolute dimensions*

D *unit of measure*

E *output size*

F *print dimensions*

G *resolution*

H *constrain proportions*

I *resample image*

J *interpolation method*

K *auto button*

L *linked values*

Image→Image Size may be the most essential and challenging command in all of Photoshop. This is because it serves two very important and very different purposes. First, **Image Size** lets you change the *pixel dimensions*, which indicate the number of pixels contained in an image. Second, it permits you to set the *resolution*, which is the number of pixels that get packed into an inch on the page. Whether you change just the resolution or both the resolution and the pixel dimensions hinges on the **Resample Image** check box (I). Here's how the options inside the **Image Size** dialog box work:

A pixel dimensions

The first rule of image editing is that more pixels means more flexibility. With lots of pixels, you have greater latitude to crop, more wiggle room when correcting colors and retouching blemishes, and more detail and clarity when printing. The **Pixel Dimensions** area in the **Image Size** dialog box tells you how many pixels an image contains. If the **Resample Image** check box (I) is turned on, you can also increase or reduce the quantity of pixels.

622 x 524 pixels (325,928 total pixels), 300 pixels per inch

78 x 66 pixels (5,148 total pixels), 37.5 pixels per inch

B image size in memory

Lots of pixels are good, but they come at a price. More pixels mean a larger file size, both on disk and in your computer's memory (or *RAM*). A full-color image that measures 2,550 by 1,700 pixels weighs in at 12.5 megabytes (MB). In comparison, a typical new computer comes equipped with 128MB of RAM, so 10 percent of the RAM is gobbled up by this one image. Factor in the other stuff your computer is doing—running Photoshop, running other programs—and the RAM may be full. If an image exceeds the amount of RAM allotted to it, your computer slows down.

The image size data tells you how much room the image takes up in RAM. If **Resample Image** (I) is turned on, the number inside parentheses tells you how big the image was before you chose **Image Size**.

C absolute dimensions

The **Width** and **Height** values show the dimensions of the image in pixels. You can change these values only if **Resample Image** (I) is turned on. Usually, if you're going to change the number of pixels in an image, you want to reduce the number (called *downsampling*) to decrease the file size, particularly if you want to e-mail the image or post it on the Web. Increasing pixels (*upsampling*) is tantamount to inventing pixels out of thin air—it increases file size but does little to help the appearance of the image.

D unit of measure

When editing pixel dimensions, you can select from two units of measure, **Pixels** and **Percent**.

> *tip* On the PC, press **tab** to advance to this option, then press the ↑ or ↓ key to change the setting.

E output size

These options control how large the image will print. If you're planning on posting your image to the Web, you can ignore these options.

F print dimensions

Enter the width and height of your final printed image. This goes not only when printing from Photoshop, but when importing into other programs, too.

This time, you can select from every unit of measure *except* pixels. When modifying the **Width** value, select **Columns** to match the image to a specified number of columns in a QuarkXPress or InDesign document (as introduced in Rulers & Units on page 21).

G resolution

This value determines the number of pixels that print per inch (abbreviated *ppi*) or per centimeter (*ppc*). Raising or lowering the value when **Resample Image** (I) is turned on changes the number of pixels in the image; to change the resolution without changing pixels, turn **Resample Image** off.

H constrain proportions

Turn this check box on to change the width and height of an image by the same percentage. If you want to make the image tall and thin or short and fat, turn **Constrain Proportions** off. This option is dimmed when **Resample Image** (I) is turned off.

I resample image

Turn this check box on to change the number of pixels in an image, known generically as *resampling*. Turn the option off to change the print size and resolution without affecting pixel count.

J interpolation method

When **Resample Image** (I) is active, Photoshop has to recalculate, or *interpolate*, the new pixels in the image. Tell Photoshop how to perform its calculations using this pop-up menu. If in doubt, select **Bicubic**. Otherwise, read Resample An Image on page 24 to see recommendations on each setting.

K auto button

Click this button to let Photoshop do the thinking for you. I don't recommend this option; it's far better to learn how to use **Image Size** properly.

L linked values

The chain icon shows you that changing one value changes the linked one(s) as well. When **Constrain Proportions** (H) is active, the **Width** and **Height** values are linked. When **Resample Image** (I) is off, **Width**, **Height**, and **Resolution** are linked.

steps **Resample An Image**

The **Image Size** command is a great way to reduce the size of an image so that you can post it on the Web, e-mail it to a friend or colleague, or simply make it more manageable.

1 **get image**
Open an image, preferably a large one. My image weighs in at 12.5MB, far too big to post on the Web.

2 **choose image size**
Choose **Image➡Image Size** to display the **Image Size** dialog box.

> *tip* On the PC, try the shortcut **alt+I, I**. (Press **alt+I** and then press the **I** key.) Or right-click the image window title bar and choose **Image Size**.

3 **select resample image**
Select the **Resample Image** check box. In most cases, you'll want to leave the pop-up menu set to **Bicubic**, which considers all available pixels when calculating new ones. Skip **Bilinear**, which merely considers fewer pixels. Ostensibly, it's quicker, but not enough to notice. On rare occasions, you may want to try **Nearest Neighbor**, which makes no attempt to interpolate but rather keeps some pixels and throws away others. This is helpful when you want to retain crisp lines and text that get slightly blurred when using **Bicubic**.

4 **set resolution**
When **Resample Image** is checked, changing the **Resolution** value also messes up the **Width** and **Height** values. So if you intend to print the image, it's a good idea to get the **Resolution** setting out of the way first. As for the exact resolution value you should use, refer to Select The Ideal Resolution on the facing page for recommendations.

5 **change pixel dimensions**
Change the **Width** and **Height** values, either at the top or middle of the dialog box. I like to work with **Percent** selected as my unit of measure so I can gauge the relative change to the size of the image. Watch the **Pixel Dimensions** number in parentheses (A, page 22) so you know the size of the image in memory. For Web or e-mail use, keep it under 2MB.

6 **click OK**
Or press **enter** (Win) or **return** (Mac) to apply your changes. If the result isn't to your liking, don't worry; just choose **Edit➡Undo** and try again.

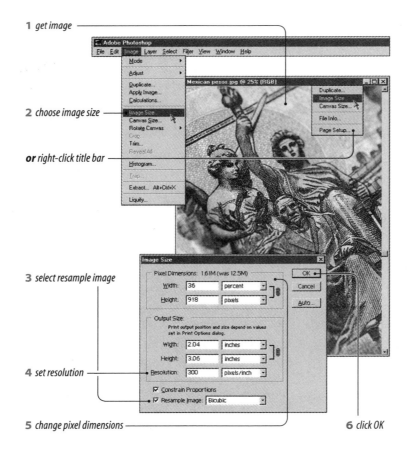

1 *get image*

2 *choose image size*

or right-click title bar

3 *select resample image*

4 *set resolution*

5 *change pixel dimensions*

6 *click OK*

steps Change The Print Size

As often as not, you have no desire to change the number of pixels in an image; you just want to change how it looks on the page. By changing the resolution, you can print the image larger or smaller without adding or subtracting so much as a single pixel.

Repeat steps 1 and 2 on the facing page. Then do the following:

3 deselect resample image

Turning off this check box ensures that no pixels are harmed in the resizing of this image. The **Pixel Dimensions** options (A, page 22) become unavailable, so all you're left with is the **Output Size** settings.

4 change output size settings

Notice the link icon (L, page 23) now extends to include **Width**, **Height**, and **Resolution**. So it doesn't matter in what order you edit the values—each affects the other two. If you're not sure what **Resolution** value to use, consult the table in Select The Ideal Resolution below.

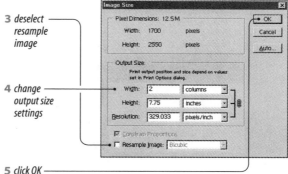

3 deselect resample image

4 change output size settings

5 click OK

5 click OK

If you've done everything correctly, the image looks the same now as it did before you chose **Image Size**. This is because you changed the way the image prints; the on-screen appearance remains unaffected.

> **tip** One final tip: When working in the **Image Size** dialog box, press **alt** (Win) or **option** (Mac) to change the **Cancel** button to **Reset**. Click this button to restore the settings that appeared when you entered the **Image Size** dialog box.

Select The Ideal Resolution

Commercial printers use patterns of circular dots called *halftones* to simulate shades of color. The halftone dots are arranged in rows; the number of dots in an inch is called the *screen frequency*. As a rule of thumb, the resolution of an image should ideally be 2 times the screen frequency, but you can get away with as low as 1.5 times. If you go higher than 2.5 times, you're just wasting memory and printing time. Accordingly, here are a few suggested resolutions for different printing environments. Bear in mind, these are just suggestions. If some other setting looks good, trust your eyes.

printer	ideal resolution	no lower than	no higher than
300-ppi laser printer	120 ppi	90 ppi	150 ppi
600-ppi laser printer	180 ppi	135 ppi	225 ppi
newsprint	180 ppi	135 ppi	225 ppi
coated magazine stock	267 ppi	200 ppi	330 ppi
color inkjet printer	300 ppi	240 ppi	400 ppi
super-fine coated stock	350 ppi	260 ppi	440 ppi

The Rotate Canvas Commands

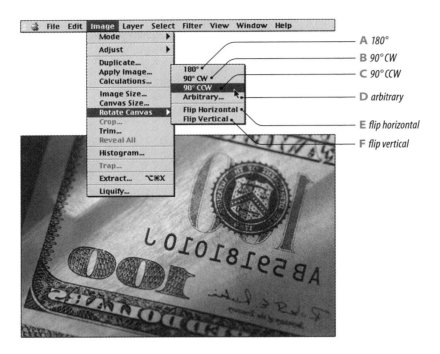

A *180°*
B *90° CW*
C *90° CCW*
D *arbitrary*
E *flip horizontal*
F *flip vertical*

Choose **Image**➝**Rotate Canvas** to display a sub-menu of commands that permit you to rotate or flip an image in its entirety. These commands are designed to fix pictures that are scanned or photographed sideways, as well as flip slides and transparencies that are digitized wrong side up.

A 180°
If an image is truly upside-down, like a person standing on his head, choose **180°** to spin it back on its feet. On the PC, you can choose this command from the keyboard by pressing **alt+I, E, 1**.

B 90° CW
Choose this command to rotate the image 90 degrees clockwise—that is, a quarter turn to the right, from 12 to 3 o'clock. On the PC, press **alt+I, E, 9**.

C 90° CCW
This command rotates the image 90 degrees counterclockwise, which is a quarter turn to the left, from 12 to 9 o'clock. The alt-key equivalent is **alt+I, E, 0**.

D arbitrary
This badly named command does the opposite of what its name implies. Whereas the word *arbitrary* means anything from careless to despotic, the **Arbitrary** command is both precise and judicious. Choose it to display a dialog box that invites you to enter a specific rotation value. When doing so, keep in mind that 360 degrees is a full circle. You can also select **°CW** to rotate to the right or **°CCW** to rotate to the left.

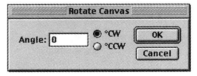

E flip horizontal
Use this command to fix wrong-reading text, as in the case of the image above. On the PC, press **alt+I, E, H**.

F flip vertical
Choose **Flip Vertical** or press **alt+I, E, V** to swap the top and bottom halves of the image.

Straighten A Crooked Image

The **Image→Rotate Canvas** commands make quick work of righting pictures that are flipped or on their sides. However, if a photograph is crooked, it's more likely to be off by a degree or two than by a whopping 90 degrees. Obviously, the solution is to apply a slight rotation with the **Arbitrary** command. But how do you decide how much rotation to apply? The answer lies with the measure tool.

1 select measure tool

Click and hold on the eyedropper tool icon on the right side of the toolbox. Then select the measure tool from the flyout menu. Or if you prefer, press **shift-I** repeatedly until the measure tool is active.

2 drag along axis

Drag with the measure tool along an element that should be absolutely horizontal or vertical. The division between ground and sky usually works best, but buildings and other vertical objects work fine as well. After you draw a measure line, you can adjust it by dragging one of the two endpoints.

3 note angle value (optional)

The moment you start dragging with the measure tool, Photoshop displays the **Info** palette, which tracks the angle and distance of the measure line using the **A** and **D** values. Take a quick glance at the **A** value, but don't bother to memorize it. Photoshop has already assigned the angle to memory for you.

4 choose arbitrary

Choose **Image→Rotate Canvas→Arbitrary**. Alternatively on the PC, you can press **alt+I, E, A**. Either way, Photoshop displays the **Rotate Canvas** dialog box with an **Angle** value already in place. The **°CW** or **°CCW** radio button is already selected as well. These settings reflect the exact angle of the line you drew with the measure tool.

5 click OK

Or press **enter** (Win) or **return** (Mac). Assuming you measured correctly, Photoshop rotates the image so it's exactly straight. It does not, however, rotate the measure line. To hide the measure line, just click a different tool.

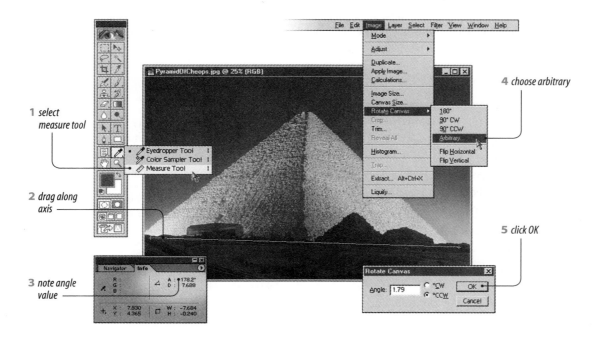

1 select measure tool

2 drag along axis

3 note angle value

4 choose arbitrary

5 click OK

The Crop Tool

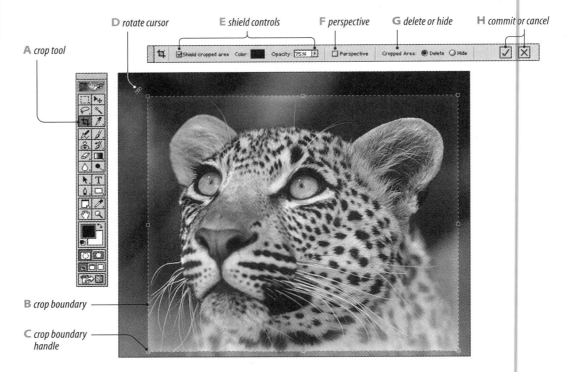

A *crop tool*

D *rotate cursor*   E *shield controls*   F *perspective*   G *delete or hide*   H *commit or cancel*

☑ Shield cropped area   Color: Opacity: 75%   ☐ Perspective   Cropped Area: ⦿ Delete ○ Hide   ☑ ☒

B *crop boundary*

C *crop boundary handle*

A professional photographer backs up a step or two after framing a subject in the viewfinder so she has some room to crop. Photoshop provides a special tool for this purpose: the crop tool.

A crop tool

Click this icon or press the **C** key to select the crop tool, which clips away extraneous or distracting background elements.

B crop boundary

Drag with the crop tool to create a rectangular *crop boundary*. Use this boundary to define the portion of the image that you want to retain.

C crop boundary handle

Drag a handle to resize the crop boundary; press **shift** while dragging to resize it proportionally.

D rotate cursor

Drag outside the perimeter of the dotted line to rotate the crop boundary.

E shield controls

Photoshop 6 covers the area to be cropped away in a translucent *shield*. Use the shield controls in the options bar to turn the shield on or off, specify its color, and adjust its opacity.

F perspective

Select this option to make the crop boundary handles move independently of each other, useful for removing a perspective distortion from a cropped image.

G delete or hide

You can choose to permanently delete or temporarily hide the cropped portion of the image. For more information, read Hide Instead Of Crop on page 31.

H commit or cancel

Click the check mark or press **enter** (Win) or **return** (Mac) to crop the image. Regardless of the shape of the boundary, the cropped image comes out rectangular. Click **X** or press **esc** to abandon the operation.

⟨steps⟩ Crop Away Extraneous Details

After you rotate an image using the **Arbitrary** command, as outlined in Straighten A Crooked Image on page 27, Photoshop leaves wedges of color in the rotation's wake. To get rid of these decidedly unsightly wedges, crop them into oblivion.

1 select crop tool
Click the crop tool icon or press the C key.

2 draw crop boundary
Drag inside the image window to draw a rectangle around the portion of the image you want to keep. As you do, you enter the *crop mode*. From this point on until you press **enter** or **esc**, most of Photoshop's commands and palettes are unavailable.

3 drag inside to move
Drag inside the crop boundary to move it.

4 drag handle to scale
Drag a handle to resize the boundary. Press **shift** and drag to resize proportionally.

⟨tip⟩ Press **alt** (Win) or **option** (Mac) while dragging to resize the boundary with respect to the central *crop origin* (6).

5 drag outside to rotate
By dragging outside the crop boundary, you can straighten and crop an image in one operation.

⟨tip⟩ Press **shift** while dragging outside the crop boundary to constrain the angle of rotation to 15-degree increments.

6 drag origin
The crop origin serves as the center of rotation. It's also the center when **alt**- or **option**-dragging a handle.

7 click commit
Click the check mark in the options bar, choose **Image➡Crop**, double-click inside the crop boundary, press **enter** (**return** on the Mac), *or* select a different tool to complete the crop operation.

1 *select crop tool*   2 *draw crop boundary*   3 *drag inside to move*   4 *drag handle to scale*   5 *drag outside to rotate*   6 *drag origin*   7 *click commit*

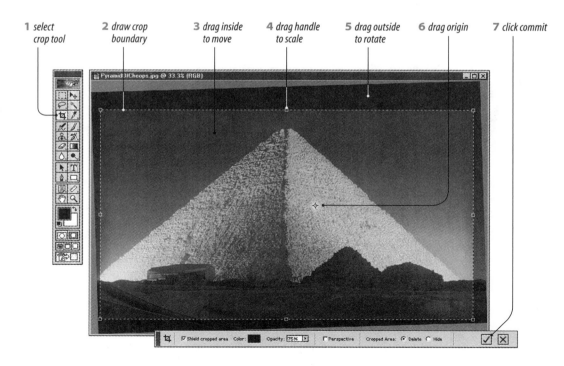

Match One Image To Another

Photoshop lets you crop an image to a specific size and resolution. Just select the crop tool and enter **Width**, **Height**, and **Resolution** values in the options bar prior to drawing a crop boundary. Likewise, you can crop one image (Image B) to match the size and resolution of another (Image A). Assuming both images are open, here's how it works:

1 select crop tool
Click the crop tool icon or press the C key.

2 crop image A
Crop the first image, Image A, as desired. If you want to change the resolution, visit **Image➟Image Size**.

3 click front image
Click the **Front Image** button in the options bar. Photoshop loads the size and resolution information from Image A into the options bar.

4 click image B
Click inside Image B or choose its name from the **Window** menu to bring it to the foreground.

5 draw crop boundary
Photoshop constrains the crop boundary to the same proportions as Image A. So if Image A is oriented horizontally, the crop boundary will be horizontal as well. You can scale and rotate the boundary, but you can't monkey with its height or width.

6 press enter or return
Once you get the crop boundary the way you want it, press **enter** (Win) or **return** (Mac) to **apply** the crop.

> *tip* Photoshop keeps the size and resolution information even after you crop the image. To remove all constraints from the crop boundary, click the **Clear** button in the options bar.

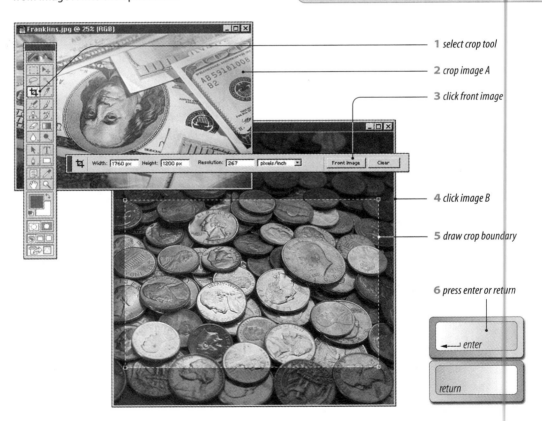

1 *select crop tool*

2 *crop image A*

3 *click front image*

4 *click image B*

5 *draw crop boundary*

6 *press enter or return*

ⓢsteps Hide Instead Of Crop

Normally, cropping deletes a portion of the image. But in Photoshop 6, you can opt to merely hide the cropped areas, leaving them available for future retrieval. There's just one caveat—hiding only works with layers. So here's what you do:

1 select crop tool
Once again, press the C key.

2 double-click background layer
Photoshop deletes cropped portions of the flat Background layer without exception, so you need to convert it to a floating layer. If the **Layers** palette is not visible, press **F7**. Then double-click **Background**.

3 click OK
A dialog box appears, asking you to name the new layer. Enter a name if you like, and then click **OK**.

4 draw crop boundary
As usual, you can move, scale, and rotate the crop boundary to taste.

5 select hide
Select the **Hide** radio button in the options bar. This ensures that Photoshop retains all pixels throughout the layered portions of the image.

6 click commit
Or press **enter** (Win) or **return** (Mac).

The image looks as if the cropped pixels have been deleted. But in truth, they're still there. To confirm that the pixels remain intact, choose **Image� Reveal All**. Photoshop expands the canvas to accommodate all pixels in all layers. You can likewise expand the canvas using **Image➡Canvas Size**, as explained in The Canvas Size Command on page 32.

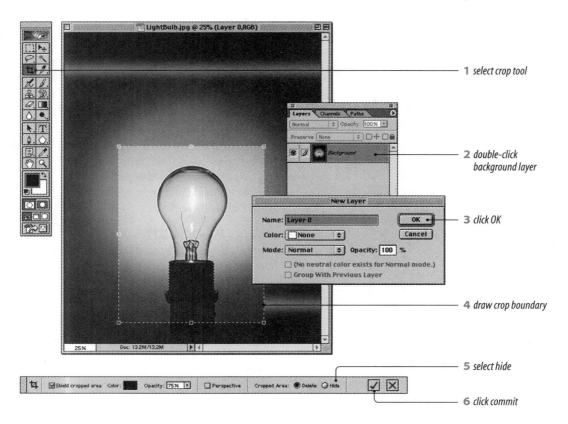

1 *select crop tool*

2 *double-click background layer*

3 *click OK*

4 *draw crop boundary*

5 *select hide*

6 *click commit*

The Canvas Size Command

A *current size*

B *new size*

C *desired canvas dimensions*

D *unit of measure*

E *anchor grid*

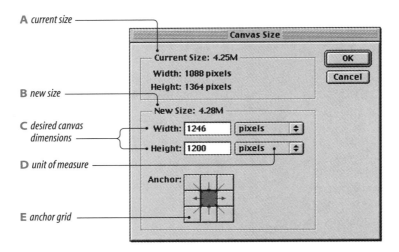

In Photoshop, the *canvas* defines the physical limitations of the image. To see the canvas boundary first-hand, drag outward from the lower-right corner of the image window to expand the window beyond the confines of the image.

canvas boundary

resize image window

When you crop an image, you make the canvas smaller. But you can also make the canvas larger. To enlarge or reduce the canvas independently of the image, choose **Image➡Canvas Size**.

A current size

The first part of the **Canvas Size** dialog box lists the canvas dimensions in the prevailing unit of measure (discussed in Rulers & Units, page 20) and the image size in memory (The Image Size Command, page 23).

B new size

Use the **New Size** options to change the dimensions of the canvas.

C desired canvas dimensions

Enter new values into the **Width** and **Height** option boxes to expand or reduce the size of the canvas. In most cases, you'll want to increase the canvas dimensions. If your goal is to reduce the canvas, you can better see what you're doing using the crop tool.

However, in the event you do reduce the canvas size, Photoshop warns you that "some clipping will occur." This is a bit misleading—**Canvas Size** deletes pixels from the Background layer only; pixels on all other layers are merely hidden.

D unit of measure

Change the unit of measure by selecting an option from either of these pop-up menus.

E anchor grid

The **Anchor** grid lets you position the image on the resized canvas. Click the center of the grid to center the image; click a side or corner to add or subtract pixels in the opposite side or corner of the canvas. The arrows show how the canvas will be affected. Arrows pointing out indicate canvas expansion; arrows pointing in show cropping.

(steps) Add A Border

Canvas Size isn't the only command in Photoshop that lets you add a border around an image. But it is the one that provides you with the most control.

1 press D, press X

When you expand an image with **Canvas Size**, Photoshop fills the new pixels with the background color. Pressing D makes the foreground color black and the background color white; pressing X switches the colors, so the background color is black. If you want to make the border something other than black, set the background color using the **Color** palette.

2 choose canvas size

Choose **Image→Canvas Size** to display the **Canvas Size** dialog box.

> **tip** The PC version of Photoshop offers two shortcuts for **Canvas Size**. Press alt+I, S. Or right-click on the title bar and choose **Canvas Size**.

3 select pixels (optional)

Select **Pixels** from the **Width** and **Height** pop-up menus to ensure a border of uniform thickness.

4 add to width & height

Add twice the thickness of your border to both the **Width** and **Height** values. For example, to make a 4-pixel border, increase each value by 8.

5 click OK

Photoshop fills the new pixels with the background color, resulting in an even border all the way around.

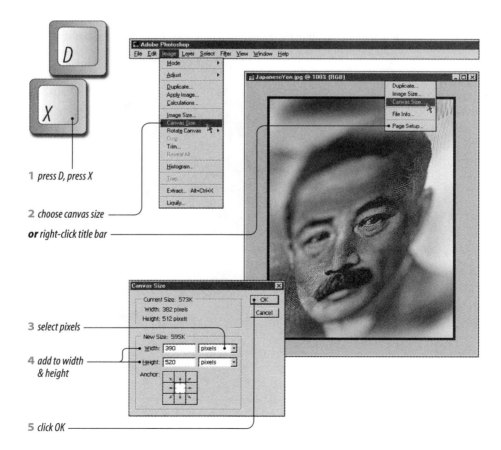

1 press D, press X

2 choose canvas size

or right-click title bar

3 select pixels

4 add to width & height

5 click OK

steps Trim Away White Space

Prior to Photoshop 6, it was a royal pain in the neck to trim white space from an image. Now, it's downright simple, thanks to the **Trim** command.

1 get image
Open an image with lots of empty space, like the one below. Even blurry edges are no problem for **Trim**.

2 choose trim
You'll find the **Trim** command in the **Image** menu.

3 select color to delete
Photoshop asks you which color you want to delete. If an image includes layers, you can delete the trans-

parent pixels. Otherwise, you can delete the color assigned to the very first (upper-left) or last (lower-right) pixel in the image. If your image is surrounded by trim color, like mine, any **Based On** option will do.

4 decide where to trim
Select the sides of the image you want to trim. Most likely, you'll want to select all four check boxes.

5 click OK
Photoshop crops the pixels around the perimeter of the image that match the color specified with the **Based On** option (3). The result is the smallest possible canvas that fully accommodates the image.

1 get image

2 choose trim

3 select color to delete

4 decide where to trim

5 click OK

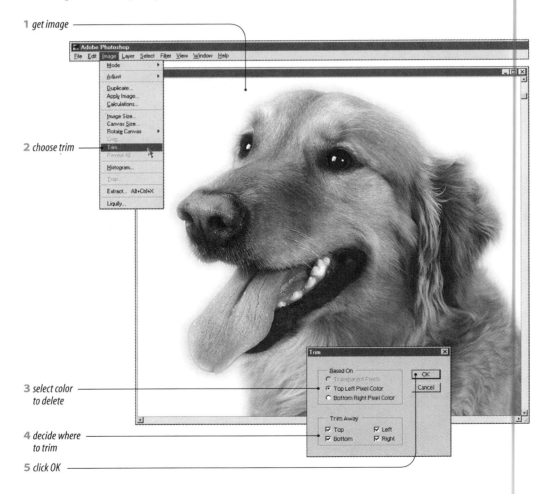

chapter

3

Open, Navigate, Save

Sections @ A Glance

Discover how to open an image captured with a scanner or digital camera, magnify the image on screen, scroll to a hidden area, and save the image in a few essential file formats.

Most programs are at least sometimes in the business of creating files. You start with a blank document or spreadsheet or drawing and you build your masterpiece. But you almost never create a new document in Photoshop. 999 out of 1,000 times, you begin your day in Photoshop by opening an existing photograph or scanned image. That's an image editor for you—begin with an image, end with an image, and nothing but image in between.

This chapter introduces you to a typical Photoshop session. I show you how to open an image file stored on disk. Then I tour you through the navigation functions, including enough keyboard shortcuts to suit any working style. And finally, I show you how to save your work so you can place it inside another document, share it with a colleague, or archive it for later retrieval. This is a day in the life of Photoshop.

35

The Open Command, Windows

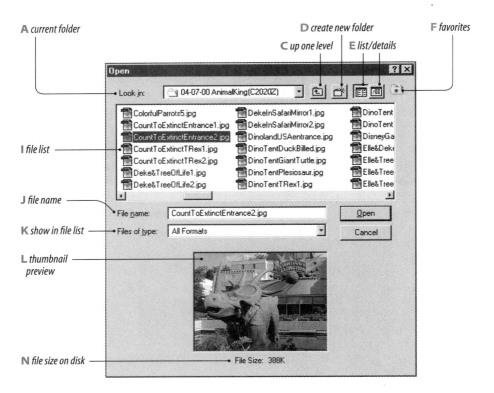

A *current folder*

D *create new folder* **F** *favorites*

C *up one level* **E** *list/details*

I *file list*

J *file name*

K *show in file list*

L *thumbnail preview*

N *file size on disk*

Choose **File➡Open** to open an image saved on a disk, hard drive, or networked volume. Alternatively, you can press **ctrl+O** (Win) or **command-O** (Mac). Photoshop displays the **Open** dialog box, which lets you locate and select an image to open. The dialog box is *non-modal*, which means you can switch to the desktop or some other program if you're having difficulty locating a file, without having to first close the dialog box.

> *tip* On the PC, you can open an image by double-clicking anywhere in the empty application background (see page 2 of The Photoshop Desktop). Press **alt** and double-click to display the **Open As** dialog box, which lets you specify a format other than the one indicated by the file's extension. For example, you might use **Open As** to open a file saved on the Macintosh with no extension. Press **ctrl** and double-click to create a new image.

A current folder

Here is the name of the folder that contains the selected image. Click to see a list of folders that contain this folder. Select one to ascend up from the current folder. On the PC, you also can see other volumes (G).

B sort order (Macintosh)

Click this button on the Mac to switch the order of files in the file list (I) from A–Z to Z–A.

C up one level (Windows)

Click this button on the PC to ascend out of the current folder into the folder that contains it.

D create new folder (Windows)

Click this button to create and name a new folder.

E lists or details (Windows)

Click the first button to organize the file list (I) into several columns. Click the second button to see the size, save date, and other details about each file.

The Open Command, Macintosh

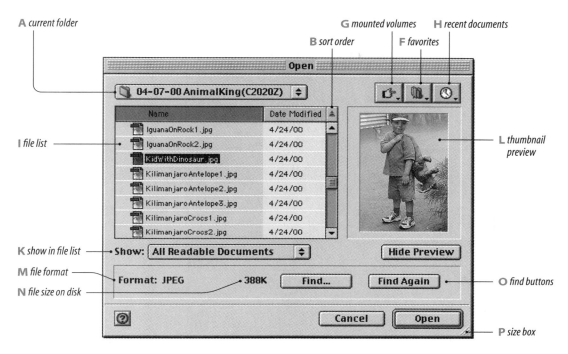

A *current folder*

B *sort order*

G *mounted volumes*   H *recent documents*

F *favorites*

I *file list*

L *thumbnail preview*

K *show in file list*

M *file format*

N *file size on disk*

O *find buttons*

P *size box*

F favorites
If you plan to visit a particular folder often, click this button and choose **Add Favorite** (Win) or **Add To Favorites** (Mac). Also use this button to choose a previously saved favorite.

G mounted volumes (Macintosh)
Volumes are disks and networked items available to your computer. Click this button on the Mac to display a menu of available volumes. Use the current folder (A) pop-up menu to access volumes on the PC.

H recent documents (Macintosh)
Click here to see a list of recently opened images.

I file list
The file list shows all files in the current folder (A) that Photoshop thinks it can open. Click a file to select it. Or type the first few letters in the file's name.

J file name (Windows)
The Windows version of Photoshop lists the name of the image selected in the file list (I).

K show in file list
Use this pop-up menu to change which images you can see in the file list (I).

L thumbnail preview
The *thumbnail preview* shows what the selected file looks like. A thumbnail must be saved with the image, as explained on page 44 of The Save Command.

M file format (Macintosh)
This is the format the selected image was saved in. On the PC, you can tell the format from the file extension.

N file size on disk
This item tells you the size of the selected file on disk. Note that the image expands in RAM when opened.

O find buttons (Macintosh)
On the Mac, click the **Find** button to search for a file by name. On the PC, press the **windows** key and F.

P size box (Macintosh)
Drag here to resize the dialog box.

Scroll Bars & Hand Tool

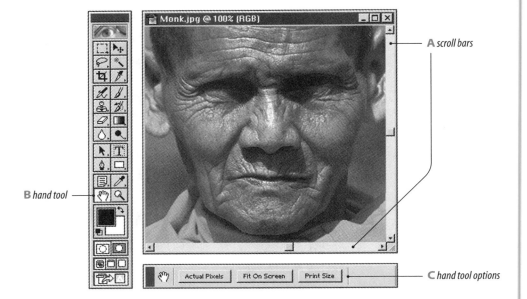

A *scroll bars*

B *hand tool*

C *hand tool options*

Anytime the image window is smaller than the image, some portions of the image are necessarily hidden on screen. The scroll bars and hand tool permit you to reveal hidden areas.

A scroll bars
Each of the scroll bars includes a moving scroll box and two scroll arrows, one at either end. Drag a scroll box, click an arrow, or click inside the scroll bar to scoot the image up, down, or sideways.

B hand tool
Drag with the hand tool to move the image dynamically. This is by far the easiest way to scroll.

tip The **H** key selects the hand tool. The spacebar enables the hand tool when another tool is active.

C hand tool options
Click the buttons in the options bar to adjust the view size, as discussed in View Commands on page 40.

Page Up & Page Down

If the scroll bars and hand tool aren't enough to satisfy your scrolling needs, here are a few shortcuts that allow you to pan inside the window without once touching the mouse. Note that the table is geared toward Windows users. If you use a Macintosh, press **command** instead of **ctrl**.

scroll	keystroke	scroll	keystroke
to upper-left corner	home	to lower-right corner	end
up one screen	page up	left one screen	ctrl+page up
up a few pixels	shift-page up	left a few pixels	ctrl+shift+page up
down one screen	page down	right one screen	ctrl+page down
down a few pixels	shift-page down	right a few pixels	ctrl+shift+page down

Zoom In, Zoom Out, Zoom Tool

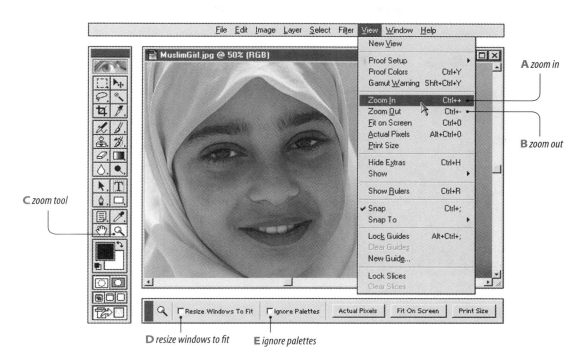

C *zoom tool*

A *zoom in*

B *zoom out*

D *resize windows to fit*   E *ignore palettes*

If you think all those scrolling tricks are a bit much, you haven't seen anything yet. Photoshop devotes more energy to zooming than it does to scrolling. The most essential of the many zoom functions are the **Zoom In** and **Zoom Out** commands and the ubiquitous zoom tool. Here's how they work:

A zoom in
Choose **View➞Zoom In** to magnify the foreground image. The command works in predefined increments, as indicated in the title bar. 100% is the most representative, showing one image pixel for every screen pixel.

B zoom out
Choose **View➞Zoom Out** to reduce the view size.

> *tip* Press **ctrl** plus the + key to zoom in and **ctrl** plus – to zoom out. Both zoom without resizing the window. To zoom the window and image together, press both **ctrl** and **alt**. On the Mac, it's the opposite. Press **command** with + or – to resize the window; add **option** to leave the window unchanged.

You can change the window resizing behavior. Choose **Edit➞Preferences➞General** and change the setting of **Keyboard Zoom Resizes Windows**. By default, it's checked on the Mac and unchecked on the PC.

C zoom tool
Click with the zoom tool to zoom in, **alt**-click (Win) or **option**-click (Mac) to zoom out. Drag to identify the area you want to magnify. Unless you specify otherwise (D), the window size remains unchanged.

> *tip* Press Z to select the zoom tool. Press **ctrl+ spacebar** (Win) or **command-spacebar** (Mac) to get the tool temporarily. Add **alt** or **option** to zoom out.

D resize windows to fit
Select this check box in the options bar to resize the window when clicking with the zoom tool.

E ignore palettes
Turn on this option to scale the image window with no regard for the palettes on the right side of the screen.

View Commands

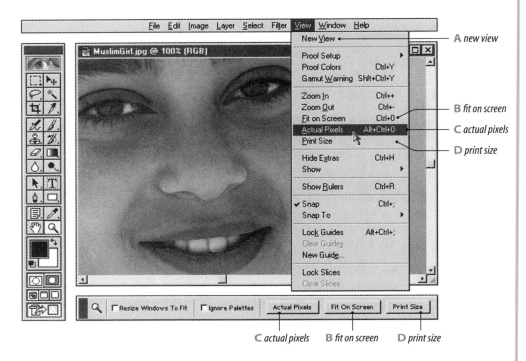

A *new view*

B *fit on screen*

C *actual pixels*

D *print size*

C *actual pixels*   **B** *fit on screen*   **D** *print size*

Zoom In, **Zoom Out**, and the zoom tool aren't the only options for magnifying an image inside Photoshop. Other commands in the **View** menu let you quickly switch to a different view size or create an entirely new window for the image.

A new view

Choose the **New View** command to create a new window for the foreground image. You still have just one image, but you have multiple windows into it. One window might be zoomed in and the other zoomed out, providing you with close up and far away views at the same time.

> *tip* To create a copy of the foreground image that you can edit entirely independently of the original, choose **Image→Duplicate**.

B fit on screen

View→Fit on Screen zooms the image to the highest magnification level that permits the entire image to be visible on screen.

> *tip* Other ways to fit the image on screen include double-clicking the hand tool icon in the toolbox, and pressing **ctrl+0** (Win) or **command-0** (Mac).

C actual pixels

Choose **Actual Pixels** to switch to the 100% view size. This is the most accurate view of the image because it shows you one image pixel for every screen pixel.

> *tip* To switch to the 100% view size, double-click the zoom tool icon in the toolbox or press **ctrl+alt+0** (Win) or **command-option-0** (Mac).

D print size

Choose **Print Size** to see the image at the size it will ostensibly print. Due to fluctuations in screen resolution, this command is generally meaningless.

> *tip* To gain access to any command but **New View** when a tool other than the hand or zoom tool is active, press the **spacebar** and right-click (Win) or **control**-click (Mac).

The Navigator Palette

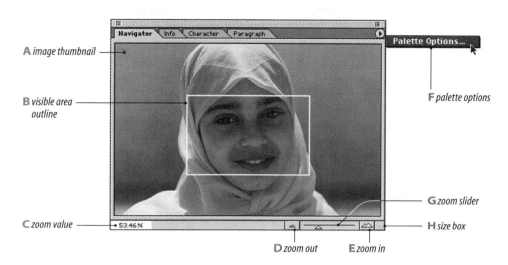

A *image thumbnail*

B *visible area outline*

C *zoom value*

F *palette options*

G *zoom slider*

H *size box*

D *zoom out*　E *zoom in*

To make sure all bases are covered, Photoshop gives you the **Navigator** palette (**Window➡Show Navigator**), which lets you scroll and zoom in a miniature copy of the image. It's like working with a zoomed out window created using **View➡New View**, but with some additional controls.

A image thumbnail
The central portion of the **Navigator** palette is consumed by a thumbnail of the image. Photoshop regularly updates the thumbnail to show all edits, so you can trust that it's accurate.

B visible area outline
The red rectangle shows the portion of the image visible in the foreground window. Drag the rectangle to scroll the image. Click to quickly center the outline to a new location, a real help when working at high levels of magnification.

> *tip* Press the **ctrl** (Win) or **command** (Mac) key and drag in the image thumbnail (A) to draw your own rectangle, thus changing the view size.

C zoom value
The zoom value tracks all magnification adjustments. You can also enter your own zoom value, accurate to 0.01 percent.

D zoom out
Click this icon to zoom out from the image, just as if you had **alt**- or **option**-clicked with the zoom tool.

E zoom in
Click here to magnify the image incrementally, as when clicking in the image window with the zoom tool.

F palette options
Choose **Palette Options** from the **Navigator** palette menu to display a dialog box inviting you to change the color assigned to the visible area outline (B). You can select a predefined color or click in the square swatch to define a color of your own.

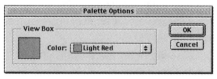

G zoom slider
Drag the triangle under the zoom slider to change the view size on the slide, as it were. As with all magnification adjustments, the new view size is reflected by the zoom value (C).

H size box
By default, the image thumbnail (A) is awfully dinky. If you want to make it bigger, drag here.

The Save Command, Windows

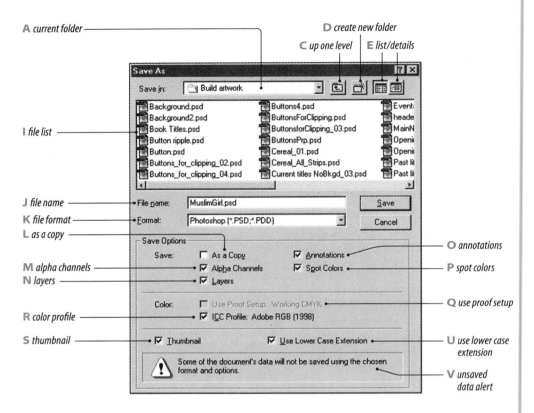

A *current folder*

D *create new folder*

C *up one level*   E *list/details*

I *file list*

J *file name*
K *file format*
L *as a copy*

M *alpha channels*
N *layers*

R *color profile*

S *thumbnail*

O *annotations*
P *spot colors*

Q *use proof setup*

U *use lower case extension*

V *unsaved data alert*

The simple act of saving ensures that you can use an image over and over for years to come. Photoshop is such a proponent of saving that it gives you four ways to approach the process:

Choose **File➡Save**, or press **ctrl+S** (Win) or **command-S** (Mac), to save your recent changes in place of the previous version of the image stored on disk.

Choose **File➡Save As**, or press **ctrl+shift+S** or **command-shift-S**, to display the dialog box above, which lets you specify the name of the saved image and the data that gets saved with it.

Press **ctrl+alt+S** or **command-option-S** to display this same dialog box with **As a Copy** (L) turned on, which saves an independent copy of the image.

Choose the **Save for Web** command to prepare an image so it can be posted on a Web site, as discussed in Chapter 18, Save For The Web.

Like the **Open** dialog box, the **Save** dialog box is devoted largely to the task of navigating from disk to disk and folder to folder. So it's not surprising that many **Save** options duplicate **Open** options. In the name of saving a few trees, the following pages focus on options unique to the **Save** dialog box.

A current folder
Use this option and the others in the top portion of the dialog box (B through I) to specify the disk and folder where you want to save the file. For more information, see The Open Command on pages 36 and 37.

J file name
Enter the name of the file that you want to create on disk. Windows permits you to enter a few hundred characters; the Mac tops out at 31. On the Mac, be sure not to replace the three-character extension (T) if you want the file to be compatible with Windows.

The Save Command, Macintosh

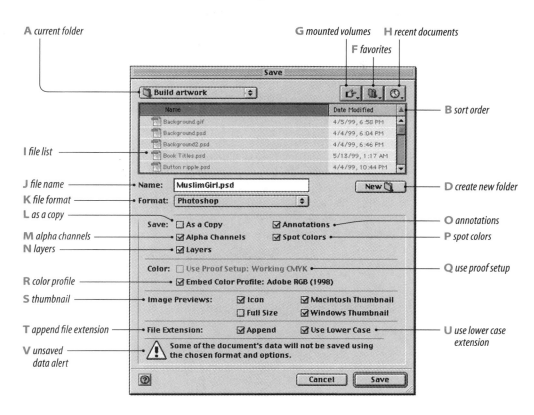

A *current folder*

G *mounted volumes* **H** *recent documents*

F *favorites*

B *sort order*

I *file list*

J *file name*

K *file format*

L *as a copy*

D *create new folder*

M *alpha channels*

N *layers*

O *annotations*

P *spot colors*

Q *use proof setup*

R *color profile*

S *thumbnail*

T *append file extension*

U *use lower case extension*

V *unsaved data alert*

K file format

An image file is a sequence of data stored on disk. The *file format* is the way the data is organized. The format you choose determines the information Photoshop can save and whether other programs can reliably interpret the image. Although Photoshop can save an image in more than a dozen formats, only a few are worth knowing about. The best are PSD, TIFF, JPEG, and PDF, as discussed on pages 45 through 48.

L as a copy

Select this specific check box to create an entirely independent file on disk. This means the next time you choose **File➡Save**, Photoshop updates the previously saved file and leaves the version saved using **As a Copy** unchanged. The advantage is that you can save several steps in the creation of an image knowing that each step will remain separate and intact.

M alpha channels

Chapter 9, Define Channels & Masks, shows how you can use *masks* to define intricate selections, helpful when editing hair and other fine details. To make a mask, you create a new *alpha channel* inside the **Channels** palette. Check the **Alpha Channels** option in the **Save** dialog box to save the masks with the image. This check box and the three that follow (N, O, & P) are not available when saving an image in the JPEG format, as in Save A JPEG Image on page 47.

N layers

As explained in Chapter 8, Create & Modify Layers, Photoshop lets you add independent layers of pixels and text to an image. To save these layers, select the **Layers** check box. Otherwise, the appearance of the image is preserved, but the independent layers are merged into a so-called *flat* image.

O annotations

Photoshop 6 lets you add notes to an image using the notes and audio annotation tools (as in The Annotate Tools on pages 50 and 51 of Chapter 4). You can save these notes by selecting the **Annotations** check box.

P spot colors

As explained in Add A Spot Color (pages 258 and 259), you can introduce additional inks to a CMYK image by creating separate channels of color. To save these so-called *spot colors*, select the **Spot Colors** check box.

Q use proof setup

Select this check box to convert an image to the color proofing environment specified using **View➞Proof Setup**. The option is available only when saving an image in the EPS or PDF format, as I examine in Save A PDF Document on page 48.

R color profile

This option lets you save a *color profile* with the image. Colors vary radically from one screen or printer to another. A color profile identifies the source of the colors in an image, so another program can convert the colors and maintain consistency from one computer to the next. For more information, read Color Settings on pages 58 and 59 of Chapter 4.

S thumbnail

The **Thumbnail** (Win) and **Image Previews** (Mac) options let you save reduced versions of an image so that you can preview the file before opening it. To see these options, you must first visit **Edit➞Preferences➞Saving Files** and select **Ask When Saving** from the **Image Previews** pop-up menu.

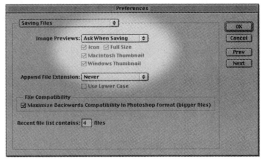

Photoshop for Windows lets you save just one kind of preview, which is visible from inside the **Open** dialog box. But on the Mac, you can save any of four kinds

of thumbnails, including an icon that's visible from the desktop and thumbnails for both the Mac and Windows **Open** dialog boxes. The remaining check box, **Full Size**, creates a large thumbnail that has such narrow use it's better left turned off.

T append file extension (Mac)

The three-letter *file extension*—such as **.psd** or **.tif**—permits a PC application to identify the format of an image file. On the Mac, an extension isn't necessary; however, I recommend you go ahead and use one in case you decide to open the image on a PC at some later point in time. To tell Photoshop to automatically append a file extension to the end of a file name, select the **Append** check box. (If this option is not available, choose **Edit➞Preferences➞Saving Files** and select **Ask When Saving** from the **Append File Extension** pop-up menu.)

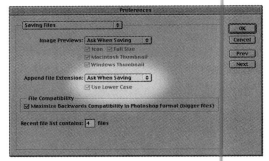

U use lower case extension

Select this check box to use lowercase (**.psd**) instead of uppercase (**.PSD**) letters in a file extension. Lower-case extensions are the better choice because they ensure compatibility across all computer platforms.

V unsaved data alert

An exclamation point at the bottom of the **Save** dialog box tells you that some information will not be saved with the file according to your specifications. Sometimes the solution is to select more check boxes; other times you need to select a different file format (such as PSD or TIFF). But just because you see the exclamation point doesn't necessarily mean you have reason to worry. For example, you might select **As a Copy** (L) and turn off **Layers** (N) in order to save a flattened version of the image. But so long as you also take care to save a layered version of the image, as explained on the facing page, you're covered.

🔵 Save A Native Photoshop File

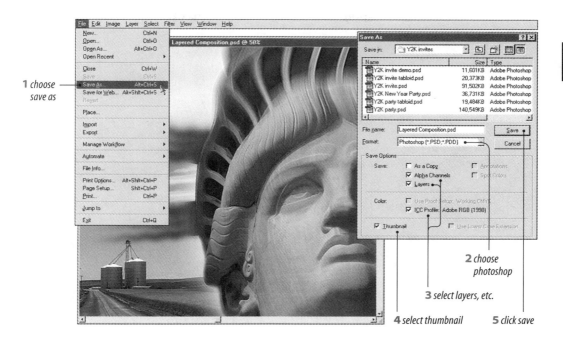

1 *choose save as*

2 *choose photoshop*

3 *select layers, etc.*

4 *select thumbnail*

5 *click save*

Every program has a file format that it prefers over all others. This so-called *native format* permits the application to not only store anything you create, but also save files quickly and with little fuss. The *Photoshop format*—also known by its file extension *PSD* (short for Photoshop document)—is Photoshop's native format. Unless you plan to import an image into another program, you should save it in the PSD format. And even then, you may want to create a back-up PSD file just to be safe.

1 choose save as
If this is your first time saving to the PSD format, choose **File➡Save As** to bring up the **Save** dialog box. After the first save, you can update the file just by pressing **ctrl+S** (Win) or **command-S** (Mac).

2 choose photoshop
Choose **Photoshop** from the **Format** pop-up menu. This is **Photoshop (*.PSD; *.PDD)** on the PC. The program automatically appends **.psd** to the end of the filename. If not, turn on **Append** (T) on the Mac.

3 select layers, etc.
Select all available check boxes except **As A Copy** in the central portion of the dialog box. Depending on your image, these may include **Alpha Channels** (M), **Layers** (N), **Annotations** (O), **Spot Colors** (P), and **Profile** (R). If you see an alert message (V), something isn't selected.

4 select thumbnail
On the Mac, select **Macintosh Thumbnail** at least. You might also select **Icon** and **Windows Thumbnail**.

5 click save
Photoshop saves the native PSD file.

> 📍 By default, when saving a layered PSD file, Photoshop tacks on a flat version of the image as well. This increases the file size by as much as 50 percent without providing any meaningful benefit. To save space on your hard disk, choose **Edit➡Preferences➡Saving Files**. Then turn off the check box **Maximize backwards compatibility in Photoshop format**.

steps Save A TIFF Image

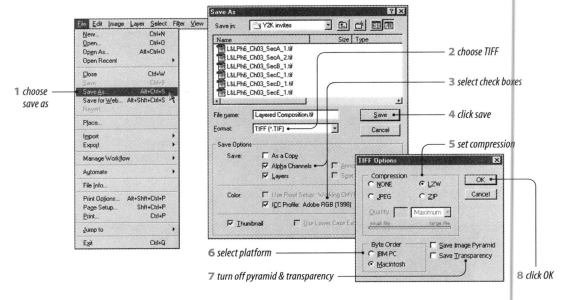

1 choose save as

2 choose TIFF

3 select check boxes

4 click save

5 set compression

6 select platform

7 turn off pyramid & transparency

8 click OK

PSD is great for saving images that you plan on editing inside Photoshop. But to open or import an image into another program, you need to save the file using a more standardized format. When placing an image into **QuarkXPress**, **InDesign**, or another publishing program, the best standardized format is *TIFF*, short for *tag image file format*.

1 choose save as
Alternatively, you can press **ctrl+alt+S** (Win) or **command-option-S** (Mac).

2 choose TIFF
On the PC, this option reads **TIFF (*.TIF)**.

3 select check boxes
The options available to you depend on your preferences. If you choose **Edit→Preferences→Saving Files** and turn on **Enable advanced TIFF save options**, you can save all data, including layers. Otherwise, **Layers** and **Annotations** are dimmed. In the event you do select **Layers**, Photoshop includes a flattened image to ensure compatibility with programs that don't recognize layers. This makes TIFF an ideal format for saving layered images for use outside Photoshop.

4 click save
This brings up the **TIFF Options** dialog box.

5 set compression (optional)
TIFF lets you reduce the size of the file by applying a **Compression** option. **LZW** and **ZIP** are *lossless*, meaning that they reduce file size without changing a single pixel in the image. **JPEG** is *lossy*, meaning that it achieves smaller file sizes by reorganizing pixels. Your best bet is the widely compatible and lossless **LZW**. Note: **ZIP** and **JPEG** are available only if **Enable advanced TIFF save options** (3) is checked.

6 select platform
Select whether you intend to use this file on a PC or a Mac. If you don't know, don't worry about it. Most programs support PC and Mac TIFF files alike.

7 turn off pyramid & transparency
The first check box saves multiple versions of an image with incrementally lower resolutions. The second retains transparent areas. Unless you have a reason for doing otherwise, leave both options off.

8 click OK
Photoshop takes a few moments to save the TIFF file.

steps Save A JPEG Image

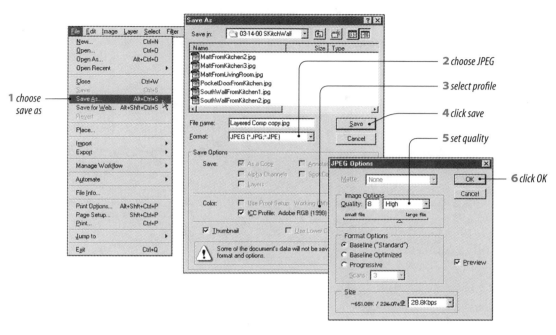

1 *choose save as*

2 *choose JPEG*

3 *select profile*

4 *click save*

5 *set quality*

6 *click OK*

Pronounced *jaypeg*, the *JPEG* format is exceptionally versatile. Although it cannot accommodate layers, channels, or annotations, it is the one format applicable to both print media and the Web. Because it permits you to compress a file to its absolute smallest, JPEG is perfect for archiving scans, digital photos, and other raw images.

1 choose save as
As always, this brings up the **Save** dialog box.

2 choose JPEG
On the PC, choose **JPEG (*JPG; *.JPE)**. If the image includes layers or other special information, Photoshop automatically selects **As a Copy** and adds the word **copy** to the name to show you that it's about to create an independent file on disk. If you decide to update this file in the future, you'll need to again choose **File➞Save As**.

3 select profile
Although JPEG can't handle layers and other data, it can accommodate the color profile.

4 click save
Click **Save** to display the **JPEG Options** dialog box, which asks you to specify how much JPEG compression you want to apply.

5 set quality
JPEG pits image quality against file size. A higher **Quality** setting results in a larger file; a lower setting saves disk space but makes for a rattier looking image. For printing and archiving, I recommend a **Quality** setting of 8 or better. Lower settings are acceptable for the Web, as discussed in Save A Photograph In JPEG on pages 268 and 269 in Chapter 18.

> *tip* To preview the effect of a **Quality** setting, select the **Preview** check box. Be sure to wait for the image to update in the image window.

6 click OK
The **Format Options** are designed primarily for Web images. However, whether you're bound for print or the Web, the default **Baseline ("Standard")** setting is safest. So click **OK** to save the file.

steps Save A PDF Document

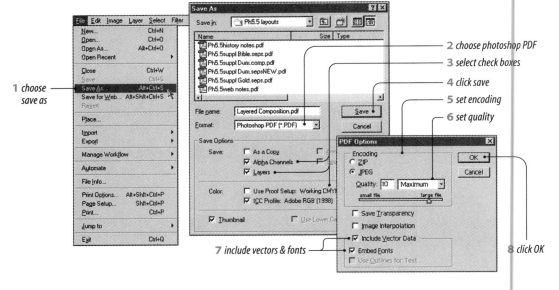

1 choose save as

2 choose photoshop PDF

3 select check boxes

4 click save

5 set encoding

6 set quality

7 include vectors & fonts

8 click OK

Previous to Version 6, Photoshop accommodated pixels only. Now the program enables you to create vector-based paths and text that will render at the full resolution of your printer, as explained in Chapter 11, Draw Vector Shapes. Both the PSD and TIFF formats can save this vector information, but neither can transfer vectors effectively to another program. The best format for exporting Photoshop vectors for use in the wider world of print and Web design is the *portable document format*, or *PDF*.

1 choose save as
Naturally, you have to choose **Save As** to switch to a new file format.

2 choose photoshop PDF
Photoshop calls its version of PDF **Photoshop PDF** to distinguish it from the multi-page PDF files that you can create using mainstream electronic publishing programs.

3 select check boxes
Like PSD and TIFF, PDF lets you save layers, channels, and annotations. Plus it goes one better, adding **Use Proof Setup**, which converts a saved image to CMYK.

4 click save
This brings up the **PDF Options** dialog box.

5 set encoding
You can compress pixels in one of two ways. Choose **ZIP** to apply lossless compression; choose **JPEG** for lossy. The latter, **JPEG**, is typically the better choice, since it permits you to keep file size to a minimum.

6 set quality
As when saving a straight JPEG file (discussed in Save A JPEG Image on page 47), you'll want to specify a **Quality** value of 8 or higher.

7 include vectors & fonts
The first check box (available only if the image lacks a Background layer) retains any transparent areas. The second, **Image Interpolation**, upsamples low-resolution images during printing and should be left off. Of more practical use are **Include Vector Data**, which saves vector shapes, and **Embed Fonts**, which includes typeface definitions so the file can be printed from any system with all fonts intact.

8 click OK
Photoshop saves the image so it can be opened in any program that supports PDF, notably **Adobe Acrobat**.

Personalize Photoshop

The word *software* says it all. Unlike hardware, which is an immutable and inanimate object, software is in a perpetual state of transition, capable of radical mutation at a moment's notice. Photoshop 6 is a case in point. So different is it from its predecessor that many features may seem altogether foreign to artists who have been using the program for years.

But lest you think Adobe's engineers are the only ones capable of transforming Photoshop, this is an exceptionally versatile piece of software that invites you to mold and adapt it to fit your specific needs. In addition to being able to merge palettes, adjust tools, and change how images are saved, you have at your disposal **Preferences**, **Preset Manager**, and **Color Settings**—commands whose sole purpose is to finesse the behavior of the program. It's your agenda; Photoshop just wants to make it happen.

The Annotate Tools

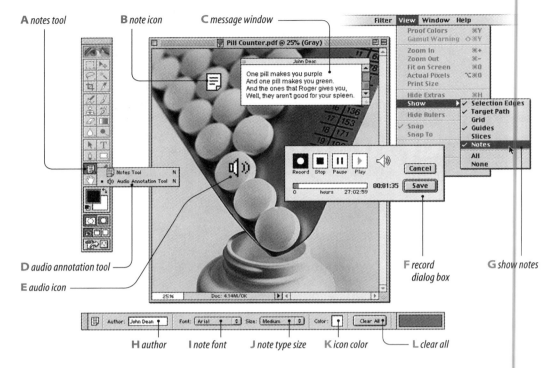

A notes tool   **B** note icon   **C** message window

D audio annotation tool
E audio icon

F record dialog box   **G** show notes

H author   **I** note font   **J** note type size   **K** icon color   **L** clear all

The journey toward personalizing Photoshop begins with a single image. The new annotation tools let you add private reminders as well as missives to other artists who may edit the image. You can even save an image in the PDF format (as explained in Save A PDF Document on page 48) and hand off the file to a client, who in turn can open and further annotate the file in **Adobe Acrobat 4** and later.

A notes tool
The notes tool lets you add text notes to an image. Click with the tool anywhere inside the image to start a new note; drag to make a new note and define the size of the message window (C).

B note icon
The note icon shows that there's a message in the image. Double-click the icon to display the corresponding message window (C). You can also drag the icon to move it to the exact portion of the image to which the note refers.

C message window
Enter your message into this window. Change the font (I), type size (J), and other attributes from the options bar. When you finish, close the message by clicking the box in the upper-left corner of the window. Don't worry, you can always restore the message by double-clicking the note icon (B).

D audio annotation tool
Click and hold on the notes tool icon in the toolbox to display a flyout menu offering the alternative audio annotation tool. Click with this tool to display the record dialog box (F), which lets you add a voice message. It's a nifty feature, no doubt, but before you get too carried away with it, bear in mind that audio notes increase the file size dramatically. By comparison, text notes take barely any space at all.

tip Press N to select the notes tool (A) from the keyboard. Press **shift-N** to switch between the notes and audio annotation (D) tools.

E audio icon

This icon shows that the image contains an audio annotation. Assuming your speakers are turned on, double-click this icon to listen to the message. Press **esc** to stop the sound.

Note that you cannot edit an audio note the way you can a text note. If you don't like a voice message, click **Clear All** (L) to delete it and create a new audio note.

F record dialog box

Clicking with the audio annotation tool displays the record dialog box. On the Mac, click the **Record** button to begin recording your voice. Some Macs, such as PowerBooks, include built-in microphones, so you can record without hooking up any additional hardware. Other Macs require separate mikes. When you finish speaking, click **Stop**, and then click **Save**.

On the PC, make sure you have a mike cabled to your sound card. If you have more than one sound card, choose **Start➡Settings➡Control Panel** and double-click the **Multimedia** icon to confirm the settings. When you're sure everything's in order, return to Photoshop, click with the audio annotation tool, and click the **Start** button. To stop recording, click **Stop**.

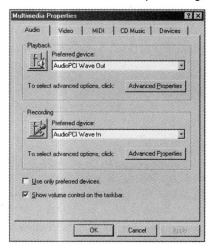

G show notes

Hide or show all notes with **View➡Show➡Notes**. A check mark shows whether or not the notes are visible.

> (tip) You can also hide notes by pressing **ctrl+H** (Win) or **command-H** (Mac). This invokes the **Hide Extras** command, which hides selection outlines, guides, and other non-printing items. To show the hidden extras, press **ctrl+H** or **command-H** again.

H author

Use this option to assign an author to a note. By default, Photoshop enters the name of the licensed user of the program (bad news for those of you who entered **Kilroy** or **Mr. Ed** during installation).

I note font

Choose the typeface that you want to assign to a selected text note. If no note is selected, your **Font** choice affects the next note you create. Either way, the pop-up menu affects all text in the note, not just the highlighted letters. This option and the next are available only when the notes tool is active; you cannot assign a font to an audio annotation.

J note type size

Choose from five type sizes for a selected text note, ranging from **Smallest** (illegibly small) to **Largest** (quite big). Text notes do not change in size when you zoom in and out , so be sure to use a combination of size and font that you can read without zooming.

K icon color

By default, annotation icons are colored with yellow. You can change the color assigned to a selected note icon by clicking the **Color** swatch in the options bar. Then define a color using the **Color Picker** dialog box, according to the rules spelled out in The Color Palette on pages 80 through 82 of Chapter 6.

L clear all

Click the **Clear All** button to delete a selected note. Photoshop asks if you're sure. Click **OK** if you are.

> (tip) Alternatively, you can delete a note by clicking its icon and pressing **backspace** (Win) or **delete** (Mac). Great tip, but it doesn't always work. If a selection or path is active, Photoshop deletes that instead. Luckily, **Clear All** always deletes notes.

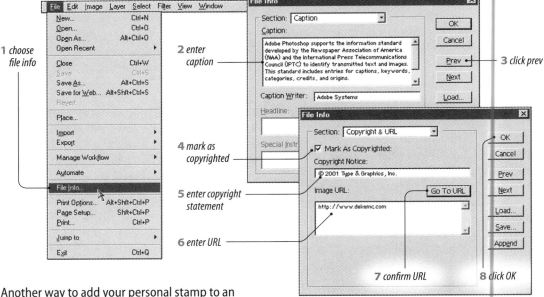

1 *choose file info*

2 *enter caption*

3 *click prev*

4 *mark as copyrighted*

5 *enter copyright statement*

6 *enter URL*

7 *confirm URL*

8 *click OK*

Another way to add your personal stamp to an image is to brand it with a copyright statement. Ever concerned to protect its users, Photoshop lets you add a copyright and Web site address with every image you make.

1 choose file info
On the PC, press **alt+F** and then **I**.

2 enter caption (optional)
The **Caption** field invites you to type anything from a sentence to several paragraphs about the image. This is your opportunity to add a commercial message or describe the subject of the photograph. Fill in **Caption Writer** to give yourself credit. To print image and caption, choose **File➡Print Options**, as explained on page 253 of The Print Options Command.

3 click prev
Or press **ctrl+6** (Win) or **command-6** (Mac) to view the sixth panel in the dialog box, **Copyright & URL**.

4 mark as copyrighted
Check this box to mark the image with a copyright symbol (©) in its title bar and preview box (introduced in Image Preview & Status Bar on page 15).

5 enter copyright statement
Enter the name of the copyright holder. The standard form is copyright symbol/date/copyright holder, as in "© 2001 Type & Graphics, Inc." To access the © on the PC, press and hold the **alt** key, press the numerical sequence 0-1-6-9 on the keypad, and then release **alt**. It's easier on the Mac—just press **option-G**.

6 enter URL
If you have a Web site, enter the address (known in the parlance as the *Universal Resource Locator*) in the **Image URL** option box. Enter the full address, such as **http://www.dekemc.com**, or just enough to get by, as in **funpix.com**.

7 confirm URL (optional)
Click the **Go To URL** button to launch a browser and check out your site. This is also how others can use the image to get to your Web site. Note that you must be connected to the Internet for this option to work.

8 click OK
Then save your image in any format. Even a JPEG file can accommodate a copyright and URL.

The Preferences Commands

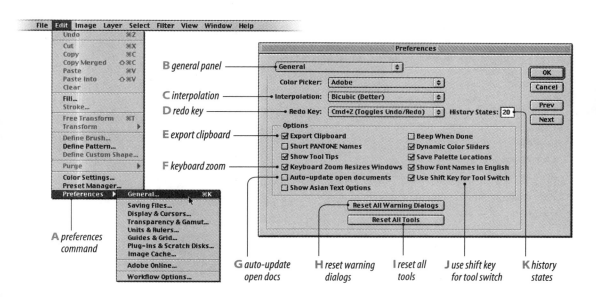

A *preferences command*

B *general panel*

C *interpolation*

D *redo key*

E *export clipboard*

F *keyboard zoom*

G *auto-update open docs*

H *reset warning dialogs*

I *reset all tools*

J *use shift key for tool switch*

K *history states*

Preferences are just that—settings you can adjust to fit your particular and sometimes ephemeral predilections. Where Photoshop is concerned, you can express your most inconsequential proclivities until the tiniest of the cow's fleas comes home. This isn't to say preferences are a waste of time; in fact, they can be very useful. It's just that you don't have to come to grips with every single one of them. In the next few pages, I cover what I consider to be the best of the preference settings, which is still an awful lot. The others you can safely ignore and leave set as they are by default.

A preferences command

Choose **Edit➡Preferences** to display a submenu of commands. Choose any one of them to display a specific panel of the vast **Preferences** dialog box.

> *tip* Better yet, press **ctrl+K** (Win) or **command-K** (Mac) to display the **General** panel. Then switch to another panel by pressing **ctrl** or **command** and a number—**ctrl+2** switches to **Saving Files**; **command-3** takes you to **Display & Cursors**. To display the **Preferences** dialog box and switch to the panel last used, press **ctrl+alt+K** or **command-option-K**.

B general panel

This panel contains all the settings that don't fit anywhere else. Ironically, they're often the most useful. Press **ctrl+1** (Win) or **command-1** (Mac) to return here.

C interpolation

This option decides how a scaled image is rendered. **Bicubic** ensures the smoothest results; **Nearest Neighbor** is good for retaining high-contrast edges. Your decision affects the behavior of the **Image Size** and **Free Transform** commands, among others. To learn more, see Resample An Image on page 24.

D redo key

You can change the shortcut for **Edit➡Redo** to match those offered by other programs. But I wouldn't; doing so assigns a non-standard shortcut to the **Undo** command, making it less accessible. For more information, see Chapter 15, Work With History.

E export clipboard

Every program has its own *Clipboard*, which is where items duplicated using **Edit➡Copy** are stored. When you switch programs, the Clipboard is transferred to the system. The problem is, Photoshop lets you copy enormous images that can bring your system to its

Preferences, Saving & Display

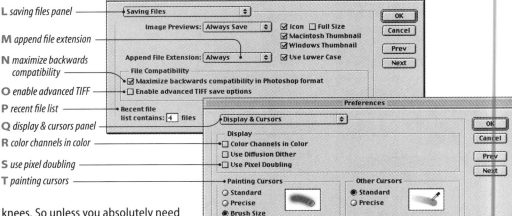

L *saving files panel*

M *append file extension*

N *maximize backwards compatibility*

O *enable advanced TIFF*

P *recent file list*

Q *display & cursors panel*

R *color channels in color*

S *use pixel doubling*

T *painting cursors*

knees. So unless you absolutely need to paste an image into another program, turn **Export Clipboard** off.

F keyboard zoom

Select whether you want to resize the image window when you press **ctrl** with **+** or **–**, as in Zoom In, Zoom Out, Zoom Tool on page 39 of Chapter 3.

G auto-update open docs

You and a coworker use networked computers to edit a single image that resides on a server. Your coworker chooses **Save**. If this check box is on (bad), your version of the image updates, wiping out your edits. If the check box is off (better), you are warned the source image has changed and given the option of updating.

H reset warning dialogs

When Photoshop presents you with a warning, you often have the option to select **Don't Show Again** so the program will stop heckling you. If you later decide you want to be heckled after all, click this button.

I reset all tools

Click this button to restore the default settings for all Photoshop's tools. You can perform this same operation by choosing **Reset All Tools** from the options bar.

J use shift key for tool switch

By default, pressing **shift** with a letter key switches between tools that share a slot in the toolbox. For

example, **shift-M** switches between the rectangular and elliptical marquee tools. Turn this check box off if you'd prefer to switch tools by pressing M alone.

K history states

This value specifies the number of operations you can undo from the **History** palette per open image.

L saving files panel

Click **Next**, or press **ctrl+2** (Win) or **command-2** (Mac), to change how files are opened and saved.

M append file extension (Macintosh)

Select **Always** to ensure that all files saved from the Mac version of Photoshop will also work on the PC.

N maximize backwards compatibility

Turn this option off to minimize the sizes of your PSD files! See Save A Native Photoshop File on page 45.

O enable advanced TIFF

Select this option to save layers with TIFF files, as well as apply ZIP and JPEG compression.

P recent file list

Photoshop shows your most recent work in **File➡ Open Recent** so you can easily reopen the images. Raise this value as high as **30** to remember more images; enter **0** to remain covert.

Preferences, Scratch Disks & Memory

U *plug-ins &*
scratch disks panel

V *additional plug-ins*

W *scratch disks*

X *memory & image*
cache panel

Y *physical*
memory usage

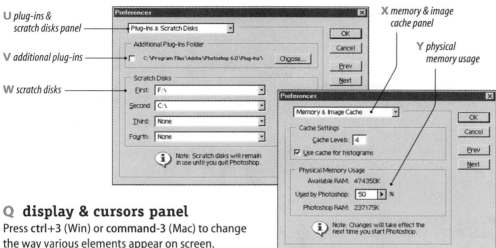

Q display & cursors panel

Press **ctrl+3** (Win) or **command-3** (Mac) to change the way various elements appear on screen.

R color channels in color

Normally, the component images in the **Channels** palette are shown as grayscale. Select this check box to colorize the channels so you can see them as Photoshop sees them. Channels are the subject of Chapter 9, Define Channels & Masks.

S use pixel doubling

Select this option if you want to temporarily down-sample an image when you move a layer or drag a slider triangle in a color adjustment dialog box.

T painting cursors

These options affect the cursor when a paint or edit tool is active. The cursor may look like the tool icon (**Standard**), a cross (**Precise**), or a circle the size of the active brush (**Brush Size**). The last setting is the best. Press **caps lock** to temporarily get **Precise**.

U plug-ins & scratch disks panel

The next few panels are devoted mainly to measurements and guides, as explained on page 21 of Rulers & Units. Press **ctrl+7** (Win) or **command-7** (Mac) to leap-frog beyond them to **Plug-Ins & Scratch Disks**.

V additional plug-ins

Like most applications, Photoshop is a bunch of programs working together. Entire squadrons of subprograms, or *plug-in modules*, are located inside folders

with names like **Helpers**, **Required**, and **Plug-Ins**. If you want Photoshop to load another folder of plug-ins during start up, select this check box and click the **Choose** button to locate the folder on disk.

W scratch disks

When Photoshop runs out of real memory (or *RAM*, as on page 23 of The Image Size Command), it starts gobbling up space on your hard drive. This so-called *scratch disk* space represents Photoshop's reserve of *virtual memory*. If you run out of scratch disk, it's game over, so a little up-front management is a great idea. If your computer provides more than one hard disk, select the disks in the order you want Photoshop to use them, starting with the disk that does *not* contain the Photoshop application or your operating system.

X memory & image cache panel

Press **ctrl+8** (Win) or **command-8** (Mac) to view the final essential preference setting.

Y physical memory usage (Windows)

When RAM becomes scarce, Photoshop battles with the Windows operating system to see who gets the memory. You can specify how much RAM Photoshop can grab and keep by entering a **Used by Photoshop** value. Exit Photoshop and restart the program to make the new setting take effect.

The Preset Manager

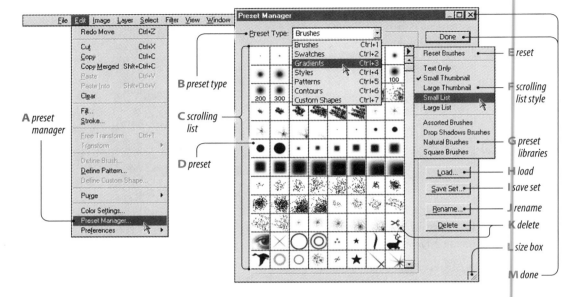

B *preset type*

C *scrolling list*

D *preset*

A *preset manager*

E *reset*

F *scrolling list style*

G *preset libraries*

H *load*

I *save set*

J *rename*

K *delete*

L *size box*

M *done*

Photoshop 6 introduces *presets*, which are collections of brushes, color swatches, gradients, and other attributes made widely available to tools and commands throughout the program. Photoshop automatically installs a handful of libraries representing each category of preset in the **Presets** folder inside the **Photoshop 6.0** folder.

A preset manager

Choose **Edit➡Preset Manager** (or press alt+E, M on the PC) to display the **Preset Manager** dialog box, which lets you load and save preset libraries, as well as delete and rename individual presets. The one thing you can't do is create a new preset; for that, consult the options bar (N through R).

B preset type

Choose the category of preset you want to manage. These include brushes for the paint and edit tools, patterns for the rubber stamp tool, custom shapes for the vector drawing tools, and so on.

C scrolling list

These are the presets available to the selected category (B). If the list is empty, choose a library (G).

D preset

The scrolling list shows previews of each available preset. Click a preset to select it; **shift**-click to select multiple presets. You can likewise deselect a preset by **shift**-clicking on it.

E reset

Click the arrowhead above the scroll bar to display a menu. Choose **Reset** to restore the scrolling list to its default collection for the selected category (B).

F scrolling list style

Choose one of these options to change the appearance of the presets in the scrolling list. You can view presets by name (**Text Only**), thumbnail, or name and thumbnail together (the two **List** options).

G preset libraries

The bottom of the menu lists other preset libraries in this category. Choose a library to load it. Then decide if you want to replace all presets in the scrolling list or click **Append** to add the new presets to the list.

H load

To load a library not found in the menu, click this button and search for the library on disk.

Presets In The Options Bar

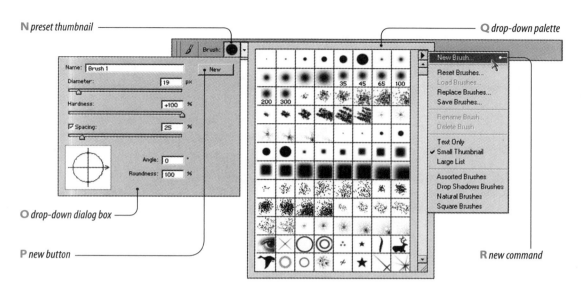

N *preset thumbnail*

Q *drop-down palette*

O *drop-down dialog box*

P *new button*

R *new command*

I save set

To create your own library, select the desired presets in the scrolling list and click **Save Set**. To trade libraries created on the Mac with the PC, be sure the preference setting **Append File Extension** is set to **Always** (see Preferences, Saving & Display on page 54).

J rename

Double-click a preset or click the **Rename** button to assign a different name to a selected preset.

K delete

Click here to delete one or more selected presets. But be careful! You can't undo this operation, and there's no **Cancel** button. The only way to retrieve a deleted preset is to reload it from a library on disk.

> *tip* Deleting may be dangerous, but it's not difficult. Press the **alt** (Win) or **option** (Mac) key and click with the scissors cursor to delete a preset.

L size box

Drag here to resize the **Preset Manager** dialog box.

M done

Click either **Done** or the Windows close box to close the dialog box and accept all changes.

N preset thumbnail

To create a new preset or edit an existing one, select a tool that uses the preset and refer to the options bar. Above I've selected the paintbrush tool and clicked the **Brush** preset thumbnail.

O drop-down dialog box

A single click of the preset thumbnail may be all it takes to edit the preset. Clicking the **Brush** thumbnail drops down a dialog box from the options bar (see Brush Size & Shape, page 96). Clicking a gradient thumbnail displays a floating dialog box (Make Your Own Gradient, pages 88 and 89). Other presets are defined using commands, as I explain in later sections.

P new button

Click the **New** button to make a new preset rather than edit an existing one.

Q drop-down palette

Click the triangle next to the preset thumbnail (N) to see a palette of presets. The palette remains available until you press **enter** or **esc** or again click the triangle.

R new command

Choose **New** from the drop-down palette menu to display a dialog box of present creation options.

Color Settings

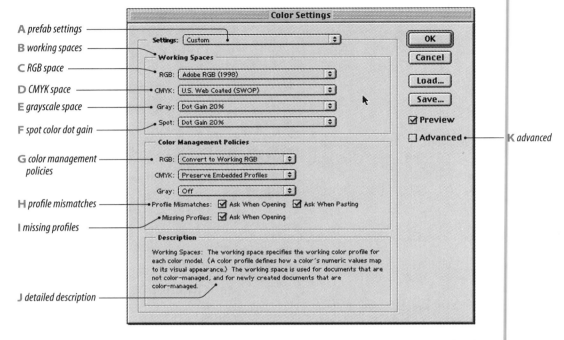

A *prefab settings*

B *working spaces*

C *RGB space*

D *CMYK space*

E *grayscale space*

F *spot color dot gain*

G *color management policies*

H *profile mismatches*

I *missing profiles*

J *detailed description*

K *advanced*

Color management determines whether the colors you see on screen are representative of the colors you'll later see in print or on the Web. Initially, this might not make a lick of sense. Shouldn't Photoshop be able to display accurate colors without asking you to set preferences? After all, your preference will always be "yes, make the colors accurate." Sadly, it's more complicated than that. You're talking about matching your monitor to thousands of possible monitors and printers, all of which generate colors differently. Photoshop's solution is to ask you to choose **Edit➡Color Settings** (alt+E, G on the PC) and respond to the survey in the **Color Settings** dialog box. Here's how it works:

A prefab settings

If color management seems overly technical and you want to get it over with as quickly as possible, choose a **Settings** option and let Photoshop recommend the best settings for you. If you're a Web designer, choose **Web Graphics Defaults**. If most of your images go to print, choose one of the **Prepress Defaults** options—

U.S., **Europe**, or **Japan**. I strongly advise that you steer clear of the other options.

B working spaces

Photoshop generates accurate colors by converting them from a *working space* to your monitor. The working space emulates the display of colors on a different monitor or printer. These options therefore establish a source (the working space) and a destination (your monitor), which is precisely what Photoshop needs to make informed color manipulations.

C RGB space

The letters *RGB* stand for red, green, and blue, the primary colors of light. Your monitor projects light onto red, green, and blue phosphors that coat the inside of the screen. Therefore, your monitor is said to be an *RGB device*. Scanners and digital cameras are likewise RGB devices, because they capture light using red, green, and blue receptors. As a result, every digitized photograph starts out as an RGB image.

The **RGB** pop-up menu in the **Working Spaces** area defines how an RGB image (the source) is displayed on your monitor (the destination). You can choose from several sources, but the most popular are **sRGB** and **Adobe RGB**. The default, **sRGB**, represents a baseline PC monitor, great for anticipating the appearance of Web images. **Adobe RGB** is based on a high-definition TV screen, making it capable of displaying a wider range of colors, better suited to professional printing.

D CMYK space

CMYK stands for cyan, magenta, yellow, and black, the so-called *process-color* inks used to create full-color pages in commercial printing. Before submitting an image to a commercial printer, you need to convert the image to CMYK using **Image➞Mode➞CMYK Color**, as in Prepare A CMYK Image To Place In A Publishing Program on pages 254 and 255.

The **CMYK** option in the **Working Spaces** area defines a source for CMYK images. The default setting, **U.S. Web Coated (SWOP)**, is designed to accommodate commercial *web offset printing* (nothing to do with the World Wide Web) with coated paper stock. If you intend to use uncoated stock, choose **U.S. Web Uncoated**. Otherwise, consult with your print house.

E grayscale space

When creating a black-and-white publication, choose **Image➞Mode➞Grayscale** to convert your images to shades of gray. This speeds printing and eliminates potential problems. Black-and-white printing uses black ink only, so color management is simpler. If you look closely at a printed image, you'll see tiny dots, or *halftone cells*. When the ink hits the paper, it expands these dots slightly, resulting in the phenomenon called *dot gain*. Select the dot gain you expect from the **Grayscale** pop-up menu. Higher values tell Photoshop to lighten the image to account for darker printing.

If you're creating grayscale images strictly for the Web, select one of the **Gamma** options. **Gamma 2.2** most accurately anticipates PC monitors.

F spot color dot gain

Spot colors are additional inks beyond CMYK. Like grayscale, you need to account for dot gain. To learn more, read Add A Spot Color on pages 258 and 259.

G color management policies

When Photoshop saves an image, it embeds a *color profile*, which explains the working space (B) in which the image was last edited. Photoshop also reads this profile when opening an image. So what happens when the embedded profile doesn't match the working space? The answer lies in **Color Management Policies**. Select from **Off**, which ignores the embedded profile; **Preserve Embedded Profiles**, which uses the profile as the working space for the image; and **Convert To Working**, which converts the colors in the image from the profile space to the working space.

H profile mismatches

The **Color Management Policies** are somewhat moot, however, because Photoshop goes ahead and asks you to confirm your decisions every time it opens an image in which the profile does not match the working space (below). To tell Photoshop to stop bugging you, turn off **Ask When Opening**. From then on, it just tells you what it's doing, as an FYI. **Ask When Pasting** controls whether Photoshop bugs you when you copy an image from one space and paste it into another.

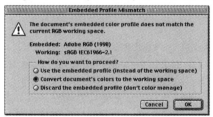

I missing profiles

Not all images contain profiles. When you open an image without one, Photoshop asks you if you'd like to assign the file a profile next time you save it, or just leave it alone. The correct answer: Assign that profile.

J detailed description

If you don't like my explanations, hover your cursor over an option and read the **Description** text.

K advanced

Check here to decide how Photoshop tweaks colors from one working space to the next. These options are wisely hidden; you don't need to get involved.

⬤steps Ensure Accurate Color

Now that you understand what the **Color Settings** options do, the following steps explain how to best put them to work to achieve predictable color:

1 open adobe gamma
Photoshop ships with a program called **Adobe Gamma** that lets you calibrate your monitor. This way, Photoshop knows the proper destination for its color conversions. On the PC, choose **Start➡Settings➡Control Panel**, then double-click **Adobe Gamma**. On the Mac, choose **Apple➡Control Panels➡Adobe Gamma**.

2 select control panel, click next
This displays all the options in one window.

3 set gamma sliders
Turn off **View Single Gamma Only**. Then squint your eyes and use the sliders to make the inner colors match the outer ones in each of the three color swatches.

4 click OK
And name the new monitor settings file.

5 display color settings
Choose **Edit➡Color Settings** to display the **Color Settings** dialog box.

6 choose adobe RGB
If you're like most artists, you do a lot of Web work one day and a lot of print work the next. If so, the best general-purpose RGB space is **Adobe RGB**.

7 choose CMYK space
If you know what print house you'll be working with, consult your press operator about the optimal **CMYK** setting. Otherwise, choose **U.S. Web Coated (SWOP)**.

8 set color management policies
It's generally considered a good idea to convert RGB images. But CMYK images are designed for specific printers and should therefore remain unchanged. Grayscale images rarely need management. Set **RGB** to **Convert To Working RGB**; set **CMYK** to **Preserve Embedded Profiles**; set **Gray** to **Off**. Turn off the **Profile Mismatches** and **Missing Profiles** check boxes.

9 click save, name file, add comment
It's a good idea to save your settings so you can access them later. After you name the file, click **Save** again. Then enter a comment if you like and click **OK**. From now on, your saved settings are listed as a **Settings** option; the comment appears in the **Description** area.

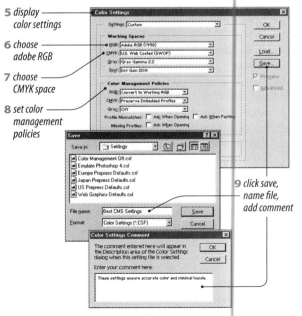

1 open adobe gamma
2 select control panel, click next
3 set gamma sliders
4 click OK

5 display color settings
6 choose adobe RGB
7 choose CMYK space
8 set color management policies
9 click save, name file, add comment

Make Selections

Whether your intention is to correct part of a photo or create some wholly impossible visual effect, you need a selection tool. Armed with one of these, you can draw a *selection outline,* which isolates one portion of an image from the rest. The area inside the selection outline is vulnerable to your edits; the area outside is not. This is how you change the color of a dress, sharpen the focus of a face in the crowd, or put a dog's head on a man's body.

Selections are so critical that Photoshop devotes 15 tools, a palette, and an entire menu to their creation and modification, all of which I discuss in this chapter. But that's not all. If you can't get a selection just right, Photoshop supplies a line of masking and extraction capabilities, discussed in Chapter 9, Define Channels & Masks. One way or another, you'll select exactly the portion of the image you have in mind.

61

The Marquee Tools

A *marquee tool slot*
B *rectangular marquee tool*
C *elliptical marquee tool*
D *single row & column tools*
E *selection states*
F *feather*
G *antialiasing*
H *size constraint*
I *marquee*

Rectangular Marquee Tool M
Elliptical Marquee Tool M
Single Row Marquee Tool
Single Column Marquee Tool

ELittle watercolor.jpg @ 50% (RGB)

Feather: 0 px ☑ Anti-aliased Style: Fixed Size Width: 64 px Height: 64 px

Photoshop's marquee tools permit you to draw selection outlines in the shape of rectangles and ovals. The tools are wonderfully easy to use—just drag to make a perfect geometric shape—so they serve as a perfect jumping off point for learning about some of the finer points of selections.

A marquee tool slot

Photoshop devotes the very first slot in the toolbox to the marquee tools. Click and hold to display a flyout menu of alternate tools.

B rectangular marquee tool

Press **M** to select the default resident of the marquee tool slot, which lets you draw rectangular selections, well suited to editing screen shots or merely isolating portions of a layer. Press **shift** when drawing a marquee to draw a square. Press **alt** (Win) or **option** (Mac) to draw outward from the center.

> *tip* When drawing with any marquee tool, press the **spacebar** to move the shape on the fly, great for getting a selection outline exactly in position.

C elliptical marquee tool

Press **shift-M** to switch to the elliptical marquee tool. Then drag in the image window to draw an oval selection outline. Press **shift** to draw a circle; press **alt** or **option** to draw outward from the center; press the **spacebar** to move the oval on the fly.

D single row & column tools

The remaining marquee tools let you select an entire row (horizontal) or column (vertical) of pixels. In each case, the row or column measures just one pixel tall or wide and the entire width or height of the image. Ostensibly, these tools permit you to isolate random lines of scanner garbage. But between you and me, I've never found a compelling use for either of them.

E selection states

Normally, dragging with a marquee tool creates a new selection outline. Alternatively, however, you can add to an existing selection, subtract from it, or retain only the intersection of the existing selection and the new outline. For more information, read Add, Subtract, Restrict on page 69.

F feather

Normally, a selection outline represents a crisp delineation between the selected and protected areas in an image. To assign a gradual transition to the next selection outline you draw, enter a value into the **Feather** option. Higher values result in softer transitions. See Antialias & Feather below for more information.

G antialiasing

Imagine you have a bag of blocks. I ask you to build me a big rectangle. No problem, right? Next, I ask you to build a circle. No matter how hard you try to make the perimeter of the shape smooth, it comes out jagged. Substitute pixels for blocks and you have an idea of the problem facing Photoshop. Rectangular selections are easy, but how does it draw a smooth oval when each and every pixel is square? The solution is to turn on the **Anti-aliased** check box, which tells Photoshop to blur the selection of the outer ring of pixels. It's like making the blocks around the perimeter of the circle semi-transparent. The translucent blocks blend into the background, softening the shape. Note

that *antialiasing*, as it's called, is applicable to curved selections only; when using the rectangular marquee tool (B), the **Anti-aliased** check box is dimmed.

H size constraint

Suppose you want to select an area according to a specific *aspect ratio*—say, 4 parts wide for every 3 parts tall. Choose **Constrained Aspect Ratio** from the **Style** pop-up menu and enter 4 and 3 into the **Width** and **Height** option boxes, respectively. Your next marquee will measure 4/3 as wide as it is tall, the same proportions as a computer screen. If you would rather specify an exact size, such as 640 by 480 pixels, choose **Fixed Size** and enter 640 and 480 into the **Width** and **Height** option boxes. To return to an unconstrained marquee, choose **Normal**.

I marquee

Photoshop traces the *marquee* (a.k.a. selection outline) with a pattern of animated dashes, informally known as marching ants. The pixels inside the marquee are said to be *selected*; the pixels outside the marquee are *deselected*.

Antialias & Feather

Most folks have never heard the word *antialiasing*, and while *feather* sounds familiar, it means something altogether different when the topic is Photoshop as opposed to, say, poultry. Yet both are ways to modify selections to achieve authentic, photographic transitions.

On the right, I dragged each of three kinds of selections against a white background. The difference is all in the edges.

J jagged edges

If Photoshop were incapable of softening selection outlines, every curved edge would appear jagged, with stair-stepped transitions around the selected portion of the image.

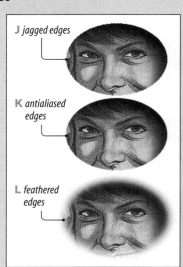

J *jagged edges*

K *antialiased edges*

L *feathered edges*

K antialiased edges

Antialiasing partially selects the outer ring of pixels to create a slight fade between the selection and the area around it. Because the ring of antialiasing is never more than one pixel thick, the edges appear at once well-defined and smooth.

L feathered edges

If antialiasing is soft, feathering is downright blurry. It fades the selection over a range of pixels, as defined by the **Feather** value. The value represents a radius, which means that it takes at least twice that distance to complete the effect. The figure shows a **Feather** value of 6, so the fade extends a bit beyond 12 pixels.

The Lasso Tools

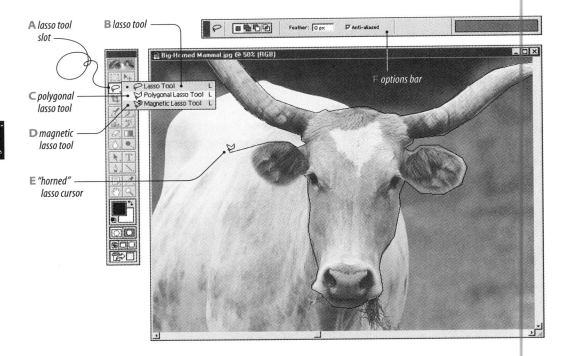

A *lasso tool slot*

B *lasso tool*

C *polygonal lasso tool*

D *magnetic lasso tool*

E *"horned" lasso cursor*

F *options bar*

Few image elements are rectangular or oval. To accommodate more common free-form elements, like the steer's head above, Photoshop provides the lasso tools.

tip Draw a polygon with the standard lasso tool by pressing the **alt** key (or **option** on the Mac) and clicking. Alternate between **alt-clicking** and dragging to combine straight and free-form sides.

A lasso tool slot
Click and hold the lasso icon to display a flyout menu containing three tools, each of which draws selection outlines of any size or shape.

B lasso tool
Click the lasso icon or press the L key to select the standard version of the lasso tool. Drag inside the image window to draw a free-form selection outline.

C polygonal lasso tool
Press **shift-L** to switch to the polygonal lasso tool. Then click repeatedly inside the image window to set corners in a straight-sided selection (also called a free-form *polygon*). To complete the selection, click at the first point in the outline. Or double-click to create a new corner and finish the selection in one action.

D magnetic lasso tool
Press **shift-L** again to get the magnetic lasso tool, which traces the contours of an image element based on its coloring. For a hands-on tour, see Draw A Magnetic Lasso on the facing page.

E "horned" lasso cursor
The cursor changes to show you which lasso tool is active. The "horned" lasso indicates that you're drawing a straight-sided selection, either with the polygonal or standard lasso tool.

F options bar
Most of the lasso options are the same as those available to the marquee tools (The Marquee Tools, **pages 62 and 63**). But a few are unique to the magnetic lasso, as I show on the facing page.

⬬steps Draw A Magnetic Lasso

Every so often, an element stands out from its background so clearly that you think surely Photoshop must be able to see it as well as you do. That's when you should take up the magnetic lasso tool.

1 get image
Open an image with strong color distinction between the foreground element and its background.

2 select magnetic lasso tool
If necessary, press shift-L.

3 click to set first point
Click anywhere along the outline of the foreground element. I clicked on the horn of the steer; for no particular reason, this is where I decided to start.

4 move cursor around image
You do *not* need to drag. After your initial click, you need only move the mouse around the image element—much less taxing on your hands and wrists than dragging, I assure you. You need only click to set a significant point in the selection outline.

> *tip* In addition to your click points, the magnetic lasso adds points automatically. These points bind the outline around the image element. If you don't like where Photoshop sets the last point, press the **backspace** (Win) or **delete** (Mac) key.

5 adjust width value
Of all the items in the options bar, the **Width** value is far and away the most useful. It determines the thickness of the area examined by the magnetic lasso as you move the cursor. For general tracing, the default **Width** value is fine, but for tight areas like the hairs around the steer's ears, you need to lower the value.

> *tip* Lower the **Width** value on the fly by pressing the [key (to the right of P). Each [lowers the value by 1. Raise the value incrementally by pressing].

6 click first point
This closes the shape to create the finished selection. Or double-click to connect the first and last points.

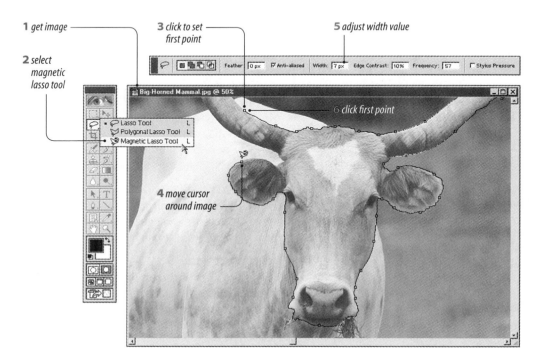

1 *get image*

2 *select magnetic lasso tool*

3 *click to set first point*

5 *adjust width value*

Big-Horned Mammal.jpg @ 50%

6 *click first point*

4 *move cursor around image*

Lasso Tool   L
Polygonal Lasso Tool   L
Magnetic Lasso Tool   L

Feather: 0 px   ✓ Anti-aliased   Width: 7 px   Edge Contrast: 10%   Frequency: 57   ☐ Stylus Pressure

The Magic Wand

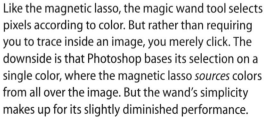

A *magic wand tool*

B *tolerance* — **C** *antialiasing* **D** *contiguous* — **E** *use all layers*

F *eyedropper*

G *sample size*

Like the magnetic lasso, the magic wand tool selects pixels according to color. But rather than requiring you to trace inside an image, you merely click. The downside is that Photoshop bases its selection on a single color, where the magnetic lasso *sources* colors from all over the image. But the wand's simplicity makes up for its slightly diminished performance.

A magic wand tool

Press the **W** key to select the magic wand. Then click in a uniformly colored portion of an image to select it.

B tolerance

This number defines the range of selected colors, as measured in *brightness levels*. A **Tolerance** of 32 tells the wand to spread the selection 32 levels lighter and 32 levels darker. Raise or lower the **Tolerance** to increase or decrease the range of the next selection.

C antialiasing

Soften the edges of the selection by turning on this check box. For jagged edges, turn the option off.

D contiguous

Normally, the wand selects *contiguous* (adjacent) pixels only. So if two orange pumpkins are separated by a green field, the wand selects one pumpkin and not the other. To select both, turn off **Contiguous**.

E use all layers

To base the selection on colors from all visible layers, check this option. To source colors from the active layer only, turn the option off. To learn more about layers, read Chapter 8, Create & Modify Layers.

F eyedropper

Curiously, the magic wand options aren't the only ones that affect the wand tool. Select the eyedropper tool (by pressing the I key) to see one more.

G sample size

This pop-up menu appears in the options bar when the eyedropper tool is active. It controls the number of colors on which the magic wand bases its selections. **Point Sample** sources just the color of the pixel you click; **5 by 5 Average** sources 25 colors in all.

Grow, Similar, Modify

If clicking with the magic wand tool selects too much of an image, your best bet is to lower the **Tolerance** value and try again. But if the wand selects too little, Photoshop provides a wealth of commands that expand the size of a selection:

1 get image
Open an image that contains a high degree of color contrast, like my orange pumpkin set against a backdrop of greens and browns.

2 select magic wand tool
Press the W key.

3 click image element
Click what seems to be the most medium-colored pixel in the element that you want to select. That way, Photoshop has lots of room to go lighter and darker as it expands the selection.

4 choose grow
Choose **Select ➡ Grow** to expand the selection by the amount specified in the **Tolerance** option box.

It's as if the selected pixels were the source colors for another magic wand selection. If the selection doesn't grow enough, choose **Select ➡ Grow** again.

5 choose similar
Select ➡ Similar is just like the **Grow** command, except that it jumps across differently colored areas to incorporate non-adjacent pixels that fall inside the **Tolerance** range. In the case of my pumpkin, **Similar** lets me select the orange pixels that lie on the other side of the green stem.

6 choose smooth
A typical magic wand selection suffers lots of loose pixels around its perimeter. To smooth these away, choose **Select ➡ Modify ➡ Smooth**. Photoshop presents you with a **Radius** option. Enter the thickness of the gnarliest edge in the selection and click **OK**.

7 choose expand or contract
Finally, to expand or contract the selection outline by a specific number of pixels, choose one of these commands. Both are great for last-minute adjustments.

1 get image

2 select magic wand tool

3 click image element

4 choose grow

5 choose similar

6 choose smooth

7 choose expand or contract

Essential Selection Commands

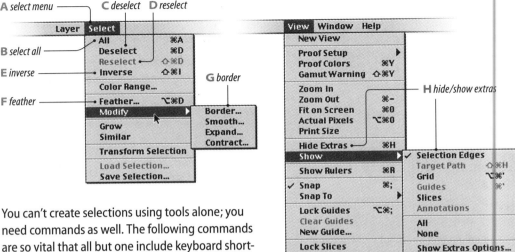

A *select menu*   C *deselect*   D *reselect*

B *select all*

E *inverse*

G *border*

F *feather*

H *hide/show extras*

You can't create selections using tools alone; you need commands as well. The following commands are so vital that all but one include keyboard shortcuts. In time, you'll use them without even thinking.

A select menu

Naturally, the bulk of the selection commands reside in the **Select** menu. If you're ever in doubt as to how to edit a selection, look here.

B select all

Select➡**All** selects every pixel in the active layer. But given that most of Photoshop's commands affect an entire layer when no pixel is selected, what's the purpose of selecting everything when you can achieve the same results by selecting nothing? Well, there are a few commands that require a selection, most notably **Cut** and **Copy**. To copy an entire layer to the Clipboard, for example, choose **Select**➡**All** and then **Edit**➡**Copy**. That's **ctrl+A**, **ctrl+C** (Win) or **command-A**, **command-C** (Mac).

C deselect

To deselect all pixels in an image, press **ctrl+D** (Win) or **command-D** (Mac). Alternatively, you can click in the image with the lasso or marquee tool.

D reselect

After deselecting an image, you can reinstate the most recent selection by pressing **ctrl+shift+D** (Win) or **command-shift-D** (Mac). Creating a new selection disables **Reselect** until you next deselect the image.

E inverse

Select➡**Inverse** reverses a selection, selecting everything that isn't selected and deselecting everything that is. For instance, suppose you want to select everything but the sky. Just click in the sky with the magic wand and press **ctrl+shift+I** or **command-shift-I**.

F feather

Press **ctrl+alt+D** or **command-option-D** to feather an existing selection outline. This is usually more convenient than feathering in advance using the **Feather** value in the options bar.

G border

Of the **Select** commands, **Border** is the least essential. I mention it only because of what it *doesn't* do. Rather than draw a border around a selection, as its name implies, it selects the border. Draw a border using **Edit**➡**Stroke**, as in The Stroke Command on page 90.

H hide/show extras

Press **ctrl+H** (**command-H** on the Mac) to hide the marching ants and other extras so you can better see your image. Or hide just the ants using **View**➡**Show**➡ **Selection Edges**. Choose **View**➡**Show**➡**Show Extra Options** to control exactly what **ctrl+H** hides.

Add, Subtract, Restrict

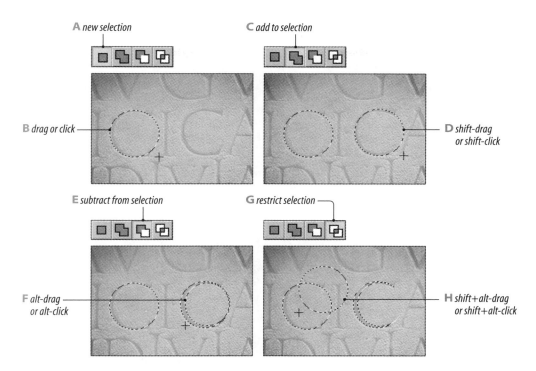

A *new selection*

C *add to selection*

B *drag or click*

D *shift-drag or shift-click*

E *subtract from selection*

G *restrict selection*

F *alt-drag or alt-click*

H *shift+alt-drag or shift+alt-click*

The selection state buttons (The Marquee Tools, page 62) let you combine marquees to create complex selections. Once you glean how they work, you can perform each technique from the keyboard.

A new selection
The default setting replaces the old selection with the new selection, regardless of the tool you use.

B drag or click
When no key is pressed, drag with a marquee or lasso tool, or click with the magic wand, to replace the old selection with a new one.

C add to selection
Select this button to add one selection outline to another. Both old and new selections are retained.

D shift-drag or shift-click
To add outlines without resorting to the **Add to Selection** button, press the **shift** key and drag with a marquee or lasso tool or click with the wand.

E subtract from selection
This button lets you subtract the next selection outline you draw from the existing ones.

F alt-drag or alt-click
Press the **alt** (Win) or **option** (Mac) key and drag with a marquee or lasso tool to subtract the new selection from any existing outlines. It's an ideal way to carve holes into selections, as in the case of the **C** above. When using the magic wand, **alt**- or **option**-click.

G restrict selection
The **Restrict Selection** button finds the intersection of the new selection outline and any existing ones.

H shift+alt-drag or shift+alt-click
Press both **shift** and **alt** (or **shift** and **option** on the Mac) and drag with the marquee or lasso tool to find the intersection between the new outline and the existing ones. This permits you to restrict a selection to a smaller space. When armed with the wand tool, press **shift** and **alt** (or **shift** and **option**) and click.

Move & Transform Outlines

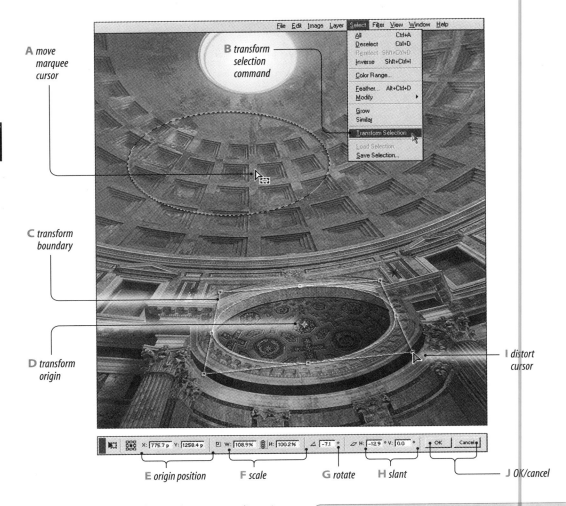

A *move marquee cursor*

B *transform selection command*

C *transform boundary*

D *transform origin*

I *distort cursor*

File Edit Image Layer Select Filter View Window Help

All — Ctrl+A
Deselect — Ctrl+D
Reselect — Shft+Ctrl+D
Inverse — Shft+Ctrl+I

Color Range...

Feather... — Alt+Ctrl+D
Modify

Grow
Similar

Transform Selection

Load Selection...
Save Selection...

X: 775.7 p   Y: 1258.4 p   W: 108.9%   H: 100.2%   ∠ -7.1   H: -12.5   V: 0.0   OK   Cancel

E *origin position*   **F** *scale*   **G** *rotate*   **H** *slant*   **J** *OK/cancel*

Photoshop stands out from other image editors in that it treats a selection outline with as much care as the selected pixels. You can undo changes made to a selection. You can also edit selection outlines independently of pixels. Photoshop lets you move, scale, or rotate a selection outline without affecting the pixels inside. Or you can move and clone selection and pixels together. Here's what I mean:

A move marquee cursor

Get the marquee, lasso, or wand tool, then drag a selection outline to move it independently of the image.

tip Nudge the outline in 1-pixel steps by pressing the ←, ↑, →, or ↓ key. Press **shift** with an **arrow** key to move the outline in 10-pixel increments.

B transform selection command

If a marquee doesn't properly match an image, you may need to do more than nudge it. To scale, rotate, or otherwise *transform* the outline independently of the image, choose **Select➧Transform Selection**.

C transform boundary

Choosing **Transform Selection** results in a *transform boundary*, which you use to modify the marquee.

Move & Clone Pixels

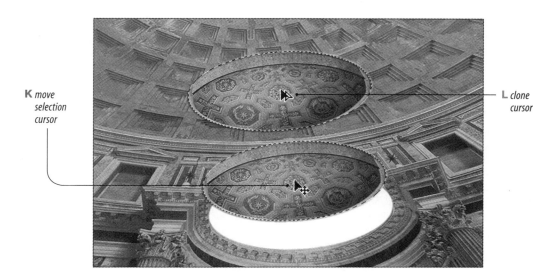

K *move selection cursor*

L *clone cursor*

D transform origin
Drag the target-shaped *transform origin* to move the center of the transformation.

E origin position
Photoshop lists the coordinate position of the origin at the beginning of the options bar. Click in the grid to move the origin from the center of the transform boundary (C) to one of the corners or sides.

F scale
Change the **W** or **H** value to resize the selection outline. If you want to scale the outline proportionally, click the chain to link **W** and **H** into alignment. You can also drag one of the eight handles on the boundary to scale the selection, or **shift**-drag to scale proportionally. The **W** and **H** values update automatically.

G rotate
Enter a value here or drag outside the boundary to rotate the outline. This comes in really handy when using the marquee tools. Oval shapes are common in photographs, but they're usually at an angle.

H slant
You can slant a selection outline by entering values in the **H** and **V** option boxes. Or press the **ctrl** (Win) or **command** (Mac) key and drag a side handle.

I distort cursor
Press **ctrl** (**command** on the Mac) and drag a corner handle to distort the outline. This is a perfect way to mold a marquee to fit an image. It's like scaling, rotating, and slanting at once. In fact, the options bar tracks a distortion by updating all values.

> *tip* Press **ctrl+shift** (**command-shift** on the Mac) while dragging a handle to constrain a distortion. Press **ctrl+alt** (**command-option**) to move opposite handles. Or press **ctrl+shift+alt** (**command-shift-option**) to achieve a perspective effect.

J OK/cancel
Press **enter** (Win) or **return** (Mac) to accept the transformation. Press **esc** to cancel.

K move selection cursor
To move the selected pixels, press **ctrl** (or **command** on the Mac) and drag the selection. The **ctrl** key gets the move tool, as in The Move Tool on page 107.

L clone cursor
When you move selected pixels, you leave a hole in their wake. To avoid this, press **ctrl+alt** (**command-option** on the Mac) and drag the selection. This moves a copy of the selection, a process called *cloning*.

steps Replace One Image Element...

Virtually all Hollywood movie posters feature an actor's head on a model's body. And virtually all these compositions happen in Photoshop. Here's how to use the selection tools to replace one head—or anything else for that matter—with another.

1 get images
Open the images you want to merge. I intend to put the pouting girl's face on the body builder's body.

2 select element to replace
Though it may sound counterintuitive, it's usually easiest to start by selecting the thing you want to replace. I select the body builder's head with the lasso and elliptical marquee tools.

3 drag outline into other image
After you finish drawing the selection outline, drag it from the first image window and drop it in the second. Now you can use it to select the replacement head.

4 choose transform selection
In all likelihood, the selection outline doesn't precisely fit the replacement head. Given that it's mostly a matter of the selection being the wrong size and orientation, you can make the outline and head jibe by choosing **Select➥Transform Selection**.

5 scale & rotate
Drag the handles to scale; drag outside the transform boundary to rotate. Be sure to scale the selection outline so it fits inside the new head.

6 note scale & rotate values
Later, you'll have to reverse the scale and rotation so the new head fits the old one. So get a Post-it and jot down the scale and rotate values from the options bar.

7 click OK
After you get the values—whatever you do, don't skip that step (6)—press **enter** (Win) or **return** (Mac).

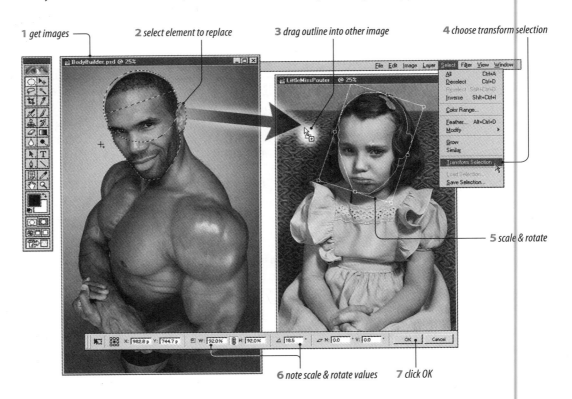

1 *get images* 2 *select element to replace* 3 *drag outline into other image* 4 *choose transform selection*

5 *scale & rotate*

6 *note scale & rotate values* 7 *click OK*

...With Another

8 add to selection
By making the selection slightly smaller than the replacement head (5), you gave yourself some wiggle room. Now incorporate additional details by pressing **shift** while dragging with a marquee or lasso tool.

9 ctrl-drag selection to first image
To import the selected head into its new home, press **ctrl** (**command** on the Mac) and drag the head from the second image window and drop it into the first.

10 choose free transform
Choose **Edit➡Free Transform** to scale and rotate the replacement head (see Free Transform, page 109).

11 enter scale & rotate values
Invert the values that you scribbled on your Post-it note and enter them into the options bar. In my case, the 18.5° rotation translates to –18.5°; the 92% scaling translates to $1/0.92 = 108.7\%$. Or just wing it!

12 click OK
Photoshop redraws the pixels to your specifications.

From this point on, it's a matter of editing the imported image to taste. I used a layer mask to merge the two images (Layer-Specific Masks, page 131). Then I corrected the skin tones using **Image➡Adjust➡Curves** (The Curves Command, pages 200 and 201).

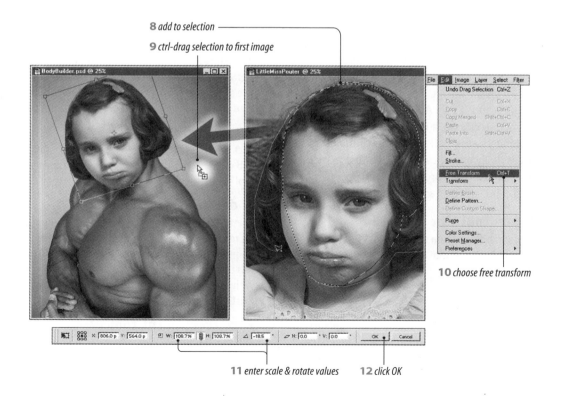

8 add to selection

9 ctrl-drag selection to first image

10 choose free transform

11 enter scale & rotate values   12 click OK

The Pen Tools

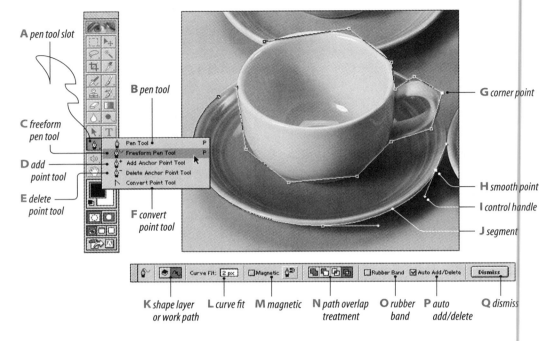

A *pen tool slot*

B *pen tool*

C *freeform pen tool*

D *add point tool*

E *delete point tool*

F *convert point tool*

G *corner point*

H *smooth point*

I *control handle*

J *segment*

Pen Tool · P
Freeform Pen Tool · P
Add Anchor Point Tool
Delete Anchor Point Tool
Convert Point Tool

Curve Fit: 2 px   Magnetic   Rubber Band   Auto Add/Delete   Dismiss

K *shape layer or work path*   **L** *curve fit*   **M** *magnetic*   **N** *path overlap treatment*   **O** *rubber band*   **P** *auto add/delete*   **Q** *dismiss*

There's one last selection tool that's admittedly more complicated but also several times more precise than the tools we've examined so far. The pen tool lets you construct selection outlines one point at a time, much as in **Adobe Illustrator**. And unlike the marquee, lasso, and wand tools, the pen does not limit you to creating selection outlines. You can just as easily export *clipping paths* that mask the image inside other programs. Read Draw & Export A Clipping Path on page 260 to find out how.

A pen tool slot
Click and hold the pen tool icon to display a flyout menu of five tools that let you draw and edit precise selection outlines.

B pen tool
Press P to select the standard pen tool, which lets you draw complex lines and shapes known as *paths*. Click and drag inside the image to define corners (G) and smooth arcs (H) one *anchor point* at a time. Photoshop automatically joins the points with *segments* (J).

C freeform pen tool
Press **shift-P** to switch to the freeform pen tool, which lets you draw free-form outlines, much like the lasso. The difference is, when you release, Photoshop automatically assigns points and segments to the path.

D add point tool
Click a segment in an existing path to insert a point and gain more control over the path. Position a pen tool over a segment to get this tool automatically.

E delete point tool
Points afford more control, but they can make the path more jagged and slow printing. To delete an anchor point and smooth out a segment, click the point with this tool. This is a great way to simplify paths created with the freeform pen tool. Move a pen tool over an existing point to activate the delete point tool.

F convert point tool
This tool lets you change a point long after you create it. Click a smooth point (H) to convert it to a corner (G). Drag a corner point (G) to get a smooth arc (H).

> **tip** The pen tool provides access to the add, delete, and convert point tools. Move the pen cursor over a segment (J) in a selected path to get the add point tool; move it over a point to get the delete point tool. Press **alt** (Win) or **option** (Mac) with the pen over a point to get the convert point tool.

G corner point

Tracing a shape with the pen tool is a matter of setting down anchor points. The simplest kind of point is the *corner point*. Just click to create one.

H smooth point

A corner point results in a sharp corner. But what if you want an arc, as on the outline of a circle? Drag with the pen tool to create a *smooth point*, which ensures a continuous arc.

I control handle

As you drag to create a smooth point, two levers emerge from the point. These so-called *control handles* control the curvature of a segment. The farther you drag away from the point, the longer the control handle and the more the segment curves.

J segment

Photoshop automatically draws a segment between the new point you create and the one that preceded it. A straight segment joins two corner points; if either point is a smooth point, the segment curves.

> **tip** Photoshop permits you to create a hybrid of a corner point and a smooth point called a *cusp point*, which is a point at which curved segments meet to form a sharp corner. Drag like you're making a smooth point. Then midway into the drag, press **alt** or **option** and move the control handle in another direction.

K shape layer or work path

The options bar offers a pair of buttons before you start drawing with the standard pen tool. The first permits you to make a new shape layer (as explained in Pen Tool Shapes on page 161). The second button results in a path. For now, select the second button.

L curve fit

When using the freeform pen tool, this setting specifies the maximum distance between your freehand drawing and the final path. Low values result in more precise paths; high values result in smoother paths.

M magnetic

Again available when using the freeform pen, this check box enables the magnetic pen tool. It works like the magnetic lasso (Draw A Magnetic Lasso, page 65), except that the outcome is a path. Click the magnetic pen icon to display a list of options. Remember, adjust the **Width** value by pressing the [and] keys.

N path overlap treatment

After you draw a path with a pen tool, Photoshop presents you with four buttons that let you change the behavior of any overlapping areas in the paths.

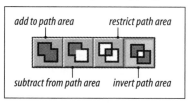

add to path area   *restrict path area*

subtract from path area   *invert path area*

By default, **Invert Path Area** is active. This treats overlaps as holes; so if you convert the paths to a selection (V), the overlaps are deselected. The second to last button, **Restrict Path Area**, is just the opposite; it treats non-overlaps as deselected. The **Add to Path Area** button adds paths together, overlaps and all. Select a single path and click **Subtract from Path Area** to make the path carve holes in the others.

O rubber band

When using the standard pen tool, select this check box to have Photoshop draw a segment between your cursor and the last point you drew. If you're new to paths, **Rubber Band** makes it easier to predict the outcome of clicking or dragging with the pen tool.

P auto add/delete

Check this option if you want to be able to use the pen tool to insert and delete points in an existing path, as described in the Tip at the top of this page.

The Paths Palette

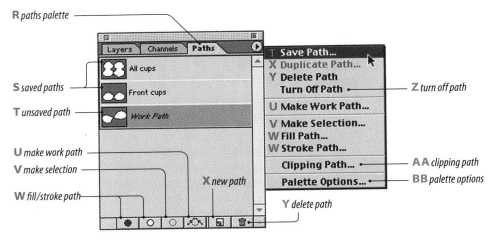

R *paths palette*

S *saved paths*

T *unsaved path*

U *make work path*

V *make selection*

W *fill/stroke path*

X *new path*

T Save Path...
X Duplicate Path...
Y Delete Path
Turn Off Path — **Z** *turn off path*
U Make Work Path...
V Make Selection...
W Fill Path...
W Stroke Path...
Clipping Path... — **AA** *clipping path*
Palette Options... — **BB** *palette options*

Y *delete path*

Q dismiss

There are three ways to complete a path: First, click or drag on the first point in the path, which *closes* the path to make a shape. Second, press **ctrl** (Win) or **command** (Mac) and click off the path. This deactivates the path and leaves it *open*. Third, click **Dismiss**—or press **enter** (Win) or **return** (Mac)—to deactivate the path and hide it. It's not gone for good; click **Work Path** (T) in the **Paths** palette to redisplay the path.

R paths palette

Choose **Window→Show Paths** to see the **Paths** palette, which lets you manage your paths.

S saved paths

Photoshop lets you save hundreds of paths with an image. Each saved item in the **Paths** palette may contain one or more paths. It's like having a reservoir of selection outlines in case you want to reselect an image element in the future.

T unsaved path

The **Work Path** item represents a group of paths that has not yet been saved. It's dangerous to have **Work Path** hanging around; if you dismiss it and start drawing a new path, the previously unsaved paths disappear. So when you get a moment, be sure to save the paths, either by choosing **Save Path** from the palette menu or by double-clicking the **Work Path** item.

U make work path

Click this button or choose **Make Work Path** to convert a selection to a path. Photoshop presents you with the **Tolerance** option which, like the freeform pen's **Curve Fit** (L), defines how many pixels the path can vary from the selection outline. While convenient, selection-to-path conversions are rarely successful; you're better off drawing paths with the pen tool.

V make selection

Photoshop may not do a good job of converting selections to paths, but it does a terrific job of converting paths to selections. Select a path and click this button. Or better yet, press **ctrl** (**command** on the Mac) and click a path name. Or press **ctrl+enter** (**command-return**) to convert the active path.

> *tip* Use the keyboard tricks explained in Add, Subtract, Restrict on page 69 to combine paths with selections. Press **ctrl+shift+enter** (**command-shift-return**) to add the active path to an existing selection. Press **ctrl+alt+enter** (**command-option-return**) to subtract. Finally, press **ctrl+shift+alt+enter** (**command-shift-option-return**) to retain the intersection.

W fill/stroke path

Click the **Fill Path** button to fill the selected paths with the foreground color, according to the path

The Arrow Tools

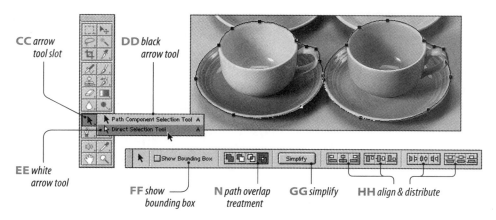

CC *arrow tool slot*

DD *black arrow tool*

EE *white arrow tool*

FF *show bounding box*

N *path overlap treatment*

GG *simplify*

HH *align & distribute*

overlap treatment settings (N). More interesting is the **Stroke Path** button, which paints along the path with the paint or edit tool selected in the toolbox. Alternately, you can **alt**- or **option**-click the button to select from a list of possible tools.

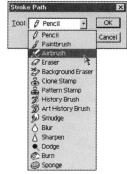

X new path
Click this button to create a new set of paths. Press **alt** or **option** and click to name the paths.

Y delete path
Click the little trash can to delete the selected paths; **alt**- or **option**-click to delete without a warning.

Z turn off path
To create a new **Work Path** item, you have to hide all other paths. To do so, choose **Turn Off Path** or click in an empty area of the palette below the named paths.

AA clipping path
Choose this command to save a clipping path, as in Draw & Export A Clipping Path on page 260.

BB palette options
This command lets you resize the path thumbnails. Press **alt** or **option** and choose **Palette Options** to see a magical sprite whose sole purpose is to amuse.

CC arrow tool slot
Click and hold to select from two tools that Photoshop calls the path component and direct selection tools. I prefer plain old black and white arrows.

DD black arrow tool
Press **A** to get the black arrow. Click to select an entire path; **shift**-click to select multiple paths. Drag a path to move it; **alt**- or **option**-drag to clone it. To delete a selected path, press **backspace** (Win) or **delete** (Mac).

EE white arrow tool
Press **shift-A** to switch to the white arrow, which lets you modify individual points and control handles. Drag off a path to create a marquee; any points inside the marquee become selected.

FF show bounding box
When the black arrow is active, select this check box to surround the selected paths with a *bounding box*. Drag a handle to scale the paths; drag just outside the box to rotate; press **ctrl** or **command** and drag a handle to slant or distort.

GG simplify
Click this button to combine all visible paths according to the path overlap treatment settings (N).

HH align & distribute
Use the first six buttons to align two or more selected paths into columns or rows. The remaining buttons *distribute* (evenly space out) three or more paths.

Draw & Save A Path Selection

If you managed to plow through all those pen tool and **Paths** palette options, I commend you. Fortunately, however, most of them fall under the heading of optional equipment. They're nice to have around, but you won't be needing them on a regular basis. Here's how to select an area with the pen tool:

1 get image
The pen tool is best suited to selecting geometric objects with clearly defined edges. Anything with lots of sharp corners and smooth surfaces is great. Complex elements are fine, but beware of wispy details like leaves and hair. For those, you need to create a mask, as I show in Chapter 9, Define Channels & Masks.

2 select pen tool
Press the P key.

3 create work path
If necessary, click the **Create Work Path** button in the options bar. In all likelihood, it's already active.

4 draw path outline
Trace along the outline of the element you want to select with the pen tool. Position anchor points at corners and in the middle of long arcs. For the best results, draw your path slightly on the inside of the element. That way, you won't pick up stray colors from the background. Closed paths work best when drawing selections, so finish up by clicking or dragging the first point in the path.

> **tip** If you make a mistake, press **ctrl** (Win) or **command** (Mac) to temporarily access the white arrow tool, and then drag an anchor point or control handle to adjust the shape of the path.

5 display paths palette
If the **Paths** palette is not available, press **F7** to display the **Layers** palette and then click the **Paths** tab.

6 name path
Double-click the **Work Path** item in the **Paths** palette. Then enter a name for your path and click **OK**.

7 make selection
Click this button or press **ctrl+enter** (Win) or **command-return** (Mac) to convert the path to a selection outline. The path remains intact in case you decide to use it again.

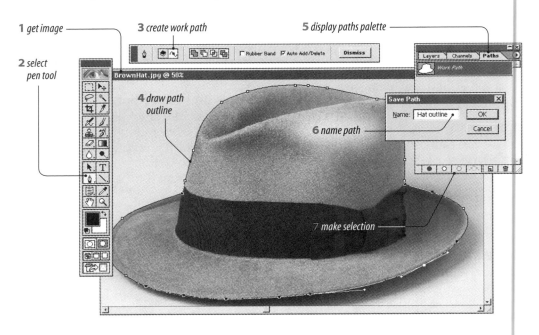

1 *get image*
2 *select pen tool*
3 *create work path*
4 *draw path outline*
5 *display paths palette*
6 *name path*
7 *make selection*

Apply Color & Gradients

When it comes to coloring pixels, your most convenient options are *fill* and *stroke*. **Edit➧Fill** colors selected pixels. Imagine pouring paint into a selection and you pretty much get the idea. If a single color isn't enough, you can apply a *gradient*, in which one color fades gradually into another. Meanwhile, **Edit➧Stroke** traces color around the perimeter of a selection, great for drawing outlines.

Fill and **Stroke** are relatively easy to use. The bigger trick is defining a color in the first place. Three or four carefully chosen base colors, called *primaries*, blend to form literally millions of others. Orange results from one mixture of primaries, purple from another. It takes some experience to get reliable results. Fortunately, the lessons learned in this chapter have practical applications throughout not only Photoshop, but other publishing applications as well.

79

The Color Palette

A *color palette* F *color sliders* G *brightness levels*

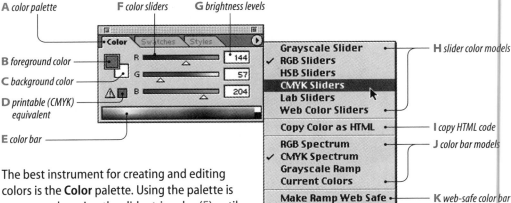

B *foreground color*

C *background color*

D *printable (CMYK) equivalent*

E *color bar*

H *slider color models*

I *copy HTML code*

J *color bar models*

K *web-safe color bar*

The best instrument for creating and editing colors is the **Color** palette. Using the palette is as easy as dragging the slider triangles (F) until the desired color pops up in the foreground swatch (B). Or probe deeper and learn how to get the exact color you want:

A color palette

Click the **Color** tab or press **F6** to display the palette.

B foreground color

Photoshop keeps track of two colors at a time. The first of these, the *foreground color*, is applied by the paintbrush, airbrush, paint bucket, and other painting tools. Click this swatch to make the foreground color active, and then edit it in the **Color** palette.

C background color

Click this swatch to edit the *background color*, which is applied by the eraser tool. The background color also fills the hole left when you move a selection, as in Move & Clone Pixels on page 71 of Chapter 5.

D printable (CMYK) equivalent

By default, the **Color** palette lets you mix colors using the primaries red, green, and blue, known collectively as *RGB*. Although well suited to screen images, the RGB primaries permit you to create colors that won't print accurately using cyan, magenta, yellow, and black (*CMYK*). When this occurs, a caution triangle appears, flanked by the closest CMYK color. Click either the triangle or the swatch to replace the RGB color with the CMYK equivalent. For more information, see RGB Versus CMYK on page 82.

E color bar

Click a color in this bar to replace the active color. Press **alt** (**option** on the Mac) and click to change the inactive color. For example, if the foreground swatch (B) is active, **alt**-click to change the background color (C).

> **tip** By default, the color bar shows CMYK colors. To switch to another model, right-click (**control**-click on the Mac) and choose another option. Or **shift**-click to cycle from one model to the next.

F color sliders

Click in a slider bar or drag a slider triangle to adjust a color visually. The slider bars update to show you what color you'll get if you click or drag a triangle to a given spot.

G brightness levels

When you click or drag a slider (F), the value to the right of it updates automatically. Or enter your own values. The RGB values represent *brightness levels* from 0 (darkest) to 255 (lightest). When working in CMYK, the numbers show *ink densities* from 0 (lightest) to 100 (darkest) percent.

H slider color models

Choose one of these commands to change the color model used by the slider bars. For black-and-white work, choose **Grayscale Slider**. For color work, the best setting is **RGB** or **CMYK Sliders**.

Eyedroppers & Color Controls

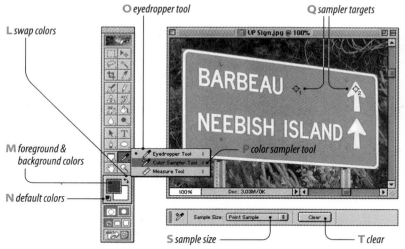

O *eyedropper tool*

Q *sampler targets*

L *swap colors*

M *foreground & background colors*

N *default colors*

P *color sampler tool*

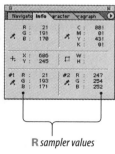

R *sampler values*

S *sample size*

T *clear*

Choose **Web Color Sliders** only when creating Web graphics specifically for old-style 8-bit (256-color) monitors. Otherwise, choose **RGB Sliders**.

I copy HTML code
Designers who code their own Web pages can use Photoshop to capture HTML colors. Choose **Copy Color as HTML** to convert the color specified in the **Color** palette to HTML and copy the HTML code to the Clipboard. (The color shown on the facing page translates to COLOR="#9039CC".) Then switch to your HTML editing program and choose **Edit➞Paste**.

J color bar models
Choose a command to change the color model used by the color bar (E). Better yet, **shift**-click the color bar.

K web-safe color bar
This command reduces the color bar to the 216 colors common to 8-bit monitors on the Mac and PC.

L swap colors
Click the double-arrow icon in the toolbox to swap the foreground and background colors. To access this option from the keyboard, press the X key.

M foreground & background colors
Rather than activating a color, as in the case of the foreground and background swatches in the **Color**

palette (B & C), clicking one of these swatches displays the large and complex **Color Picker** dialog box. I recommend you avoid it—the **Color** palette is just as capable and several times more convenient.

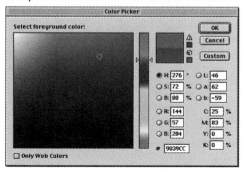

N default colors
Click here to reset the default foreground and background colors, black and white, respectively. If you prefer to work from the keyboard, press the D key.

O eyedropper tool
In addition to defining a color in the **Color** palette, you can lift a color directly from the image. To do so, select the eyedropper tool (or press the I key) and click in the image window. The clicked color becomes the new foreground color. To lift a background color, **alt**-click (**option**-click on the Mac) in the image.

P color sampler tool

Click and hold the eyedropper icon to display a flyout menu that includes the color sampler tool. Or press shift-I to select the tool from the keyboard. Use the tool to target multiple colors in the image window.

Q sampler targets

Click in the image window with the color sampler tool to add crosshair targets. Create up to four targets in all. Drag a target to move it to a different location.

R sampler values

Clicking with the color sampler tool automatically displays the **Info** palette, which lists the primary color ingredients for each sampler target (Q). Change the color model for the target by clicking the tiny eyedropper icon in the **Info** palette and choosing an option, such as **CMYK Color**.

Note that the sampler values remain visible even when you switch to a different tool. To hide these values without deleting the sampler targets, choose **Hide Color Samplers** from the **Info** palette menu. Choose **Show Color Samplers** to bring back both the sampler targets and values.

S sample size

When using either the eyedropper or the color sampler tool, the options bar offers the **Sample Size** pop-up menu. Choose **3 by 3 Average** to average the colors of nine pixels centered on the click point; choose **5 by 5 Average** to average 25 pixels. Return to the default **Point Sample** option to lift the color of the single pixel on which you click.

T clear

Click this button to delete any and all sampler targets (Q) from the image window.

> *tip* The **Clear** button is useful, but what if you want to delete a single sampler target and leave the others intact? The solution is to first select the color sampler tool (P). Then press **alt** (Win) or **option** (Mac) and click the target.

RGB Versus CMYK

Photoshop provides several different ways to represent colors. The most fundamental of these *color models* are *RGB* and *CMYK*, designed to mimic your monitor and your printer, respectively.

RGB is the color model of light. Pure red, green, and blue primaries are measured in brightness levels from 0 to 255, for a total of 256 variations. It's based on the way computers work. A total of 8 *bits* is devoted to each primary. A bit conveys just 2 variations, 0 or 1, so 8 bits translates to $2^8 = 256$. Add red, green, and blue together, and you get 24 bits, or $256^3 = 16.7$ million possible color permutations.

RGB is called the *additive color model*—higher brightness levels produce lighter colors. Set the R, G, and B values to **255** and you get white. Set them all to **0** to get black.

CMYK is RGB's opposite. This *subtractive color model* applies cyan, magenta, yellow, and black ink to a white page to build up colors, just like a commercial printer. Higher ink densities mean darker colors. Set C, M, Y, and K to **0%** to get white. Set C, M, and Y to **60%** and K to **100%** to get a rich black. The total amount of CMYK ink shouldn't exceed 300%—doing so can result in smeared colors during printing.

A third model, *Lab*, emulates neither monitor nor printer and is said to be *device independent*. The L stands for *luminosity*; *a* and *b* are variables. Theoretical in nature, Lab is useful here for comparative purposes. The table below shows a few sample colors and their recipes in the three color models. Experiment to discover others.

color	RGB recipe	CMYK recipe	Lab recipe
bright yellow	R:255, G:255, B:0	C:0, M:0, Y:100, K:0	L:100, *a*:0, *b*:120
vivid orange	R:255, G:128, B:0	C:0, M:40, Y:80, K:0	L:80, *a*:60, *b*:85
emerald green	R:0, G:180, B:0	C:80, M:0, Y:100, K:0	L:60, *a*:−120, *b*:120
deep violet	R:100, G:0, B:160	C:50, M:100, Y:0, K:0	L:30, *a*:60, *b*:−60
drab brown	R:120, G:80, B:60	C:40, M:70, Y:80, K:15	L:40, *a*:20, *b*:20
neutral gray	R:128, G:128, B:128	C:45, M:40, Y:40, K:10	L:50, *a*:0, *b*:0

The Swatches Palette

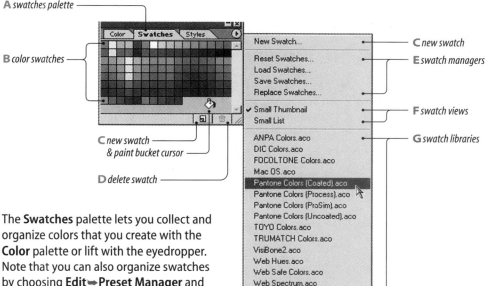

A swatches palette

B color swatches

C new swatch & paint bucket cursor

D delete swatch

C new swatch

E swatch managers

F swatch views

G swatch libraries

The **Swatches** palette lets you collect and organize colors that you create with the **Color** palette or lift with the eyedropper. Note that you can also organize swatches by choosing **Edit→Preset Manager** and selecting **Swatches** from the **Preset Type** pop-up menu. Changes you make in the **Preset Manager** dialog box are reflected in the **Swatches** palette, and vice versa.

A swatches palette
Press **F6** and click the **Swatches** tab to display the palette. Or choose **Window→Show Swatches**.

B color swatches
The main body of the **Swatches** palette sports a collection of colored squares, or *swatches*. Click a swatch to replace the foreground color; **alt**-click (**option**-click on the Mac) to change the background color. Double-click a swatch to give it a new name.

C new swatch & paint bucket cursor
Click the page button or choose **New Swatch** to save the foreground color as a swatch. Or move your cursor over an empty space in the palette and click with the paint bucket. To skip naming the color, press **alt** (Win) or **option** (Mac) as you click.

> *tip* Shift-click a swatch to replace it with the foreground color. You can also right-click (**control**-click on the Mac) to access the **New Swatch** command.

D delete swatch
Drag a swatch to the trash can to delete it.

> *tip* You can likewise delete a swatch by pressing **ctrl** (Win) or **command** (Mac) and clicking it.

E swatch managers
Choose one of these commands to load or save swatch libraries on disk. **Reset Swatches** restores Photoshop's default collection of 122 swatches. See The Preset Manager on pages 56 and 57 for more information on loading and saving preset libraries.

F swatch views
You can view swatches as colored squares (**Small Thumbnails**) or by name (**Small List**). The name view gives you a better feeling for the purpose of Photoshop's default swatches.

G swatch libraries
Photoshop ships with several predefined libraries of color swatches, including spot colors from industry-standard **Pantone** and CMYK colors from **Trumatch**. Choose the desired library to load its color swatches.

The Fill Command

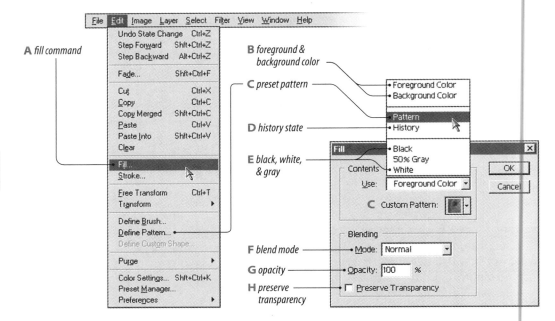

A *fill command*

B *foreground & background color*
- Foreground Color
- Background Color

C *preset pattern*
- Pattern

D *history state*
- History

E *black, white, & gray*
- Black
- 50% Gray
- White

F *blend mode*

G *opacity*

H *preserve transparency*

Once you define the foreground or background color that you want to use, you can apply the color to the image using **Edit→Fill** or one of several **backspace** (Win) or **delete** (Mac) key techniques. If a portion of the image is selected, Photoshop fills the selection. If no portion of the image is selected, Photoshop fills the entire image or layer.

A fill command

Choose **Edit→Fill** to display the **Fill** dialog box. Here you can specify not only which of several colors to apply, but also how to apply them.

> *tip* Under Windows, you can choose the **Fill** command by pressing **alt+E, L**. But here's an even handier trick that works on both platforms: **shift+backspace** (Win) or **shift-delete** (Mac).

B foreground & background color

Select an option from the **Use** pop-up menu to tell Photoshop what you want to use to fill the selection or layer. Of the first two options, one applies the foreground color and the other, the background color.

C preset pattern

Choose the **Pattern** option to apply a preset pattern. If the option is dimmed, no pattern is yet defined. Press **esc** and choose **Edit→Preset Manager** to load a pattern library stored on disk (as in The Preset Manager on pages 56 and 57). Or define your own pattern by selecting an area with the rectangular marquee tool and choosing **Edit→Define Pattern**. Back inside the **Fill** dialog box, select the desired pattern from the **Custom Pattern** pop-up palette, and then press **enter** (Win) or **return** (Mac) to close the palette.

D history state

Choose **History** to fill a selection or layer with the active source state in the **History** palette. If the option is dimmed, the source state is not applicable to the current image. To learn more, read Chapter 15, Work With History.

E black, white, & gray

The last three options in the **Use** pop-up menu apply black, medium gray, or white, useful when the foreground and background colors are set to something other than their defaults.

Backspace & Delete

F blend mode

The **Mode** pop-up menu defines how Photoshop blends the fill color(s) with the existing colors in the selection or layer. *Blend modes* are a large topic, covered at length in The Blend Modes on pages 137 through 139 of Chapter 10.

G opacity

You can make the fill translucent by lowering the **Opacity** value. For more information, see The Opacity Value on page 136.

H preserve transparency

When working with a layer, some pixels may be transparent, and others may be opaque. To fill selected pixels according to their opacity—and leave any transparent pixels unfilled—select the **Preserve Transparency** check box. Read Chapter 8, Create & Modify Layers, to learn more.

> **tip** Immediately after applying the **Fill** command, you have the opportunity to change the opacity and blend mode. Choose **Edit➞Fade Fill** or press **shift+ctrl+F** (**command-shift-F** on the Mac) and make the desired changes.

I backspace (Win)/delete (Mac)

You can access many of the functions in the **Fill** dialog box using shortcuts that involve the **backspace** key (**delete** on the Mac). To fill a selected area in the Background layer with the background color, press **backspace** on its own.

J ctrl+backspace/cmd-delete

When working on a layer, the **backspace** key deletes pixels. Fortunately, you can fill an area on a floating layer with the background color by pressing **ctrl+backspace** (**command-delete** on the Mac).

K alt+backspace/option-delete

To fill a selection or layer with the foreground color, press **alt+backspace** (**option-delete** on the Mac).

Windows keyboard

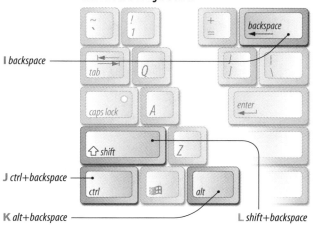

Macintosh keyboard

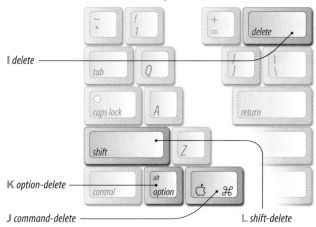

> **tip** Press **ctrl+alt+backspace** (**command-option-delete** on the Mac) to fill an area with the active history state (D). But don't press **ctrl+alt+delete**!

L shift+backspace/shift-delete

Add the **shift** key to one of the preceding tricks (J or K) to preserve the transparency of a layer. For example, pressing **shift+alt+backspace** fills all but the transparent pixels with the foreground color.

The Paint Bucket Tool

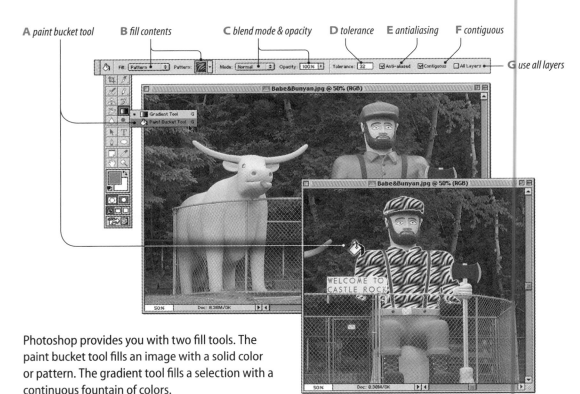

A *paint bucket tool*   B *fill contents*   C *blend mode & opacity*   D *tolerance*   E *antialiasing*   F *contiguous*

G *use all layers*

Photoshop provides you with two fill tools. The paint bucket tool fills an image with a solid color or pattern. The gradient tool fills a selection with a continuous fountain of colors.

A paint bucket tool

Press **shift-G** to select the paint bucket, which shares a flyout menu with the gradient tool (H). Then click in a uniformly colored portion of an image to fill it. It's as if you selected an area with the magic wand tool (The Magic Wand, page 66) and pressed **alt+backspace**.

B fill contents

Use the **Fill** pop-up menu in the options bar to select whether to fill an area with the foreground color or a pattern. Assuming you've loaded a pattern using the **Preset Manager** or **Define Pattern** command (as in The Fill Command on page 84), you can select a repeating pattern from the **Pattern** option.

C blend mode & opacity

Select a blend mode and then enter an **Opacity** value to blend the fill colors with the existing colors in the image. See pages 136 through 139 of Chapter 10, Blend & Stylize Layers, for more information.

D tolerance

Raise or lower the **Tolerance** value to expand or contract the range of the paint bucket tool. For reference, a value of 128 pretty much fills in an entire image.

E antialiasing

Check **Anti-aliased** to soften the edges of the area filled with the paint bucket tool. See Antialias & Feather on page 63 to see how this check box works.

F contiguous

When this check box is on, the paint bucket fills adjacent pixels only. To fill Paul Bunyan's shirt and hat at the same time, I turned **Contiguous** off.

G use all layers

When off, this option fills an area based on the contents of the active layer. Turn on **Use All Layers** to take into account all visible layers. Either way, however, the paint bucket affects the active layer only.

The Gradient Tool

H *gradient tool*   J *gradient picker*   K *gradient style*   C *blend mode & opacity*   L *reverse*   M *dither*   N *transparency*

I *gradient preview*

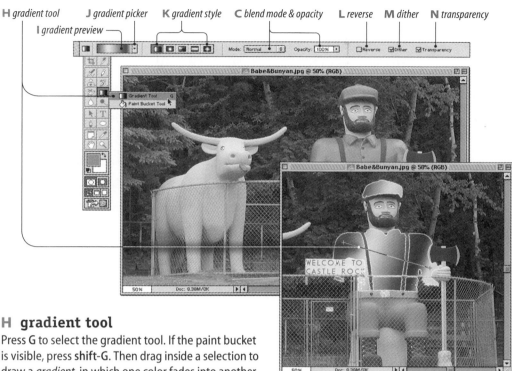

H gradient tool
Press **G** to select the gradient tool. If the paint bucket is visible, press **shift-G**. Then drag inside a selection to draw a *gradient*, in which one color fades into another. If no selection is active, the gradient fills the entire image or layer. The distance and direction of your drag determines the length and angle of the gradient fill.

I gradient preview
By default, the gradient fades from foreground to background color. To design your own gradient—using any colors you like—just click on the gradient preview. To learn how it works, read Make Your Own Gradient on pages 88 and 89.

J gradient picker
Click the down-pointing arrowhead to the right of the gradient preview to display a drop-down palette of preset gradient fills. You can load additional presets by choosing one of the commands from the bottom portion of the drop-down palette menu.

K gradient style
Photoshop provides five *gradient styles*, which are ways in which colors fade into each other, as on right.

L reverse
Select this check box to reverse the order of colors in the gradient. This is frequently helpful when drawing black-to-white gradients. I selected **Reverse** to create each of the examples below. Had I not, black would appear in the center and white around the outside.

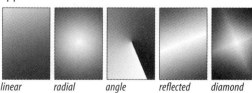

linear   radial   angle   reflected   diamond

M dither
This option mixes up colors in a gradient to prevent harsh transitions, known as *banding*.

N transparency
You can build translucent areas into a gradient. Use this check box to turn the translucency on and off.

steps Make Your Own Gradient

Gradual color transitions are commonplace elements in digital photographs. So it's no surprise that Photoshop takes gradients very seriously, supplying one of the most powerful gradient creation environments on the market. Here's how to create a colorful, credible gradient fill:

1 select gradient tool
Click the gradient tool icon or press the **G** key.

2 click gradient preview
This displays the **Gradient Editor** dialog box.

3 select base preset (optional)
The **Gradient Editor** provides a handful of preset gradients. You can access still more by choosing a command from the bottom portion of the **Presets** menu (identified by the arrowhead in a circle). Feel free to select one of these presets as a jumping off point.

4 edit color stops
The squares below the main gradient bar represent key colors in the gradient, which Photoshop calls *color stops*. Drag a color stop to move it; **alt**-drag (**option**-

drag on the Mac) to clone it. Click below the gradient bar to add a new stop. Select an option from the **Color** pop-up menu to link the stop to the foreground or background color. Or click the **Color** swatch to specify a custom color of your own. Click outside the **Gradient Editor** to lift a color from the image.

> *tip* You can delete a color stop by dragging it sharply away from the gradient bar. If you then think better of it, press **ctrl+Z** (or **command-Z** on the Mac) to undo the deletion.

5 edit midpoints
The diamonds represent *midpoints*, the point at which one color fades exactly halfway into the next. Drag the diamond to make a color fade faster or slower.

6 edit transparency stops
The squares above the main gradient bar are transparency stops. They permit you to create a gradient that blends in and out of the image. Create, move, clone, and delete transparency stops just as you do color stops (4). To modify the translucency of a stop, select it and enter a new **Opacity** value.

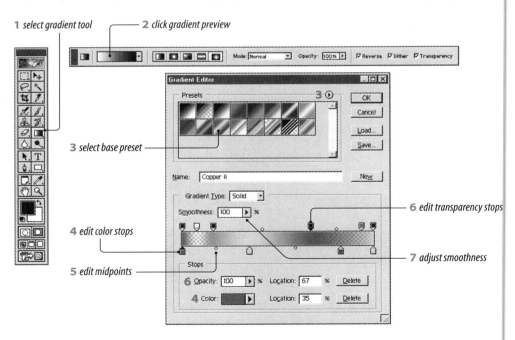

1 *select gradient tool*

2 *click gradient preview*

3 *select base preset*

4 *edit color stops*

5 *edit midpoints*

6 *edit transparency stops*

7 *adjust smoothness*

7 adjust smoothness (optional)

This option determines how colors transition into one another. A **Smoothness** of 0% results in a flat fade, in which every incremental color gets equal weight. While that sounds good, it results in sudden visual drop offs, particularly when fading to light colors. Better to raise the **Smoothness** value and stretch out transitions based on their proximity to color stops.

8 generate noise gradient (optional)

Photoshop 6 introduces a new kind of gradient called a *noise gradient*. Random in nature, a noise gradient is useful for introducing experimental or arbitrary effects. If you're interested, select **Noise** from the **Gradient Type** pop-up menu. If not, skip ahead to create your new gradient (13).

9 adjust roughness

A noise gradient is a random progression of colors. To blur one color into the next so the gradient appears more smooth, lower the **Roughness** value. Raise the value to sharpen the color transitions.

10 edit color range (optional)

You can limit the color range of a gradient by adjusting the **R**, **G**, and **B** sliders. Or change the color model to work with other sliders. If your colors are completely off base, use **Randomize** (12) to generate new colors, and then revisit this step.

11 set options

The **Restrict Colors** check box limits the gradient to printable CMYK colors. For a more vibrant gradient, turn this check

box off. If you're feeling adventurous, you can introduce random levels of translucency into a gradient by selecting the **Add Transparency** check box.

12 click randomize

Don't like the colors in a noise gradient? Click the **Randomize** button. Still not satisfied? Click **Randomize** again. Every click of this button instructs Photoshop to generate a new gradient using an altogether different set of colors.

13 enter name & click new

When you get a gradient you like, enter a name for it into the **Name** option box. Then click the **New** button. The new gradient appears in the **Presets** list. You can likewise add a new gradient by merely clicking in an empty area of the **Presets** list.

> *tip* Weird as it may sound, you can't replace an existing preset. To edit a preset, therefore, you have to create a new gradient and delete the previous one. How do you delete a preset? Press the **alt** (Win) or **option** (Mac) key and click it.

14 click OK

When you finish making gradients, click **OK**. Or click **Cancel**. Regardless of how you leave the **Gradient Editor**, Photoshop saves your changes to the presets.

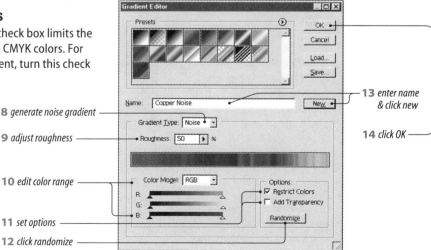

8 *generate noise gradient*

9 *adjust roughness*

10 *edit color range*

11 *set options*

12 *click randomize*

13 *enter name & click new*

14 *click OK*

The Stroke Command

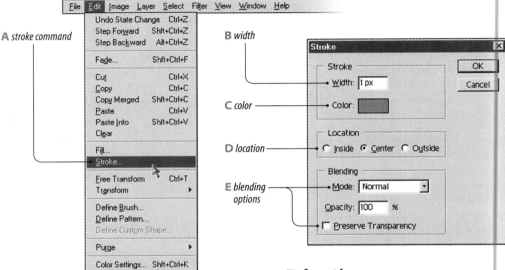

A *stroke command*

B *width*

C *color*

D *location*

E *blending options*

The **Edit➞Stroke** command works in one of two ways. It traces an outline around the selected portion of an image. Or, if no selection is active, it traces the boundaries of a layer. You need either a selection or a layer to stroke.

A stroke command

Choose **Edit➞Stroke** (or press **alt+E, S** on the PC) to display the **Stroke** dialog box.

B width

Enter the thickness of the desired stroke, in pixels. If the selection is antialiased, Photoshop draws a soft stroke. If the selection is jagged (drawn with **Antialiased** turned off), the stroke is jagged. Feathered selections get a blurry stroke, and so on.

C color

By default, this swatch shows the active foreground color. Click the swatch to display the **Color Picker** dialog box, which lets you select a different color.

> *tip* Move the cursor outside the **Color Picker** dialog box and click to lift a color from the image.

D location

The **Location** options determine whether Photoshop draws the stroke entirely inside the selection, entirely outside, or centers the stroke on the selection outline.

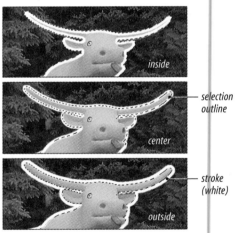

inside

selection outline

center

stroke (white)

outside

E blending options

Use these options to set the blend mode and opacity of the stroke (Chapter 10, Blend & Stylize Layers). Check **Preserve Transparency** to leave transparent portions of a layer unstroked. To adjust the blend mode and opacity of the stroke immediately after applying the **Stroke** command, choose **Edit➞Fade Stroke**.

Paint & Retouch

Sections @ A Glance

Learn how to apply colors
with Photoshop's paintbrush,
pencil, and airbrush tools.
I also show you how to use
the edit tools, which let you
smear, blur, sharpen, lighten,
darken, and duplicate pixels
in an image.

Photoshop provides a wealth of commands that automatically correct the appearance of an image according to your specifications and numerical input. There's nothing wrong with these commands—in fact, with few exceptions, they're extraordinarily useful. But all the automation in the world can't eliminate the need for old-fashioned artistic labor.

That's why Photoshop gives you just shy of a dozen tools that you can use to apply color and edit pixels inside an image. Every one of the tools responds like a brush—that is to say, you drag your mouse and the tool paints pixels inside the image window.

If your fine motor skills aren't all you wish they were, don't worry. I show you lots of ways to constrain and articulate your brushstrokes. While I wouldn't go so far as to paint a piece of artwork from scratch inside Photoshop, it is a powerful retouching environment.

The Paint Tools

F *brush preview* G *brush picker* H *blend mode* I *opacity* J *wet edges* K *auto erase* L *brush dynamics*

A *airbrush tool*

B *paintbrush tool*

C *pencil tool*

Paintbrush Tool B
Pencil Tool B

McFarlands&Car.jpg @ 50% (Gray)

D *brush cursor*

E *brushstrokes*

The three constants of Photoshop are the airbrush, paintbrush, and pencil. This trio represents the only category of tools that has remained constant since Adobe first introduced Photoshop in 1990. But that's not to say the tools haven't changed since then. Every update expands the paint tools' capabilities, and Photoshop 6 is no exception.

A airbrush tool

The airbrush lays down a stream of paint in the foreground color. Its main difference from the paintbrush (B) is that it paints continuously, even when you hold the cursor still.

tip The airbrush sprays a jet of color. So press the J key to select the airbrush tool from the keyboard.

B paintbrush tool

The paintbrush tool applies the foreground color, but only so long as you drag. That's often a good thing because it means you end up with a constant coating of color. In fact, of the three paint tools, the paintbrush is the most predictable, versatile, and utilitarian.

C pencil tool

Sharing a slot with the paintbrush is the pencil, which paints a jagged line, regardless of the active brush (F).

tip By default, the pencil draws a line 1-pixel thick, great for making precise changes. To correct a single aberrant pixel, just click. The shortcut for the paintbrush and pencil is the **B** key. Press **shift-B** to switch between the two tools.

D brush cursor

By default, Photoshop updates the cursor to reflect the size and shape of the active brush (F). This helps you to predict the outcome of your drags. If you'd prefer to see a cursor in the shape of the tool icon, choose **Edit➥Preferences➥Display & Cursors** and select **Standard** from the **Painting Cursors** options. Or press **caps lock** for a crosshair cursor.

E brushstrokes

Regardless of which tool is used to create it, a painted line in Photoshop is called a *brushstroke*. The image below shows examples of the three kinds of brushstrokes you can create with the paint tools.

airbrush

paintbrush

pencil

F brush preview

Each of the paint tools works by firing off a rapid succession of colored spots, spaced very closely to create the illusion of a constant line. The spot is called the *brush*. Click this preview of the brush to display the drop-down brush editor.

G brush picker

Click the down-pointing arrow to the right of the brush preview to display a drop-down palette of preset brushes. You can select a brush, delete a preset, or load additional brushes from disk. For complete information on selecting and editing brushes, see Brush Size & Shape on pages 96 and 97.

H blend mode

By default, the paintbrush and pencil apply opaque brushstrokes in the foreground color. Airbrush lines are somewhat translucent, but you can change this. Select an option from the **Mode** pop-up menu to blend the foreground color with the existing colors in the image, as I show in Mode, Opacity, Pressure, & Exposure on pages 98 and 99.

I opacity

Another way to blend the foreground color with the colors in the image is to reduce the **Opacity** value. Any number below 100 percent results in a translucent brushstroke. When using the airbrush tool, the **Opacity** option changes to **Pressure**, which controls not only the opacity of the stroke but also the amount of paint emitted when the cursor is held still. Read Mode, Opacity, Pressure, & Exposure on pages 98 and 99 for additional tips and information.

J wet edges

This check box appears in the options bar when the paintbrush tool is active. Select **Wet Edges** to make the brushstroke translucent and trace an opaque edge around its perimeter. It mimics the effect in watercolor where paint washes toward the outside of the brushstroke. Combine this option with different blend modes (H) to get a wide variety of effects.

wet edges off

wet edges on

K auto erase

When using the pencil, select this check box to paint with the background color if and only if you begin your drag on a pixel colored in the foreground color. The effect is the pencil either applies or erases the foreground color, as in old-style painting programs.

L brush dynamics

Use this pop-up palette to make Photoshop respond to a pressure-sensitive tablet, as in Custom Brush & Dynamics on page 97.

The Edit Tools

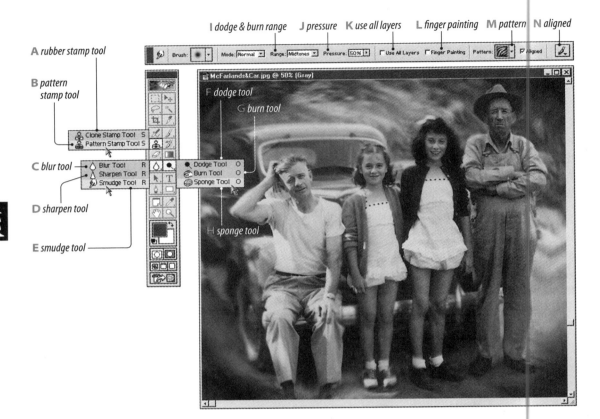

A *rubber stamp tool*

B *pattern stamp tool*

C *blur tool*

D *sharpen tool*

E *smudge tool*

F *dodge tool*

G *burn tool*

H *sponge tool*

I *dodge & burn range*   J *pressure*   K *use all layers*   L *finger painting*   M *pattern*   N *aligned*

Clone Stamp Tool S
Pattern Stamp Tool S

Blur Tool R
Sharpen Tool R
Smudge Tool R

Dodge Tool O
Burn Tool O
Sponge Tool O

McFarlands&Car.jpg @ 50% (Gray)

Painting tools are all very well and good, but Photoshop is first and foremost an image editor. So it's no surprise that Photoshop devotes more tools to the task of editing than painting. Seven of Photoshop's eight edit tools modify the pixels in an image; only one, a seldom-used variation on the rubber stamp tool (A) that paints with preset patterns (B), applies new colors.

A rubber stamp tool

Also called the clone stamp tool, the rubber stamp clones pixels in an image. Press the **alt** (Win) or **option** (Mac) key and click in the image to set the source point. Then drag to clone the source in a different area of the image. Strange as this may sound, the rubber stamp is in fact the most useful of the edit tools, ideally suited to retouching, as in Retouch An Old Photograph on pages 101 and 102.

B pattern stamp tool

Drag with the pattern stamp tool to paint with a preset pattern. Note that you must load a preset pattern (M) before using the tool.

> *tip* You can select a stamp tool from the keyboard by pressing the S key. Assuming **Use Shift Key for Tool Switch** is selected in the **Preferences** dialog box (as by default), press **shift-S** to switch back and forth between the rubber stamp and pattern stamp tools.

C blur tool

Drag with the blur tool to reduce the focus of the image. Like the airbrush, the blur tool works continuously so long as the mouse button is down, even if you hold the mouse in place. So you can click and hold in an image until you achieve a desired effect.

D sharpen tool

The sharpen tool increases the focus of an image. But be careful—the sharpen tool has a habit of over-sharpening very quickly. Either reduce the **Pressure** setting (J) or drag very briefly over your image.

stamp   blur   sharpen   smudge   dodge   burn

E smudge tool

Drag with the smudge tool to smear pixels. Raise the **Pressure** value (J) to smear pixels farther as you drag. (Note that you have to drag the tool for it to work; it does nothing when you hold it still.)

> **tip** The keyboard shortcut for the blur, sharpen, and smudge tools is R. Press **shift-R** to cycle from blur to sharpen to smudge and back to blur.

F dodge tool

Drag with the dodge tool to lighten badly lit areas, such as a face shadowed by a hat. Raise the **Exposure** setting (J) to lighten colors more rapidly; lower the setting to achieve greater subtlety. Specify exactly which colors to lighten using the **Range** option (I).

G burn tool

Just as burning toast makes it darker, the burn tool darkens colors in an image, useful for creating shadows and dark frames. The **Range** (I) and **Exposure** (J) options work the same as they do for the dodge tool.

H sponge tool

Drag with the sponge tool to change the vibrancy of colors in an image. Set the **Mode** option in the options bar to **Desaturate** to leech away saturation, which leaves colors more gray. Set the **Mode** to **Saturate** to make colors more vivid.

> **tip** Press the letter O to select the current occupant of the dodge tool slot. Press **shift-O** to cycle between the dodge, burn, and sponge tools.

I dodge & burn range

The **Range** option appears when the dodge or burn tool is active. By default, **Midtones** is active, which limits changes to the medium colors in an image. This prevents colors from becoming flat-out white in the highlights or black in the shadows. Select **Highlights** to affect just the lightest colors; select **Shadows** to lighten or darken the darkest colors.

J pressure

The **Pressure** value appears when the blur, sharpen, smudge, or sponge tool is active. If the dodge or burn tool is active, the option changes to **Exposure**. Select a stamp tool and Photoshop offers an **Opacity** value. See Mode, Opacity, Pressure, & Exposure on pages 98 and 99 for complete information on each.

K use all layers

As always, you can edit just one layer at a time. But with **Use All Layers**, you can take multiple layers into account. For example, select this check box when using the smudge tool to smear the contents of one layer into another. You can likewise blur, sharpen, and clone between layers.

L finger painting

Available when using the smudge tool, this option paints a bit of foreground color at the beginning of a smudge. Raise the **Pressure** setting to lengthen the smudge of foreground color.

> **tip** Press **alt** (Win) or **option** (Mac) and drag to finger paint when the check box is off.

M pattern

Click here to select a preset pattern or load patterns from disk when using the pattern stamp tool (B).

N aligned

This check box aligns cloning or patterning applied in separate brushstrokes with one of the stamp tools (A & B). The result is that one brushstroke matches up perfectly with another. Turn off the option when you want to clone several places from a single source, as demonstrated in Retouch An Old Photograph on pages 101 and 102.

Brush Size & Shape

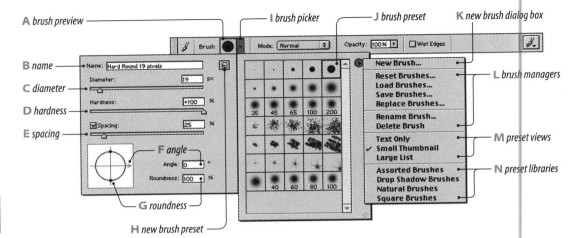

A *brush preview* — | I *brush picker* | J *brush preset* | K *new brush dialog box*

B *name* — Name: Hard Round 19 pixels

C *diameter* — Diameter: 19 px

D *hardness* — Hardness: +100 %

E *spacing* — Spacing: 25 %

F *angle* — Angle: 0 °

G *roundness* — Roundness: 100 %

H *new brush preset*

New Brush...
Reset Brushes...
Load Brushes...
Save Brushes...
Replace Brushes...
Rename Brush...
Delete Brush
Text Only
✓ Small Thumbnail
Large List
Assorted Brushes
Drop Shadow Brushes
Natural Brushes
Square Brushes

L *brush managers*
M *preset views*
N *preset libraries*

The foremost ingredient in a brushstroke drawn with a paint or edit tool is the brush itself. The brush determines the thickness, softness, and calligraphic skew of the stroke. If you define a custom brush (O), you can venture even further, creating rough sketch lines and stamped shapes. Fortunately, Photoshop gives you plenty of ways to design the right brush for the job.

A brush preview

Click the brush preview to display the *brush editor*, which lets you edit the size (C) and shape (F and G) of a brush or create a new preset (H). When you finish editing the brush, press **enter** (Win) or **return** (Mac).

B name

Change the name of the brush, or enter a name for a new brush. Note that multiple brushes can have the same name.

C diameter

Use the slider bar or enter a number to change the diameter (width) of the brush, in pixels. The thickest a brush can be is 999 pixels.

> *tip* Press a bracket key to change the diameter of a brush on the fly. Press [to reduce the diameter or] to increase it. The increment of each keystroke varies as a percentage of the present diameter.

D hardness

The **Hardness** option defines the softness of a brush. A value of **100%** results in an antialiased brush; **0%** results in a blurry brush. Photoshop's default presets are set to one of these two extremes, but incremental **Hardness** values such as 25% or 75% are often more useful for producing credible edits.

> *tip* To change the **Hardness** value on the fly, press **shift** with a bracket key. Press **shift-[** to decrease the hardness by 25 percent; press **shift-]** to increase the hardness by the same amount.

E spacing

As I mentioned on page 93 of The Paint Tools, the paint and edit tools fire off a rapid succession of closely spaced brushes. You can modify this spacing as a percentage of the **Diameter** value. For example, suppose the **Diameter** is 20 pixels and the **Spacing** is 25%, as by default. This tells Photoshop to apply a brush of color every 5 pixels (25 percent of 20). A lower value results in closer spacing, but it can also prevent Photoshop from keeping up with your drags.

> *tip* To get a feel for how **Spacing** works, turn off the check box that precedes the option and drag with the paintbrush in the image window. Photoshop lays down a sequence of brushes, spaced strictly according to the speed of your drag.

Custom Brush & Dynamics

O *define brush*   P *custom brush spacing*   Q *brush dynamics*

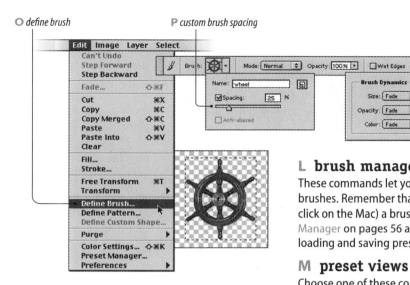

F angle

Edit the **Angle** value or drag the gray arrow in the lower-left box to pivot the brush. This option is meant to be used in combination with **Roundness** (G).

G roundness

Enter a new **Roundness** value or drag the handles on the circle in the box to make the brush shorter than it is wide. When combined with the **Angle** option (F), you can create calligraphic brushes.

H new brush preset

Click this button to make a new brush. Otherwise, pressing **enter** (Win) or **return** (Mac) modifies an existing preset.

I brush picker

Click the down-pointing arrowhead to display a palette of brush-management options (J through N).

J brush preset

Click a brush in the palette to paint with it. Each of the three paint tools and eight edit tools keeps track of its own independent brush.

K new brush dialog box

Choose **New Brush** to display a dialog box that offers the same options as the brush editor (B through G).

L brush managers

These commands let you load, save, or delete preset brushes. Remember that you can **alt-click** (**option-click** on the Mac) a brush to delete it. See The Preset Manager on pages 56 and 57 for more information on loading and saving preset libraries.

M preset views

Choose one of these commands to view the brushes by name only (**Text Only**), brush preview (**Small Thumbnail**), or both (**Large List**).

N preset libraries

Photoshop ships with a few brush libraries. Choose the desired library to load its brushes. **Assorted Brushes** contains a collection of custom brushes (O).

O define brush

To create your own brush, draw it on a separate layer. Then select it with the rectangular marquee tool and choose **Edit➡Define Brush**. Photoshop adds the brush to its list of presets.

P custom brush spacing

To edit a custom brush, select it from the brush picker (I) and then click the brush preview (A). You can change the **Spacing** (E). If the custom brush is sufficiently small, you can apply **Anti-aliased**.

Q brush dynamics

Click the far right button in the options bar to vary the size, opacity, or color of a brushstroke. To fade a brushstroke over a specified distance, choose the **Fade** option. If you own a *pressure-sensitive drawing tablet*, select **Stylus** from a pop-up menu. From that point on, easing up on the *stylus* (tablet pen) causes the brushstroke to fade.

Mode, Opacity, Pressure, & Exposure

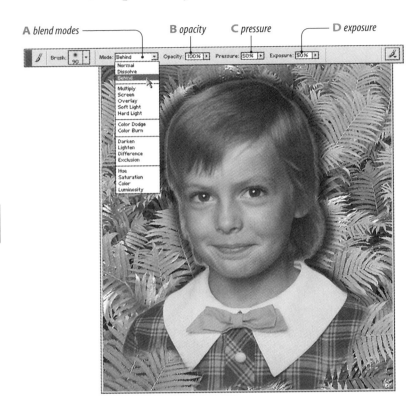

A *blend modes* B *opacity* C *pressure* D *exposure*

When you edit images, the last thing on your mind is math. Yet it's the first thing on Photoshop's mind. Granted, virtually any computer program can be described as a mathematics factory, but it's particularly true of Photoshop, where several thousand colors may be compared, multiplied, subtracted, and merged in a single brushstroke. The **Mode**, **Opacity**, **Pressure**, and **Exposure** options give you access to all kinds of mathematical trickery. Some functions, such as **Multiply**, use math to simulate real-life effects; others, like **Difference**, invite you to create effects that would otherwise be impossible.

A blend modes

When using the airbrush, paintbrush, pencil, or one of the two stamp tools, the **Mode** pop-up menu lists a total of 18 *blend modes*, which mix the foreground or cloned colors with the existing pixels in the image. The number of modes slims to seven when the blur,

sharpen, or smudge tool is active; none are applicable to the dodge, burn, and sponge tools. Blend modes take on greater significance when applied to layers, which is why I examine each and every one of them in The Blend Modes on pages 137 through 139 of Chapter 10. In the meantime, here are the handful of modes that produce interesting effects when used with the paint and edit tools:

❖ **Normal**: Selected by default, **Normal** makes no attempt to apply fancy math to the brushstroke. It's essentially like turning the blend mode off.

❖ **Dissolve**: Use this mode with a feathered brush to paint a pattern of loose pixels that resemble iron filings in a sandbox. Press **shift+alt+X** (**shift-option-X** on the Mac) to select **Dissolve** when a paint or stamp tool is active.

❖ **Behind**: When working with a layer, use the **Behind** mode (**shift+alt+Q**) to paint behind the pixels in the layer. Above, I painted black behind the girl's head.

The Fade Command

E fade command   F fade dialog box

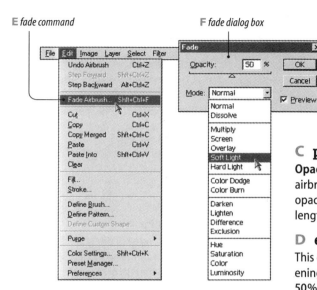

B opacity

Reduce the **Opacity** to create a translucent brushstroke with the paintbrush, pencil, or one of the two stamp tools. The **Opacity** value works with the blend mode to create more than 1,000 variations.

C pressure

Opacity changes to **Pressure** when you select the airbrush, blur, sharpen, or sponge tool. It controls the opacity and intensity of each effect, as well as the length of a smear applied with the smudge tool.

D exposure

This option controls the amount of lightening or darkening applied by the dodge or burn tool. A value of 50% or less is best for most work. After all, you can always brush in more if needed.

> **tip** Regardless of which paint or edit tool you're using, you can change the **Opacity**, **Pressure**, or **Exposure** setting from the keyboard. Just press a number key while the tool is selected. For example, press **4** for 40%. Press two numbers in a row for greater precision, such as **4, 6** for 46%.

E fade command

The blend mode and other options affect the next brushstroke you draw. To change a brushstroke *after* you draw it, choose **Edit➡Fade** or press **ctrl+shift+F** (**command-shift-F** on the Mac). Note that this command is operative immediately after you apply a brushstroke and affects the most recent brushstroke drawn. If you so much as click with another tool, the **Fade** command dims to gray.

F fade dialog box

The **Fade** dialog box offers **Opacity** and **Mode** options, permitting you to blend a brushstroke with the original image. Note it's always **Opacity**; never **Pressure** or **Exposure**. This means you can fade a smudge tool brushstroke, but you can't shorten the length of its smear.

❖**Multiply & Screen**: These two are opposites. **Multiply** darkens blended colors as if they were overlapping inks. So cyan plus yellow makes green (as in CMYK). **Screen** lightens blended colors as if they were lights projected on a monitor. Red plus green makes yellow (as in RGB). Use **Multiply** (**shift+alt+M**) to create a magic marker effect; use **Screen** (**shift+alt+S**) to produce a highlight.

❖**Darken & Lighten**: When used with the blur, sharpen, or smudge tool, **Darken** (**shift+alt+K**) preserves those colors that are darker than the pre-edit pixels; **Lighten** (**shift+alt+G**) preserves those colors that are lighter.

❖**Difference**: Make the foreground color white and paint with the **Difference** mode (**shift+alt+E**) to invert colors as you drag over them. Use other colors to get psychedelic effects. Only black does nothing.

❖**Color**: The **Color** mode (**shift+alt+C**) colorizes an image. Start with a grayscale photo, choose **Image➡Mode➡RGB** to convert it to RGB, and paint away.

> **tip** To advance from one mode to the next, press **shift-plus (+)** when a paint or edit tool is active. To apply the previous mode, press **shift-minus (–)**. And don't worry about doing permanent damage—you can always return to **Normal** by pressing **shift+alt+N** (**shift-option-N** on the Mac).

Paint A Frame Inside A Selection

You can mask off an area by selecting it. The selection acts as a stencil—paint all you like inside the selection and not a drop will spill outside. One use for this technique is to create a custom frame:

1 select rectangular marquee
For a round frame, get the elliptical marquee tool.

2 select frame boundary
Draw an outline around the image. The outline should match the inside edge of your prospective frame.

3 choose feather
Or press **ctrl+alt+D** (**command-option-D** on the Mac). Then enter a **Radius** of 12 or higher to fade the edge of the frame and press **enter** (**return**).

4 choose inverse
Or press **ctrl+shift+I** (**command-shift-I** on the Mac).

This selects the area outside the image, which is where you want to paint your frame.

5 select paintbrush
Because of its even painting style and soft edges, the paintbrush is generally the best tool for painting a frame. But you can use the airbrush as well.

6 select spatter brush
By default, Photoshop offers a series of six custom **Spatter** brushes, designed to lend a traditional feel to your brushstrokes. Select one of these or another brush of your choosing from the brush picker.

7 paint in selection
Paint inside the selected area of the image. Scribble back and forth to get a rough look, as in the image below. No matter how random or wild your gestures, Photoshop keeps the paint inside the selection.

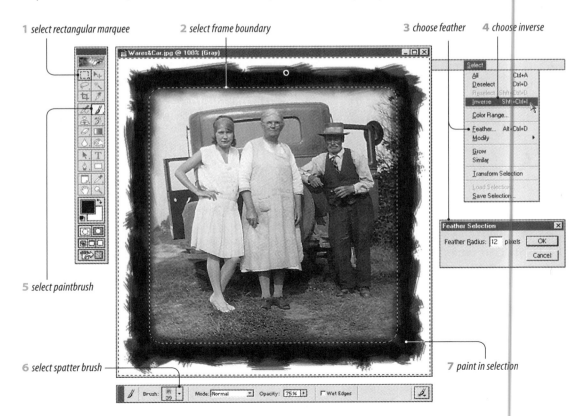

1 *select rectangular marquee* 2 *select frame boundary* 3 *choose feather* 4 *choose inverse*

5 *select paintbrush*

6 *select spatter brush*

7 *paint in selection*

⬭steps Retouch An Old Photograph

One of the miracles of digital imaging is the ability to take something old and make it new again. The idea is that a typical photograph—even one that is substantially damaged—contains all the visual information you need to fix it. This means you can wash away imperfections and rebuild lost details by cloning the existing pixels in the photo. Cloning requires a bit of work, but it's a heck of a lot easier than trying to paint new details with an airbrush.

1 select rubber stamp
This tool clones pixels from one location to another. By effectively painting an image with the image itself, the rubber stamp manages to convey a degree of photographic realism that's unmatched by other tools.

2 click brush preview
Photoshop's preset brushes are either hard-edged or blurry. A hard brush results in sharp edges around cloned brushstrokes; a blurry brush results in smeared transitions that appear incongruous with the surrounding film grain. For the best effect, design your own brush.

3 set hardness
Set the hardness to somewhere between 50% and 75%. This affords your brushstrokes some softness without becoming altogether blurry.

> *tip* Don't forget, you can adjust the hardness of a brush on the fly by pressing **shift-[** or **shift-]**, great for making quick adjustments without any fuss.

1 select rubber stamp   *2 click brush preview*   *3 set hardness*   *4 turn off aligned*

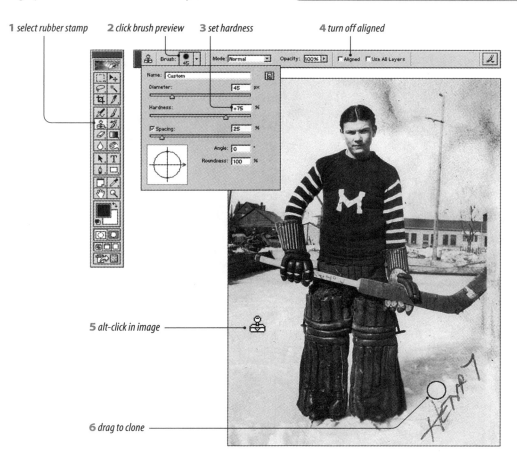

5 alt-click in image

6 drag to clone

4 turn off aligned

Turning off **Aligned** lets you clone several times in a row from a single pristine spot in the image.

5 alt-click in image

Press **alt** (Win) or **option** (Mac) and click to set the source point for your cloning. This is not an optional step; you must set a *from* point before you can clone part of an image *to* a new location.

6 drag to clone

The point at which you begin dragging sets a relative alignment between the *from* and *to* points for the duration of the brushstroke. As you drag, Photoshop identifies the *from* location with a cross, so you're constantly aware exactly what it is you're cloning.

7 adjust blend mode & opacity

From here, it's a matter of alt-clicking (**option**-clicking on the Mac) to set the source and then dragging

to clone—over and over again. Your success will depend largely on your artistic inclination and willingness to practice, but there are a few tips I can pass along. For starters, bear in mind that you can adjust the **Mode** and **Opacity** settings to mix the cloned pixels with the original ones, great for subtle changes.

8 choose new view

It helps to zoom into your image to adjust fine details, but it's equally nice to see a far-away view. By choosing **View➡New View**, you can have both.

9 keep your drags short

The restored tip of the hockey stick is a series of clicks and short drags around the outer edge. Not every click works, which is why you have **Edit➡Undo**.

10 burn shadow

I darkened the base of the shadow with the burn tool. Don't hesitate to bring in other edit tools to assist.

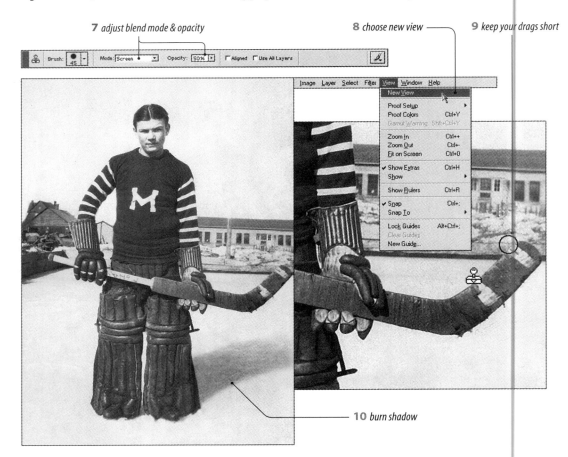

7 *adjust blend mode & opacity*   **8** *choose new view*   **9** *keep your drags short*

10 *burn shadow*

Create & Modify Layers

Every digital photograph starts out as a *flat* image, in which every pixel resides on a single plane. But as soon as you begin combining images together, you create *layers*, which are independent images stacked one in front of the other. A document that contains layers is called a *layered composition*.

Photoshop's reliance on layers makes for an exceedingly flexible (if sometimes confusing) working environment. So long as an image remains on a layer, you can move, transform, edit, align, reorder, or blend it with other layers for an independent period of time. No change need be permanent.

But layers come at a price. Because they are actually independent images, each layer consumes space on disk and in memory. That's why you can merge multiple layers into one and even flatten an image, as this chapter explains.

The Layers Palette

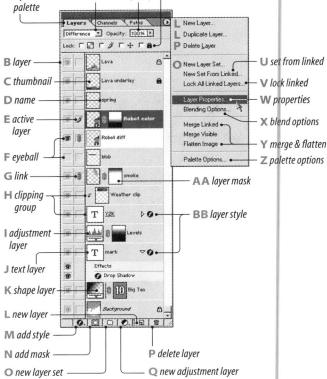

A *layers palette*
R *blend mode*
S *opacity*
T *lock boxes*
B *layer*
C *thumbnail*
D *name*
E *active layer*
F *eyeball*
G *link*
H *clipping group*
I *adjustment layer*
J *text layer*
K *shape layer*
L *new layer*
M *add style*
N *add mask*
O *new layer set*
P *delete layer*
Q *new adjustment layer*
U *set from linked*
V *lock linked*
W *properties*
X *blend options*
Y *merge & flatten*
Z *palette options*
AA *layer mask*
BB *layer style*

Given the important role that layers play in Photoshop, it's no surprise that the **Layers** palette is a rather busy place. The following are brief introductions to its many options.

A layers palette

Choose **Window➞Show Layers** or press the **F7** key to display the **Layers** palette.

B layer

The named items in the **Layers** palette are layers. Drag a layer up or down the list to change its order in the stack. The layer listed first in the palette is foremost in the stack, in front of all others. The layer named **Background** is the base layer, forever located at the bottom of the stack. If an image contains a Background layer and nothing else, it is flat.

C thumbnail

Photoshop shows a thumbnail view of every layer. Choose **Palette Options** (Z) to resize the thumbnails.

D name

To identify its contents, every layer has a name. Change the name by choosing **Layer Properties** (W).

E active layer

Click a layer to activate it. A paintbrush shows this is the one and only layer you can paint or edit. The few operations that cross multiple layers rely on linking (G).

F eyeball

Click an eyeball to hide the layer to the right of it. When the layer is hidden, the eyeball disappears. Click where the eyeball should be to show the layer.

> **tip** Alt-click (**option-click** on the Mac) to hide all layers except the layer to the right of the eyeball.

G link

A chain icon to the right of the eyeball marks a layer as *linked* to the active layer (E). All linked layers move and transform at once (Move & Arrange Layers, page 107). Click in this column to link or unlink other layers.

H clipping group

When you *group* layers in Photoshop, something special happens. The bottom layer in the group (whose name appears underlined, as in **Y2K**) *masks* the contents of the grouped layers above it (**Weather clip**). This means pixels in the grouped layers are visible where the bottom layer is opaque and hidden where the bottom layer is transparent. To learn more, see Use One Layer To Clip Another on page 134 of Chapter 9.

I adjustment layer

If in place of the usual thumbnail (C) you see a special icon, the layer is an *adjustment layer*, which is a color adjustment that you can edit long after applying it. See Adjustment Layers on pages 209 and 210.

J text layer

Photoshop relegates text to an independent layer. The big **T** shows that you can edit the text using the type tool. Read Chapter 12, Create & Edit Type.

K shape layer

A second thumbnail showing a shape against a gray background (like the **10**) denotes a *shape layer*, which is a vector-based path that prints at the full resolution of your printer. See Chapter 11, Draw Vector Shapes.

L new layer

Click this button to create an empty layer, automatically named **Layer 1** or the like. Then fill, stroke, or paint the layer as desired. To assign a more meaningful name as you create a layer, choose **New Layer** from the palette menu. You can also alt-click (**option-click** on the Mac) the **New Layer** button, or press **ctrl+shift+N** (**command-shift-N** on the Mac).

This dialog box also lets you copy the layer to a new document: Choose **New** from the **Document** pop-up menu, name the document, and click **OK**.

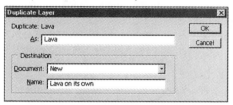

M add style

Click here to display a pop-up menu that lets you add a *layer style*—such as a drop shadow or the like (BB)—to the active layer. See Chapter 10, Blend & Stylize Layers, for complete information.

N add mask

Click here to temporarily hide portions of a layer or layer set (O) with a *layer mask* (AA), as in Layer-Specific Masks on page 131. If part of the layer is selected, clicking the **Add Mask** button converts the selection to a mask, thus hiding everything outside the mask.

O new layer set

This button creates a *layer set*, which lets you arrange layers into a folder, as in Layer Sets on page 106.

P delete layer

Click the trash button to delete the active layer, mask, or set. A warning asks you if you're sure you want to go through with it. To skip this message, drag the layer and drop it on the trash button, or press **alt** (**option** on the Mac) and click the button.

Q new adjustment layer

Click this button to display a pop-up menu of specialty layers. The first three are *dynamic fill layers*, typically associated with shape layers (K). The remaining commands represent adjustment layers (I). See Chapters 11 and 13 for complete discussions of each.

R blend mode

Use the pop-up menu at the top of the **Layers** palette to change the *blend mode*, which governs the way the pixels in the active layer or layer set (O) mix with those in the layers below. See The Blend Modes on pages 137 through 139 of Chapter 10 for explanations of each.

S opacity

Lower the **Opacity** value to make a layer translucent. The Opacity Value on page 136 tells the whole story.

T lock boxes

These four check boxes protect certain attributes of the active layer. The first **Lock** box ensures that you can't paint outside the boundaries of a layer, as in Paint Inside & Behind A Layer on page 132. The second prevents you from altering the contents of a layer. The third prevents you from moving or transforming a layer. And the fourth locks everything.

U set from linked

Choose **New Set From Linked** from the palette menu to unite all linked layers (G) into a set.

V lock linked

This command locks all linked layers (G). A dialog box asks you which attributes you want to lock (T).

W properties

Choose this command to change the layer name. You can also assign a color for visual reference.

X blend options

Choose **Blending Options** to display a dialog box of blend modes and layer styles, covered in Chapter 10.

> *tip* Double-click a layer name to display the **Blending Options** dialog box. Press **alt** (Win) or **option** (Mac) and double-click to access **Layer Properties**.

Y merge & flatten

Choose **Merge Down** or press **ctrl+E** (**command-E** on the Mac) to combine the active layer with the layer below it. If the layer is linked or part of a set, the command merges all layers linked or set together. **Merge Visible** (**ctrl+shift+E**) combines all visible layers but leaves the hidden ones intact. Choose **Flatten Image** to merge all layers and delete the hidden ones.

> *tip* Press **ctrl+alt+E** (**command-option-E** on the Mac) to imprint the active layer onto the layer below. If layers are linked, the lowest linked layer gets the imprint. Meanwhile, **ctrl+shift+alt+E** imprints all visible layers onto the active one.

Z palette options

This command changes the thumbnail size. Or right-click (**control**-click on the Mac) in an empty area below the layer names and choose a thumbnail size.

AA layer mask

A *layer mask* lets you paint transparent areas without harming a single pixel in the layer. A chain between the layer thumbnail (C) and the mask indicates that the two are linked and will move together.

BB layer style

A florin (*f*) shows that a layer style has been applied (M). Click the triangle to the left of the florin to see exactly what styles have been applied.

Layer Sets

Navigating through a list of a dozen or so layers can prove confusing. Fortunately, you can create a set (O or U) and drag and drop layers into it. Then edit the layers as a set as follows:

CC pass through

This option respects the blend modes applied to the individual layers. Or choose another mode to override all layers in the set.

DD linked sets

Link sets together, or even link individual layers to a set.

EE expand & collapse

Click this triangle to view or hide the contents of a set.

FF hidden set

Click the eyeball to hide all layers in a set. Click that spot again to bring the layers back to life.

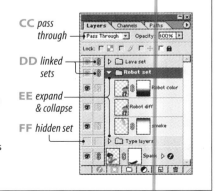

CC *pass through*

DD *linked sets*

EE *expand & collapse*

FF *hidden set*

Move & Arrange Layers

A *move tool*   B *auto switch*   C *bounding box*   D *align linked layers*   E *distribute linked layers*

F *stacking order commands*

G *move tool shortcut menu*

Photoshop lets you move layers in a handful of ways. You can drag a layer up, down, or sideways. You can move the layer forward or backward in the stacking order. And you can align and distribute linked layers into regular rows and columns.

A move tool

Drag with the move tool to move the active layer and any layers linked to it. If a set is active in the **Layers** palette, drag to move all layers in that set. If part of a layer is selected, drag inside the selection outline to move only the selected pixels; drag outside the selection to move both layer and outline together.

> *tip* Press the **V** key to select the move tool. Or better yet, press and hold **ctrl** (**command** on the Mac) and drag to move a layer when using any other tool. To clone a layer, **ctrl+alt**-drag it (**command-option**-drag on the Mac).

If a layer refuses to budge, it's likely locked with the **Lock Position** (third) or **Lock All** (fourth) check box.

B auto switch

Check **Auto Select Layer** to switch to a layer when you click with the move tool on any part of that layer in the image window. Problem is, you end up switching when you don't mean to. There are better ways (G).

C bounding box

Turn on **Show Bounding Box** to surround the selection or active layer with a dotted *bounding box* and eight handles. The bounding box lets you transform a layer without choosing a command, but the move tool has to be active for it to work.

D align linked layers

Use these buttons to align all linked layers to the active layer. Alternatively, you can choose commands from the **Layer➥Align Linked** submenu.

E distribute linked layers

The next set of buttons evenly spaces (or *distributes*) linked layers. Three or more layers must be linked.

F stacking order commands

Choose a command from the **Layer➥Arrange** submenu to move the active layer toward the front or back of the image. Or memorize the shortcuts, which appear in the submenu. All shortcuts involve **ctrl** (or **command** on the Mac) and a bracket key, **[** or **]**.

G move tool shortcut menu

It's often difficult to find the layer that goes with an element in the image window. To make it easier, right-click on the element with the move tool (**control**-click on the Mac). A shortcut menu shows you all layers that contain pixels at the spot where you clicked.

> *tip* You can also switch layers by pressing **alt** (**option** on the Mac) in place of **ctrl** in the stacking shortcuts (F). To activate the next layer up, press **alt+]**. **Shift+alt+[** selects the Background layer.

The Transform Commands

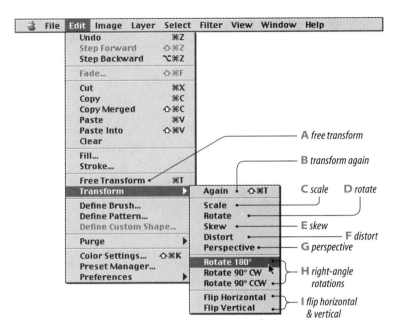

A *free transform*
B *transform again*
C *scale*   D *rotate*
E *skew*
F *distort*
G *perspective*
H *right-angle rotations*
I *flip horizontal & vertical*

for transforming a layer to match one that was transformed earlier. To repeat a transformation from the keyboard, press **ctrl+shift+T** (Win) or **command-shift-T** (Mac).

C scale

Choose **Scale** to produce a bounding box with eight handles (J). Drag a handle to resize the image. Press **shift** and drag a corner to resize the image *proportionally*—by the same amount horizontally and vertically. Press **alt** (Win) or **option** (Mac) to scale with respect to the origin (K), positioned in the center of the image. Drag the origin to move it to a different spot.

tip When you get the effect you want, press **enter** (Win) or **return** (Mac). Press the **esc** key to cancel the transformation. This likewise applies to **Rotate** (D), **Skew** (E), **Distort** (F), **Perspective** (G), and **Free Transform** (A).

Transformations are ways of modifying the geometry of an image. They include scaling, rotating, and other operations that can be expressed numerically—in percentage points, degrees, and so on.

You invoke a transformation by choosing a command from the **Edit** menu. If part of the image is selected, Photoshop transforms the selected pixels only. Otherwise, it transforms the entire layer. If the layer is linked to other layers, all linked layers transform simultaneously. If a set is active, Photoshop transforms all layers in that set.

A free transform

The most efficient of the **Transform** commands is **Free Transform**, which gives you access to every kind of transformation Photoshop offers. The downside is that it takes a little practice to get used to. See Free Transform on the facing page for complete details.

B transform again

This command repeats the most recently applied transformation. (If you haven't yet transformed anything, **Transform Again** is dimmed.) It is especially useful

D rotate

After choosing this command, drag to rotate the image. Press **shift** to constrain the angle of the rotation to a multiple of 45 degrees. Photoshop always rotates around the crosshair-shaped origin. Drag the origin to move the center of rotation.

tip If you change your mind about the kind of transformation you want to apply, right-click (**control**-click on the Mac) in the image window and choose a different transformation from the shortcut menu. It's a great way to switch from, say, rotating to scaling, or vice versa.

E skew

After you choose this command, drag a side handle to slant an image. Drag a corner handle to make a constrained distortion. The command is identical to **Perspective** (G), but the corner handles move independently of each other.

F distort

If you find **Skew** too constraining, choose **Edit➡ Transform➡Distort**. Then you can drag any of the handles completely independently of each other to stretch the image with unfettered abandon.

> **tip** Press **shift** to constrain a distortion along an axis. Press **alt** (Win) or **option** (Mac) to distort opposite handles simultaneously.

G perspective

To create a *perspective* effect, in which the image appears to decline toward a vanishing point, choose **Edit➡Transform➡Perspective**. Drag a side handle to slant the image, as when using **Skew** (E). Drag a corner handle to distort two corners in opposite directions, as if the image is leaning in space.

> **tip** When using one of the previous transformation commands (A & C through G), drag inside the bounding box to move the selection or layer. This permits you to exactly align a transformation.

H right-angle rotations

Choose one of these commands to rotate an image by a multiple of 90 degrees (also known as a *right angle*). If it helps to think of a clock, **90° CW** rotates from 12 o'clock to 3 o'clock; **90° CCW** rotates to 9 o'clock; **180°** rotates the image to 6 o'clock, or upside down.

I flip horizontal & vertical

Choose **Edit➡Transform➡Flip Horizontal** to swap the left and right sides of the shape. Choose **Flip Vertical** to reflect the image on its head.

> **tip** To rotate or flip *all* layers in an image, linked or not, choose a command from the **Image➡Rotate Canvas** submenu, as in The Rotate Canvas Commands on page 26 of Chapter 2.

Free Transform

Choose **Free Transform** (A) or press **ctrl+T** (**command-T** on the Mac) to display a bounding box that lets you do anything:

J handle

Drag a handle to scale the selection or layer. **Shift**-drag to scale proportionally; **alt**-drag to scale from the origin (K).

K origin

Drag the origin—which determines the center of rotations and other transformations—to move it.

L rotate cursor

Move the cursor outside the bounding box to get the rotate cursor. Then drag to rotate the selection.

M distort cursor

Press **ctrl** (**command** on the Mac) and drag a handle to distort or skew the image. Press **ctrl+shift+alt** (**command-shift-option**) and drag a corner handle to achieve a perspective effect.

N move cursor

Position the cursor inside the bounding box and drag to move the image.

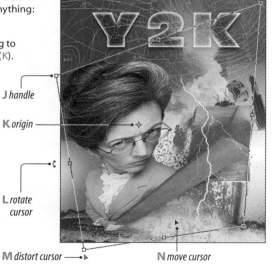

J handle

K origin

L rotate cursor

M distort cursor *N move cursor*

✦steps✦ Scale, Rotate, Distort, & Flip

Free Transform is as powerful as all the other transformation commands put together. So very likely, it's the one you'll use most often. Here's how to use **Free Transform** to scale, rotate, and distort an image element inside a layered composition:

1 get images

Open the image you want to transform and the image you want to serve as the backdrop. For my part, I intend to combine the robot with the **Y2K+10** composition to the right of it.

2 select element to add

I selected the robot with the lasso tool. Don't fret too much about the accuracy of your selection outline. Transforming the element will soften the edges, and you can always finesse them later.

3 drag & drop selection

Use the move tool to drag the selection from one image window to the other. If another tool is active,

press **ctrl** (Win) or **command** (Mac) to temporarily get the move tool, and then drag the selection. Be sure to begin your drag inside the selection, so that the cursor shows a pair of scissors. Photoshop introduces the dropped selection as a new layer, as explained on page 112 of Build A Layered Composition.

4 prepare layer

If you want to transform multiple layers at a time, link the layer or add it to a set. For my part, I renamed the layer by **alt-double-clicking** it (**option**-double-clicking on the Mac).

5 choose free transform

Choose **Edit➞Free Transform** or press **ctrl+T** (**command-T** on the Mac) to initiate the transformation.

6 scale & move

Generally speaking, your first chores are to scale the layer to fit the composition and move it into roughly the desired position. For example, my robot was way

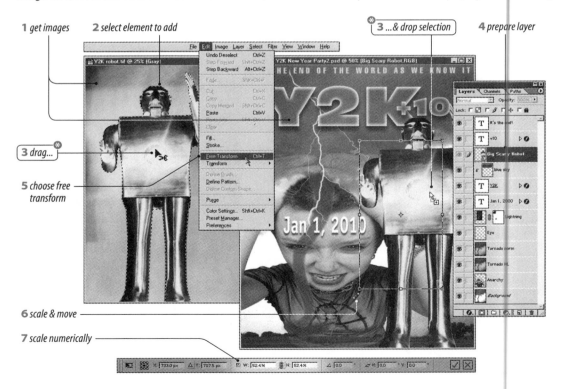

1 *get images* **2** *select element to add* **3** *...& drop selection* **4** *prepare layer*

3 *drag...*

5 *choose free transform*

6 *scale & move*

7 *scale numerically*

too large to fit the composition, so I **shift**-dragged a corner handle to reduce the robot proportionally to 52.4 percent of its original size.

7 scale numerically (optional)

If you want to scale the layer by specific percentage values, enter them into the **W** and **H** option boxes in the options bar. To scale the layer proportionally, click the link icon between the **W** and **H** values.

8 rotate

Move your cursor outside the rectangular bounding box to get the rotate cursor. Then drag to rotate the layer. If you prefer, you can enter a degree value into the **Rotate** option box in the options bar. If you do, be aware of three rules: A positive value rotates the layer in a counter-clockwise direction. A negative value rotates the layer clockwise. And there are 360 degrees in a circle, which means that a value of 360° rotates the layer back to its original position.

9 drag origin (optional)

Notice that the layer rotates around the origin, which looks like a small crosshair target. Feel free to drag the origin to a different location if you want to change the center of the rotation.

10 distort

Press the **ctrl** key (**command** on the Mac) and drag a corner handle to perform a distortion. You can also **ctrl**-drag a side handle (including those at the top or bottom) to slant the layer. To distort two opposing corner handles, press **ctrl+alt** (**command-option**) and drag. Add **shift** to constrain the drag, great for slants and perspective distortions.

tip While working in the free transform mode, Photoshop permits you to undo the single most recent operation. Choose **Edit➞Undo** or press **ctrl+Z** (Win) or **command-Z** (Mac).

11 right-click (optional)

Dragging handles isn't always the best way to apply a transformation. If you find yourself struggling to flip a layer or rotate it 90 degrees, for example, you're better off choosing a command. Right-click (Win) or **control**-click (Mac) in the image to display a shortcut menu of commands familiar from The Transform Commands on pages 108 and 109. I chose **Flip Horizontal** to create a mirror image of the robot.

12 click commit

When you're finished transforming, apply your changes by clicking the check mark in the options bar, or by pressing **enter** (Win) or **return** (Mac). Assuming **Bicubic** is selected in the **Preferences** dialog box (see page 53 of The Preferences Commands), Photoshop renders a smooth version of the transformed layer.

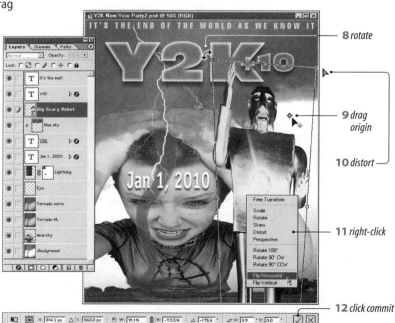

8 *rotate*

9 *drag origin*

10 *distort*

11 *right-click*

12 *click commit*

steps Build A Layered Composition

To bring it all home, the next three pages show how to assemble a typical layered composition in Photoshop. Bear in mind, there are lots of different ways to work. The following steps are presented merely as an example:

1 get images
Open the images that you want to combine. One image will serve as the backdrop (in my case, the French doors); the others will become floating layers inside the composition (the man and hot dog).

2 select images
Use Photoshop's selection tools to select the image elements that you want to turn into layers. I used the pen tool to select both the man and the hot dog.

3 drag & drop images
With the move tool, drag each selection into the back-drop window. Press **shift** as you drop to center the selection in the backdrop. Don't like to drag and drop? Then press **ctrl+C** to copy the selection, switch to the backdrop window, and press **ctrl+V** to paste.

4 name layers
After creating the layers, it's a good idea to take a moment and name them. This makes it easier to identify and switch between layers. Press the **alt** key (**option** on the Mac) and dou-ble-click the layer in the **Layers** palette. Enter a name and select a color to highlight the layer. I used yellow to distin-guish these initial layers from any that might come later.

1 get images

2 select images

3 drag & drop images

4 name layers

5 choose save as

To avoid losing any work, save your composition to a layer-friendly format. Press **ctrl+shift+S** (**command-shift-S** on the Mac) and then set the **Format** option to **Photoshop**. Check the **Layers** option and click **Save**.

6 scale & move layers

Transform and position the layers as desired, according to *Scale, Rotate, Distort, & Flip* on pages 110 and 111. Notice that large layers remain fully intact beyond the boundaries of the image window. The **Shaved guy** layer extends down to the man's feet, even though we can't see anything beyond his torso.

> *tip* To expand the canvas size to show all pixels in all layers, choose **Image→Reveal All**.

7 make new layer

I had the urge to give the man a halo. If you similarly decide to hand-draw an element, be sure to give it its own layer. This permits you to edit the element without harming other portions of your artwork.

Photoshop positions the new layer in front of the active layer. So I selected the **Shaved guy** layer and **alt**-clicked (or **option**-clicked) the **New Layer** button at the bottom of the **Layers** palette. Then I assigned the layer a name and color.

8 draw marquee

The easiest way to make a soft halo is to stroke an elliptical marquee. So I drew the shape with the elliptical marquee tool. Then I used **Select→Transform Selection** to rotate the marquee a few degrees.

9 feather & stroke

I chose **Select→Feather** and applied a **Radius** of 12 pixels. Then I used **Edit→Stroke** to apply a white, 32-pixel-thick outline. The result was a glowing halo. Thanks to the fact that I had the foresight to create a new layer (7), I still to this day have the opportunity to adjust the placement and shape of the halo as I see fit. Only layers provide this kind of flexibility.

10 make new layer (page 114)

Next, I wanted to create a shadow behind the hot dog. Ctrl-clicking (**command**-clicking on the Mac) the **New Layer** button creates a layer in back of the active layer. So I selected the **Hotdog** layer and **ctrl+alt**-clicked (**command-option**-clicked) to create and name the new **Dog shadow** layer.

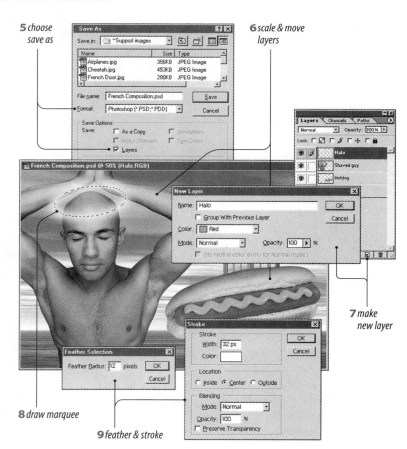

5 choose save as

6 scale & move layers

7 make new layer

8 draw marquee

9 feather & stroke

11 select horizon

I wanted to paint the shadow strictly within the ground of the Background layer, so I selected the area with the rectangular marquee tool. The horizon was absolutely flat, so the rectangular marquee tool worked perfectly.

12 airbrush shadow

I pressed the **D** key to make the foreground color black. Next, I selected the airbrush tool and set the **Pressure** to 20 percent by pressing the 2 key. Then I brushed in the black shadow. Because I cordoned off the area I wanted to paint with a marquee, I only had to swipe the airbrush back and forth and I was done.

13 select doors

Finally, I wanted to achieve the surreal effect of creating a doorway through the hot dog. I could have carved a hole in the hot dog to reveal the doors. But it seemed easier to place the doors on their own layer and move it in front of the hot dog. I started by switching to the Background layer (**shift+alt+[** under Windows, **shift-option-[** on the Mac). Then I selected the doors with the pen tool.

14 choose layer via copy

There are two ways to move a selection to its own layer. You can copy the selection and immediately paste it (**ctrl+C, ctrl+V** under Windows; **command-C, command-V** on the Mac). Or you can save a keystroke and press **ctrl+J** (Win) or **command-J** (Mac), the shortcut for **Layer➡New➡Layer via Copy**. The marching ants disappear to show that you now have a new layer.

tip To name the layer as you create it, press **ctrl+alt+J** (command-option-J on the Mac). You can also press **ctrl+shift+J** to cut the selection to a new layer, leaving a hole in its wake, great for cutting down on file size. Press **ctrl+shift+alt+J** to name the cut layer.

15 adjust stacking order

Drag the layer in the **Layers** palette to move it in front of the element you want to cover. Or press **ctrl+]** a few times to move the active layer forward incrementally.

10 *make new layer*

11 *select horizon*

12 *airbrush shadow*

13 *select doors*

14 *choose layer via copy*

15 *adjust stacking order*

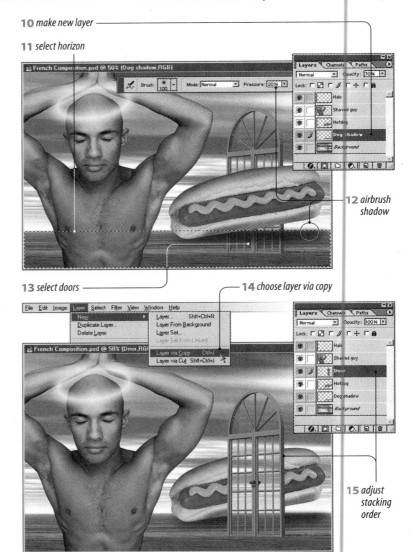

Define Channels & Masks

Photoshop's selection tools are adept and practical (see Chapter 5, Make Selections). They let you select basic forms, isolate areas of color, and trace smooth objects. But when it comes to selecting intricate or delicate edges—both commonplace in the natural world—the lasso is too sloppy, the wand is too approximate, and the pen is way too much work.

The solution is *masking*, which permits you to use an image to select itself. Unlike layers and other core features, masking isn't restricted to one palette; it's peppered all over Photoshop. You can sample a color range, scrub with an eraser, drape a ruby-colored "quick mask" over an image, assign transparency to a layer, or edit a mask as an independent image. In this chapter, I'll show you when and how to use each of these techniques to achieve the credible, organic compositions for which Photoshop is famous.

115

The Color Range Command

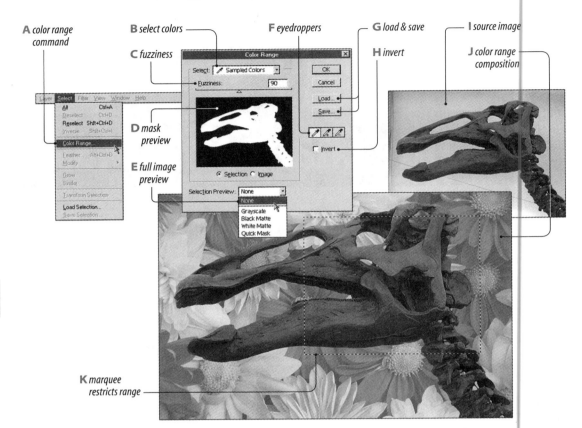

A *color range command*

B *select colors*

C *fuzziness*

D *mask preview*

E *full image preview*

F *eyedroppers*

G *load & save*

H *invert*

I *source image*

J *color range composition*

K *marquee restricts range*

The best introduction to masking is the **Color Range** command. Essentially an enhanced version of the magic wand, **Color Range** lets you adjust the range of colors you want to select until you get it just right. It also measures colors in a more sophisticated manner than the wand to provide smoother selection outlines. Meanwhile, **Color Range** previews your selection as a black-and-white mask (D).

A color range command

Choose **Select** ➡ **Color Range** (or press alt+S, C under Windows) to display the **Color Range** dialog box.

B select colors

Choose an option from the **Select** pop-up menu to select a predefined range of colors or brightness levels. For example, **Yellow** selects all the yellows in the image; **Highlights** selects just the lightest colors; **Out Of Gamut** selects the colors that can't be printed with CMYK inks. These options can be useful, but they disable the **Fuzziness** slider (C) and eyedropper tools (F), thus prohibiting you from modifying the selection to better suit your needs. For ultimate control, leave this option set to **Sampled Colors**.

C fuzziness

This slider is a variation on the **Tolerance** value that accompanies the magic wand tool (see The Magic Wand on page 66). Like **Tolerance**, **Fuzziness** spreads the selection across a range of brightness levels. Raise the value to expand the selection; lower the value to reduce the selection. But there are two important differences: First, **Tolerance** modifies the next selection, not the current one; **Fuzziness** changes the ongoing selection. Second, the wand selects all colors that fall inside the **Tolerance** range to the same degree; **Color Range** gradually fades selection as colors drift to the outer edge of the **Fuzziness** range. As a result, you get soft transitions, as witnessed by the flowers selected and set against a black background below.

magic wand selection   *color range selection*

D mask preview

By default, this preview shows how the selection looks when expressed as a mask. The white region is selected; the black region is not. Gray pixels are partially selected. This might seem like a weird way to express a selection outline, but it's actually more precise. Where marching ants show only the halfway mark between the selected and deselected portions of an image, a mask shows the wide range of selection, from fully selected to partially selected to not at all.

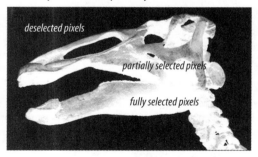

deselected pixels

partially selected pixels

fully selected pixels

Use the radio buttons below the preview to see the mask (**Selection**) or a reduced version of the image.

E full image preview

Choose **Grayscale** to fill the image window with the mask. The two **Matte** options set the selected pixels against a black or white background, great for testing edges. **Quick Mask** shows the mask as a ruby-colored overlay (as in The Quick Mask Mode on page 122). Choose **None** to return to the normal image.

F eyedroppers

Click in the image window to specify the color upon which **Color Range** bases its selection, as when clicking with the magic wand. You can even click inside the mask preview (D).

> *tip* The dialog box supplies two additional eyedroppers so you can add and subtract colors in the selection, but you need never use them. Armed only with the main eyedropper, click to start a new selection, **shift**-click to add colors, or **alt**-click (**option**-click on the Mac) to subtract colors.

You can likewise **shift**-drag to add a range of colors or **alt**-drag to subtract. If you make a mistake, just press ctrl+Z (command-Z on the Mac) to undo it.

G load & save

Click the **Save** button to save the sampled colors and **Fuzziness** value. Click **Load** to open a saved file. To use the file on a PC, it must end in the extension **.axt**.

H invert

Select this option to reverse the selected and deselected pixels. **Shift**-clicking with the eyedropper then subtracts from the selection, turning **Color Range** into a deselection machine. Use **Invert** when it's easier to isolate the colors you *don't* want to select, as in the case of my dinosaur skeleton.

I source image

By way of example, here's the image as it appeared before I selected it with the **Color Range** command.

J color range composition

And here's the selected dinosaur layered against a contrasting background. As you can see, **Color Range** is capable of producing excellent selections.

K marquee restricts range

One final tip: To restrict the area affected by **Color Range**, select an area before choosing the command. The marquee tool is perfect for this purpose.

The Eraser Tool

A *eraser tool* B *brush* C *eraser mode* D *opacity* E *wet edges* F *erase to history* G *brush dynamics*

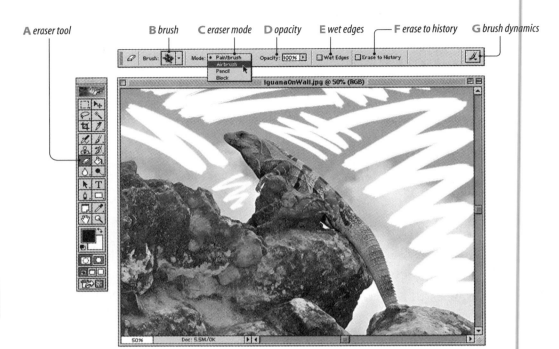

Photoshop provides three eraser tools, all of which purport to erase background elements from an image. You can then move the remaining foreground element into a new composition.

A eraser tool

Of the three erasers, the standard eraser tool is the most humdrum. When editing a flat image, it's little more than a paint tool that uses the background color. If you're working on a layer, the tool erases away pixels, leaving transparency in its wake. Press the E key to select the eraser from the keyboard.

B brush

Click the down-pointing arrow to select a preset brush. Or click the brush preview to design your own. Remember, you can resize the brush without resorting to presets by pressing the bracket keys, [and].

C eraser mode

Unlike other paint tools, the eraser does not support blend modes (Mode, Opacity, Pressure, & Exposure, pages 98 and 99). Instead, use the Mode option to

emulate any of the three paint tools. A fourth mode, **Block**, erases with a square cursor that remains a fixed size regardless of how far you zoom in or out.

D opacity

Although you can't change the blend mode, you can create a translucent brushstroke by reducing the **Opacity** value. Press a number key to adjust the value from the keyboard.

E wet edges

When the **Mode** option (C) is set to **Paintbrush**, select **Wet Edges** to paint a translucent brushstroke with more opaque edges. When erasing a layer with a soft brush, the result is a sort of glowing effect.

F erase to history

The eraser has a trick up its sleeve: When you select this check box—or press **alt** (Win) or **option** (Mac) when dragging with the eraser—the eraser reverts the image to the source state in the **History** palette. Nifty as this is, the function is better served by a more capable tool, namely The History Brush on page 234.

Background & Magic Erasers

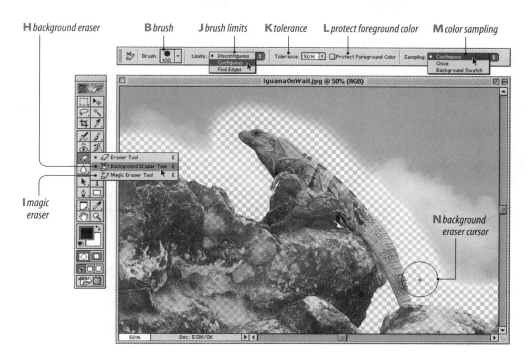

H *background eraser* **B** *brush* **J** *brush limits* **K** *tolerance* **L** *protect foreground color* **M** *color sampling*

I *magic eraser*

N *background eraser cursor*

G brush dynamics
Click this option to vary the size and opacity of an eraser stroke, either by fading it over a specified distance or linking it to stylus pressure. The latter requires a pressure-sensitive drawing tablet, sold separately.

H background eraser
Press **shift-E** to switch to the background eraser, which samples colors from an image and erases them as you drag (N). If an image is not already on a floating layer, Photoshop layers the image automatically.

I magic eraser
Press **shift-E** again to get the magic eraser. Click in the image window to make a range of colors transparent. It's like clicking with the magic wand tool and pressing **backspace** (Win) or **delete** (Mac).

J brush limits
The magic eraser options are based on those for the magic wand (The Magic Wand, page 66). Those for the background eraser are unique, however, starting with **Limits**. You can erase only adjacent background colors (**Contiguous**) or all background colors (**Discontiguous**). Use **Find Edges** to enhance edge details. The default, **Discontiguous**, is generally the best.

K tolerance
Raise this value to erase more colors; lower the value when erasing around fragile details, such as hair.

L protect foreground color
Turn this option on to avoid erasing the foreground color, whatever it may be.

M color sampling
The cursor (N) samples the colors to be erased. It can sample colors continuously as you drag (**Continuous**), once at the beginning of each drag (**Once**), or merely erase the background color (**Background Swatch**).

N background eraser cursor
At the center of this cursor is a cross. Drag the cross over the colors you want to sample. Photoshop erases matching colors that fall inside the brush outline. Soft brushes usually produce the best results.

steps Extract An Image Element

Another method for isolating an image element is the **Extract** command. Like the background eraser, it deletes the background from a layer. Like **Color Range**, it acts like a miniature program, rife with complex options. Luckily, the options are relatively straightforward, so long as you follow these steps:

1 choose extract
Choose **Image➡Extract**, or press **ctrl+alt+X** (Win) or **command-option-X** (Mac). Photoshop displays the **Extract** window, complete with image preview.

2 select edge highlighter
Start off by identifying which part of the image you want to extract. Select the edge highlighter tool from the left side of the window. Or press the B key.

3 select smart highlighting
The **Smart Highlighting** check box helps to identify strong edges in the image. If the element you want to extract isn't well defined, leave this check box off.

4 trace image element
Trace around the foreground element. Be sure to trace a complete, unbroken outline. If the element is cropped, highlight to the edges of the photograph.

> *tip* If **Smart Highlighting** is off, you may find it easier to **shift**-click around the element rather than drag. Shift-clicking draws straight lines.

Press **[** or **]** to reduce or enlarge the brush—even in the middle of a drag! A small brush is better for intricate details. If you make a mistake, press **ctrl+Z** (Win) or **command-Z** (Mac) to undo. Or press E for the eraser.

5 select fill tool
After tracing the image, press G to select the fill tool.

6 click inside highlighter outline
The outline fills with blue. If the blue leaks outside the outline, there's a break in the outline. Fix the break with the edge highlighter tool (4) and try filling again.

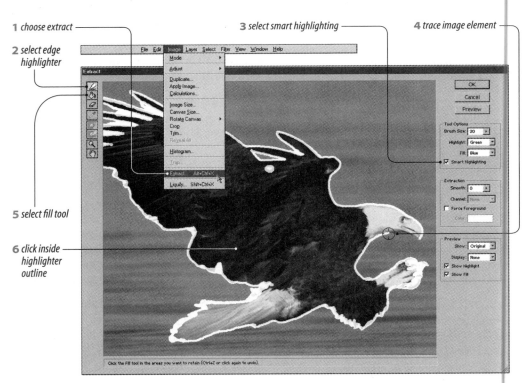

1 *choose extract*

2 *select edge highlighter*

3 *select smart highlighting*

4 *trace image element*

5 *select fill tool*

6 *click inside highlighter outline*

7 click preview

Once you achieve an unbroken outline with a contained fill, click the **Preview** button to tell Photoshop to automatically extract the image.

8 set matte

After the preview completes, examine the extracted edges for defects. By default, Photoshop sets the image against a checkerboard pattern. For a more helpful black or white background, choose **Black Matte** or **White Matte**. Or press the F key to cycle through the various **Display** options.

9 apply cleanup tool

You have two tools to fix any problems you find. Press C to select the cleanup tool, then drag to erase pixels in the same way as the background eraser. **Alt**-drag (Win) or **option**-drag (Mac) to make pixels visible.

10 apply edge touchup

For more automation, press **T** for the edge touchup tool, which automatically adjusts pixels along the highlight outline (4). To access other pixels, **ctrl**-drag (Win) or **command**-drag (Mac) to move the outline.

> *tip* Need more precision from the cleanup or touchup tools? Press [to reduce the brush size. Or press a number key to reduce the pressure setting.

11 click OK

When you like what you see, click the **OK** button. The result is a layer with a transparent background.

12 drag & drop

To get the full effect, press **ctrl** (Win) or **command** (Mac) and drag the extracted layer into another image. Use the background eraser to make repairs.

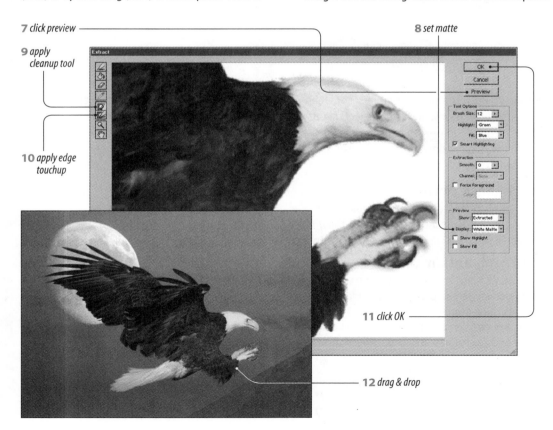

7 *click preview*

9 *apply cleanup tool*

10 *apply edge touchup*

8 *set matte*

11 *click OK*

12 *drag & drop*

The Quick Mask Mode

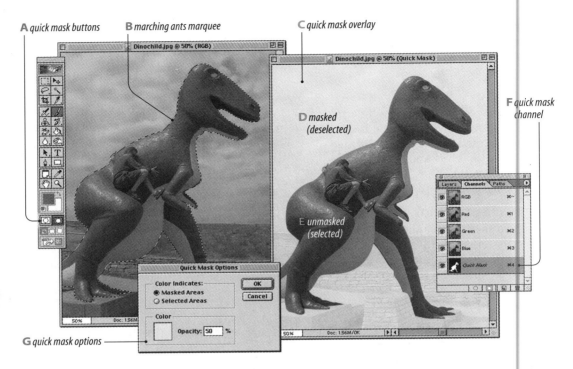

A *quick mask buttons*   **B** *marching ants marquee*   **C** *quick mask overlay*

D *masked (deselected)*

E *unmasked (selected)*

F *quick mask channel*

G *quick mask options*

Photoshop's *quick mask mode* is nothing more than an alternative way to view and edit a selection outline. Enter the mode to view the selection as a mask, edit the mask as desired, and then exit the mode to see the updated selection outline.

A quick mask buttons

Click the right-hand button to enter the quick mask mode; click the left-hand button to return to the *standard mode*. Or just press Q to toggle between the two.

B marching ants marquee

In the standard mode, the marching ants trace the boundary between those pixels that are at least 50-percent selected and those that are not. You can edit the marquee using a dedicated collection of tools and commands, as in Chapter 5, Make Selections.

C quick mask overlay

Press Q to see the quick mask version of the selection. The ruby-colored overlay shows the wide range of selection, from 100-percent selected to completely

deselected. The mask is an independent image, so you can edit it using any tool or command in Photoshop, including the paint and edit tools.

D masked (deselected)

By default, a ruby-colored overlay covers the deselected, or *masked*, portions of the image. Paint with black to add to the mask.

E unmasked (selected)

Where there is no overlay, the pixels are selected, or *unmasked*. Paint or erase with white to unmask.

F quick mask channel

The quick mask appears as a temporary item in the **Channels** palette, which I introduce in The Channels Palette on pages 125 and 126.

G quick mask options

The ruby overlay may get lost in predominantly red images. To change the overlay color, double-click one of the quick mask buttons (A), and then click the color swatch in the **Quick Mask Options** dialog box.

Refine A Selection With Quick Mask

The quick mask mode lets you direct all of Photoshop's tools and commands to the task of editing a selection outline. These steps show how to finesse a complex marquee using the paint and fill tools.

1 get image
Open the image that contains the element you want to select. Feel free to select an image with lots of color and a busy background, attributes that might confuse Photoshop's automated functions. But stick with smooth edges. We'll get to hair later (Define A Mask From Scratch, pages 128 through 130).

2 choose color range
The quick mask mode works best when you have a rough selection in place. Your best bet for this purpose is **Select→ Color Range** (The Color Range Command, pages 116 and 117), but you can use the magic wand as well. Don't worry about creating a perfect selection; you just need a jumping off point.

3 enter quick mask mode
Press Q to coat the deselected portions of the image with a red overlay, often called a *rubylith*.

4 select paintbrush
The most basic tool for editing a quick mask is the paintbrush. Press the B key to get it.

5 set foreground color
Press D to get the default foreground and background colors, black and white. Then press X to switch the foreground color to white. Painting with white erases away the rubylith, thus unmasking areas.

1 get image

2 choose color range

3 enter quick mask mode

4 select paintbrush

5 set foreground color

6 paint mask

6 paint mask

Add to the selected area by painting with white. To apply more rubylith, press the **X** key to make the foreground color black. Then paint to mask areas.

> **tip** Feel free to use the selection tools to cordon off areas. For example, I selected the triceratops's horns with the lasso tool before painting.

7 select gradient tool

Press **G** to get the gradient tool, which is perfect for creating gradual transitions in the quick mask mode.

8 select foreground to transparent

Click the down-pointing arrow in the options bar to display a pop-up menu of gradient presets, and then choose the **Foreground to Transparent** item. Also press the **D** key to make the foreground color black.

9 draw gradient

Drag wherever you want something to fade into view. I dragged upward at the base of the triceratops's feet. This way, the feet will start out deselected and fade into view, ideal for layering the dinosaur against tall grass. Because you selected **Foreground to Transparent** (8), you add to the mask without harming the selected regions.

10 hide RGB

The quick mask is a standard mask laid on top of an image. To view the mask by itself, go to the **Channels** palette and turn off the eyeball in front of **RGB**. The selected areas appear white; the deselected areas appear black.

> **tip** To hide the image from the keyboard, press the tilde (~) key. Press ~ again to view image and mask together.

11 exit quick mask

When you arrive at a satisfactory mask, press **Q** to return to standard mode.

12 drag & drop

Use the move tool to drag and drop the selection into a new background image.

13 select burn tool

To make the triceratops better mesh with its new backdrop, I selected the burn tool from the toolbox...

14 paint shadow

...and then I painted the layer behind the triceratops to create a soft shadow.

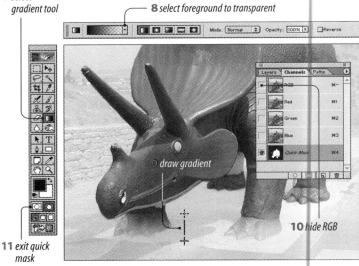

7 select gradient tool

8 select foreground to transparent

9 draw gradient

10 hide RGB

11 exit quick mask

12 drag & drop

13 select burn tool

14 paint shadow

The Channels Palette

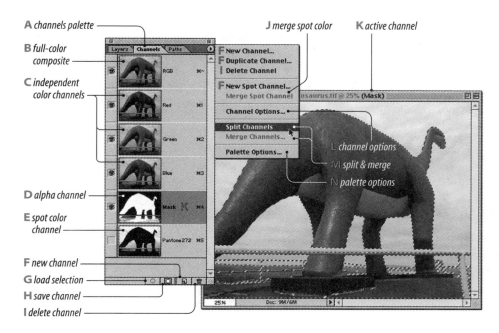

A *channels palette*
B *full-color composite*
C *independent color channels*
D *alpha channel*
E *spot color channel*
F *new channel*
G *load selection*
H *save channel*
I *delete channel*
J *merge spot color*
K *active channel*
L *channel options*
M *split & merge*
N *palette options*

The only difference between the quick mask mode and "real" masking is that the former is temporary and the latter is permanent. A quick mask does not get saved with an image; a mask created in the **Channels** palette does.

A channels palette

Choose **Window➡Show Channels**. Or press F8 to get the **Layers** palette and click the **Channels** tab. The result is the **Channels** palette, which shows the individual *channels* of color (C) that make up an image.

B full-color composite

The item at the top of the **Channels** palette isn't a channel, but rather a combination of channels called a *composite*. Click it to see the full-color image. The composite is named after the prevailing color mode, most likely **RGB** or **CMYK**. To change the mode, choose a command from the **Image➡Mode** submenu.

C independent color channels

When you print a CMYK image, the printer outputs the cyan, magenta, yellow, and black inks in separate passes. So it's not surprising that Photoshop treats

each ink as a separate channel. Likewise, an RGB image comprises separate channels for the red, green, and blue primaries. Whether CMYK or RGB, each channel is an independent 8-bit image, which means that it contains $2^8 = 256$ brightness variations. It's like having several grayscale images at your disposal, any one of which may serve as the basis for a mask.

> *tip* If the **Channels** palette is hidden, you can switch between channels from the keyboard. Press **ctrl+1** (**command-1** on the Mac) to switch to the Red channel in an RGB image or the Cyan channel in a CMYK image. **Ctrl+2** takes you to the Green or Magenta channel, and so on. To return to the full-color composite, press **ctrl+tilde (~)**.

D alpha channel

Named after a formula for calculating transparent pixels, an *alpha channel* is any channel beyond the three or four required to express color in an image. In other words, it's an extra channel that contains a mask. Press **ctrl** and the number of the alpha channel to switch to the channel from the keyboard. Use the eyeball icons to view image and mask together.

E spot color channel

Photoshop lets you create specially colored text or logo elements by adding a channel of color beyond the standard RGB or CMYK. To find out how, read Add A Spot Color on pages 258 and 259 of Chapter 17.

F new channel

Click this button to add a new alpha channel to an image. Press **ctrl** (Win) or **command** (Mac) and click to add a spot color channel (E). Photoshop lets you create up to 24 channels in all.

> *tip* To name a new channel as you create it, choose **New Channel** from the palette menu, or press **alt** (Win) or **option** (Mac) and click the **New Channel** button. To duplicate a channel, drag it and drop it onto the button.

G load selection

After designing a mask, click this button to convert the mask to a selection outline. Only then can you use the mask to edit the image. See Save & Load A Selection on the facing page for more information.

H save channel

Click here to convert the selection outline to a mask. Again, see the facing page for a demonstration.

I delete channel

Click the trash can to delete the active channel (K). Press **alt** (Win) or **option** (Mac) and click to delete the channel without warning. Note that you can delete alpha channels and spot colors only. If a color channel is active, the trash can is dimmed.

J merge spot color

Select a spot color channel and choose **Merge Spot Color** from the palette menu to convert the spot color to its nearest RGB or CMYK equivalent and mix it in with the existing colors in the image. Use this command when you want to absorb the spot color into the image and eliminate the extra printed plate.

K active channel

Click a channel name or press its **ctrl**-key shortcut to activate it. The active channel name appears in the title bar, next to the image and layer name.

> *tip* You can activate and edit multiple channels at a time. Just click one and **shift**-click the others.

L channel options

Choose **Channel Options** or double-click an active alpha channel to change the name of the channel, as well as specify the color and opacity of the overlay when viewing mask and image together (D). By default, black represents masked areas and white represents unmasked. Choose **Selected Areas** to invert that, coloring the unmasked areas in black instead.

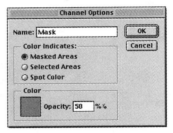

To convert an alpha channel to a spot color, click the **Spot Color** option. Double-click a spot color channel to substitute a new spot color. See Add A Spot Color, pages 258 and 259.

M split & merge

The **Split Channels** command separates each channel into its own image window. The command is applicable to flattened images only. **Split Channels** is meant to be used in tandem with **Merge Channels**, which puts the channels back together again. Just for fun, try splitting an RGB image. Then merge the channels and choose **Lab Color** from the **Mode** pop-up menu. The effect is generally psychedelic.

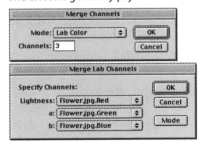

Merge Channels is also useful for assembling archived images in which color plates have been saved as separate files.

N palette options

Choose this command or right-click (**control**-click on the Mac) in the empty area below the channel names to change the size of the thumbnails.

Save & Load A Selection

Masking gives you more freedom when editing selection outlines. But only by loading the mask as a selection can you use it to edit pixels in an image. With this in mind, the following steps explain how to save a selection as an alpha channel, edit it, and convert the channel back to a selection.

1 draw selection outline

It took me a fair amount of time to trace the tyrannosaurus rex skeleton with the polygonal lasso tool. I reckon if I spend more than a couple of minutes creating a selection outline, it's worth saving.

2 choose save selection

Choose **Select➡Save Selection**. Or alt-click (**option-click** on the Mac) the **Save Channel** button (H). This permits you to convert the selection to an alpha channel and give the channel a name.

3 switch to mask

Click the new channel in the **Channels** palette. If you're working in the RGB mode and this is your first alpha channel, press **ctrl+4** (**command-4** on the Mac).

4 deselect & modify

Although you converted the selection to a mask, the marching ants remain intact. Press **ctrl+D** (**command-D**) to dismiss them and give yourself free reign to paint or edit the mask without constraint. For my part, I used **Filter➡Blur➡Gaussian Blur** to soften the selection outline and **Filter➡Noise➡Median** to round off the corners. I also touched up a few spots with the paintbrush.

5 ctrl-click mask

To convert the mask to a selection, choose **Select➡Load Selection**. Better yet, click the **Load Selection** button (G). Better still, press **ctrl** (Win) or **command** (Mac) and click the mask in the **Channels** palette.

6 switch channels, drag & drop

Switch back to the full-color composite by pressing **ctrl** (Win) or **command** (Mac) and the **tilde (~)** key. The selection outline survives the journey, permitting you to drag the masked element and drop it against a different background with the move tool.

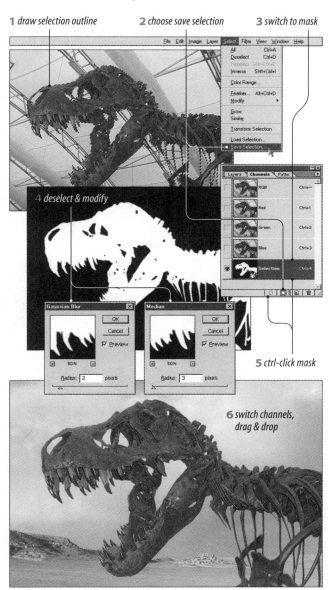

1 *draw selection outline*   2 *choose save selection*   3 *switch to mask*

4 *deselect & modify*

5 *ctrl-click mask*

6 *switch channels, drag & drop*

⬤steps Define A Mask From Scratch

Working from selection outlines is all very well and good, but the true power of masking resides in its ability to use the image to select itself. These steps show how to take a color channel from an RGB photograph and finesse it into a complex, naturalistic mask. Use this technique to select hair and other wispy details when **Color Range** and **Extract** fail.

1 survey channels

Press **ctrl**+1, 2, and 3 (**command**-1, 2, and 3 on the Mac) to peruse the color channels and decide the best candidate for a mask. Select the channel with the most contrast between the foreground element and its background, as in the Blue channel below.

2 duplicate channel

After selecting the channel you want to use, duplicate it by dragging it onto the **New Channel** button along the bottom of the **Channels** palette.

3 choose invert

Remember, white represents selected pixels and black represents the mask. If the areas you want to select are darker than those that you don't—as is likely—choose **Image➟Adjust➟Invert** (or press **ctrl**+**I**) to swap the blacks and whites.

4 copy red channel

When selecting people (regardless of race), you can boost skin tones in the mask using the Red channel.

1 *survey channels*

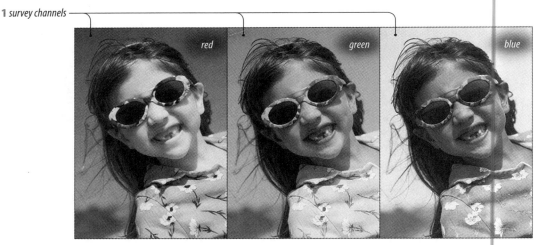

red   green   blue

2 *duplicate channel*

3 *choose invert*

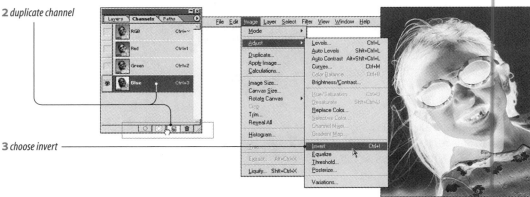

Press ctrl+1 to switch to the Red channel. Then press ctrl+A and ctrl+C to copy the channel. On the Mac, press command-1, A, C.

5 paste into mask

Press ctrl+4 to switch to the mask channel (assuming you're working in RGB). Then press ctrl+V to paste the Red channel into it. Press command-4, V on the Mac.

6 choose fade

Now it's time to blend the two channels together. Choose Edit➡Fade to display the Fade dialog box.

Set the Opacity to 50% and the Mode to Screen. This retains the brightest portions of both channels.

7 select burn tool

Press shift-O two or more times to get the burn tool.

8 paint shadows

Select Shadows from the Range pop-up menu in the options bar. Then paint the portion of the image you want to mask to darken the darkest pixels. For the best results, paint fast with a large, soft brush. Click places that need just a touch of extra darkness.

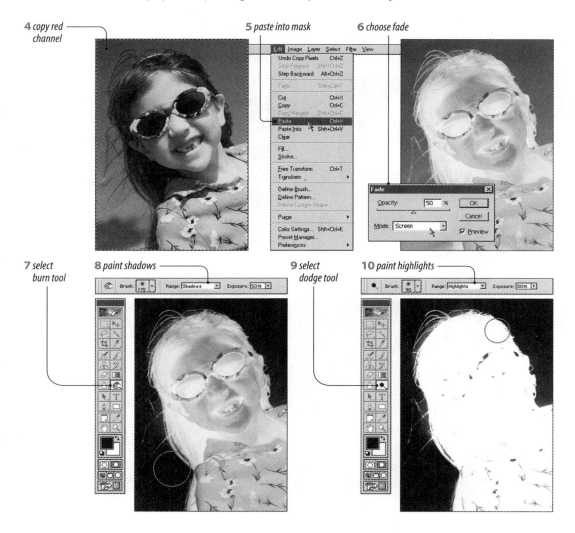

4 copy red channel

5 paste into mask

6 choose fade

7 select burn tool

8 paint shadows

9 select dodge tool

10 paint highlights

9 select dodge tool

Press **shift-O** twice more for the dodge tool.

10 paint highlights

Set the **Range** option to **Highlights**, permitting you to lighten the lightest pixels in the mask. Then paint the area that you want to select. Again, a big soft brush tends to work best.

11 touch up mask

Use the paintbrush to touch up any remaining smudges and ragged edges in the mask. Note that when working in a mask, pressing the D key produces a default foreground color of white, which adds to the selection. Press X to fill in the mask with black.

12 switch to full-color composite

Press **ctrl+~** (**command-~** on the Mac) to switch to the standard composite view of the image.

13 ctrl-click mask

Load the selection from the mask channel by pressing **ctrl** (**command** on the Mac) and clicking the mask in the **Channels** palette.

> **tip** If a selection already exists, you can add the mask to the selection by **ctrl+shift**-clicking the mask. Subtract the mask by **ctrl+alt**-clicking. Find the intersection by **ctrl+shift+alt**-clicking.

14 drag & drop

Ctrl-drag (**command**-drag) the selection against a new background, apply a special effect, or perform any other operation that strikes you as desirable.

Don't think for a moment this is the only way to mask an image. To explore other techniques, consult *Photoshop 6 Bible* from IDG Books Worldwide or the Total Photoshop video series from **www.totaltraining.com**.

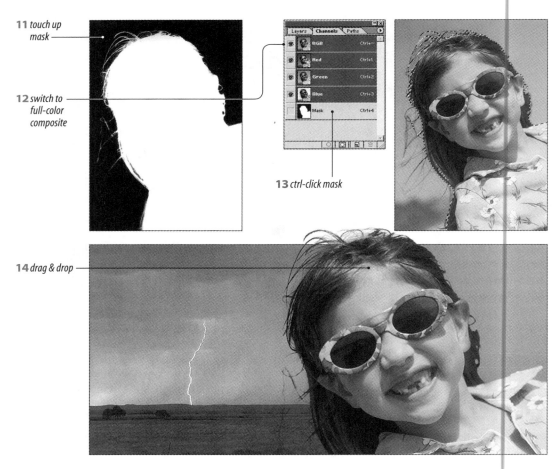

11 *touch up mask*

12 *switch to full-color composite*

13 *ctrl-click mask*

14 *drag & drop*

Layer-Specific Masks

The primary purpose of masking is to create sophisticated selection outlines. However, you can also use a mask to assign transparency to one or more layers. Each of the following *layer-specific masks* allows you to permanently delete pixels or temporarily hide them.

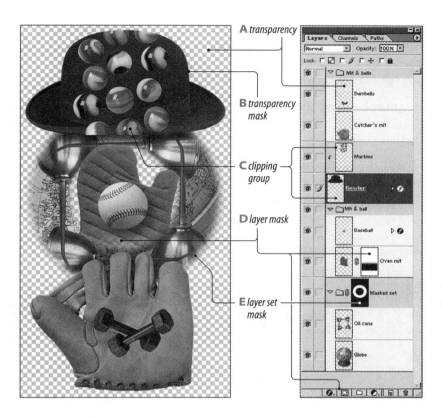

A *transparency*

B *transparency mask*

C *clipping group*

D *layer mask*

E *layer set mask*

A transparency
When you select part of an image and place it on its own layer, the pixels outside the selection become transparent, permitting you to see down to the pixels underneath. In areas where all pixels are transparent—which occurs only when the composition lacks a Background layer—Photoshop shows a checkerboard pattern that says "nothing's here." To change the checkerboard colors, press **ctrl+K, ctrl+4** (**command-K, 4** on the Mac).

B transparency mask
The boundary between opaque and transparent areas in a layer is called the *transparency mask*. Add to the transparency by painting away pixels with one of the erasers (see pages 118 and 119). Once deleted, you can restore pixels using the history brush (The History Brush, page 234) or **Edit➥Undo**.

C clipping group
Photoshop lets you mask multiple layers using a single transparency mask. In the image above, for example, the bowler hat masks the marbles. This is called a *clipping group*, as I demonstrate in Use One Layer To Clip Another on page 134.

D layer mask
If you want the freedom to edit the transparency of a layer well into the future, assign a *layer mask*. Click the **Add Mask** button, and then paint inside the new mask. Paint with black to hide pixels; paint with white to bring them back. Click the layer thumbnail to return to the image; click the mask thumbnail to edit the mask. For a way to create and use a layer mask, see Paste An Image Into A Selection on page 133.

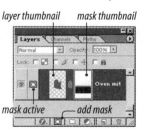

layer thumbnail   *mask thumbnail*

mask active   *add mask*

E layer set mask
You can also assign a mask to an entire set of layers. All layers in the set subscribe to the transparency specified in the layer set mask.

steps Paint Inside & Behind A Layer

Although you can't manipulate it directly, the transparency mask is a working mask. Not only can you paint inside it, just as if it were a selection outline, you can also paint glows and shadows behind it.

1 select paint tool
The airbrush and stamp tools are likewise good candidates for this technique.

2 adjust brush & opacity
I used a big, soft brush and an **Opacity** of 50%.

3 lock transparent pixels
Select the layer to edit. Then turn on the first **Lock** box in the **Layers** palette. This activates the transparency mask so it serves as a kind of selection outline.

4 paint inside mask
Thanks to the **Lock** option (3), the paint in my image stayed completely inside the Eiffel Tower statuette.

5 change layer
Click another layer to make it active. And be sure this time that all **Lock** options are turned off.

6 select behind mode
Choose **Behind** from the **Mode** pop-up menu in the options bar. This creates the inverse effect of **Lock**, painting exclusively outside the transparency mask.

7 paint behind mask
I set the foreground color to white and painted glows in the **Liberty** and **Pagoda** layers. In each case, only transparent pixels in the active layer were affected.

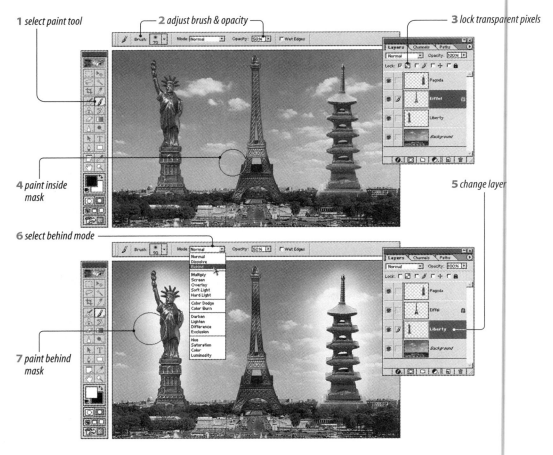

1 select paint tool

2 adjust brush & opacity

3 lock transparent pixels

4 paint inside mask

5 change layer

6 select behind mode

7 paint behind mask

Paste An Image Into A Selection

Selections and masks are so intertwined that one can become another in a flash. The following steps show a couple of ways to turn a selection into a layer mask using variations on the **Paste** command.

1 switch to quick mask mode
Press Q to paint a new selection outline.

2 draw gradient with gradient tool
Press the **G** key, then draw a gradient in the quick mask mode. I drew mine from right to left. When I exited the quick mask mode, the left portion of the image became selected, fading gradually to the right.

3 copy image
Switch to another image, then press **ctrl+A, ctrl+C**.

4 choose paste into
Return to the selected image and press **ctrl+shift+V** to paste a new layer and convert the selection into a layer mask. It's as if you pasted into the gradient.

5 select foreground element
I used the lasso tool to select the men shaking hands.

6 copy, paste outside
Copy a second image and return to the selected one. Then press **alt** (**option** on the Mac) and choose **Paste Into**. This pastes the image outside the selection.

7 touch up masks
Press **ctrl+** to switch to the active layer's mask and finesse it as desired with the paintbrush. Press **ctrl+~** to exit the mask and edit the layer.

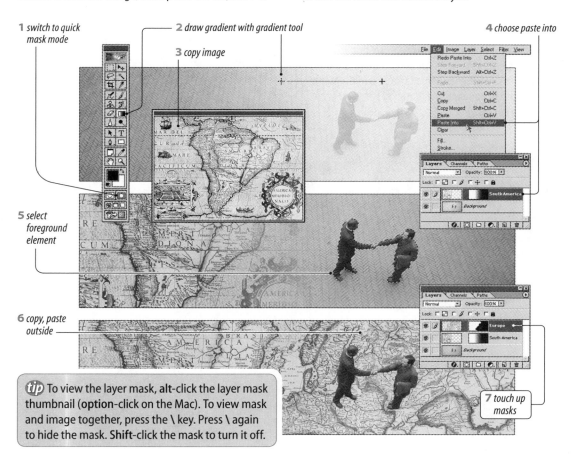

1 switch to quick mask mode

2 draw gradient with gradient tool

3 copy image

4 choose paste into

5 select foreground element

6 copy, paste outside

7 touch up masks

tip To view the layer mask, **alt**-click the layer mask thumbnail (**option**-click on the Mac). To view mask and image together, press the \ key. Press \ again to hide the mask. **Shift**-click the mask to turn it off.

🫧 **Use One Layer To Clip Another**

To *clip* a layer is to mask it with the contents of another layer. Wherever the clipping layer is opaque, the layer above it is visible; wherever the clipping layer is transparent, the layer above is hidden. The upshot is that you can use one image to fill another. Photoshop calls this pairing of layers a *clipping group*. Here's how to make one:

1 assemble composition
Stack the layers in your composition in the order you see fit. Make sure the image that you want to clip (the *contents* layer) and the image that will mask it (the *clipper*) are on separate layers. In my case, I wanted to fill the white face outline with the map image. So I painted the face on one layer and pasted the map onto another.

2 move contents above clipper
When creating a clipping group, Photoshop requires the mask to be at the bottom. So go to the **Layers** palette and drag the contents layer above the layer that will clip it. For example, I moved the **Map** layer above the **Face** layer.

3 group with previous
After selecting the contents layer (in my case, **Map**), choose **Layer➥Group with Previous** or press the shortcut, **ctrl+G** (Win) or **command-G** (Mac). Alternatively, you can press **alt** (Win) or **option** (Mac) and click the horizontal line between the contents and clipper layers, as shown below. Either way, Photoshop clips the contents layer to fit inside the transparency mask of the layer behind it.

4 adjust opacity & blend mode
I reduced the **Opacity** value to 50% to create an equal mix of map and white face outline. Note, however, that the face outline remains opaque. The opacity of the clipping group as a whole depends on that of the clipper. Read Chapter 10, Blend & Stylize Layers, for more information.

> **tip** To release the contents layer from the clipper, select either layer and press **ctrl+shift+G** (Win) or **command-shift-G** (Mac). Or drag the contents layer to another position in the stack. (Dragging the clipper moves all layers in the group.)

1 *assemble composition*   **2** *move contents above clipper*   **3** *group with previous*   **4** *adjust opacity & blend mode*

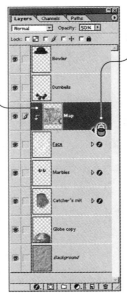

Blend & Stylize Layers

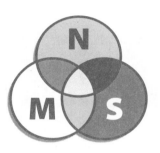

Throughout Photoshop, some operations are permanent, and others are temporary. Painting with a brush, for example, is a permanent modification. Although you can undo or erase the brushstroke, it changes the color and opacity of pixels in a way that you can't reverse in a different Photoshop session. In contrast, a temporary operation—such as assigning a blend mode to a layer—is forever changeable. Select **Multiply**, quit Photoshop, restart the program, and you can still return to the **Normal** mode.

From **Opacity** to blend modes, **Blending Options** to the **Styles** palette, every operation in this chapter is temporary. This means two things: First, it's impossible to make a mistake, so feel free to experiment. Second, due to their mathematical nature, temporary effects take less time to apply and consume less space on disk than traditional pixel-level changes. Flexible and fast, this is Photoshop at its best.

The Opacity Value

A *translucent layer*   **B** *opacity value*   **C** *opacity slider*

The most readily available of Photoshop's tempo-rary layer effects are the **Opacity** value and blend modes, which mix the colors in the active layer (anything other than Background) with the colors in the layers below. Perched at the top of the **Layers** palette, these simple pixel calculations let you achieve almost 2,000 stylistic variations. You may not be able to predict the outcome of every one of them, but so what? If you don't like one blend mode, you can painlessly switch to another. So give them a try and see what happens.

A translucent layer

The opacity of every pixel on a layer is defined by the layer's transparency mask (see Layer-Specific Masks, page 131). You can further reduce the layer's opacity using the **Opacity** value (B). A layer that is anything but 100 percent opaque is considered *translucent*— that is, somewhere between opaque and transparent.

B opacity value

Enter a value between 1 and 100 percent into the **Opacity** option box. Lower values melt the active

layer into the layers behind it. If reducing the **Opacity** value doesn't produce the desired effect, then it's time to check out the blend modes (E through U).

> **tip** To adjust the **Opacity** value without going to the trouble of clicking in the option box, press a number key when any tool other than a paint or edit tool is active. Press 1 for 10%, 2 for 20%, up to 0 for 100%. Press two numbers in a row for a specific percentage, such as 3 then 4 for 34%.

C opacity slider

Click the right-pointing arrowhead to the right of the **Opacity** value to display a slider bar. Drag the triangle to adjust the value dynamically.

D blend mode pop-up menu

Click the word in the upper left corner of the **Layers** palette—by default, **Normal**—to display a pop-up menu of 17 blend modes (E through U).

E normal

The **Normal** mode is essentially no mode at all. No special calculation is applied to the pixels, other than

The Blend Modes

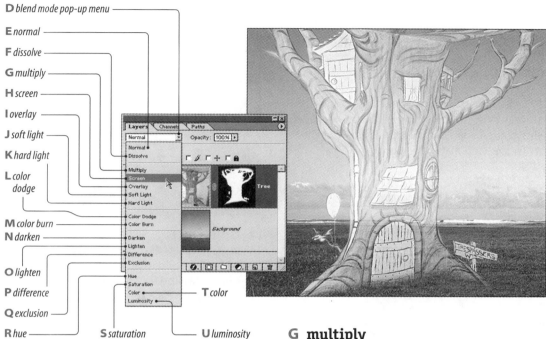

D *blend mode pop-up menu*

E *normal*

F *dissolve*

G *multiply*

H *screen*

I *overlay*

J *soft light*

K *hard light*

L *color dodge*

M *color burn*

N *darken*

O *lighten*

P *difference*

Q *exclusion*

R *hue*

S *saturation*

T *color*

U *luminosity*

that imposed by the **Opacity** value (B). If your blend mode experiments go haywire and you need a safe retreat, return to the **Normal** mode.

normal

dissolve

F dissolve

When **Normal** is active, translucent pixels—whether defined by the transparency mask, layer mask, or the **Opacity** value—mix gradually with the pixels behind them. **Dissolve**, on the other hand, represents trans-lucency by randomly scattering opaque and transpar-ent pixels, a technique known as *dithering*.

G multiply

Imagine that you transferred the active layer to a 35mm slide and all layers below it to another slide. Now position one slide in front of the other and hold them up to the light. The light has to pass through two layers of film, so one slide darkens the other. This is the effect produced by **Multiply**. To see the mode in action, read Multiply The Dark Stuff on page 141.

multiply

screen

H screen

This time, take those same two slides from before (G) and place them in separate projectors. Shine the two projectors at the same screen so the slides exactly overlap. Because each projector brightens the environment, one slide lightens the other. The **Screen** mode mimics this effect, as in Screen The Light Stuff on page 140.

I overlay

This and the two modes that follow—**Soft Light** (J) and **Hard Light** (K)—combine elements of **Multiply** (G) and **Screen** (H). **Overlay** in particular darkens the darkest colors and lightens the lightest colors to create an even merging of images. Select this mode when reducing the **Opacity** value (B) doesn't quite deliver the effect that you're looking for.

overlay

soft light

hard light

J soft light

If **Overlay** (I) produces too bright of an effect, try the **Soft Light** mode. Although similar to **Overlay** at a reduced **Opacity** setting, **Soft Light** results in more muted colors with softer transitions. It's the perfect mode for creating ghosted effects.

K hard light

This mode is the inverse of **Overlay** (I), meaning that applying one to the active layer produces the same effect as applying the other to the layers below. For example, applying **Hard Light** to a tree in front of a meadow produces the same effect as reversing the layers and applying **Overlay** to the meadow. So where **Overlay** emphasizes the background, **Hard Light** emphasizes the active layer. The upshot is, if **Overlay** proves too subtle, give **Hard Light** a try.

L color dodge

Named after the dodge tool, this mode adds brightness levels from the active layer to those of the layers below. Essentially an exaggerated version of the **Screen** mode, **Color Dodge** turns the lightest pixels in a layer into a white-hot flash.

color dodge

color burn

M color burn

This mode subtracts the brightness levels of the active layer from the layers below. If **Color Dodge** turns an image into a flash bulb, **Color Burn** is the stain left on your retina after the flash is over.

N darken

Choose this mode to display only those pixels in the active layer that are darker than the pixels behind them. Unlike **Multiply**, **Darken** doesn't mix colors, except to the extent that it's calculated in each color channel independently. So use **Darken** when you want to hide the light pixels and show the dark ones.

darken

lighten

O lighten

This mode displays only those pixels in the active layer that are lighter than their counterparts in the layers below. Choose **Lighten** when you want to hide the dark pixels and show the light ones.

P difference

True to its name, this mode finds the difference between the brightness levels on the active layer and those on the layers below. The result is a kind of photographic negative, where the affected pixels invert the pixels behind them. Give it a try when you're in the mood for something distinctly unconventional.

difference

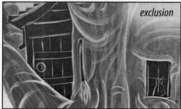
exclusion

Q exclusion

Like **Difference** (P), **Exclusion** uses the active layer to invert those behind it. The difference is that this mode sends all medium colors to gray. Use it when you want to leech color out of a **Difference** effect.

R hue

Use this mode to mix the core colors, or *hues*, from the active layer with the saturation and luminosity values of the layers below. For complete information on hue, saturation, and luminosity, read The Hue/Saturation Command on pages 190 and 191 of Chapter 13.

S saturation

The term *saturation* refers to the intensity of colors, from their most vivid to drab gray. This mode mixes the saturation values from the active layer with the hue and luminosity of the layers below.

T color

Combining the two modes preceding it (R & S), **Color** blends the hue and saturation of the active layer with the luminosity of the layers behind it. This is the perfect mode when you want to use a layer to colorize the image below.

U luminosity

The inverse of the **Color** mode (T) is **Luminosity**. It mixes the *luminosity* (the lightness or darkness) of the pixels in the active layer with the hue and saturation values from the layers below. It's like imprinting a grayscale image onto the colors from another image. Together, hue, saturation, and luminosity make up the *HSL* color model, explained in The Hue/Saturation Command on pages 190 and 191.

Keyboard Tricks

If you can modify the translucency of a layer from the keyboard without highlighting the **Opacity** value (B), it follows that you can adjust the blend mode from the keyboard as well. Press **shift-plus** (+) to advance from one blend mode to the next in the order that they appear in the blend mode pop-up menu (D). Press **shift-minus** (–) to step backward through the blend modes. These keystrokes are useful for browsing through the blend modes. But if you know the specific mode you want, you're better off knowing the shortcuts shown in the table on the right.

blend mode	win keystroke	mac keystroke
normal	shift+alt+N or L	shift-option-N or L
dissolve	shift+alt+I	shift-option-I
multiply & screen	shift+alt+M & S	shift-option-M & S
overlay	shift+alt+O	shift-option-O
soft light	shift+alt+F	shift-option-F
hard light	shift+alt+H	shift-option-H
color dodge & burn	shift+alt+D & B	shift-option-D & B
darken & lighten	shift+alt+K & G	shift-option-K & G
difference & exclusion	shift+alt+E & X	shift-option-E & X
hue & saturation	shift+alt+U & T	shift-option-U & T
color	shift+alt+C	shift-option-C
luminosity	shift+alt+Y	shift-option-Y

🟢steps Screen The Light Stuff

Aside from **Normal**, the blend modes you'll probably find yourself using most are **Screen** and **Multiply**. Why? For the simple reason that they're incredibly useful. Use **Screen** anytime you want to keep the light stuff and drop out the dark stuff; use **Multiply** to drop out the light stuff and keep the dark stuff. Here's what I mean:

1 add highlight
After opening a photo of a wide-open eye, I wanted to replace the pupil with a bright highlight. So I created a new layer and drew a white-to-transparent gradient with the gradient tool set to the radial style (see The Gradient Tool, page 87).

2 reduce opacity
You might think you have to apply **Screen** to properly blend the highlight. But because the layer contains white pixels only, there are no dark colors to drop out, and **Normal** and **Screen** would look the same. So if there's any mixing to do, use the **Opacity** value.

3 import new layer
Where **Screen** comes in handy is when blending multicolored layers. So drag one in from an open image window. For my part, I selected a photo of the Earth with the elliptical marquee tool and blurred the outline with **Select➡Feather**. Then I used the move tool to drag and drop it onto the eye.

4 scale & position
It's a rare occasion when the height and width of a dropped image precisely matches its new background. So press **ctrl+T** (Win) or **command-T** (Mac) to enter the free transform mode. Then scale, rotate, and move the layer so it matches the rest of your composition. I scaled the Earth so it fit exactly inside the iris of the eye.

5 apply screen
The Earth contains a wide range of brightness levels, from brilliant whites to deep blues trending toward black. To drop out the dark colors, press **shift+alt+S** (Win) or **shift-option-S** (Mac) to apply the **Screen** mode. (If the shortcut doesn't work, press M to get the marquee tool and try again.) Why not apply the **Lighten** mode instead? Because **Lighten** shows light pixels and hides dark ones, resulting in harsh transitions between the two. **Screen**, on the other hand, introduces translucency gradually, thus ensuring incremental, organic transitions.

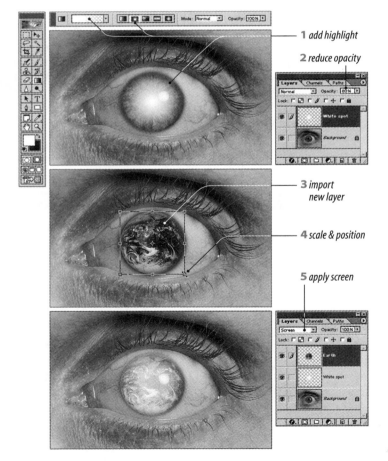

1 *add highlight*

2 *reduce opacity*

3 *import new layer*

4 *scale & position*

5 *apply screen*

6 import, scale, & position

This time, import an image that you want to use to darken your composition. I decided to imprint the face of a stopwatch onto the iris. Again using the elliptical marquee tool and **Feather** command, I selected the face of a stopwatch and **ctrl**-dragged it into my eye composition (equivalent to dragging with the move tool). Naturally, the stopwatch wasn't the proper size and shape, so I scaled it and positioned it using **Edit ➡ Free Transform**.

7 apply multiply

To drop out the light colors in the layer, press **shift+alt+M** (Win) or **shift-option-M** (Mac). Assuming a selection tool is active, this applies the **Multiply** mode to the new layer. The light colors melt away, leaving softly transitioning dark colors that simply aren't possible with the **Darken** mode.

8 duplicate layer

Applying **Multiply** to the stopwatch resulted in a rounded clock face that followed the contours of the iris. However, the effect looked a bit flimsy. If this happens to you, duplicate the layer by dragging it onto the **New Layer** button at the bottom of the **Layers** palette. The effect of two layers of stopwatch multiplied one on top of the other made a much stronger impact—maybe too strong. So I pressed the 5 key to back off the **Opacity** of the duplicate layer to 50%.

9 scan logo

Multiply is great for burning in scanned logos. Like so many corporate emblems, the one on right is tattered and torn, a last-known copy that's seen better days. No problem. I scan it and clean it up using a combination of the **Levels** command (Adjust Brightness Using Levels, pages 197 through 199) and the rubber stamp (The Edit Tools, pages 94 and 95).

10 import logo, apply multiply

You might think that part of importing a logo into a composition is selecting it. But assuming yours is a typical black-and-white piece of art, there's no need. After importing the logo into the eye and rotating it into position, I applied the **Multiply** mode. All the white non-logo stuff turned invisible, leaving only the dark logo elements. Note that I added the light area inside the moon by drawing a circle on a separate layer behind the moon and filling it with white.

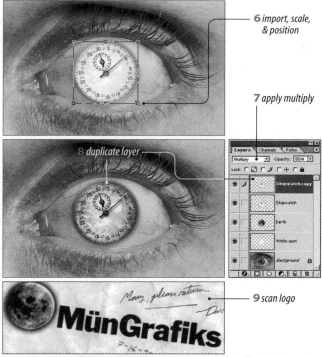

6 *import, scale, & position*

7 *apply multiply*

8 *duplicate layer*

9 *scan logo*

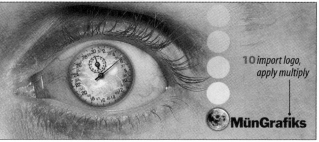

10 *import logo, apply multiply*

Blending Options

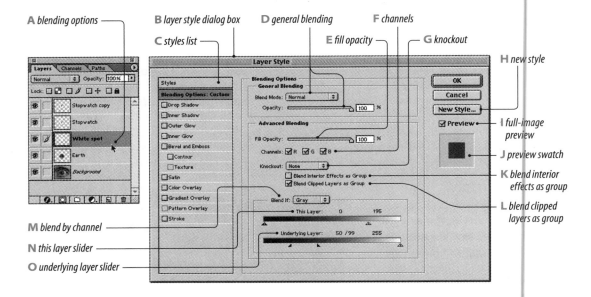

A *blending options*

B *layer style dialog box*

C *styles list*

D *general blending*

E *fill opacity*

F *channels*

G *knockout*

H *new style*

I *full-image preview*

J *preview swatch*

K *blend interior effects as group*

L *blend clipped layers as group*

M *blend by channel*

N *this layer slider*

O *underlying layer slider*

Most programs would be satisfied with 17 blend modes, but not Photoshop. The program devotes incomparable energy to the task of expanding your ability to blend layers. Blessed with well over 100 options, the **Layer Style** dialog box (B) is so vast that I spend the rest of this chapter explaining it.

A blending options

To advance to the next level of blending, double-click the name of a layer in the **Layers** palette or choose **Blending Options** from the palette menu. Doing so displays the **Layer Style** dialog box (B).

B layer style dialog box

This dialog box offers an unprecedented 13 panels of options, 12 of which are devoted to *layer effects* such as drop shadows, glows, and so on. The remaining **Blending Options** panel (above) lets you hide color channels, modify the interaction of distant layers, and adjust the visibility of specific ranges of colors.

C styles list

Use this list to apply effects and switch between the dialog box's 13 panels. To return to the first panel (above), click **Blending Options** at the top of the list.

tip Switch between items in the list by pressing **ctrl** (**command** on the Mac) and a number. For example, **ctrl+1** displays the **Drop Shadow** panel, **ctrl+2** displays **Inner Shadow**, all the way to **ctrl+0** for **Stroke**. Unlike clicking, the keystrokes switch between effects without activating them.

D general blending

These options duplicate the blend mode and **Opacity** options in the **Layers** palette. They blend all pixels and effects assigned to a layer in unison.

E fill opacity

This option fades pixels in a layer independently of any effects. This means by setting the **Fill Opacity** to **50%**, you can make the layer translucent while leaving its drop shadow unchanged. **Fill Opacity** also works with **Knockout** (G) to bore through layers.

F channels

Use these check boxes to hide a layer inside one or more channels. They can prove especially handy when editing CMYK images. By turning off the **K** check box, for example, you can limit effects that may overwhelm an image by adding too much black.

G knockout

A *knockout* is a layer that carves holes in the layers behind it. First, use the **Fill Opacity** (E) to specify the translucency of the knockout. Lower values result in more piercing holes. Then set the **Knockout** option to **Shallow** to bore through one layer set or clipping group to the bottom of the next. Or use **Deep** to bore to the next logical stage, potentially as far as the Background layer. Below, I created a new layer, drew a feathered circle using the elliptical marquee tool, and filled the circle with white. (The specific color doesn't matter, but it must be filled.) Then I set the **Fill Opacity** to 0% and the **Knockout** to **Deep**, which exposed the pupil in the Background image.

feathered circle

fill opacity: 0%, knockout: deep

H new style

Click this button to save the current collection of blending and effects settings as a style, as discussed in Create & Apply A Layer Style on pages 155 and 156.

I full-image preview

Select this check box to see the effects of your settings in the image window. **Preview** is very helpful for learning how to use options such as **Fill Opacity** (E) and **Knockout** (G).

J preview swatch

This swatch shows how the effect will look as a preset icon in the **Styles** palette. Don't sweat it if the swatch doesn't look particularly representative—the swatch shows effects much better than blending settings.

K blend interior effects as group

An *interior effect* is one that exists inside the perimeter of a layer, such as an inner shadow or glow or an overlay effect (pages 152 and 153). Select this check box to blend the effects with the layer before blending them with the rest of the image. Turn it off to blend the interior effects evenly with all layers. Also worth noting, when this check box is on, the **Fill Opacity** value (E) modifies interior effects; when off, it doesn't.

L blend clipped layers as group

When selected, Photoshop blends all layers in a clipping group and then blends the clipping group as a whole with the rest of the composition. This means the blend mode assigned to the bottom layer in the group affects all other grouped layers. To respect each layer's blending independently of the bottom layer, turn **Blend Clipped Layers as Group** off.

M blend by channel

The **Blend If** pop-up menu governs the scope of the two slider bars below it (N & O). When set to **Gray**, the sliders affect all colors uniformly. Or choose a color channel to edit the brightness levels in that channel independently of the others.

N this layer slider

This slider bar provides another mechanism for dropping out colors in the active layer. Drag the light triangle to the left to make the lightest pixels invisible; drag the black triangle to the right to the make darkest pixels invisible. It's analogous to the **Lighten** and **Darken** blend modes, except with precise control.

O underlying layer slider

Whereas the previous slider hides pixels on the active layer, this one shows pixels from the layers below. The light triangle forces the visibility of light colors from below; the black triangle forces dark colors.

> *tip* Both sliders result in harsh transitions between hidden and visible pixels. To soften the transitions, press **alt** (Win) or **option** (Mac) and drag a triangle. It separates in half to show the points at which the visibility begins and ends.

steps Mask Colors With Blending Options

The primary purpose of Photoshop's **Blending Options** is to provide you with a means to temporarily mask colors inside a layer. In these steps, I show how to use the most important options, **Blend If** (6) and **Knockout** (8).

1 assemble layered image

You'll need a composition with two or more overlapping layers to see the effects of **Knockout** (8). For convenience's sake, I organized my layers into a set (**Iris elements**). You can, too, but it's not essential.

2 create set

Click the **New Set** button to add a folder to the **Layers** palette. This will establish a limit for **Knockout** (8).

3 import layer

Drag a layer into the composition from another image. Then move the layer into the set (2). I introduced the **Vortex** layer and placed it in the set called **Knockouts**.

4 display blending options

Double-click the new layer to display the **Layer Style** dialog box with **Blending Options**.

5 apply mode & opacity

I wanted to drop out the dark colors in the vortex, so I applied **Screen**. I also reduced the **Opacity** to 80%.

6 hide colors via sliders

Screen fades dark colors, but the only color it completely hides is black. To hide other colors, use the **Blend If** sliders. I dragged the black **This Layer** triangle to 60, which hid

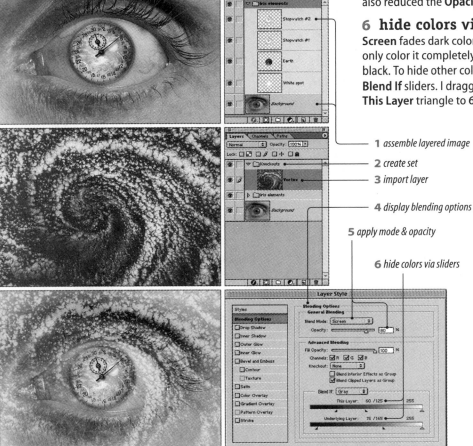

1 *assemble layered image*

2 *create set*

3 *import layer*

4 *display blending options*

5 *apply mode & opacity*

6 *hide colors via sliders*

pixels as bright as 60 and darker. To soften the transitions, I pressed **alt** (**option** on the Mac) and dragged the right half of the triangle to 125. Next, I set the two halves of the black **Underlying Layer** triangle to 15 and 165 to force the visibility of eyelashes and other dark elements from lower layers.

7 create knockout layers

What if you want to mask shapes instead of color ranges? Then create one or more *knockout layer*s in the same set as the layers you want to hide. To mask the eyeball, I created a new layer in the **Knockouts** set

and painted black inside the eye. To mask the pupil, I created a second layer and painted white. Either black or white will do; I used both to tell the masks apart.

8 knock out layer set

I wanted to use the black eye to carve a hole in the Vortex layer only. So I double-clicked on the black layer and set the **Blend Mode** option in the **Layer Style** dialog box to **Screen**. This made the black invisible, and where pixels are invisible, the mask goes into effect. Then I set the **Knockout** to **Shallow**, punching a hole through all layers in the set, but no farther.

9 drill to background

On page 143, I showed how to drill a hole to the Background by setting the **Knockout** for the **Pupil** layer to **Deep**. But this time, instead of setting the **Fill Opacity** to 0%, I set the **Blend Mode** to **Multiply**. Either way, the white pixels become transparent and mask all the way down.

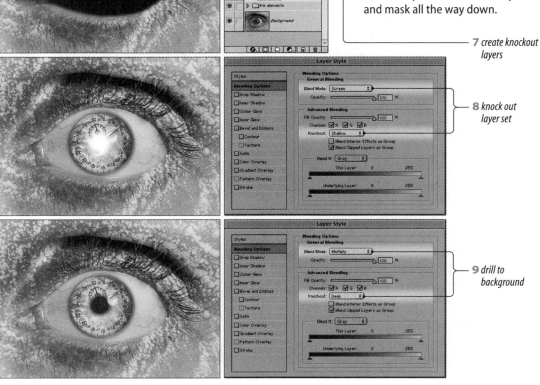

7 *create knockout layers*

8 *knock out layer set*

9 *drill to background*

Drop Shadow

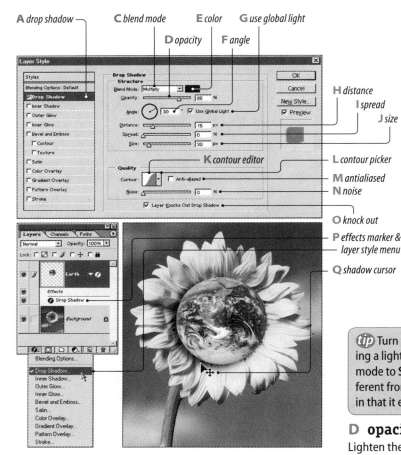

A *drop shadow* —   **C** *blend mode*   **E** *color*   **G** *use global light*

D *opacity*   **F** *angle*

H *distance*
I *spread*
J *size*

K *contour editor*
L *contour picker*
M *antialiased*
N *noise*

O *knock out*
P *effects marker & layer style menu*
Q *shadow cursor*

double-click a name in the **Layers** palette and click the **Drop Shadow** option on the left side of the **Layer Style** dialog box.

B inner shadow
The second kind of shadow is the *inner shadow*. Pictured on the facing page, an inner shadow appears inside the layer, as if the part of the image lies in the shade.

C blend mode
Shadows darken their surroundings, so the default blend mode is **Multiply**. But you can assign any mode you like.

> *tip* Turn a shadow into a glow by selecting a light color (E) and changing the mode to **Screen**. This kind of glow is different from those on pages 148 and 149 in that it extends in a single direction.

D opacity
Lighten the shadow by reducing its **Opacity** setting. Use the slider or enter a value.

E color
Click here to display the **Color Picker** dialog box, which lets you change the color of your shadow. If the blend mode is set to **Multiply**, you can select any color and be guaranteed it will darken the image.

> *tip* Click outside the **Color Picker** in the image window to lift a color from the image.

F angle
Use the **Angle** wheel and value to change the direction in which Photoshop casts the shadow. The angle affects the placement of the light source, so a value of 45° casts the shadow down and to the left.

We now embark on a tour of Photoshop's extensive list of *layer effects*, which continues to the Stroke section on page 154. Layer effects automate the application of various interior and border decorations that help to set a layer apart from its background. These effects adjust automatically any time you move or modify a layer, they are forever editable, and they take up little room in memory. Our tour begins with shadows.

A drop shadow
Photoshop offers two kinds of shadows. The first of these, *drop shadows*, are shadows cast by the layer onto the layers in back of it. To apply a drop shadow,

Inner Shadow

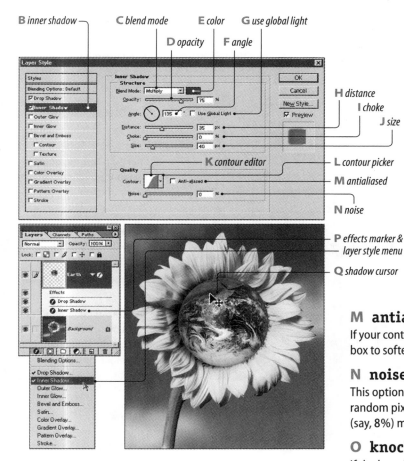

B *inner shadow*
C *blend mode*
D *opacity*
E *color*
F *angle*
G *use global light*
H *distance*
I *choke*
J *size*
K *contour editor*
L *contour picker*
M *antialiased*
N *noise*
P *effects marker & layer style menu*
Q *shadow cursor*

J size
Expand or reduce the size of the shadow with this option. Larger shadows tend to be softer.

K contour editor
The **Contour** option controls the way the shadow fades. Click here to design your own contour.

L contour picker
Better yet, just select a contour from the list of presets. To avoid harsh edges, select the contour shown in the figure, known as **Gaussian**.

M antialiased
If your contour has corners, select this check box to soften them. Otherwise, ignore it.

N noise
This option dithers the shadow, adding random pixels of transparency. A little noise (say, **8%**) matches the film grain of a photo.

O knock out
If the layer is translucent, select this check box to make sure you can't see the drop shadow through it. Or turn the check box off to see the drop shadow and layer mix.

P effects marker
After you click **OK**, the shadow appears in the **Layers** palette. Use the eyeball to hide and show the effect. Double-click the shadow name or select it from the **Layer Style** pop-up menu to edit it.

Q shadow cursor
You can move the cursor outside the **Layer Style** dialog box and drag the shadow in the image window. Photoshop updates the **Angle** (F) and **Distance** (H) values automatically.

G use global light
Select **Use Global Light** to subscribe to a universal light source throughout the image for all directional effects. When the check box is on, changing the **Angle** value affects all other effects that subscribe to this option as well. Turn off **Use Global Light** to edit the angle of a single shadow by itself.

H distance
Enter the distance that the shadow is cast here.

I spread/choke
This option expands a drop shadow or contracts an inner shadow. Raising the value makes the shadow larger and sharper. For soft shadows, **0%** is best.

Outer Glow

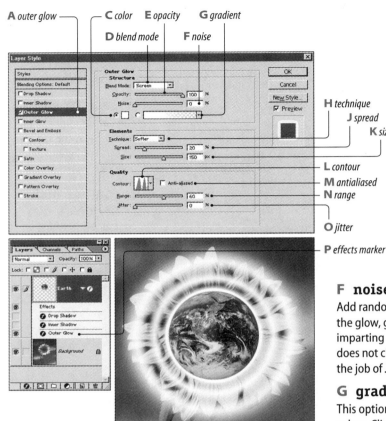

A *outer glow* — C *color*   E *opacity*   G *gradient*
D *blend mode*   F *noise*

H *technique*
J *spread*
K *size*

L *contour*
M *antialiased*
N *range*

O *jitter*

P *effects marker*

In theory, *glows* are bright halos that emanate from a layer. However, by changing the color and blend mode (C & D), you can turn a glow into a shadow or vice versa. So here's the scoop: A glow is a non-directional effect that emanates evenly in all directions. In contrast, shadows are cast at an angle.

A outer glow
Double-click a layer and select this option to create an *outer glow* that fills the transparent portion of a layer.

B inner glow
Pictured on the facing page, an *inner glow* extends inward from the edges of a layer.

C color
Select this radio button to fill the glow with a solid color. Click the swatch to change the color.

D blend mode
The default blend mode for a glow is **Screen**. To make a non-directional shadow, select a dark color (C) or gradient (G) and set the mode to **Multiply**.

E opacity
Use this value to adjust the translucency of the most opaque colors in the glow.

F noise
Add random pixels of transparency to dither the glow, great for matching film grain or imparting a gritty look. Note that this option does not change the color of the pixels; that's the job of **Jitter** (O).

G gradient
This option fills the glow with a fountain of colors. Click the bar to edit the colors and define your own gradient; click the down-pointing arrowhead to select a preset.

H technique
Select **Softer** to append a slight blur to the glow, which reduces the chance of obvious corners around the effect. The **Precise** setting removes this additional blur, which creates tighter glows around highly articulated layer outlines, common with text.

I source
Available only when applying an inner glow, the **Source** option decides whether the glow emanates outward from the **Center** or inward from the **Edge**. On the facing page, I set a black-to-white gradient emanating inward from the perimeter of the planet. The **Screen** mode (D) makes the black transparent.

Inner Glow

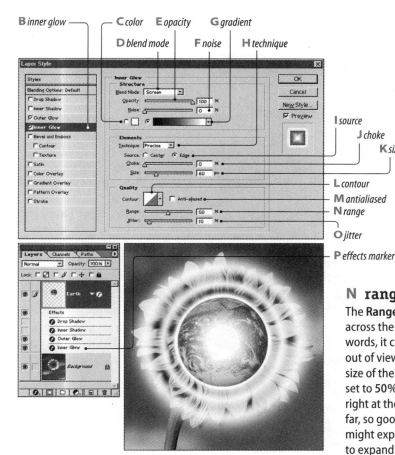

B *inner glow* — C *color* E *opacity* G *gradient*
D *blend mode* F *noise* H *technique*

I *source*
J *choke*
K *size*
L *contour*
M *antialiased*
N *range*
O *jitter*
P *effects marker*

facing page zigzags up and down three times, which results in a central glow and two rings. Click the **Contour** preview to define a custom contour; click the down-pointing arrowhead to select a preset.

M antialiased

This check box softens edges within a glow, as are evident when using a stair-stepped contour (L). Most contours are smooth, however, in which case you can safely leave **Anti-aliased** turned off.

N range

The **Range** slider bar maps the contour (L) across the size (K) of the glow. In other words, it changes the way colors fade in and out of view without changing the overall size of the effect. When the **Range** value is set to 50%, the midpoint of the contour sits right at the middle of the glow's radius. So far, so good. However, contrary to what you might expect, you lower the **Range** value to expand the glow and raise the value to contract it.

J spread/choke

Spread or choke the glow to move an outer glow outward or an inner glow inward with respect to the perimeter of the layer. Raising this value gradually reduces the softness of the glow, regardless of the **Technique** setting (H).

K size

Use this option to make the glow larger or smaller. As always, bigger glows tend to be softer because there's more room to blur.

L contour

The **Contour** setting controls how the glow fades in and out of view. For example, the contour on the

O jitter

Raise this value to introduce randomly colored pixels into a glow filled with a gradient (G). Note that the gradient must contain multiple colors for **Jitter** to work. The option does not affect a solid color (C) or a gradient that fades to transparency.

P effects marker

Photoshop adds an effects marker to the **Layers** palette for each kind of glow that you apply.

> *tip* Drag an effects marker and drop it beneath another layer to copy the effect to the other layer. Drag an effects marker to the trash to delete it.

Bevel & Emboss

A *bevel & emboss* B *style* E *direction* G *soften*
C *technique* D *depth* F *size*

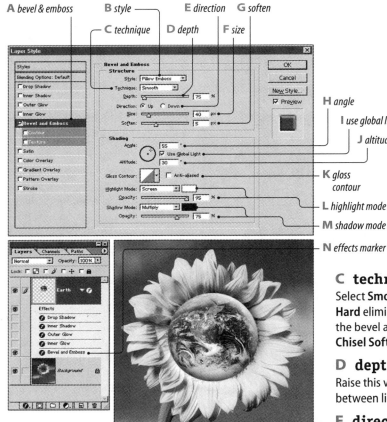

H *angle*
I *use global light*
J *altitude*
K *gloss contour*
L *highlight mode*
M *shadow mode*
N *effects marker*

B style

This pop-up menu offers five styles of bevel: **Outer Bevel** affects the transparent pixels outside a layer; **Inner Bevel** works inside the layer. **Emboss** applies both an inner and outer bevel. **Pillow Emboss** applies an inner bevel and then reverses the colors in the outer bevel to create a crater effect. **Stroke Emboss** creates a bevel inside an outline created using the **Stroke** option (Stroke, page 154).

C technique

Select **Smooth** to blur the bevel. **Chisel Hard** eliminates the blurring, which gives the bevel a hard edge. If it's too harsh, use **Chisel Soft** to smooth the edge slightly.

D depth

Raise this value to increase the contrast between lights and darks.

E direction

Use this option to decide which side gets the glow and which side gets the shadow.

Photoshop calls its next layer effect **Bevel & Emboss** as if to imply it's two different effects. Really, it's just one. Photoshop creates a *bevel* by tracing a highlight along one side of a layer and a shadow along the other. The so-called *emboss* is nothing more than two bevels joined together (B). For information on Photoshop's other embossing option—which does not require layers—read The Stylize Filters on page 226 of Chapter 14.

F size

The **Size** value makes the bevel grow and shrink.

G soften

Use this slider to blur the beveled edges. It produces an effect regardless of the **Technique** setting (C).

H angle

Two parameters define the position of the light source. The first, **Angle**, defines the slant at which the light hits the layer. The second is **Altitude** (J).

A bevel & emboss

Click here or press **ctrl+5** (**command-5** on the Mac) to display a giant panel of bevel options. You can further modify a bevel using **Contour** (O) and **Texture** (P).

I use global light

Select this check box to match the **Angle** value (H) to the one used for the shadow effects (see Drop

Contour & Texture

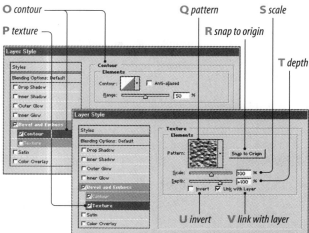

O contour

P texture

Q pattern

R snap to origin

S scale

T depth

O contour

P texture

M shadow mode
These controls affect the blend mode and translucency of the shadows.

N effects marker
A single item marks the application of **Bevel & Emboss** (A) and its subordinate **Contour** (O) and **Texture** (P) effects.

O contour
Select **Contour** to create hills and valleys in the beveled edge. The **Range** value stretches and shrinks the contour in the bevel.

P texture
Select this check box to add a texture to the surface of the layer.

Q pattern
Click here to select a preset pattern (which you define outside the **Layer Style** dialog box using **Edit➜Define Pattern**). The pattern acts as a *texture map*—light pixels indicate hills, dark pixels become valleys.

R snap to origin
Click here to align the pattern with the ruler origin (see Rulers & Units, page 20).

> *tip* Drag inside the image window to move the pattern dynamically.

Shadow, page 146). This is very useful when applying both an inner bevel and a drop shadow to the layer.

J altitude
The *altitude* is the position of the light on a half circle across the sky. A value of 90° puts the light straight overhead; 0° puts the light on the horizon.

K gloss contour
There are two **Contour** controls, one of which sculpts grooves into the beveled edge (O) and this one, which adds glossy variations to the highlights and shadows.

L highlight mode
Edit the blend mode and **Opacity** of the highlights.

S scale
This option enlarges or reduces the texture map.

T depth
Use this value to adjust the contrast between lights and darks as well as the direction of the hills and valleys. Values nearing 0% soften the contrast.

U invert
Click here to invert the hills and valleys—or just enter a negative **Depth** value (T).

V link with layer
Select this check box to attach the texture to the layer so it moves when you drag the layer.

Satin & Color

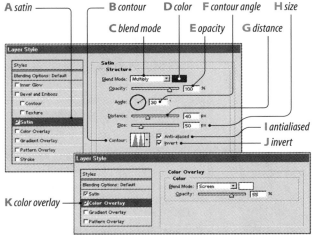

A *satin* — B *contour*   D *color*   F *contour angle*   H *size*

C *blend mode*   E *opacity*   G *distance*

I *antialiased*
J *invert*

K *color overlay* —

A *satin*

K *color overlay*

a lot of wiggle in it, such as one of the **Cone**, **Ring**, or **Slope** presets. Try loading the **contours.shc** file for additional presets.

C blend mode
This option and **Opacity** (E) are constants throughout the four fill effects. Since **Satin** (A) and **Color Overlay** (K) apply a single color, **Multiply** and **Screen** work well. Try the **Hard Light**, **Color**, and **Luminosity** modes with the multicolored fills (L & M).

D color
Click the color swatch to change the color of the **Satin** (A) or **Color Overlay** (K) effect.

E opacity
Enter a value to make an effect translucent.

F contour angle
Use this option to rotate the contoured fill.

> *tip* Drag inside the image window to modify the **Angle** (F) and **Distance** (G) values automatically.

G distance
This option defines the *offset*, which is how two contours intersect. To get a feel for it, set the value to **0** and then press the ↑ key to raise the value in 1-pixel increments.

The next series of layer styles are strictly interior effects. The first two, **Satin** (A) and **Color Overlay** (K), fill the layer with a coating of color. The difference is that **Satin** includes a **Contour** option (B) to apply color variations. The remaining effects apply gradients (L) and patterns (M).

A satin
Click here to fill a layer with a contoured wave effect. If you squint, I suppose it looks a bit like satin.

B contour
This is the option that makes **Satin** (A) work. For the best effect, be sure to select something with

H size
This value controls the size of the overall effect. Again, pressing ↑ can be a useful way to gauge how this option works, especially given that incremental adjustments can produce big differences in the effect.

I antialiased
Select this check box to smooth out jagged **Contour** settings (B), such as **Steps**, **Terraced**, and **Sawtooth**.

J invert
Normally, **Satin** (A) produces transparent waves against a colored background. To get the opposite effect—colored waves against a transparent background, as above—select the **Invert** check box.

Gradient & Pattern

L *gradient overlay*   C *blend mode*   O *reverse*   P *align with layer*

E *opacity*   N *gradient*   Q *style*

R *gradient angle*

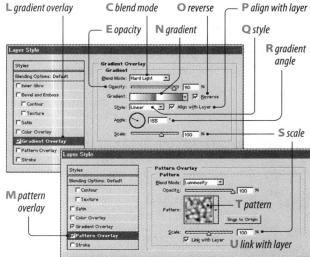

S *scale*

M *pattern overlay*

T *pattern*

U *link with layer*

L *gradient overlay*

M *pattern overlay*

N gradient

Click the down-pointing arrowhead to select a preset gradient; click the **Gradient** preview to design your own. Shown on left are examples of the **Chrome** preset.

O reverse

Select this check box to reverse the order of colors in the active gradient (N). **Reverse** comes in particularly handy when **Style** (Q) is set to anything other than **Linear**.

P align with layer

When selected, Photoshop centers the gradient in the layer, sizes the gradient to fit, and links layer and gradient so they move together. Turn the check box off to move the layer independently.

> *tip* Drag inside the image window to reposition either a gradient or pattern with respect to the layer.

Q style

Click here to specify the orientation of colors inside the gradient. See The Gradient Tool on page 87 for examples.

R gradient angle

Drag in the circle or enter a value to adjust the angle of the gradient.

K color overlay

Select this option to mix a color in with a layer using the **Blend Mode** (C), color (D), and **Opacity** (E) options. **Color Overlay** is ideally suited to coloring the transparent areas produced by **Satin** (A).

L gradient overlay

Select this option to coat a layer with a gradient.

M pattern overlay

This option coats a layer with a repeating pattern.

> *tip* For a 3-D pattern effect, select the same pattern inside the **Texture** panel (Contour & Texture, page 151). Slight beveling works best.

S scale

Use this option to size the gradient with respect to either the layer, if **Align with Layer** (P) is turned on, or the entire image, if the check box is off. When editing a pattern, the **Scale** value is measured as a percentage of the pattern's original size.

T pattern

Click the pattern preview or down-pointing arrowhead to select a preset pattern. Click **Snap to Origin** to align the pattern to the ruler's 0, 0 coordinates.

U link with layer

Select this check box to link the pattern to the layer, so the two move and transform in unison.

Stroke

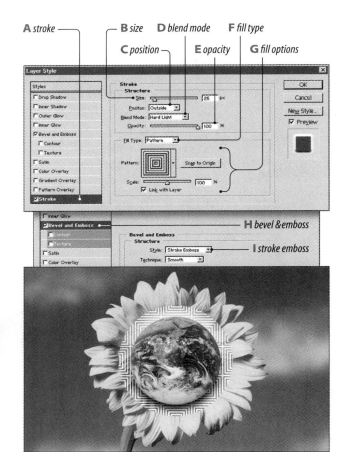

A stroke — B size   D blend mode   F fill type
C position   E opacity   G fill options

H bevel &emboss
I stroke emboss

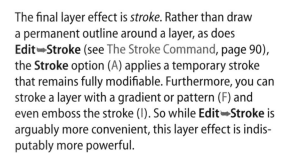

The final layer effect is *stroke*. Rather than draw a permanent outline around a layer, as does **Edit➡Stroke** (see The Stroke Command, page 90), the **Stroke** option (A) applies a temporary stroke that remains fully modifiable. Furthermore, you can stroke a layer with a gradient or pattern (F) and even emboss the stroke (I). So while **Edit➡Stroke** is arguably more convenient, this layer effect is indisputably more powerful.

A stroke
Select this option or press **ctrl+0** (**command-0** on the Mac) to trace an outline around the visible pixels in the layer.

B size
Enter a thickness for the stroke in pixels.

C position
Use this pop-up menu to specify whether Photoshop draws the stroke entirely outside the layer, entirely inside, or centers the stroke along the layer's border.

D blend mode
If you want the stroke to blend with the pixels on the layer, choose a blend mode...

E opacity
...and adjust the **Opacity** value.

F fill type
Given that fill and stroke are independent attributes, calling an option **Fill Type** when it actually defines the contents of the stroke is misleading. But the idea is sound enough: Based on your choice from this pop-up menu, Photoshop will "fill" your stroke with a solid color, gradient, or preset pattern.

G fill options
After you make a choice from the **Fill Type** pop-up menu (F), Photoshop offers you the appropriate options to explain your choice in more detail. If you select **Color**, you see a lone color swatch and that's it. Otherwise, you get the full array of gradient and pattern modifiers that I discuss in Gradient & Pattern on page 153.

H bevel & emboss
When **Stroke** is turned on (A), you can shade your stroke by pressing **ctrl+5** (**command-5** on the Mac) to access the **Bevel & Emboss** options.

I stroke emboss
Next, select **Stroke Emboss** from the **Style** pop-up menu. From then on, you have access to the standard bevel options examined in Bevel & Emboss on pages 150 and 151. The only difference is that the highlights, shadows, contours, and textures of the bevel fit entirely within the thickness (B) of the stroke.

Create & Apply A Layer Style

What good are nine pages of layer effects and a whole lot of blending options if you can't save them? None, of course, which is why you can. Photoshop lets you save all settings that can be recorded in the **Layer Style** dialog box as presets in the **Styles** palette. Here's how it works:

1 import layer

Before you can save a style, you need to establish the layer effects. So get a dummy layer to experiment on.

2 display layer style dialog box

Double-click the new layer name.

3 set up effects

This step is entirely up to you. You can add a simple drop shadow, or you can go absolutely nuts. For my part, I wanted to create a ghost effect. So I set the **Fill Opacity** to 0% to make the pixels drop away. Then I applied variations on the **Outer Glow**, **Bevel & Emboss**, and **Satin** effects.

4 tweak effects (optional)

If you exit and re-enter the dialog box as you experiment along—presumably adding new effects and turning others off—you'll notice an interesting phenomenon. The **Layers** palette tracks every effect you apply, even if you later deactivate it. In the example below, I had experimented with **Inner Shadow** and **Stroke** but then decided against them. As a result, they appear in the palette as hidden placeholders. If you're feeling tidy, you may want to delete them. Or don't, in which case be forewarned that these hidden effects will be saved with your style.

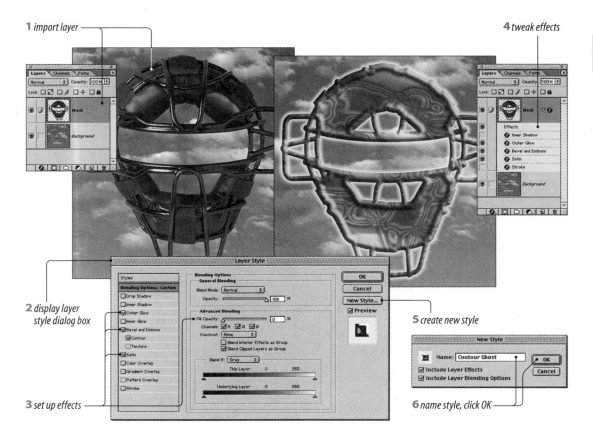

1 *import layer*

4 *tweak effects*

2 *display layer style dialog box*

3 *set up effects*

5 *create new style*

6 *name style, click OK*

5 create new style

If you happen to have the **Layer Style** dialog box open, click the **New Style** button (labeled on page 155). Otherwise, choose **Window➡Show Styles** to display the **Styles** palette. Then click in an empty portion of the palette with the paint bucket cursor. Either way, you get the **New Style** dialog box (6).

6 name style, click OK

Enter a name for the new style. If you want to save just the blending options or layer effects, turn off the appropriate check box. (Note that you can't turn off both.) Then click the **OK** button. If the **Layer Style** dialog box is open, click **OK** again to close it. Photoshop adds a preset to the **Styles** palette.

7 open another image

The new style preset transfers to any open image.

8 create new layer

By now, you've probably guessed that you can apply the style to another layer. But I want to show you something that you might not guess. So click the New Layer button at the bottom of the **Layers** palette or press **ctrl+shift+N** (**command-shift-N** on the Mac) to make a blank layer.

9 select style

Click the preset that you just created in the **Styles** palette (6). Keep an eye on the **Layers** palette and you'll see that Photoshop applies the saved blending options and layer effects to the blank layer.

10 select paintbrush

Press the B key to select the tool. Or select the pencil or airbrush if you prefer.

11 paint in image window

Drag in the image window to paint on the new layer. As you paint, Photoshop automatically applies the saved blending options and layer effects to the brush-stroke. In my case, it didn't matter what foreground color I used; because I set the **Fill Opacity** to 0% (3), the brushstroke itself was invisible. To create the reflection pictured below, I duplicated the painted layer, flipped it, and reduced the **Opacity** value.

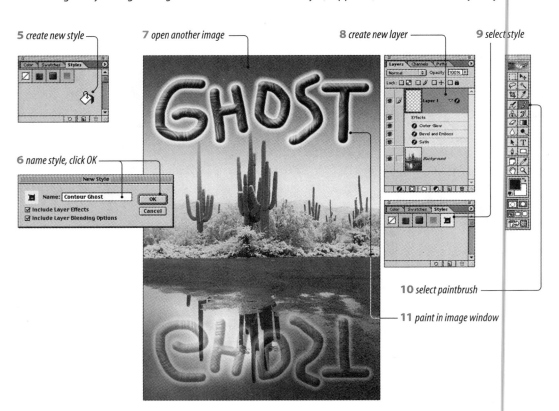

5 *create new style*

7 *open another image*

8 *create new layer*

9 *select style*

6 *name style, click OK*

10 *select paintbrush*

11 *paint in image window*

chapter

11

Draw Vector Shapes

With few exceptions, Photoshop brokers exclusively in pixels. This chapter and the next are about the exceptions. In this chapter, I show you how to create and edit vector-based shapes. In Chapter 12, we explore the world of object-oriented text.

Vector-based shapes are mathematically defined outlines that include rectangles, polygons, and even custom shapes defined with the pen tool. Often called *objects*, shapes are composed of anchor points connected by segments (see The Pen Tools on pages 74 through 77) and print at the maximum resolution of your printer. As a result, you get smooth, sharp outlines, as with the illustrations on this page.

Shapes remain fully editable inside Photoshop, so you can move and transform points long after creating them. You can likewise apply layer styles and even use a shape to mask an image. At long last, vectors and pixels are fully integrated.

157

The Shape Tools

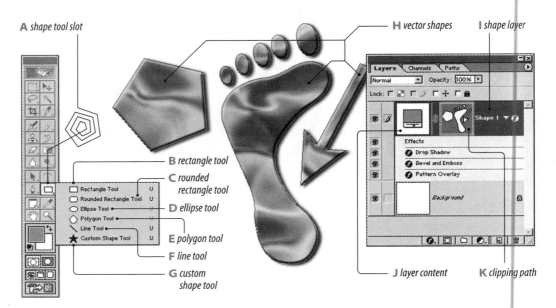

A *shape tool slot*

H *vector shapes*   I *shape layer*

B *rectangle tool*
C *rounded rectangle tool*
D *ellipse tool*
E *polygon tool*
F *line tool*
G *custom shape tool*

J *layer content*   K *clipping path*

Photoshop's shape tools let you create a variety of geometric and prefab shapes. You can express the shapes as vector-based clipping paths, standard work paths for building selections, or plain old colored pixels (L). Given the basic nature of the tools, it's amazing just how much control you have.

A shape tool slot

Click here to display a flyout menu of six shape tools that let you create everything from simple rectangles (B) to custom shapes (G). Press **shift-U** to switch tools.

B rectangle tool

Drag with this tool to draw a rectangle from corner to corner. Press the **shift** key to draw a square, press **alt** (or **option** on the Mac) to draw out from the center.

C rounded rectangle tool

This tool draws a rectangle with rounded corners. Change the **Radius** value (Q) in the options bar to modify the roundness of the corners.

D ellipse tool

The ellipse tool draws ovals. Press **shift** to draw a circle; press **alt** (or **option**) to draw from the center.

E polygon tool

Use this tool to draw geometric shapes with multiple straight sides, from a triangle up to a dodecagon and beyond. The tool always draws outward from the center; press **shift** to constrain the angle. Change the **Sides** value (Q) to add or delete sides. You can also draw stars with sharp and rounded corners (O).

F line tool

Like the other shape tools, the line tool draws filled shapes—they just happen to be long, skinny shapes. This makes Photoshop's lines more difficult to edit than traditional vector lines because you have to edit points on an outline rather than endpoints on a segment. The good news is, you can add arrowheads (P).

G custom shape tool

Drag to draw the custom shape specified in the presets pop-up palette in the options bar (R). Press **shift** to constrain the shape so it fits inside a square; press **alt** (or **option**) to draw out from the center.

> *tip* Press the **spacebar** in mid-drag to move the shape on the fly. Release the **spacebar** to return to scaling the shape, as you were before.

Shape Creation Options

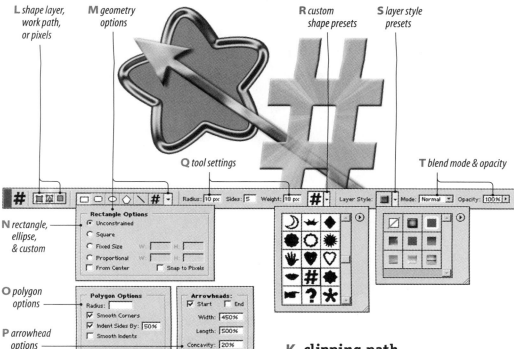

L shape layer, work path, or pixels

M geometry options

R custom shape presets

S layer style presets

Q tool settings

T blend mode & opacity

N rectangle, ellipse, & custom

O polygon options

P arrowhead options

H vector shapes

By default, Photoshop draws vector-based shapes, like those created in Illustrator or another drawing program. The difference is that you can fill them with pixel-based images and effects.

I shape layer

When you draw a vector shape, Photoshop sends it to its own specialized *shape layer*.

> *tip* After creating a shape layer, any additional shapes you draw appear on that same layer. Or press the **esc** key to dismiss the existing shapes. Then drag with a shape tool to draw a new layer.

J layer content

The first thumbnail shows the contents of the layer. Photoshop fills a new shape with the foreground color, but you can change it to a gradient or pattern (see The Change Layer Content Commands, page 162).

K clipping path

The shape itself is a clipping path that masks the contents (J) of the layer. Click this thumbnail to activate the path outlines so you can see them on screen.

L shape layer, work path, or pixels

Prior to drawing a shape, you can specify how you want Photoshop to render it using the first three buttons in the options bar. Selected by default, the first button creates a shape layer. Click the second button to add a new selection-type path to the **Paths** palette (see The Paths Palette on page 76). Click the third button to paint pixels in the active layer.

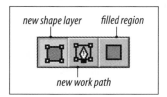

new shape layer   *filled region*

new work path

M geometry options

The options bar repeats the six shape tools, giving you an alternative to switching from the toolbox (A).

Shape Edit Options

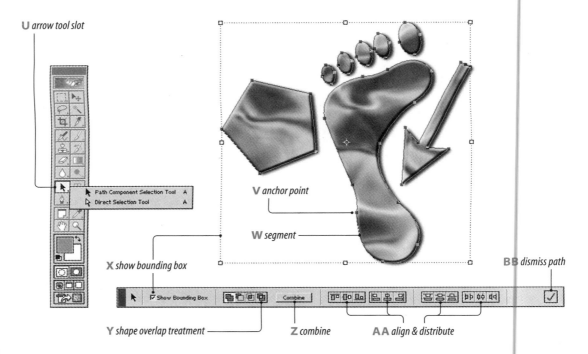

U arrow tool slot

Path Component Selection Tool A
Direct Selection Tool A

V anchor point

X show bounding box

W segment

BB dismiss path

☑ Show Bounding Box

Combine

Y shape overlap treatment

Z combine

AA align & distribute

Click the down-pointing arrowhead to the right of the tools to display a pop-up palette of options tailored to the active tool (N through P).

N rectangle, ellipse, & custom

When drawing a rectangle, ellipse, or custom shape, use these options to constrain proportions or specify an exact size. Turn on **Defined Proportions** to draw a custom shape as it was originally designed. Use **Snap to Pixels** to align a rectangle with the image pixels and avoid any risk of antialiasing.

O polygon options

When the polygon tool is active, enter a **Radius** to specify the exact size of the shape. Use **Indent Sides By** to fold the polygon into a star. The first check box rounds off the corners of the shape; the third, **Smooth Indents**, rounds off the inner folds of a star.

P arrowhead options

These options add an arrowhead to the start or end of a shape drawn with the line tool. **Width** and **Length**

are measured relative to the **Weight** value (Q), while **Concavity** dents the back side of the arrowhead.

Q tool settings

Some shapes respond to numerical adjustments. The **Radius** value affects rounded rectangles (C), **Sides** modifies polygons (E), and **Weight** goes with lines (F).

> *tip* You can edit these values from the keyboard using the bracket keys. Press the [key to lower the value by 1; press] to raise it by 1. Press shift-[or] to lower or raise the value by 10.

R custom shape presets

When drawing a custom shape, select the shape from the list of presets. You can also load additional presets from disk, as in The Preset Manager, pages 56 and 57.

S layer style presets

Because layer styles are mathematical effects, they go well with shapes. However, Photoshop renders the styles as pixels when exporting and printing.

T blend mode & opacity

These options merge a shape with the layers behind it. You can change these settings from the **Layers** palette.

U arrow tool slot

Press A to select the black arrow tool, and then click a shape outline to select the entire path. Use the white arrow to select individual points (V) and segments (W). Press **shift-A** to switch between them.

> *tip* Press **ctrl** (Win) or **command** (Mac) to get the last-used arrow tool when a shape tool is active.

V anchor point

Drag an anchor point with the white arrow tool to change the shape of the path.

W segment

Drag a straight segment to move it; drag a curved segment or its control handle to stretch it.

X show bounding box

Check this option to surround the selected shapes with transformation handles. Drag a handle to scale, drag outside to rotate, or **ctrl**-drag (**command**-drag

on the Mac) a handle to distort. Personally, I prefer to transform by choosing **Edit➠Free Transform Path**.

Y shape overlap treatment

When drawing multiple shapes on a layer, use these buttons to define the appearance of areas where shapes overlap. Press the plus key (+) to select the **Add to Shape Area** button, which fills everything. Press minus (−) to select **Subtract from Shape Area** and make a selected shape carve holes in the others. The third button, **Intersect Shape Areas**, fills overlapping areas only, while the final one, **Exclude Overlapping Shape Areas**, treats overlaps as holes.

Z combine

Click this button to combine all shapes on the active layer according to the shape overlap settings (Y).

AA align & distribute

Use these buttons to align and distribute multiple selected shapes on a single layer.

BB dismiss path

Click the check mark to dismiss a path outline, useful when you want to start a new shape layer. Alternatively, you can press **enter** (Win) or **return** (Mac).

Pen Tool Shapes

The shape tools aren't the only way to draw shapes in Photoshop. You can use the pen tool as well.

CC pen tool
Press P to get the pen tool.

DD shape layer
Click the **New Shape Layer** button in the options bar.

EE pen shape
Click and drag in the image window to draw your path as an independent, filled shape layer.

FF define custom shape
Choose **Edit➠Define Custom Shape** to save the path as a preset.

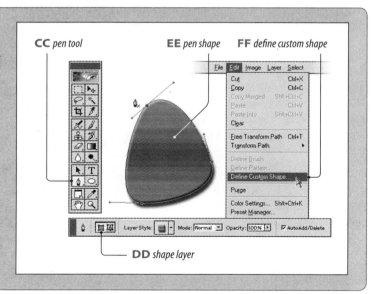

CC *pen tool*   EE *pen shape*   FF *define custom shape*

DD *shape layer*

The Change Layer Content Commands

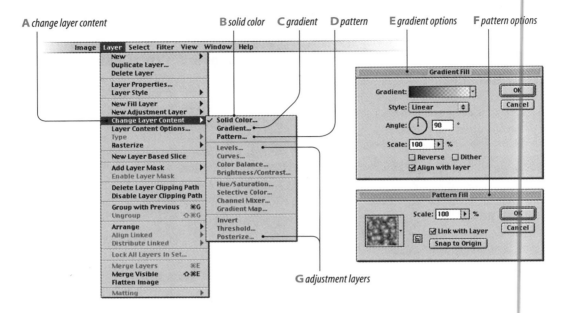

A *change layer content*   B *solid color*   C *gradient*   D *pattern*   E *gradient options*   F *pattern options*

G *adjustment layers*

When you first draw a new shape layer, Photoshop automatically colors it in the foreground color. This may lead you to believe your only options are to apply a solid color or an elaborate layer style. But in fact, you can fill the layer with a gradient or pattern just by choosing a command. Remember, regardless of which one you choose, you can assign just one fill per shape layer.

A change layer content
Photoshop calls the contents of shape layers *dynamic fills* because you can update them by choosing a command. After drawing a shape layer, choose **Layer→Change Layer Content** to display a submenu of alternative dynamic fills.

B solid color
The first command resets the fill to a solid color. It also displays the **Color Picker** dialog box, which lets you select a different color.

> *tip* If all you want to do is change the color of a shape layer, just specify a new foreground color and press alt+backspace (option-delete on the Mac).

C gradient
Choose the **Gradient** command to design a gradation using the options in the **Gradient Fill** dialog box (E).

D pattern
This command fills the shape with a repeating pattern, as defined in the **Pattern Fill** dialog box (F).

E gradient options
Select a preset from the **Gradient** pop-up menu to apply it to the active shape layer, or click the preview to create a gradient of your own. Other options work as described in Gradient & Pattern on page 153.

F pattern options
Click the pattern swatch to select a preset pattern, as in Gradient & Pattern on page 153.

> *tip* After applying a gradient or pattern, double-click the layer content thumbnail to edit the fill.

G adjustment layers
Photoshop also lets you fill a shape layer with a color adjustment. I demonstrate this in detail in Adjustment Layers on pages 209 and 210 of Chapter 13.

⬤steps Create & Edit Vector Shapes

Compared with many operations in Photoshop, drawing and editing shapes is relatively easy and a fair amount of fun. In fact, the only point that's likely to hang you up is saving. What format accommodates vectors and pixels so they can be imported into another program? As revealed in the following steps, the answer turns out to be PDF.

1 select shape tool
Press the U key or click the tool icon in the toolbox.

2 select new shape layer
Confirm that the **New Shape Layer** button is turned on. If the button is missing, a shape layer or work path is already active. Press the **esc** key to dismiss it.

3 select custom shape tool
Select it from the options bar or flyout menu.

4 select defined proportions
In the options bar, click the down-pointing arrowhead to the right of the custom shape tool. Then turn on the **Defined Proportions** radio button to maintain the original proportions of the shape.

5 load custom shapes.csh
Click the **Shape** option to bring up a palette of custom shapes. Then choose **Custom Shapes.csh** from the palette menu to load a library of predefined shapes. Photoshop will ask whether you want to replace or append the shapes; click **Append**.

6 choose crescent & layer style
With the pop-up palette still open, click the hollow **Crescent Moon Frame**. If you're drawn to some other shape, select it instead. Grab a layer style while you're at it. The style used below is **Color Target (Button)**.

7 draw shape
Drag in the image window to draw the new shape and corresponding layer. Because you selected **Defined Proportions** (4), the relative dimensions are constrained.

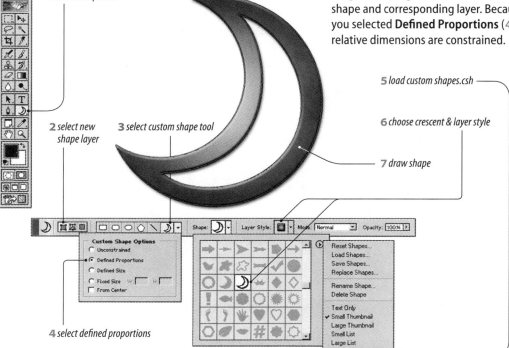

1 select shape tool

2 select new shape layer

3 select custom shape tool

4 select defined proportions

5 load custom shapes.csh

6 choose crescent & layer style

7 draw shape

8 select add to shape area

Now that you've established a shape layer, notice that the options bar has changed. Gone are the **New Shape Layer** button (2) and its cohorts. In their place are the path overlap treatment buttons. Press the plus key (same as =) to select **Add to Shape Area**, which tells Photoshop to fill all portions of all shapes.

9 select polygon tool

Click the polygon tool icon in the options bar or press shift-U four times in a row.

10 enter starfish settings

Click the down-pointing arrowhead to the right of the tool icons in the options bar. Then select **Indent Sides By** and enter **80%** to create a spiky star. Select the **Smooth Corners** check box to round off the spikes, turning the star into a starfish.

11 set sides

Set the **Sides** value to 5 to draw a five-pointed star.

> *tip* Remember, you can adjust the sides by pressing the [and] keys. Or press **shift-enter** (**shift-return** on the Mac) to highlight the **Sides** value.

12 draw starfish

Drag in the image window to draw a starfish. Because the last shape you drew was still active (7), Photoshop adds the starfish to the same layer as the crescent. The layer effects adjust to fit the additional shape.

13 press ctrl+T, ctrl-drag handle

On the Mac, press **command-T**. Or choose **Edit➡Free Transform Path**. Then press **ctrl** (Win) or **command** (Mac) and drag a corner handle to distort the shapes. Because these are vectors, you can transform them all you want without degrading the quality.

14 press enter or return

When you like what you see, press **enter** (Win) or **return** (Mac) to apply the distortion.

15 choose define custom shape

Choose **Edit➡Define Custom Shape** to save the selected paths as a custom shape.

16 name shape

After the **Shape Name** dialog box appears, enter a name for your custom shape preset. Then click **OK**.

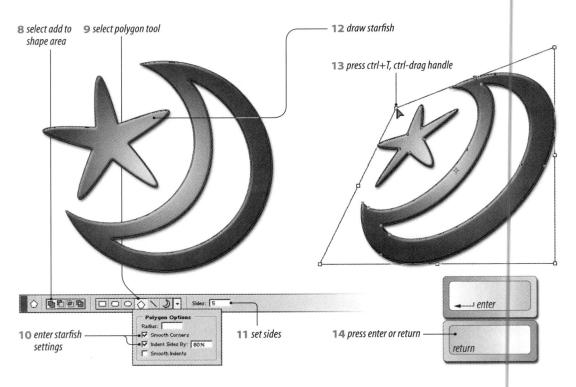

8 *select add to shape area*   **9** *select polygon tool*   **12** *draw starfish*

13 *press ctrl+T, ctrl-drag handle*

10 *enter starfish settings*   **11** *set sides*   **14** *press enter or return*

Sides: 5

Polygon Options
Radius:
☑ Smooth Corners
☑ Indent Sides By: 80%
☐ Smooth Indents

enter

return

17 select custom shape tool
If the polygon tool is still active, press **shift-U** twice.

18 choose your shape
Click the **Shape** preview, then select the custom shape that you just created (16) from the list.

19 draw, draw, draw
Draw inside the image window to create repeated instances of the custom shape. Chances are, you're still working on the same shape layer, so Photoshop expands the layer effects to keep up. If you want to make a new shape layer, press **esc** before drawing.

20 choose save as
When you finish your masterpiece, press **ctrl+shift+S**

(Win) or **command-shift-S** (Mac) to save the document. Photoshop displays the **Save As** dialog box.

21 choose PDF, select layers
Photoshop lets you save shape layers to the standard "rich" formats: PSD, TIFF, or PDF. However, of the three, only PDF can convey vectors and pixels to other programs. So choose **Photoshop PDF** from the **Format** pop-up menu. Make sure the **Layers** check box is turned on. Then click **Save**.

22 select ZIP, include vector data
Photoshop next displays the **PDF Options** dialog box. Although you can select either **ZIP** or **JPEG**, **ZIP** does the best job of retaining layer effects. Be sure to select **Include Vector Data**. Then click **OK**.

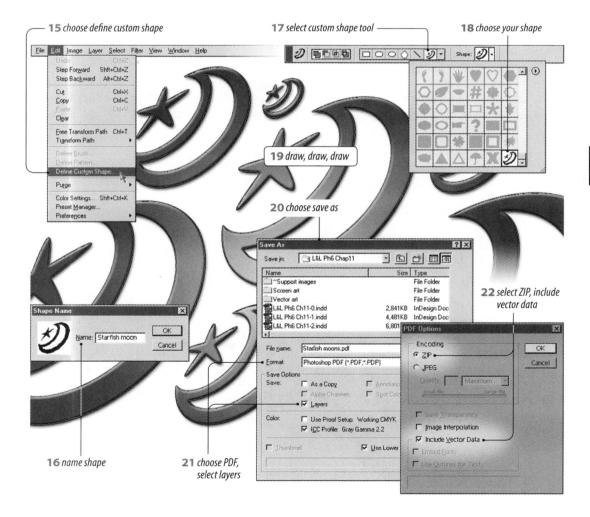

15 *choose define custom shape*

17 *select custom shape tool*

18 *choose your shape*

19 *draw, draw, draw*

20 *choose save as*

16 *name shape*

21 *choose PDF, select layers*

22 *select ZIP, include vector data*

🥚steps Paint Inside A Vector Shape

A new shape layer contains a dynamic fill (see The Change Layer Content Commands, page 162). Not only can you edit the color, gradient, or pattern via a dialog box, you can also resize it on the fly to fit a smaller or larger shape. But there are limitations. Specifically, you can't brush or edit the pixels inside a dynamic fill. Before you can hand-paint a shape, you first have to rasterize its contents.

1 make shape layer
By default, Photoshop fills the shape with a solid color. That's fine for our purposes, though you can change it to a gradient or pattern if you prefer.

2 hide overlay effects
If you applied a layer style to the shape—either from the options bar or the **Styles** palette—the dynamic fill may be obscured by one of the three **Overlay** effects. Go to the **Layers** palette and turn off any **Overlay** effects to see the fill on its own.

3 rasterize fill content
To *rasterize* a graphic is to convert it to pixels. So it follows that **Layer➞Rasterize➞Fill Content** converts the dynamic fill to colored pixels. Notice the change to the layer content thumbnail in the **Layers** palette. The little slider disappears, indicating that you can no longer edit the fill numerically. If you double-click the thumbnail, you get the standard **Blending Options**.

4 select paintbrush
Or select some other paint or edit tool.

5 specify foreground color
Adjust the values in the **Color** palette to select a color to paint with. Also adjust the blend mode and **Opacity** settings in the options bar as desired.

6 paint inside shapes
Paint the shape to hand-color it. Feel free to change colors and try out different **Opacity** values as you like. As always, Photoshop paints exactly inside the lines.

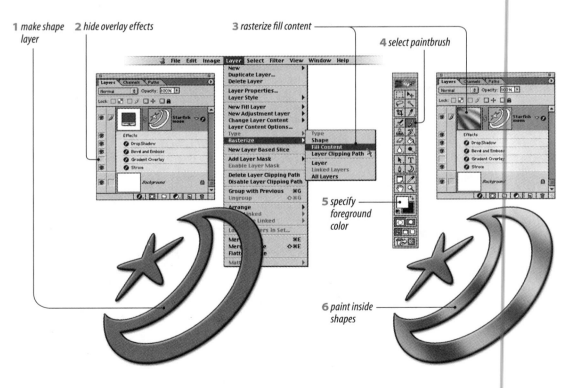

1 *make shape layer*   2 *hide overlay effects*   3 *rasterize fill content*   4 *select paintbrush*   5 *specify foreground color*   6 *paint inside shapes*

Apply A Vector Mask To An Image

There's more than one way to fill a shape with a photographic image. If you want to fill a shape you've already drawn, your best bet is to place the image on an independent layer directly in front of the shape and then press **ctrl+G** (Win) or **command**-G (Mac) to form a clipping group. But if you haven't yet drawn the shape, here's a better way:

1 get image
Open the image that you want to mask.

2 select shape tool
Select the shape tool best suited to the mask you intend to draw. I wanted to draw a rounded star, so I selected the polygon tool.

3 select new work path
Click the **New Work Path** button in the options bar. Although your final goal is to draw a shape layer, you're best off starting with a common work path.

4 set geometry options
Click the down-pointing arrowhead to display the geometry options for the active shape tool. I turned on all three check boxes for the polygon tool and set the **Indent Sides By** value to 60%.

5 draw path
Draw the desired path in the image window. If necessary, use the arrow tools and the **Free Transform** command to make the path ship-shape.

6 convert image to layer
Assuming you started with a flat image, double-click the Background layer in the **Layers** palette. Then give the layer a name and click **OK**. Photoshop converts the image into a floating layer.

7 create white background
Now the image has no background, so you need to make a new one. Press **ctrl+shift+N** (**command-shift**-N on the Mac) and click **OK** to create a new layer.

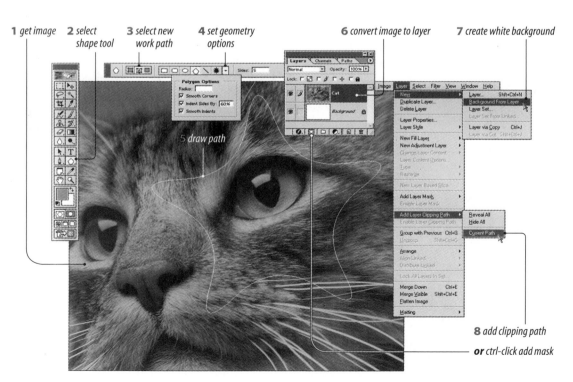

1 *get image*   **2** *select shape tool*   **3** *select new work path*   **4** *set geometry options*   **6** *convert image to layer*   **7** *create white background*

5 draw path

8 *add clipping path*

or ctrl-click add mask

Then choose **Layer➡New➡Background From Layer** to make the blank layer an empty Background layer.

8 add clipping path

Press **alt+]** (Win) or **option-]** (Mac) to ascend to the image layer. With your new path visible (5), choose **Layer➡Add Layer Clipping Path➡Current Path** to clip the photograph into the shape of the path.

> **tip** Or rather than choosing the command, press **ctrl** (Win) or **command** (Mac) and click the **Add Mask** button at the bottom of the **Layers** palette.

9 select pen tool

Want to edit or add to the shape? Not a problem. Photoshop automatically updates the mask outline to accommodate your changes. For example, I wanted to add a mouth to my cyclops cat eye. Because it's a free-form shape, I needed a free-form tool. So I started by selecting the pen tool.

10 exclude overlapping shape areas

With the new shape layer active, Photoshop doesn't ask whether you'd like to make a shape layer or work path; it knows you want to add to the shape. However, it does ask you about the nature of overlapping paths. By default, the pen tool is set to **Exclude Overlapping Shape Areas**, which creates holes where any two shapes intersect. I elected to leave this option on.

11 draw hole

Use the pen tool to draw a hole in your shape. For my part, I dragged a few times to trace three smooth points around the mouth. Because the **Exclude Overlapping Shape Areas** option was selected (10), the mouth fell away.

12 select layer style

Choose **Window➡Show Styles** to display the **Styles** palette. Then click a preset to apply a series of layer effects to the active layer. I applied the last of the default styles, **Sunset Sky (Text)**.

13 hide overlay effects

Any **Overlay** effects in the selected style obscure the image harbored inside the shape. Click the eyeball in front of the **Overlay** item in the **Layers** palette to hide the effect. Or double-click the **Overlay** item and edit the **Blend Mode** and **Opacity** settings to mix the effect with the image.

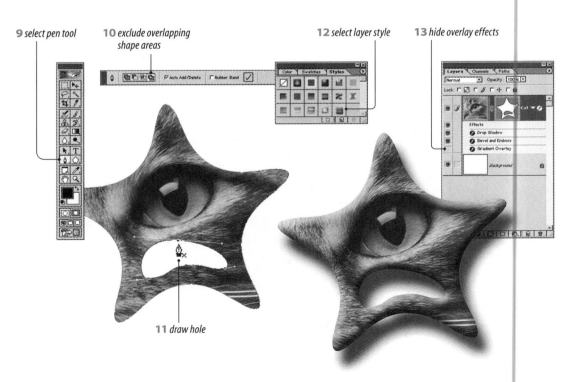

9 *select pen tool*

10 *exclude overlapping shape areas*

12 *select layer style*

13 *hide overlay effects*

11 *draw hole*

Create & Edit Type

It's fair to say that Photoshop gives you more flexibility and control over type than your average image editor. The key to Photoshop's superiority is the fact that it produces vector-based text. That means you can scale and transform type without any degradation in quality, just as you can with vector shapes.

If you're familiar with creating text in a page-layout or illustration program, you'll feel right at home with Photoshop's type controls. As in other electronic publishing programs, text in Photoshop is fully editable. So you can change words and formatting attributes, such as type size, leading, kerning, and alignment, any time you like.

What's more, you can bend and twist text along a curve, apply layer styles, and fill type with photographic images. As if all this weren't enough, you can also apply filters to type after converting it to pixels.

The Type Tool & Options

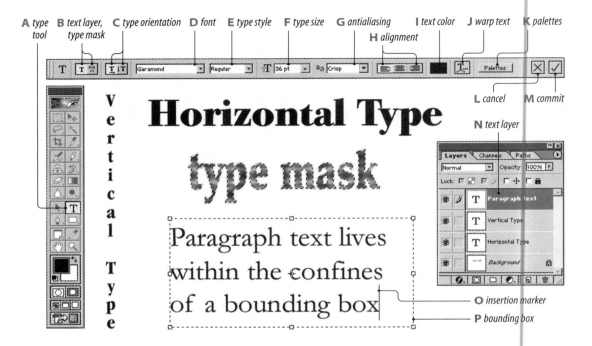

A type tool
B text layer, type mask
C type orientation
D font
E type style
F type size
G antialiasing
H alignment
I text color
J warp text
K palettes
L cancel
M commit
N text layer
O insertion marker
P bounding box

Photoshop's type tool lets you create and edit two basic kinds of vector-based text: *point text*, in which each line of type is independent of all others, and *paragraph text*, in which lines of type flow and wrap within a bounding box (P). You can also use the type tool to create text-based selection outlines (B).

A type tool
Press **T** to select the type tool. To create point text with the attributes specified in the options bar (C through I), click anywhere in the image window and begin typing. Press **enter** (Win) or **return** (Mac) to begin a new line. To create paragraph text, drag to create a bounding box and type away. When the text reaches the edge of the box, it automatically wraps to the next line. Press **enter** (Win) or **return** (Mac) to begin a new paragraph.

> *tip* To convert point text to paragraph text or vice versa, select the text layer (N) and choose **Layer→Type→Convert to Paragraph Text** or **Convert to Point Text**, respectively.

B text layer, type mask
Prior to typing with the type tool, click the first button in the options bar to create editable vector-based text on a separate text layer (N). Click the second button to create a type mask on the active layer, which you can use to select portions of an image.

C type orientation
Click the first of these two buttons to create ordinary horizontal text. Click the other button to create a vertical column of type.

D font
Use this pop-up menu to select a typeface for your text.

E type style
Choose a type style, such as **Bold** or **Italic**, from this pop-up menu.

> *tip* To quickly select a font (D) or type style (E) from the keyboard, click the current name in the **Font** or **Type Style** option box and type the first few letters of the name you want.

F type size

Choose a predefined type size from this pop-up menu or double-click the size value and enter a new one. By default, Photoshop measures type size in points. If you prefer to use pixels, enter **px** after the value. Or choose **Edit➞Preferences➞Units & Rulers** and select a new unit from the **Type** pop-up menu.

G antialiasing

To retain hard character edges, turn antialiasing off by choosing **None** from this pop-up menu. **Crisp** softens edges just a bit without sacrificing sharp contrast. At large type sizes, you may see jagged edges, in which case you might want to give **Smooth** a try. Use the **Strong** setting to increase the weight of text if anti-aliasing makes it appear thin. Note that antialiasing affects all type on a text layer.

H alignment

Use these buttons to specify how lines of text align with each other. Your options are left, center, or right for horizontal type and top, center, or bottom for vertical type. With point text, Photoshop aligns with respect to the spot you click in the image window. With paragraph text, type aligns with respect to the edges of the bounding box.

> *tip* You can change the alignment of selected text from the keyboard. Press **ctrl+shift+L, C,** or **R** (**command-shift-L, C,** or **R** on the Mac) to left align, center align, or right align text, respectively.

I text color

Click this color swatch to display the **Color Picker** dialog box. If a text layer is active (N), the color you select is applied to all text on the layer as well as the next characters you type. If one or more characters are selected, the color affects only those characters.

J warp text

Only available after you've created text, click this button to display the **Warp Text** dialog box, which lets you bend and distort text on the active layer. Read Warp Live Text Along A Curve on pages 178 and 179 to learn more about this option.

K palettes

Click this button to bring up the **Character** and **Paragraph** palettes, which contain loads of additional text formatting options. For complete details, see The Character Palette on pages 172 and 173 and The Paragraph Palette on pages 174 and 175.

L cancel

This button and the next (M) only appear in the options bar when text is selected or an insertion marker (O) is active. Click the **Cancel** button or press **esc** to exit text-editing mode without applying any changes made during the current editing session.

M commit

Click this button to apply the active text and exit text-editing mode, a process Photoshop calls *committing* text. Alternatively, you can commit text by pressing **ctrl+enter** (Win) or **command-return** (Mac) or by selecting any tool other than the type tool.

N text layer

When you first add type to an image, Photoshop automatically places it on a new text layer. If you later click or drag near the text with the type tool, Photoshop selects the text layer and activates text-editing mode. If you click or drag at a spot where no text currently exists, Photoshop creates a new text layer to hold the next characters you type.

> *tip* If you want to create new type near existing text but put it on a separate layer, you can prevent Photoshop from kicking into text-editing mode by **shift**-clicking or **shift**-dragging with the type tool.

O insertion marker

When you click or drag with the type tool, an insertion marker indicates the location where the next character you type will appear.

P bounding box

To create a bounding box, drag with the type tool or **alt**-click (**option**-click on the Mac) and enter specific **Width** and **Height** values. Drag a corner handle to scale the box. **Ctrl**-drag (Win) or **command**-drag (Mac) to scale the box and the text within it.

The Character Palette

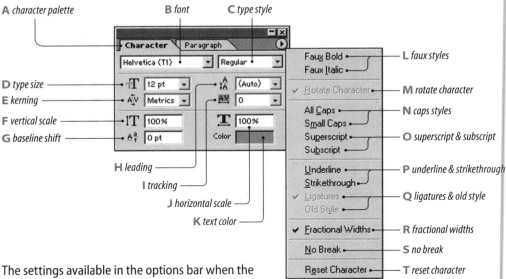

A character palette
B font
C type style
D type size
E kerning
F vertical scale
G baseline shift
H leading
I tracking
J horizontal scale
K text color
L faux styles
M rotate character
N caps styles
O superscript & subscript
P underline & strikethrough
Q ligatures & old style
R fractional widths
S no break
T reset character

The settings available in the options bar when the type tool is selected represent just a fraction of Photoshop's text formatting capabilities. In fact, the program gives you an extraordinary amount of control over the appearance of type, allowing you to apply more than a dozen other formatting attributes at both the character and paragraph levels.

A character palette

Choose **Window➞Show Character**, click the **Palettes** button in the options bar, or press **ctrl+T** (Win) or **command-T** (Mac) when in text-editing mode. Any which way, you get the **Character** palette, which lets you apply formatting to point text and paragraph text on a per-character basis. Any changes you make affect selected characters. If no text is selected, settings will be applied to the next characters you type.

B font

If your system includes two versions of a font, Photoshop distinguishes between them. **(TT)** indicates TrueType; **(T1)** indicates PostScript Type 1.

C type style

Choose one of the styles available for the selected font (B) from this pop-up menu. Your choice is also reflected in the options bar (E, page 170). If you don't see the style you're looking for, check out the additional style options in the palette menu (L through Q).

D type size

Change the size of selected text here.

> **tip** To increase or decrease the type size by 2, press **ctrl+shift+>** or **<** (**command-shift->** or **<** on the Mac). To change the type size by 10, add the **alt** key (**option** key on the on the Mac).

E kerning

Kerning is a means for adjusting the space between two characters. Because certain letters, such as T and o, appear too far apart when placed next to each other, most typefaces include instructions to space such *kerning pairs* more closely together. The default setting, **Metrics**, applies the font's built-in kerning instructions. If the prescribed spacing doesn't look right, click between the poorly spaced letters and enter a value, measured in $^1/_{1000}$'s of an *em space* (a space the width of a letter M). Negative values move characters together; positive values shift them apart.

> **tip** To increase or decrease the **Kerning** value by 20, press **alt+→** or **alt+←** (**option** on the Mac). To change the value by 100, add **ctrl** (or **command**).

F vertical scale

In addition to sizing type proportionally (D), you can change the height and width of selected characters using the **Vertical** and **Horizontal** (J) scale controls. Enter a value higher or lower than **100%** in the **Vertical Scale** option box to make selected characters taller or shorter, respectively. To return the text to its original height, enter a value of **100%**.

G baseline shift

Enter a value in this option box to move selected characters above or below the baseline. A positive value raises type; a negative value lowers it. A value of **0** applies no shift whatsoever.

H leading

Leading is the amount of space between two lines of type, measured from the baseline of the selected line to the baseline of the line above it. **Auto**, the default setting, applies a leading equal to 120 percent of the type size. So 10-point type would get 12-point leading, for example. To specify a fixed leading amount, enter a value from **0** to **5000** points in .001 increments.

> *tip* Press **alt+↓** or **↑** (**option-↓** or **↑** on the Mac) to expand or reduce the leading in increments of 2. Add **ctrl** (**command**) for increments of 10.

I tracking

Tracking works just like kerning (E), except you can apply it to long stretches of type. Raise or lower the value to increase or decrease the spacing across a range of selected characters. Note that tracking works cumulatively with kerning. So if you kern a character pair –10 and then apply –10 of tracking, the total space between the characters is –20.

J horizontal scale

Enter a value greater or less than **100%** to expand or condense the width of selected characters. To restore the normal text width, type **100%** in this option box.

K text color

Click here to apply a new color from the **Color Picker** dialog box. Or better yet, just change the foreground color and press **alt+backspace** (**option-delete**).

L faux styles

Use these two options to apply bold and italic effects to fonts that don't include bold or italic type styles, such as **Geneva** or **Symbol**. If bold and italic styles are available (C), use them instead for better results.

M rotate character

Only available for vertical type (C, page 170), this option controls the orientation of characters. When the option is turned on, as it is by default, characters appear upright. Turn the option off to rotate characters 90 degrees clockwise so they lie on their side.

> *tip* To change the orientation of an active layer of type, choose **Layer→Type→Horizontal** or **Layer→Type→Vertical**. You can also rotate the layer by choosing **Edit→Transform→Rotate**.

N caps styles

Choose **All Caps** to change selected characters of text to capital letters. The **Small Caps** option applies small capital letters, useful for formatting time (10:45 PM) and introductory text (ONCE UPON A TIME).

O superscript & subscript

These options reduce the size of selected characters and move them above (**Superscript**) or below (**Subscript**) the baseline. If you require more precise positioning, use the **Baseline Shift** option (G) instead.

P underline & strikethrough

As you would expect, **Underline** places a line below selected characters and **Strikethrough** draws a line through the middle of them. With vertical type, you get two underline options—**Underline Left** and **Underline Right**—which let you add a line to the left or right of characters.

Q ligatures & old style

These two options are only available when a typeface that includes ligatures and old style figures is selected. *Ligatures* are special letter pairs that join into one, such as fi and fl. *Old style figures* are stylized numerals, many of which extend below the baseline, such as 0123456789.

The Paragraph Palette

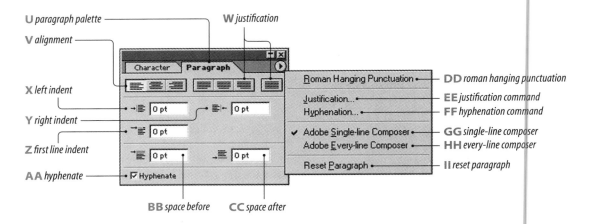

U *paragraph palette*
V *alignment*
W *justification*
X *left indent*
Y *right indent*
Z *first line indent*
AA *hyphenate*
BB *space before*
CC *space after*
DD *roman hanging punctuation*
EE *justification command*
FF *hyphenation command*
GG *single-line composer*
HH *every-line composer*
II *reset paragraph*

R fractional widths

When this option is on, as it is by default, the amount of space between characters can vary by fractions of a pixel. At small type sizes, this can result in weird spacing, in which case you should turn the option off. Note that while the **Fractional Width** option resides in the **Character** palette menu, it affects all text on the active layer and cannot be applied to selected characters. Go figure.

S no break

When you're working with paragraph text, Photoshop may need to hyphenate words at the end of a line (FF). If you want to prevent the program from ever hyphenating a certain word, select the word and choose **No Break** from the **Character** palette menu.

T reset character

Choose this command when no text is selected to return the **Character** palette to its default settings.

U paragraph palette

The **Paragraph** palette contains a host of formatting options that affect entire paragraphs. Note that some options are not applicable to point text and, therefore, are not available when point text is selected. To display the palette, choose **Window➞Show Paragraph** or press **ctrl+M** (**command-M**) when in text-editing mode. Or if the **Character** palette (A) is visible, you can simply click the **Paragraph** panel tab.

V alignment

Also duplicated in the options bar (H, page 170), these buttons control how lines of type align with each other: flush left, ragged right (first button); centered (second button); or flush right, ragged left (third button).

W justification

Only available for paragraph text, these four buttons let you *justify* paragraphs—so they fill the entire width of the bounding box—while specifying the alignment of the last line. Click one of the first three buttons to align the last line to the left, center, or right. The final button *force-justifies* the last line of text, so it fills the entire width of the bounding box.

> **tip** Press **ctrl+shift+J** (**command-shift-J** on the Mac) to justify a paragraph and left-align the last line. Press **ctrl+shift+F** to force-justify the last line.

X left indent

Enter a value in this option box to indent the entire left side of a paragraph from the edge of the bounding box for paragraph text or with respect to the spot you first clicked with the type tool for point text.

Y right indent

To indent the right side of a paragraph, type a value in this option box. Enter both **Left Indent** (X) and **Right Indent** values to reduce the width of a paragraph.

Z first line indent

To indent only the first line of a paragraph, enter a value here. This option is relative to the **Left Indent** setting (X). So if you set the left indent to 12 points and the first line indent to 6 points, the first line will be indented 18 points.

> (tip) To indent all lines *except* the first line, called a *hanging indent*, enter a positive **Left Indent** value. Then enter the negative version of that same value in the **First Line Indent** option box.

AA hyphenate

Select this check box to let Photoshop hyphenate text according to the settings specified in the **Hyphenation** dialog box (FF). Deselect the option to prevent the program from hyphenating text.

BB space before

Enter a value in this option box to set the amount of vertical space that appears before a paragraph.

CC space after

Use this option to add space after a paragraph.

DD roman hanging punctuation

Available only for paragraph text, choose this option to let punctuation marks hang slightly outside the edges of the bounding box, giving text a cleaner look.

EE justification command

Choose this command to display the **Justification** dialog box, which lets you modify the parameters Photoshop uses to justify text. Use the **Spacing** options to specify the **Minimum**, **Maximum**, and **Desired** amount of space allowed between entire words and individual letters, measured as a percentage of the default spacing.

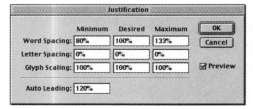

You can also permit Photoshop to alter the width of individual characters by varying the **Glyph Scaling**. But I advise you use this option sparingly, if at all, to avoid perceptible changes in the appearance of type. Finally, if you're so inclined, you can change the default **Auto Leading** value here as well.

FF hyphenation command

Choosing this command brings up the **Hyphenation** dialog box, where you can set rules for how words are hyphenated when the **Hyphenate** option (AA) is turned on. Use the option boxes to specify the minimum number of letters a word must contain to be eligible for hyphenation (**Words Longer Than**), the minimum number of characters that must appear before and after a hyphen (**After First** & **Before Last**), the maximum number of consecutive lines that can end with a hyphen (**Hyphen Limit**), and how far from the right edge of the bounding box a hyphen can appear (**Hyphenation Zone**). To prevent Photoshop from hyphenating capitalized words, deselect the **Hyphenate Capitalized Words** check box.

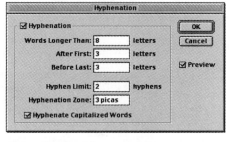

GG single-line composer

This option and the next (HH) are available only for paragraph text. Turned on by default, this feature tells Photoshop to consider one line at a time when determining where to break and hyphenate lines of text.

HH every-line composer

Choose this option to tell Photoshop to evaluate all lines in a paragraph when inserting line breaks and hyphens. The result is more evenly spaced text.

II reset paragraph

When no text is selected, choose this command to restore the **Paragraph** palette to its default settings.

⭕steps Enter & Format Type

Adding text to an image in Photoshop can be as simple as clicking with the type tool and tapping the keyboard. But for maximum flexibility and control, create text within a bounding box. Here's how:

1 select type tool
Press T or click the type tool icon in the toolbox.

2 click text layer button
Make sure the first button in the options bar is selected, as it is by default. Otherwise, you end up creating a text-based selection outline rather than editable vector type.

3 select orientation
Nine times out of ten, you'll want to create ordinary horizontal text. So click the first orientation button.

4 specify font, type style, & size
Use the first three pop-up menus in the options bar to choose a typeface, style, and size for your text. If you're not sure what you want, just wing it. You can always change these attributes later.

5 select alignment & text color
I pressed **ctrl+shift+C** (**command-shift-C** on the Mac) to create centered text. At smaller type sizes, you may want to create justified text by choosing **Window➡Show Paragraph** and selecting a justification option from the **Paragraph** palette. Then click the color swatch in the options bar or the foreground color icon in the toolbox to select a color for the text—in my case, white.

6 drag in image window
Now that your basic formatting attributes are in place, it's time to draw the bounding box. Click near the spot where you want the first letter to appear and drag to create a box roughly large enough to hold your text. Don't worry about making it exactly the right size. You can resize it later (8).

1 *select type tool* **2** *click text layer button* **3** *select orientation* **4** *specify font, type style, & size* **5** *select alignment & text color*

6 *drag in image window*

7 *enter text*

8 *resize bounding box*

9 *make edits*

7 enter text

When you release the mouse button, a box with eight handles appears with a blinking insertion marker inside it. Start typing. When the text reaches the edge of the bounding box, it wraps to the next line.

8 resize bounding box (optional)

A plus sign in the bottom-right handle of the bounding box indicates overflow text. To bring overflow text into view, drag a handle to make the box bigger.

9 make edits

To insert additional text, click at the spot where you want the text to appear and enter it from the keyboard. To replace text, drag over it to select it and then type the new text.

> *tip* To quickly select a single word, double-click it. Triple-click to select an entire line. To select all text within the bounding box, press **ctrl+A** (Win) or **command-A** (Mac).

10 adjust paragraph spacing, etc.

Now is a good time to make formatting adjustments. In my case, I reduced the type size in the second paragraph and added 8 points of paragraph spacing. Then I **ctrl**-dragged (**command**-dragged on the Mac) the bounding box to reposition the text in the image.

11 commit text

Click the check mark in the options bar to accept the text and exit the text-editing mode. Alternatively, you can press **ctrl+enter** (Win) or **command-return** (Mac); or press **enter** on the numerical keypad. If you'd rather abandon the text and start over, press the **esc** key. But be careful! Once you press **esc**, it's over—there's no way to undo it.

12 adjust blend mode & opacity

Since the text exists on a separate layer, you can create some interesting effects simply by changing the opacity and blend mode. For example, I made my text translucent by lowering the **Opacity** to 75%.

10 *adjust paragraph spacing, etc.*

11 *commit text*

12 *adjust blend mode & opacity*

Warp Live Text Along A Curve

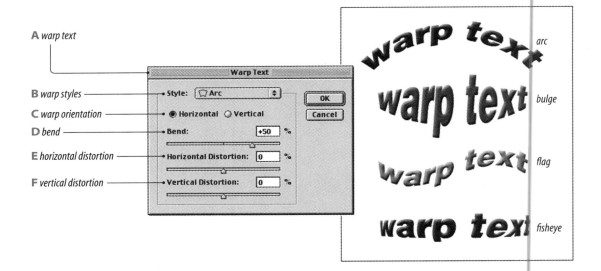

A *warp text*

B *warp styles*

C *warp orientation*

D *bend*

E *horizontal distortion*

F *vertical distortion*

arc

bulge

flag

fisheye

Photoshop doesn't limit you to creating straight rows of text. While you can't fit text to a path as you can in **Illustrator** and most other drawing and page-layout programs, you can do something most other programs can't do by bending and curving type with the **Warp Text** feature.

A warp text

Select both the type tool and a text layer. Then click the **Warp Text** button in the options bar (J, page 171) or choose **Layer▸Type▸Warp Text**. Either way, you get the **Warp Text** dialog box, which lets you bend, twist, and distort type along a curve. Applicable to both point and paragraph text, the **Warp Text** options affect all text on the active layer.

> *tip* To warp a few words from a paragraph, select the text with the type tool and press **ctrl+X** (command-X on the Mac) to cut it. Then press **enter** on the keypad to commit the type, drag with the type tool to make a new layer, and press **ctrl+V** to paste. Finally, click the **Warp Text** button.

Note that Photoshop lets you warp editable text layers only. This rules out bitmapped type (see Rasterize & Filter Type on page 182), as well as type

converted to a shape layer (**Layer▸Type▸Convert to Shape**) or work path (**Layer▸Type▸Create Work Path**). Finally, you can't warp text that contains faux bold or italic styles (L, page 173).

B warp styles

The **Style** pop-up menu contains 15 different warp styles, ranging from a simple arc to unique shapes. The small icon to the left of each style name (below) shows the basic effect of applying that style.

The figure above shows a few of the most useful styles applied to some text using the default orientation (C), bend (D), and distortion (E & F) settings. By adjusting these controls, you can create thousands of variations on the effect of each style. Photoshop automatically previews the results of your settings in the image window, permitting you to experiment with ease.

C warp orientation

After you choose a style, set the orientation of the warp. Select the **Horizontal** radio button to warp text as indicated by the icon in the **Style** menu (B). Click the **Vertical** option to rotate the warp 90 degrees, as if you had tipped the **Style** icon on its side.

arc, horizontal

arc, vertical

D bend

The **Bend** value determines the direction of the curve. The curves depicted in the **Style** icons (B) represent the default value of +50%. A value of **–50%** produces the exact opposite curve. Drag the slider bar triangle to adjust the value dynamically.

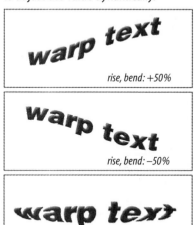

rise, bend: +50%

rise, bend: –50%

inflate, bend: +100%

inflate, bend: –70%

E horizontal distortion

This option and the next (F) enable you to create prespective effects. Enter a positive **Horizontal Distortion** value to position the origin point of the perspective to the left of the text; use a negative value to position the origin point to the right.

squeeze, bend: +50%, horiz distort: +70%

squeeze, bend: –50%, horiz distort: –50%

F vertical distortion

The **Vertical Distortion** option creates a perspective effect originating above (positive values) or below (negative values) the text. If you're feeling really radical, you can combine vertical and horizontal distortion (E) to get some pretty wacky effects.

shell lower, bend: +50%, vert distort: +50%

shell lower, bend: +50%, vert distort: –50%

wave, horiz & vert distort: +50% & –50%

> *tip* To further enhance a **Warp Text** perspective effect, choose **Edit➡Free Transform** and go nuts **ctrl**-dragging corner handles.

steps Fill Type With An Image

Photoshop gives you several ways to fill type with an image. You can convert text to shapes using **Layer➡Type➡Convert to Shape**, generate a work path using **Layer➡Type➡Create Work Path**, or use the type mask option to create a text-based selection outline. The problem with each of these techniques, however, is the text loses its editability. The solution? Use a type layer and a clipping group.

1 get image
Open the image to which you want to add text. While you're at it, get the image you'll use to fill the type and leave it open in the background.

2 select type tool
Press T to get the type tool.

3 set formatting options
Make sure the first button in the options bar is selected. Then choose a font, type style, and type size, and set other formatting options as you deem fit. Don't bother selecting a text color, though. It's irrelevant since we're filling the type with an image.

4 enter text
Images don't discriminate between point text and paragraph text, so click or drag in the image window

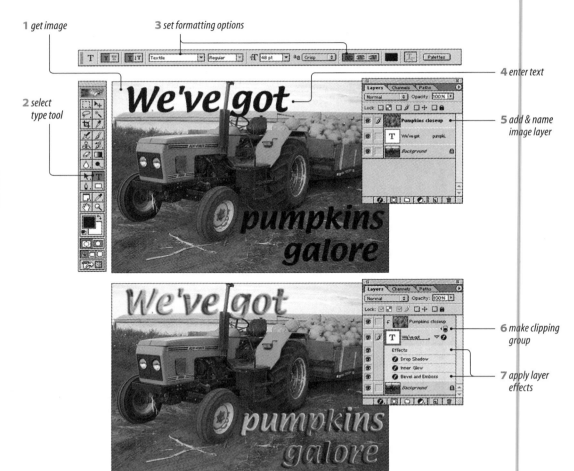

1 *get image*

3 *set formatting options*

4 *enter text*

2 *select type tool*

5 *add & name image layer*

6 *make clipping group*

7 *apply layer effects*

and type your text. Press **ctrl+enter** (Win) or **command-return** (Mac) when you're done.

5 add & name image layer

Bring to the front the image you want to fill the type—in my case, a bunch of pumpkins. Press **ctrl+A** (Win) or **command-A** (Mac) to select the image, and then cut and paste it or drag it with the move tool into the main image window. Press **alt** (**option** on the Mac) and double-click the layer in the **Layers** palette to give it a name.

6 make clipping group

The lowest layer in a clipping group masks the layers above (see Use One Layer To Clip Another on page 134), so make sure the image layer is above the type layer. Then **alt**-click (**option**-click on the Mac) the horizontal line between the two layers. Alternatively, you can select the image layer and choose **Layer ➡ Group with Previou**s or press **ctrl+G** (**command-G** on the Mac). In any case, Photoshop clips the image layer to fit inside the type.

tip The type remains fully editable, so you can change it at any time. If you want to replace the image inside the type, select the image layer or type layer and press **ctrl+shift+G** (Win) or **command-shift-G** (Mac) to ungroup the two. Then add a new image layer and group it with the type (6).

7 apply layer effects (optional)

You can enhance your filled type by applying layer effects if you like. Simply double-click the type layer and select one or more effects from the **Layer Style** dialog box. For example, I gave my pumpkin type a 3-D look by applying the **Drop Shadow**, **Inner Glow**, and **Bevel Emboss** effects. Read Type & Layer Styles below for more information.

tip You may want to experiment with adjusting the **Blend Mode** and **Opacity** settings as well. Keep in mind, the opacity of the clipper—in this case, the type layer—defines the opacity of the entire clipping group.

Type & Layer Styles

Photoshop's layer styles are exceedingly flexible and a breeze to use. And lucky for us all, they're applicable to editable vector text. The figure at right shows just a few examples of how you can employ layer effects to expand your type repertoire.

A friendly

To create this effect, I set the text against a lavendar background. Then I loaded the **Text Effects.asp** file in the **Styles** palette and applied the **Candy** preset to the text. That's all there was to it.

B emboss

Here, I started by choosing **Edit ➡ Fill** and loading the **Patterns 2.pat** file from the **Custom Pattern**

palette menu. Then I filled the background with the **Carpet** preset. Next, I created the text and applied **Layer ➡ Layer Style ➡ Bevel and Emboss**. Finally, I committed the text layer and reduced the **Opacity** value to 50%.

C mystery

To produce this ominous text effect, I began by creating some white type on a black background. Then I double-clicked the text layer in the **Layers** palette to bring up the **Layer Style** dialog box. From there, I created a linear gradient overlay at 80% **Opacity** and applied an outer bevel at a 120-degree angle. To complete the effect, I added an **Inner Shadow** set to black and **Multiply**.

steps **Rasterize & Filter Type**

Some of Photoshop's features are applicable only to pixels, such as the paint and edit tools and the commands under the **Filter** menu. In order to put these pixel-based features to work on type, you first need to convert your vector text to bitmapped type using a process called *rasterizing*. The following steps present a typical scenario:

1 get image
Any image will do. I started with a stucco pattern background image.

2 enter & prepare text
Create and format your text as usual. Throw in a layer effect or two if the mood strikes you. For my part, I used the **Layer Style** dialog box to apply pillow emboss and white stroke effects. After reducing the opacity and scaling the text slightly, I used the **Warp Text** command to make my text undulate.

3 rasterize type
Make sure the text layer is selected in the **Layers** palette and choose **Layer⟶Rasterize⟶Type**. Photoshop unceremoniously converts the text to pixels.

> *tip* The downside to rasterizing type is that you can no longer edit it, so it's a good idea to save a copy of your vector text to a separate layer before making the journey to pixels.

4 apply emboss filter
I wanted to highlight my type's edges and strip away the translucent white fill to fully reveal the gray background. This is a perfect job for the **Emboss** filter, so I chose **Filter⟶Stylize⟶Emboss**.

5 apply motion blur filter
To enhance the motion effect, I generated a soft blur using **Filter⟶Blur⟶Motion Blur**.

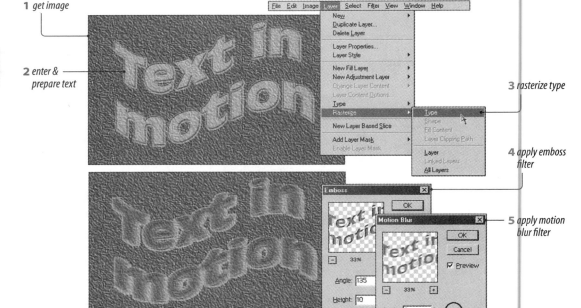

1 *get image*

2 *enter & prepare text*

3 *rasterize type*

4 *apply emboss filter*

5 *apply motion blur filter*

chapter 13

Adjust & Correct Colors

Some of the most common problems with an image revolve around color. A photo might appear dim, shot under insufficient light. It might look faded, with little contrast between lights and darks. Or a few specific colors might be out of whack. A sky might look too purple; a face might look too green.

Photoshop is a whiz at fixing colors. It permits you to rescue photographs that look beyond repair and bring to life colors you never knew were there. In imaging circles, this is called *color correction*.

You can find Photoshop's color correction commands under the **Image➡Adjust** submenu. Most of these commands are great (**Variations**, **Levels**), but a few provide vague or insufficient control (**Color Balance**, **Brightness/Contrast**). Naturally, I want you working at top form, so I'll show you the great commands and leave the vague ones to another book.

The Variations Command

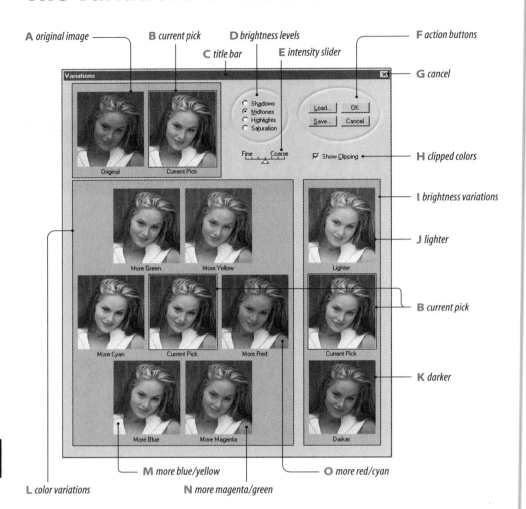

A *original image* — **B** *current pick* — **D** *brightness levels*
C *title bar* — **E** *intensity slider*
F *action buttons*
G *cancel*
H *clipped colors*
I *brightness variations*
J *lighter*
B *current pick*
K *darker*
O *more red/cyan*
M *more blue/yellow*
N *more magenta/green*
L *color variations*

Choose **Image➡Adjust➡Variations** to display the **Variations** dialog box. Designed to remove a prevalent color (called a *color cast*) and tweak the brightness of an image, **Variations** may be Photoshop's most straightforward color adjuster. Rather than previewing your corrections in the image window, as other commands do, **Variations** presents you with a collection of thumbnail previews. Your job is to click the thumbnail that looks better than the one labeled **Current Pick** (B). You can click as many thumbnails as you like and in any order.

A original image

The first thumbnail shows the image as it appeared before you chose **Variations**. To restore the image to the way it looked before you started messing with it, click this thumbnail at any time.

B current pick

This thumbnail is the one to watch. It shows how the image will look when you click **OK**. It appears in three places so you can make side-by-side comparisons with other thumbnails. Like the others, you can click it, but it won't change the image one iota.

C title bar

Drag the title bar to move the **Variations** dialog box and get a better view of the image. You can't preview **Variations** effects in the image window, but you may find it helpful to see the image at full size.

D brightness levels

Use these radio buttons to specify the range of *brightness levels* (lights and darks) that you want to modify. By default, **Midtones** is selected. This tells Photoshop to adjust only the medium colors, those between the extremes of black and white. (**Midtones** serves a similar function to *gamma*, which I explain at length in The Levels Command on pages 194 through 196.) This permits you to correct the general appearance of an image without over-lightening highlights or over-darkening shadows.

To adjust the darkest colors, select the **Shadows** option. This leaves the medium and light levels unchanged. Select **Highlights** to adjust the lightest colors independently of the medium and dark levels.

The **Saturation** option works differently than the other three. Rather than changing brightness levels, it changes the *saturation*, which is the intensity of the colors. When you select **Saturation**, Photoshop replaces the thumbnails in the central portion of the dialog box with the ones below. Click the **More Saturation** thumbnail to make the colors appear more vivid. Click **Less Saturation** to leech away the colors and make them more gray.

If the **Saturation** option doesn't deliver the effect you're looking for, try the **Hue/Saturation** command (The Hue/Saturation Command, pages 190 and 191), which provides more intuitive controls and lets you preview adjustments in the image window.

E intensity slider

This slider bar controls the force of **Variation**'s color adjustments. Move the triangle toward **Fine** to make more delicate adjustments; move it toward **Coarse** to increase the strength. The thumbnails update to reflect the new setting. By default, the triangle is set midway between **Fine** and **Coarse**, but you'll probably achieve better results by moving it one or two notches closer to **Fine**.

F action buttons

In addition to the usual **Cancel** and **OK** buttons, the **Variations** dialog box offers **Load** and **Save**. Click **Save** to save the current settings so you can apply them again and again to future images. Click **Load** to reapply settings that you've saved in the past.

G cancel (Windows)

Available to Windows users only, the close button lets you close the dialog box and cancel the operation. Mac users needn't worry—you can do the same thing by clicking **Cancel** or pressing the **esc** key.

H clipped colors

As you adjust colors—especially when using the **More Saturation** thumbnail (D)—some colors may become unprintable. That is to say, they move outside of the CMYK gamut. These colors get cut off, and are said to be *clipped*. When the **Show Clipping** check box is active, Photoshop shows the clipped colors inverted, as below.

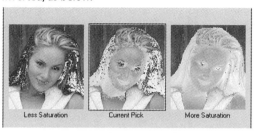

tip If you hope to print an image, avoid clipping as much as possible. But when creating an RGB image for the Web, don't worry about it. Turn off **Show Clipping** to view the colors normally.

I brightness variations

Use the thumbnails along the right side of the dialog box to make the image lighter or darker. These options are available only when **Shadows**, **Midtones**, or **Highlights** is active (D); they are hidden when **Saturation** is active.

J lighter

Click this thumbnail to make the image lighter, according to the active brightness level setting (D). If the **Midtones** radio button is active, clicking the **Lighter** thumbnail makes the medium colors lighter. To lighten the darkest colors, select **Shadows** and click **Lighter**.

> **tip** Technically, you can lighten highlights as well by selecting **Highlights** and clicking **Lighter**. But you'll rarely want to do this because you run the risk of blasting away light colors, making them white. Called *blown highlights*, these white patches are to be avoided at all costs.

K darker

Click this thumbnail to make the image darker. Select **Midtones** to darken the medium colors; select **Highlights** to darken the lightest colors. Again, you can select the **Shadows** radio button to darken shadows, but more likely than not, you'll end up making large groups of pixels black.

L color variations

When the **Shadows**, **Midtones**, or **Highlights** radio button is active (D), the central portion of the dialog box contains a total of seven thumbnails, with six color variations grouped around the **Current Pick** thumbnail. Each color variation thumbnail nudges the image toward a range of hues. Think of the colors in the rainbow wrapped into a full circle and then cut into six slices. So the **More Yellow** thumbnail represents not simply yellow, but a whole range of colors—orange, chartreuse, and so on—that have yellow at their center.

M more blue/yellow

Thumbnails that are arranged across from each other represent *complementary* colors, which means they mix to form white light. For example, **More Blue** appears on the other side of the **Current Pick** thumbnail from **More Yellow**, therefore blue and yellow

are complementary. Not only does this mean that blue and yellow light mix to form white, but it also means blue and yellow are opposites. So clicking **More Yellow** both adds yellow and subtracts blue.

The upshot is that you can use a color variation thumbnail to remove a color cast. If an image has a yellow cast, for example, click **More Blue**. Furthermore, one thumbnail undoes the effect of the other. If you click **More Yellow** and change your mind, click **More Blue** to undo it.

N more magenta/green

Magenta and green are complementary colors. So clicking the **More Magenta** thumbnail adds magenta (a bright, pinkish purple) and subtracts green; clicking **More Green** adds green and subtracts magenta.

O more red/cyan

The final pair of complementary color variation thumbnails is **More Red** and **More Cyan**. The **More Red** thumbnail adds red and subtracts cyan (a bright turquoise); **More Cyan** adds cyan and subtracts red.

Notice that these color pairs emulate the screen and print models. **More Red**, **More Green**, and **More Blue** (RGB) are paired opposite **More Cyan**, **More Magenta**, and **More Yellow** (CMY). In a perfect world, RGB and CMY are direct opposites. Because our world isn't perfect, black ink is required to balance out CMY.

ᴳᵗᵉᵖˢ Fix A Color Cast

The **Variations** dialog box is a one-stop color correction laboratory. It lets you shift whole ranges of colors as well as make changes to brightness and saturation levels. And to sweeten the deal, the thumbnail-based interface is highly intuitive. Here's a typical use for **Variations**:

1 get image

Open an image with a prominent color cast. A vintage photograph might look yellowed; a digital snapshot might appear unusually blue. You can even modify a photograph shot through a colored lens.

2 choose variations

Choose **Image→Adjust→Variations** to display the **Variations** dialog box. Windows users can choose the command from the keyboard by pressing the following sequence of keys: **alt+I, A, ↑, enter**.

3 click original (optional)

The **Variations** dialog box remembers the last correction you applied. You can work from that point if you like, but I generally prefer to clear the old correction and start from scratch. Clicking the **Original** thumbnail does exactly that.

1 *get image*

2 *choose variations*

3 *click original*

or *alt-click (option-click) reset*

4 select midtones

Select the radio button that represents the range of brightness levels you want to edit. For most jobs, **Midtones** is the only option you'll need. But even if you decide to edit shadows, highlights, or saturation levels, **Midtones** is a good place to start. You can visit the other options later (9 & 10).

5 set intensity

Set the intensity slider as desired. I generally like to nudge the slider triangle one or two notches toward **Fine**. But don't worry about getting it exactly right. You can adjust the slider as many times as you like as you work in the **Variations** dialog box.

6 set clipping

Personally, I turn **Show Clipping** off. But feel free to turn it on and off according to your needs.

7 adjust colors

Use the color variation thumbnails to change the balance of colors in the image. Keep an eye on the **Current Pick** thumbnail to judge the effects of your adjustments. Remember that opposite thumbnails undo each other, subject to the intensity slider setting. For example, you can click **More Red** at a **Coarse** intensity, and then back off the effect slightly by clicking **More Green** at a **Fine** intensity.

8 adjust brightness

Click the **Lighter** and **Darker** thumbnails to adjust the brightness of the medium colors in the image. Like opposite color variation thumbnails, **Lighter** and **Darker** are direct opposites. So clicking one undoes the effects of the other.

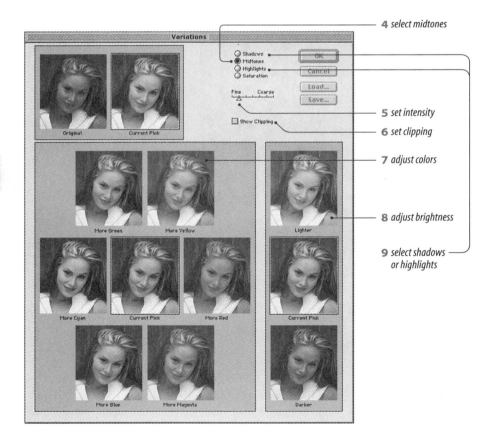

9 select shadows or highlights

Once you've had your fill of adjusting the medium brightness levels in the image, you may want to make a pass at the shadows and highlights. Select the **Shadows** or **Highlights** radio button and then click the desired color variation thumbnails. Bear in mind that you can switch between **Midtones**, **Shadows**, and **Highlights** as many times as you like.

10 select saturation (optional)

If the colors in the image are too vivid—or not vivid enough—select the **Saturation** radio button. The color variation and brightness thumbnails disappear, replaced by the **More Saturation** and **Less Saturation** thumbnails.

11 adjust saturation (optional)

Click the **More Saturation** thumbnail to make the colors in the image more vivid; click **Less Saturation** to make the colors less vivid.

Remember, **More** and **Less Saturation** are opposites, so one undoes the other. You can move the intensity slider triangle (5) to control the force of your adjustments. Finally, turn on **Show Clipping** (6) to see which colors won't translate to CMYK.

12 click save (optional)

If you want to repeat this effect on another image, click the **Save** button. Photoshop asks you to name the file and specify a location.

> 𝑡𝑖𝑝 To transfer this file from a Mac to a PC, type the extension **.ava** at the end of the filename.

13 click OK

Or press **enter** (Win) or **return** (Mac) to apply the **Current Pick** effect (B) to your image. If the result isn't what you had hoped, choose **Edit➥Undo** and again choose **Variations**. This gives you access to the most recent effect so you can tweak it to your satisfaction.

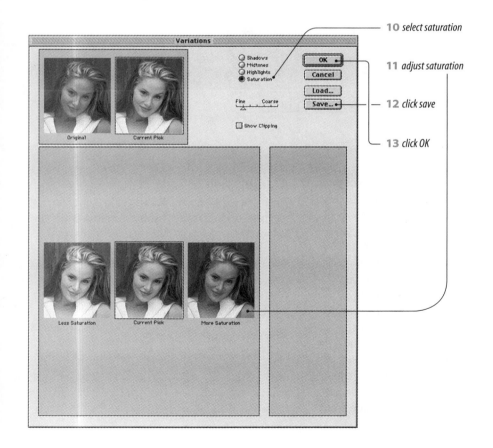

10 *select saturation*

11 *adjust saturation*

12 *click save*

13 *click OK*

The Hue/Saturation Command

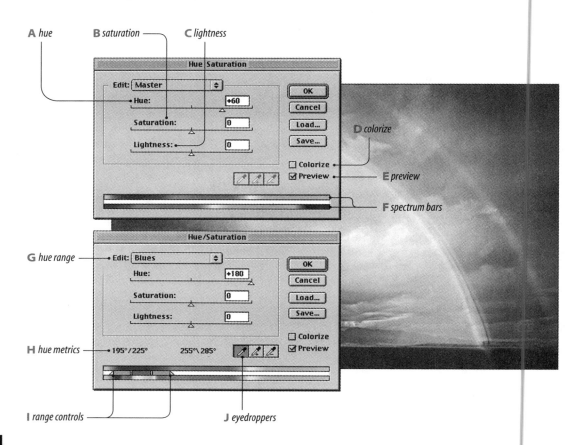

A *hue*   **B** *saturation*   **C** *lightness*

D *colorize*

E *preview*

F *spectrum bars*

G *hue range*

H *hue metrics* — 195°/225°   255°\285°

I *range controls*

J *eyedroppers*

Choose **Image➞Adjust➞Hue/Saturation** or press ctrl+U (Win) or command-U (Mac) to display the **Hue/Saturation** dialog box. While it looks very different than the **Variations** dialog box, both serve a similar purpose: to edit ranges of colors. But where **Variations** lets you focus your attention on specific brightness levels in an image using **Midtones**, **Shadows**, and **Highlights** (as in The Variations Command, page 185), **Hue/Saturation** is sensitive to variations in *hue*. Based on the notion of the *HSL color model* (short for hue, saturation, and lightness), hue is the core ingredient of a color, the quality that distinguishes red from yellow, yellow from green, and so on. Meanwhile, *saturation* is the intensity of a color and *lightness* is the shade, from light to dark. Here's how the options work.

A hue

When you see a rainbow, you're seeing the visible spectrum of hues, starting with red, then orange, yellow, green, and so on. Although the childhood *Roy G. Biv* mnemonic doesn't tell you so, the inner ring of the rainbow is identical in color to the outer ring. What you have, then, is a continuous circle of color. When the **Colorize** check box (D) is off, as by default, the **Hue** value rotates selected colors from –180° to

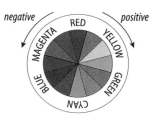

180° (or 360 degrees in all). The figure on left shows how the colors rotate, with each named color indicating a 60-degree shift.

B saturation

Use the **Saturation** slider to make colors more or less vivid. A value of +100% saturates colors to their absolute maximum; –100% leeches away the color, leaving the selection or layer gray.

If you want to make *all* layers in the image gray, choose **Image➧Mode➧Grayscale**. Photoshop throws away all but one channel, making the image much smaller. Note that this locks you into gray; before you can add color, you have to choose **Image➧Mode➧RGB Color**.

C lightness

This slider changes the brightness of colors in an image relative to their current brightness levels. A positive value lightens the darkest colors in the image without affecting white. A negative value darkens the lightest colors without affecting black. Because the **Lightness** slider is prevented from blowing away highlights and shadows, it's a great way to create faded or dimmed background images.

D colorize

Select this check box to *colorize* a selection or layer. This locks all pixels into a single hue and saturation value. A **Hue** of 0% is red, 30% is orange, and so on.

E preview

Hue/Saturation lacks the handy thumbnail previews offered by the **Variations** command. But you won't miss them. Just turn on the **Preview** check box to have Photoshop apply your changes dynamically inside the image window.

F spectrum bars

The top color bar shows the entire visible color spectrum, starting and ending with cyan, the color located at both –180° and 180° on the color wheel. The bottom bar previews what happens to these colors when the current **Hue**, **Saturation**, and **Lightness** values are applied. These *spectrum bars* are most useful when editing specific hue ranges (G).

G hue range

By default, the **Hue/Saturation** command modifies all colors in the selection or layer. However, you can

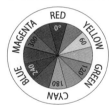

isolate a specific range of colors by choosing an option from the **Edit** pop-up menu. Each of the six options represents a 60-degree wedge from the full color wheel, as illustrated on left.

H hue metrics

The numbers tell the positions on the color wheel where the selected hue range begins and ends. These are gradual ranges. For example, the default metrics for **Reds** are 315°/345° and 15°\45°. This means the range extends 30 degrees from **345°** to **15°**. It then tapers an additional 30 degrees in either direction, thus assuring soft transitions.

I range controls

Photoshop's predefined ranges are merely jumping off points. You can modify the metrics to better suit your needs by dragging these controls. Read Recolor An Image Element on pages 192 and 193 to learn how.

J eyedroppers

Don't like metrics? Don't use them. Armed with the eyedropper, click outside the dialog box to lift a range of colors directly from the image.

⬤steps Recolor An Image Element

The **Hue/Saturation** command is best suited to recoloring specific elements in an image. It's a favorite for changing the color of clothing in mail-order catalogs. Take a picture of one sweater and then print the sweater in all five of this season's designer colors. Meanwhile, other colors—like the skin color of the guy who's wearing the sweater—remain unharmed. No masking required.

1 get image
Open an image that contains a color than needs changing. I selected a snapshot of a woman eating French fries. Everything about the photo is fine except for her dress. The camera rendered the fabric as creamy orange when it's really a bright yellow.

2 choose hue/saturation
Press **ctrl+U** (**command-U** on the Mac) to display the **Hue/Saturation** dialog box.

3 choose hue range
If you immediately start fiddling with the slider bars, you'll end up changing all colors in the image. In my case, making the dress yellower would also make the woman's skin yellower. To isolate the hue you want to change, choose its nearest equivalent from the **Edit** pop-up menu. The closest hue to orange is **Yellow**.

4 adjust hue
Tweak the **Hue** option to correct the colors in the image. Most folks have difficulty predicting hue shifts, so your best bet is to eyeball it. Press **shift-↑** and **shift-↓** to raise and lower the **Hue** value in rough increments and get a sense of where you need to go. Then press ↑ or ↓ to get the color just right.

5 adjust saturation
Some hue shifts have a tendency to exaggerate the color; others mute it. Use **Saturation** to compensate.

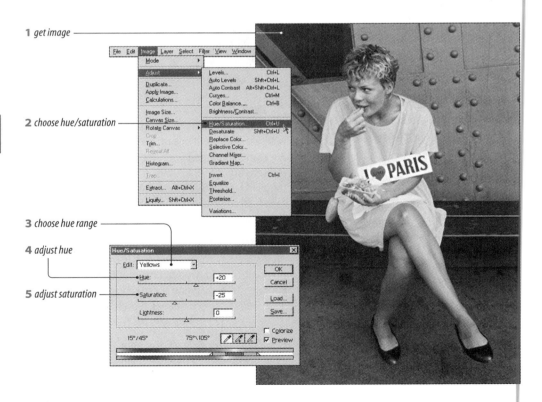

6 click with eyedropper

After setting the **Hue** and **Saturation**, you may be able to see a few problems with your hue range (3). Some colors that you meant to change aren't changing; others that you didn't, are. With eyedropper in hand (it's selected by default), click the image element that you want to modify. This defines the base color for the hue shift. To add colors, press **shift** and drag across them. If colors change contrary to your wishes, press **alt** and drag over them to protect them.

7 adjust range controls

The range controls identify the portion of the color spectrum that's open to modification. If the eyedropper doesn't quite do the trick for you, drag the triangles, the vertical bars, or even the gray areas to manually expand or contract the range. I used these items to better protect the skin tones. Some of the blonde hair continues to react, but c'est la vie.

8 adjust other ranges (optional)

Need to change another range of colors? Choose the closest equivalent from the **Edit** pop-up menu and repeat the process (4 through 7). Photoshop tracks each set of color transformations separately.

9 click save (optional)

To transfer the settings from Mac to PC, add .ahu.

10 click OK

Or press **enter** (Win) or **return** (Mac) to apply the previewed color changes to your image.

11 fade hue/saturation (optional)

After applying a hue shift, you can back it off slightly by choosing **Edit➡Fade Hue/Saturation**.

> *tip* To repeat the last applied **Hue/Saturation** settings on another image, press **ctrl+alt+U** (Win) or **command-option-U** (Mac).

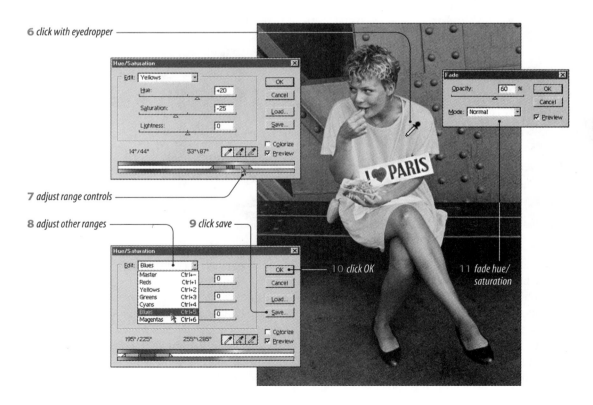

6 *click with eyedropper*

7 *adjust range controls*

8 *adjust other ranges*   9 *click save*

10 *click OK*   11 *fade hue/ saturation*

The Levels Command

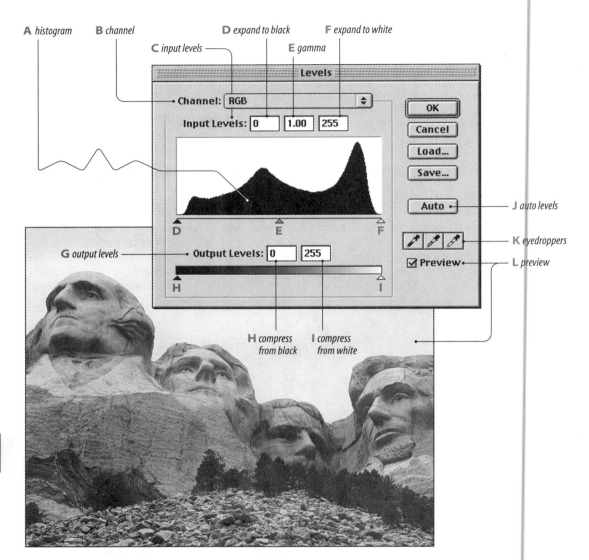

A *histogram* **B** *channel* **D** *expand to black* **F** *expand to white*

C *input levels* **E** *gamma*

G *output levels*

H *compress from black* **I** *compress from white*

J *auto levels*

K *eyedroppers*

L *preview*

The purpose of **Image➟Adjust➟Levels** is to correct the brightness and contrast of an image. Although similar in function to **Image➟Adjust➟Brightness/Contrast**, I much prefer **Levels** because it's more precise, more capable, and more accurate. Notice that I didn't say **Levels** was harder to use. Admittedly, the **Levels** dialog box offers more options than **Brightness/Contrast**, but you

can use as many or as few of those options as you like. And most of the options make your life easier, not harder. You can correct most images using nothing more than the three **Input Levels** values (C). Click the **Auto** button (J) or click in the image window with an eyedropper tool (K) to make Photoshop do some of the work. Plus you have a histogram (A) to measure your corrections. As if to hammer the point home, Photoshop blesses the **Levels** command with a keyboard shortcut: ctrl+L (Win) or **command-L** (Mac). Meanwhile, **Brightness/Contrast** has none. All in all, it's hard to imagine a more utilitarian or elegantly designed command than **Levels**.

A histogram

Whether you're editing an RGB, CMYK, or grayscale image, every channel contains 256 brightness levels, measured from 0 for black to 255 for white (see The Color Palette, pages 80 through 82). The *histogram* is a bar graph that shows how those colors are distributed. If you were to measure it, you would discover it to be exactly 256 pixels wide—that's a one pixel-wide bar for each brightness level. The first bar shows the number of black pixels, the next bar shows the number of slightly lighter pixels, and so on, all the way to white at the opposite end. The histogram isn't an option—you don't click or drag on it. Photoshop offers it as a different way of looking at the image. Read Adjust Brightness Using Levels on pages 197 through 199 to get a sense of how it might be useful.

B channel

You may wonder why the histogram shows 256 brightness levels when an image contains several million colors. The reason is that the **Levels** command adjusts colors one channel at a time. You can select the specific channel that you want to edit from the **Channel** pop-up menu. Or set **Channel** to the composite view—**RGB** or **CMYK**—to adjust the contents of each channel by the same amount. When editing a grayscale image, you have just one channel, so the **Channel** option is set permanently to **Gray**.

> *tip* To switch from one channel to another, press **ctrl** (**command** on the Mac) and a number key. For example, **ctrl+1** switches to **Red** when editing an RGB image or **Cyan** when working in CMYK.

C input levels

These three values and the corresponding slider triangles beneath the histogram (D through F) increase the contrast in an image by expanding the range of colors. You can send dark colors to black (D), light colors to white (F), and vary the brightness of medium gray (E).

D expand to black

This value tells Photoshop which brightness levels to make black. If you raise the value to **60**, as in the example below, all brightness values of 60 and darker turn black. Photoshop expands the brightness values from 61 to 254 to fill in the gaps.

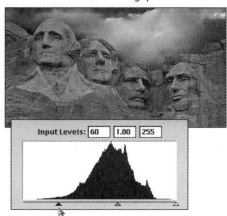

If you're not a big fan of numbers, drag the black slider triangle located under the histogram.

> *tip* You can adjust this and other brightness level values (F, H, & I) incrementally by pressing arrow keys. Press ↑ or ↓ to raise or lower the value by 1; press shift-↑ or shift-↓ to raise or lower it by 10.

E gamma

The middle **Input Levels** value is called the *gamma*. The value itself is based on a mathematical formula in which the brightness values are raised to an exponential power. By default, the value is **1.0**—any number raised to 1 equals itself, so no change occurs. Increase the value, however, and the medium colors grow lighter; decrease the gamma, and the medium colors grow darker. Black and white remain unchanged.

Measured in brightness levels, medium gray is 128, or 50% ink coverage. Below, I raised the gamma value to 1.5, which lightens it to 160, or about 63% ink. By lightening the image, I've expanded the dark pixels in the image and compressed the light pixels.

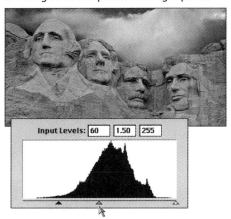

Drag the gray slider triangle to peg the point in the histogram that you want to make the new medium gray. This means you drag to the left to raise the gamma and to the right to lower the gamma.

> *tip* The arrows work a bit differently with gamma. Press ↑ or ↓ to nudge the value by **0.01**; press shift-↑ or shift-↓ to raise or lower it by **0.1**.

F expand to white

The third and final **Input Levels** value tells Photoshop which brightness levels to make white. By default, the value is 255, which makes only the very lightest pixels in each channel white. In the image at the top of the next column, I changed this value to 215, so that all brightness values of 215 and lighter turned white. Without disturbing the black pixels, Photoshop expanded the brightness values from 1 to 214 to fill in the gaps.

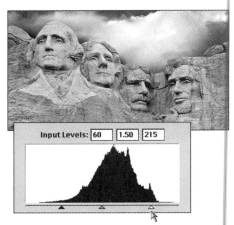

You can also expand colors to white by dragging the white slider triangle. The portion of the histogram to the right of the triangle turns white.

G output levels

After specifying which brightness levels expand to black and white, you can tweak the brightness of the darkest (H) and lightest (I) pixels.

H compress from black

Raise this value or drag the black triangle at the bottom of the dialog box to lighten the darkest colors in the image. For example, if you change the value to 128, you lighten the blackest pixels to medium gray.

I compress from white

Use this value to darken the lightest pixels in the image. This option is useful for softening highlights, as I show in the steps that begin on the facing page.

J auto levels

Click **Auto** to automatically set the black (D) and white (F) points in each of the color channels. It's the same as choosing **Image➡Adjust➡Auto Levels**.

K eyedroppers

Select an eyedropper and click in the image to set an **Input Levels** value to the brightness of the clicked pixel. As a result, the black eyedropper changes the clicked pixel to black, the white eyedropper changes it to white. The gray eyedropper is the exception. It neutralizes a pixel, removing its saturation.

L preview

Turn on the **Preview** check box to view your changes in the image window.

steps Adjust Brightness Using Levels

In the following steps, we'll look at how to correct a typical RGB image using the **Levels** command. A few of the steps work exclusively with color images. But don't worry—you can easily extrapolate the information to work with grayscale images as well.

1 get image
Open a photo that disappoints you, one you thought was going to be great but turned out drab and life-less. I selected a snapshot of a tree growing out of sheer sandstone. Sure, it's a bit flat, but just wait.

2 choose levels
Or press ctrl+L (**command**-L on the Mac) to display the **Levels** dialog box.

3 click auto
Click the **Auto** button to automatically map the dark-est colors to black and the lightest colors to white. As shown by the before and after views below, this stretches the histogram, creating gaps between the bars in the graph. Yet the **Input Levels** values don't change at all. This is because Photoshop has adjusted the brightness levels independently in each channel, as you'll see in future steps (5 through 8).

4 click with gray eyedropper
Clicking **Auto** can upset the balance of colors in an image. To correct the colors, select the gray eye-dropper tool—available only when editing a color image—and click an area that should be gray.

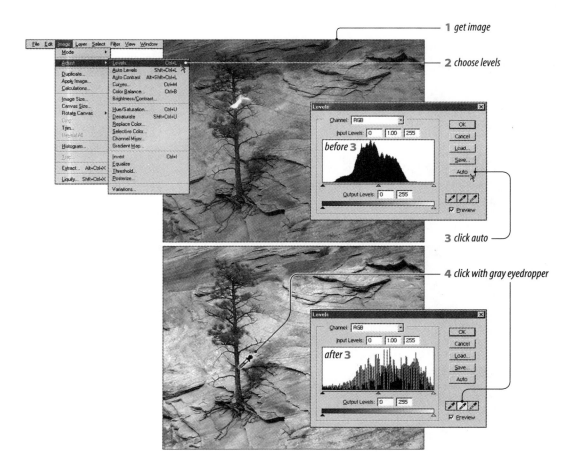

1 *get image*

2 *choose levels*

3 *click auto*

4 *click with gray eyedropper*

For my part, I clicked the tree trunk. This made the trunk gray; however, it did not change the highlights or shadows. The only way to make the grays lighter or darker is to adjust the gamma manually (7).

5 switch to red channel

Now it's time to see what the **Auto** button (3) and gray eyedropper (4) have done. Press **ctrl+1** (Win) or **command-1** (Mac) to view changes made to the red channel. Instead of seeing a stretched histogram with gaps between the bars, the histogram is relatively smooth. Better yet, the **Input Levels** values reflect the changes made thus far. It's here in the independent channels that Photoshop shows you its work.

tip If you don't like what you see, press **alt** (Win) or **option** (Mac) and click **Reset** to restore the original brightness levels. Then adjust the settings manually in the remaining steps.

6 tweak black & white

By default, the **Auto** button sends ½ percent of the darkest and lightest pixels to black and white. You can change this by pressing **alt** (Win) or **option** (Mac) and clicking **Auto**. But because every image is different, you're better off tweaking the black and white settings manually to get exactly the effect you want.

7 adjust gamma

The **Levels** command is a *non-linear* color editor. This means you can modify medium colors independently of the lightest and darkest shades. Raise the gamma value to emphasize the reds in the image; lower the gamma to downplay reds in favor of greens and blues. Don't worry if the colors drift a little; you can fix any ephemeral casts from the other channels (8).

8 fix green & blue channels

Press **ctrl+2** and **ctrl+3** to switch to the green and blue channels. Then adjust the blacks, whites, and

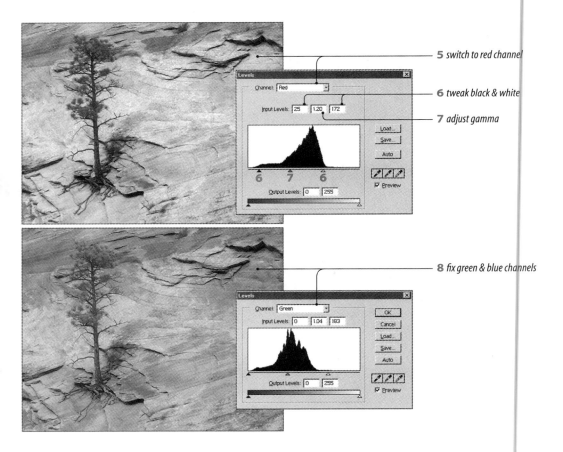

5 *switch to red channel*

6 *tweak black & white*

7 *adjust gamma*

8 *fix green & blue channels*

gammas (6 & 7). With experience, you'll learn how the adjustments interact. For example, raising the gamma in both the red and green channels emphasizes yellow; raising the gamma in both the red and blue channels brings out magenta.

9 return to composite

When the brightness of the image appears more or less balanced, press **ctrl+tilde (~)** to return to the composite view. On the Mac, press **command-tilde**. Or choose **RGB** from the **Channel** pop-up menu.

10 set output levels (optional)

Colors can drop off quickly when an image is printed. A typical commercial press has a hard time holding ink densities higher than, say, 98% or lower than 3%. Any darker, the printed image goes black; any lighter, it goes white. Fortunately, you can use the **Output Levels** values to compensate. I've nudged the black value up to **2** and the white down to **252** to slightly compress the brightness range and give the darkest and lightest colors a better chance of printing.

tip You can also set output levels using the eyedroppers. Double-click an eyedropper tool icon to specify an alternative color for black or white, or to add some color to gray. Then click with the tool in the image window to see the effect.

Note that the eyedropper output levels also affect the **Auto** button and the **Auto Levels** command.

11 click save (optional)

If you think you might want to apply these same **Levels** settings to other images, go ahead and save the settings. Mac users should be sure to append the extension **.alv** to the end of the filename.

12 click OK

Or press **enter** (Win) or **return** (Mac) to apply the current **Input Levels** and **Output Levels** settings to the various color channels in your image.

13 fade levels (optional)

As always, you can incrementally undo the **Levels** command by choosing **Edit➡Fade Levels** or pressing **ctrl+shift+F** (command-shift-F on the Mac)

tip To display the **Levels** dialog box complete with the settings you last applied, press **ctrl+alt+L** (Win) or **command-option-L** (Mac). This is especially useful for adjusting settings that you decided to reverse using **Edit➡Undo**.

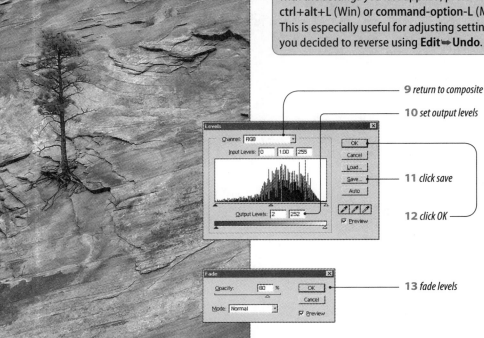

9 *return to composite*
10 *set output levels*
11 *click save*
12 *click OK*
13 *fade levels*

The Curves Command

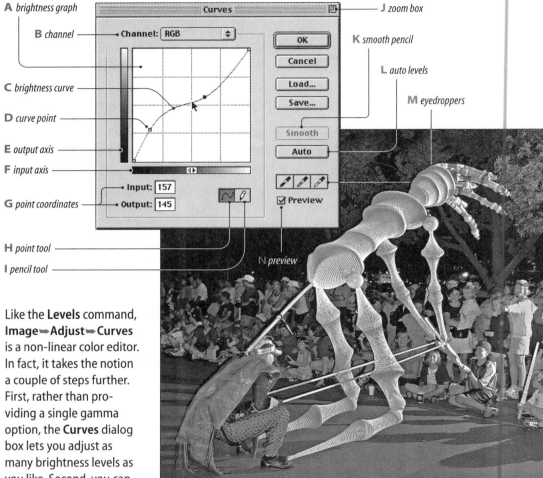

A *brightness graph*
B *channel*
C *brightness curve*
D *curve point*
E *output axis*
F *input axis*
G *point coordinates*
H *point tool*
I *pencil tool*
J *zoom box*
K *smooth pencil*
L *auto levels*
M *eyedroppers*
N *preview*

Curves
Channel: RGB
OK
Cancel
Load...
Save...
Smooth
Auto
Input: 157
Output: 145
☑ Preview

Like the **Levels** command, **Image⇒Adjust⇒Curves** is a non-linear color editor. In fact, it takes the notion a couple of steps further. First, rather than providing a single gamma option, the **Curves** dialog box lets you adjust as many brightness levels as you like. Second, you can set levels absolutely by entering specific brightness levels. Contrast this to the gamma value, which is a relative adjustment. To conserve space on screen, **Curves** sacrifices the histogram. But as with **Levels**, you get a keyboard shortcut—ctrl+M (Win) or **command-M** (Mac)—and you can preview your adjustments in the image window.

A brightness graph

The main element of the **Curves** dialog box is the brightness graph, in which you plot points along a

line (C) that represents all the brightness values in the image. You add and adjust points along this line to make colors lighter and darker.

B channel

As with the **Levels** command, **Curves** attacks an image one channel at a time. You can modify all channels by the same amount or address channels individually. To modify the brightness and contrast of one channel independently of others, as when balancing colors, choose the channel from this pop-up menu.

C brightness curve

The *brightness curve* begins as a straight line between the bottom-left and top-right corners of the graph. If you're working with an RGB image, the curve adds brightness, so higher values mean lighter colors. Thus, the bottom corner is black and the top corner is white. In CMYK, the curve adds ink, so higher values mean darker colors. The bottom corner is white and the top corner black. Note that you can reverse this (F).

D curve point

Click anywhere along the curve to add a point. If white is up (as in an RGB image), drag the point upward to lighten the colors in the image. If black is up (as in CMYK), drag the point downward to lighten colors. Continue clicking the curve to add more points. To remove a point, click it and press **backspace** (Win) or **delete** (Mac). Or just drag the point off the graph.

E output axis

The graph (A) maps the existing colors in the image (or *input levels*) to new colors (*output levels*). The vertical axis of the graph tracks the output levels. The gradation inside the vertical bar shows the orientation of your edits—if white is up, for example, raising a point makes it lighter.

F input axis

The horizontal axis of the graph plots the input levels. Drag a point from side to side to change which brightness level in the image gets changed to another level.

> *tip* As with the output axis, a gradation shows whether the graph measures brightness levels or ink densities. To switch between them, click the horizontal bar. I prefer to edit brightness levels, so I always keep white on the right, even in CMYK.

G point coordinates

The **Input** and **Output** values show the coordinates of the selected point in the graph. **Input** tells the brightness of the color as it is; **Output** tells the brightness it will be when you click **OK**. The values are measured as brightness levels (0 to 255) or ink densities (0% to 100%) based on the direction of the input axis (F).

H point tool

Photoshop lets you edit the curve (C) in one of two ways, depending on the active tool. By default, the point tool is active, which permits you to add and adjust points along the curve. Points are precise, but they have a habit of flexing the curve in ways that might not always suit your needs.

I pencil tool

To smooth out a hump in the curve, select the pencil tool and draw directly inside the graph.

> *tip* To draw a straight line with the pencil tool, click to set a point, and then press **shift** and click to set another. Then soften the corners by clicking the **Smooth** button (K).

J zoom box (Mac)/maximize (Win)

The Mac version of the **Curves** dialog box includes a zoom box. Click the box to enlarge the graph and make more detailed changes; click again to reduce the graph. On the PC, click the maximize button to enlarge the graph; click minimize to reduce it.

K smooth pencil

Click this button to smooth off the rough edges in a curve drawn with the pencil tool (I). If one click doesn't do the trick, click **Smooth** again. The button is available only when the pencil tool is active.

L auto levels

Click this button to set the darkest colors in the image to black and the lightest color to white, as when you choose **Image➡Adjust➡Auto Levels**. Visit the individual channels (B) to view and modify the curves.

M eyedroppers

Click in the image with the black or white eyedropper to make the clicked pixel either black or white. Click with the gray eyedropper to neutralize the pixel. Use the **Channel** pop-up menu (B) to see the changes.

N preview

You can lower the quality of the preview by selecting **Use Pixel Doubling** in the **Preferences** dialog box (see Preferences, Saving & Display, **pages 54 and 55**).

steps Adjust Contrast Using Curves

Just as **Levels** is great for adjusting the brightness of an image, **Curves** excels at correcting the contrast. The command is especially adept at reducing the contrast in an image marked by sudden transitions between highlights and shadows, typical of photographs captured in direct sunlight.

1 get image

For the best demonstration, open an image that you've tried without success to correct with **Levels**. Consider the example of the statues below. I've chosen **Image➡Histogram** to display the **Histogram** window, which lets me analyze the photograph without modifying it. The histogram—identical to the one in the **Levels** dialog box—shows the brightness values to be generously distributed, with plenty of blacks and whites. All **Levels** can do for this image is raise or lower the gamma, which will do nothing to bring the dark and light colors closer together.

2 choose curves

Curves alone lets you edit brightness ranges independently of each other. So press **ctrl+M** (Win) or **command-M** (Mac) to display the **Curves** dialog box.

3 add grid lines

To increase the resolution of the grid, press **alt** (Win) or **option** (Mac) and click in the brightness graph. You may also expand the **Curves** dialog box by clicking the maximize button (Win) or zoom box (Mac).

4 identify problem areas

To gauge the location of problem colors in the graph, drag in the image window. A "bouncing ball" floats up and down the curve to show where the colors fall.

5 add points

Add points by clicking along the curve. Or lift points directly from the image by pressing **ctrl** (Win) or **command** (Mac) and clicking in the image window.

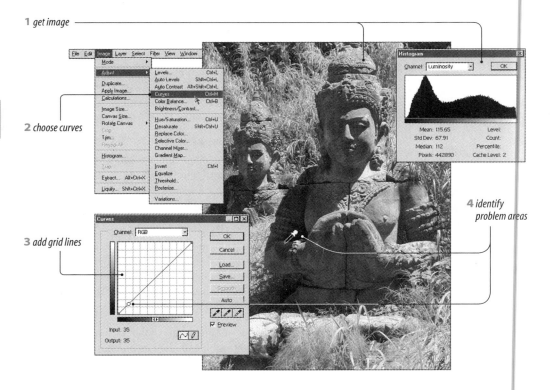

1 *get image*

2 *choose curves*

3 *add grid lines*

4 *identify problem areas*

6 adjust output value

Raise the **Output** value to lighten the point; lower the value to darken it. You can also use the arrow keys to nudge a selected point. Press ↑ or ↓ to modify the **Output** value; ← or → changes the **Input** value.

> *tip* To advance from one point to the next, press **ctrl+tab** (Win) or **control-tab** (Mac). This lets you select points without the risk of moving them.

7 click with gray eyedropper

To balance the colors, select the gray eyedropper and click a portion of the image that should be gray. Photoshop automatically adjusts the curve in each color channel to make the clicked element gray.

8 switch channels

To view the changes made by the gray eyedropper, you have to visit the individual color channels. Use the **Channel** option to switch from one to the other.

9 add & adjust points

Further balance colors as desired. To add a reference point to every color channel graph at once, turn off the gray eyedropper, and then **ctrl+shift**-click (**command-shift**-click on the Mac) in the image window.

10 draw with pencil, click smooth

If you have problems with a point flexing the curve in an undesirable way, switch to the pencil tool. Draw in the graph to create a so-called *arbitrary curve* that bends and sways independently of any points. Click the **Smooth** button to soften the transitions.

11 click save (optional)

Mac users add **.amp** to the filename to use the pencil curve on a PC. When saving a point curve, use **.acv**.

12 click OK

To repeat the most recent application of **Curves**, press **ctrl+alt+M** (**command-option-M** on the Mac).

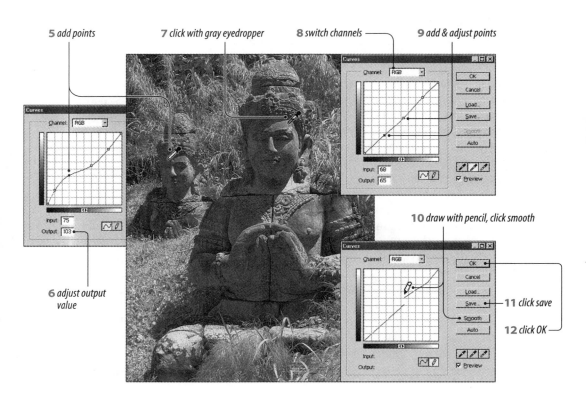

5 add points

7 click with gray eyedropper

8 switch channels

9 add & adjust points

6 adjust output value

10 draw with pencil, click smooth

11 click save

12 click OK

The Gradient Map Command

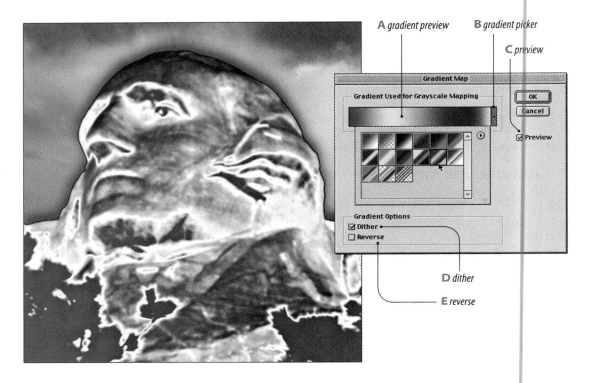

A *gradient preview*

B *gradient picker*

C *preview*

D *dither*

E *reverse*

If you're looking for something a little more outrageous, try **Image**➞**Adjust**➞**Gradient Map**. (On the PC, you can press the shortcut alt+I, A, M.) Based on the **Curves** command, **Gradient Map** applies a preset gradient as a channel-by-channel curve. Before applying the curve, Photoshop converts all colors to grays, as if you had chosen **Image**➞**Adjust**➞**Desaturate**. Then it remaps the colors according to the gradient you select in the **Gradient Map** dialog box. The examples below show the preset gradients **Black, White** and **Chrome** expressed as curves in the red channel.

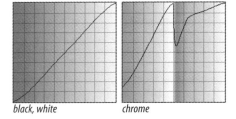

black, white   *chrome*

A gradient preview
Click the gradient preview to display the **Gradient Editor** and create your own custom gradient, as in Make Your Own Gradient on pages 88 and 89.

B gradient picker
Click here to see a pop-up palette of gradient presets. Then click a preset to apply it. I applied the **Copper** preset above. You can load additional presets by choosing a library from the palette menu.

C preview
Keep this check box turned on to see the results of your edits, even from the **Gradient Editor** dialog box.

D dither
If you encounter harsh color transitions, you may be able to smooth them out slightly with this check box.

E reverse
This option reverses the direction of the gradient.

The Channel Mixer Command

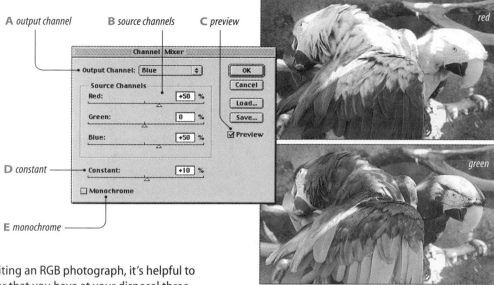

A *output channel* B *source channels* C *preview*

red

green

blue

D *constant*

E *monochrome*

When editing an RGB photograph, it's helpful to remember that you have at your disposal three independent images—one for each channel—each of which contains unique and valuable information. This means if one channel is in bad shape, you have two others that can come to its rescue. To fix one channel with the contents of the others, choose **Image→Adjust→Channel Mixer** (or press alt+I, A, X on the PC). Then use the options in the **Channel Mixer** dialog box to blend one or more color channels or mix a custom grayscale image.

A output channel

Select the channel that you want to edit from this pop-up menu. Feel free to switch back and forth between channels; Photoshop dutifully remembers the settings for each. When you select **Monochrome** (E), the only option available is **Gray**.

> *tip* Press **ctrl** (Win) or **command** (Mac) with a number to switch between channels.

B source channels

Here's where you specify how much of the red, green, and blue channels goes into the active channel (A). To maintain a consistent level of brightness, the **Red**, **Green**, and **Blue** values should add up to 100%. Any

higher and the channel grows lighter; any lower and the channel darkens. Negative values are permitted.

C preview

Keep this option on to see the results of your changes.

D constant

Use this option to add or subtract brightness when the sum of the **Source Channels** values (B) is not **100%**.

E monochrome

Select this check box to mix your own grayscale image as a combination of the color channels. The result remains a color image, so be sure to choose **Image→Mode→Grayscale** when you're done.

steps Eliminate Red-Eye

The **Channel Mixer** command is ideally suited to fixing problems that are isolated to a single channel. And the best example of a channel-specific problem is *red-eye*. At night or under dim light, a person's eyes dilate. When you shoot a photograph using a flash, the pupils don't have time to respond, so the flash passes into the eyes, hits the back of the retina, and reflects back as red. A pre-flash helps prevent this problem by shrinking pupils before the real flash. But when you're faced with red-eye in Photoshop, it's too late for a pre-flash. So here's what you do:

1 get image

Children and animals are highly prone to red-eye because their pupils dilate easily and they spend a lot of time with their eyes wide open.

2 survey channels

To prove that red-eye really is red, press **ctrl+1, 2, and 3** (**command-1, 2, and 3** on the Mac) to switch between the color channels. More likely than not, you'll find a white pupil in the red channel with virtually no sign of red-eye in the green and blue channels. This is physics working in your favor.

3 select elliptical marquee tool

Press **ctrl+~** (Win) or **command-~** (Mac) to switch back to the composite view of the image. Then press **M** and **shift-M** to select the elliptical marquee tool.

4 select irises of eyes

Zoom in as needed. Then draw an oval around the first iris, press the **shift** key, and draw an oval around the second iris. You should end up with two elliptical selection outlines.

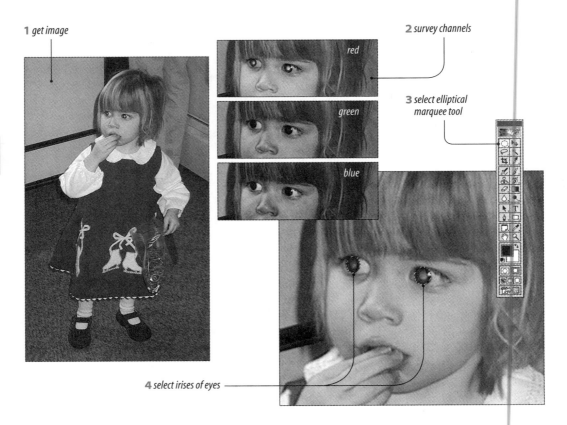

1 *get image*

2 *survey channels*

red

green

blue

3 *select elliptical marquee tool*

4 *select irises of eyes*

5 feather selection (optional)

It's not important to be terribly accurate with your selection outlines. But if you're concerned they're too sloppy, you can fudge the edges a bit by feathering them. Press **ctrl+alt+D** (Win) or **command-option-D** (Mac) to bring up the **Feather Selection** dialog box. Enter 1 or 2 pixels for the **Radius** and click **OK**.

6 hide edges

The selection is sufficiently small that the marching ants really get in the way of seeing what you're doing. So choose **View→Show→Selection Edges**—or just press **ctrl+H** (**command-H** on the Mac)—to hide the ants temporarily.

7 choose channel mixer

Remember, on the PC, you can press **alt+I**, **A**, and **X**. On the Mac, you have to choose the command.

8 set output channel to red

The **Output Channel** option is set to **Red** by default because it's the first channel in the image. Leave it this way. After all, you want to edit the red channel; the others are fine.

9 enter source channels values

In the **Source Channels** area, set the **Red** value to 0%. It's messed up; we want nothing to do with it. Then set the **Green** and **Blue** values to 50% apiece. If you want to emphasize green or blue over the other, feel free. Just make sure they add up to 100%.

10 click OK

Or press **enter** (Win) or **return** (Mac). Photoshop renders both iris and pupil black. Because the camera failed to capture the eyes' natural coloring, you can either accept the black eyes or hand-paint the irises.

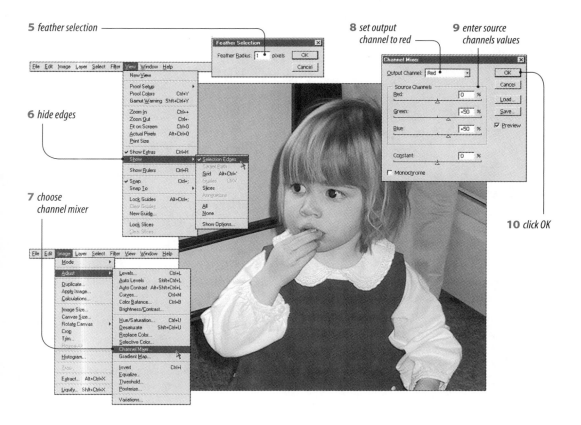

Invert, Equalize, Threshold, & Posterize

These final adjustments produce modest effects and demand very little effort. As with all of Photoshop's commands, you get what you put in—given that you can't put in much, you shouldn't expect much in return. But every so often, **Invert** (A), **Threshold** (C), and even **Equalize** (B) may come in handy.

original

A invert

B equalize

C threshold

D posterize

A invert

Choose **Image**➡**Adjust**➡**Invert** or press ctrl+I (command-I on the Mac) to reverse the brightness levels in an image. Black becomes white, white becomes black, the other levels get mapped to their opposites. Note that **Invert** cannot create a positive from a photographic negative. For that, refer to the software that came with your scanner or be prepared to tweak the colors manually.

> **tip** To invert colors selectively, press ctrl+L for **Levels**. Then exchange the **Output Levels** slider triangles, black for white, in each channel.

B equalize

This command redistributes colors so that every brightness level gets equal emphasis. The result is a flat histogram, in which each bar is roughly the same height. Though rarely useful for correcting photographs, you may find it helpful for smoothing out transitions in skies and gradients.

> **tip** To fix a photo, the better commands are **Auto Levels** and **Auto Contrast**. The former corrects blacks and whites within each channel. **Auto Contrast** corrects the composite image so as not to change the color balance.

C threshold

This command makes all colors in an image either black or white. You set a brightness level as the breaking point—anything darker becomes black, anything lighter becomes white. **Threshold** is most useful when masking.

D posterize

The least of the commands on this page, **Posterize** reduces the number of colors in an image to 255 or fewer, creating a silk-screened effect. If it sounds like a good way to produce GIF images, there's a much better way, as I explain in Save Artwork In GIF on pages 270 and 271.

Adjustment Layers

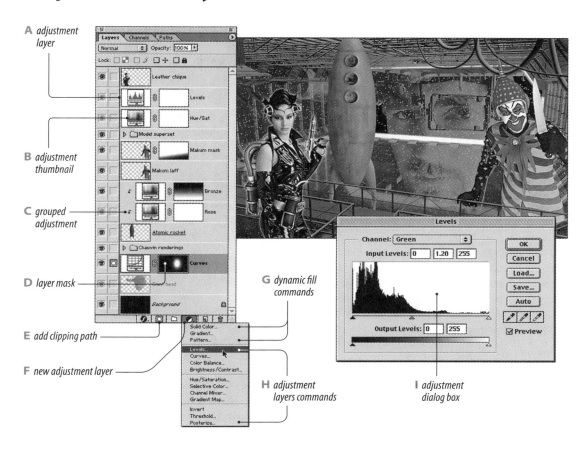

A *adjustment layer*

B *adjustment thumbnail*

C *grouped adjustment*

D *layer mask*

E *add clipping path*

F *new adjustment layer*

G *dynamic fill commands*

H *adjustment layers commands*

I *adjustment dialog box*

So far, I've discussed commands that correct one layer at a time. But as luck would have it, Photoshop lets you apply all but two of these operations to multiple layers. (The exceptions are **Variations** and **Equalize**.) You do this by establishing an independent layer of color adjustment. This appropriately named *adjustment layer* not only influences the colors of the layers behind it, but remains forever editable so long as you save the composition in one of the layer-friendly formats: native Photoshop (PSD), TIFF, or PDF. Adjustment layers are so flexible, in fact, that many designers use them to correct flat photographs. This way, if you later decide to tweak the colors to meet the demands of a different screen or printing environment, you always have

your original image on hand with the last-applied color correction ready and waiting in the wings.

A adjustment layer

You create and modify an adjustment layer in the **Layers** palette. Arrange, duplicate, or delete the adjustment layer just like any other (see Chapter 8, Create & Modify Layers). Unless part of a clipping group (C), the adjustment affects all layers behind it, all the way down to the Background layer.

B adjustment thumbnail

The first thumbnail in an adjustment layer identifies what kind of adjustment it is. From **Levels** to **Curves** to **Hue/Saturation** to **Threshold**, every adjustment gets its own unique icon.

C grouped adjustment

If you want to isolate an adjustment layer to a single layer or group of layers, make it part of a clipping group (see Use One Layer To Clip Another, page 134). This way, the adjustment won't exceed the boundaries of the layer at the bottom of the group. (FYI: Layer sets do *not* isolate adjustments.)

D layer mask

When you create a new adjustment layer (F), Photoshop automatically assigns it a layer mask (as in Layer-Specific Masks, page 131), which isolates the region affected by the adjustment. If you select an area before creating the adjustment layer, Photoshop converts the selection to a mask. From then on, painting or editing the adjustment layer changes the mask.

E add clipping path

You may notice that the **Add Mask** button remains available despite the fact that the adjustment layer already has a mask. Clicking the button adds a clipping path. Draw with a shape or pen tool to mask the adjustment with a vector-based path (as in Chapter 11, Draw Vector Shapes).

F new adjustment layer

Click the black-and-white circle at the bottom of the **Layers** palette to display a pop-up menu, and then choose an option to decide what kind of adjustment layer you want to make.

G dynamic fill commands

The first three options in the pop-up menu (F) create *dynamic fills* that you can edit by way of a dialog box. You can choose from a solid color, gradient, or pattern. To learn more about dynamic fills, read The Change Layer Content Commands on page 162.

H adjustment layers commands

The remaining 11 options create new adjustment layers. I discuss all but three of these elsewhere in this chapter. In place of **Brightness/Contrast**, I recommend you use **Levels**; in place of **Selective Color**, use **Hue/Saturation**. I normally recommend **Variations** in place of **Color Balance**, but since **Variations** is not available as an adjustment layer, **Color Balance** will have to do. The latter provides many of the same controls, but without the thumbnails.

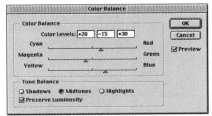

I adjustment dialog box

After you choose the desired adjustment layer (H), Photoshop displays the corresponding dialog box, which provides the usual options, down to **Preview**. Only **Invert** produces an effect without a dialog box.

Adjustment Layers & Blend Modes

Photoshop goes so far as to let you apply blend modes to an adjustment layer. When you apply any mode but **Normal**, Photoshop treats the adjustment layer as a color-corrected duplicate of the layers below. To create the bright blob behind the clown's head, I selected an area with the lasso tool, made a new **Levels** layer, and set the blend mode to **Screen**.

You can also cut holes with an adjustment layer. To burrow down to the Background stars, I double-clicked the **Levels** layer and set the **Knockout** option to **Deep**.

screened levels layer   knockout deep

Correct Colors With Layers

Adjustment layers have long been flexible and efficient, consuming very little space on disk. Now that you can save layers with a standard TIFF file, they're more attractive than ever. In fact, you may find yourself using adjustment layers for *all* your color correcting. The following steps take you through one possible application of adjustment layers, with lots of tips and insights to make it worth your while.

1 assemble composition

For purposes of this demonstration, I created a very basic composition. Starting with an old drive-in screen, I added a photo of my shadow and applied the **Multiply** blend mode. The drive-in appears projected on the ground below my shadow.

2 create invert layer

To give the drive-in a photo-negative look, I selected the Background layer, clicked the black-and-white circle at the bottom of the **Layers** palette, and chose **Invert**. The shadow above the new **Invert** layer remained unchanged.

3 create levels layer

The drive-in came out too dark, so I chose **Levels** from the adjustment layer menu and entered **2.00** for the gamma value in the **Levels** dialog box.

> *tip* To name an adjustment layer before creating it, press **alt** (Win) or **option** (Mac) and choose the desired adjustment. I gave my new **Levels** layer the name **Lighten**.

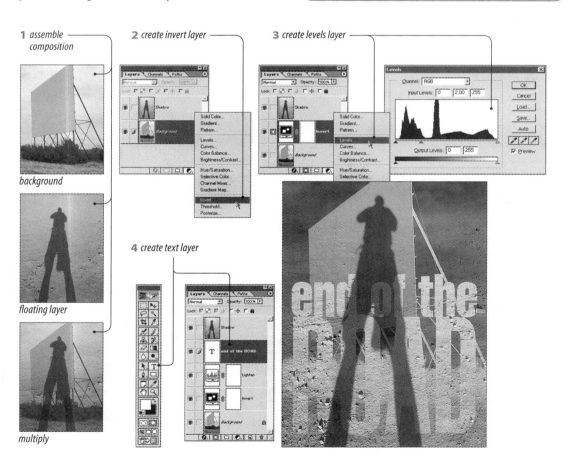

1 assemble composition

background

floating layer

multiply

2 create invert layer

3 create levels layer

4 create text layer

4 create text layer

Next I used the type tool to create a layer of text behind the shadow. Because the shadow layer uses **Multiply**, Photoshop burns it into the white letters.

5 convert text to shape

Photoshop doesn't permit you to fill type with an adjustment. But you can create an adjustment inside a shape. So I chose **Layer➝Type ➝Convert To Shape** to turn the letters into vector paths.

6 change content to invert

To swap one kind of fill for another, choose a command from the **Layer➝Change Layer Content** submenu. I wanted my letters to invert the layers behind them, so I chose the **Invert** command.

7 create threshold, group with text

To exaggerate the contrast of the colors inside the letters, I chose **Threshold** from the adjustment layer menu at the bottom of the **Layers** palette. Then I entered **128** and clicked **OK**. Because **Threshold** is an independent layer, the effect spilled outside the letters. So I pressed **ctrl+G** (**command-G** on the Mac) to group **Threshold** with the text shapes below it.

8 select dark pixels

At this point, I got a hankering to make the black portions of the letters red. I set the foreground color to black and chose **Select➝Color Range** to select the black pixels in the image.

9 create hue/saturation layer

Then I chose **Hue/Saturation** from the adjustment layer menu. Inside the **Hue/Saturation** dialog box, I turned on the **Colorize** check box and used the values shown below to make bright red. After I clicked **OK**, Photoshop automatically converted the **Color Range** selection into a layer mask, isolating the bright red coloring to the darkest portions of the letters.

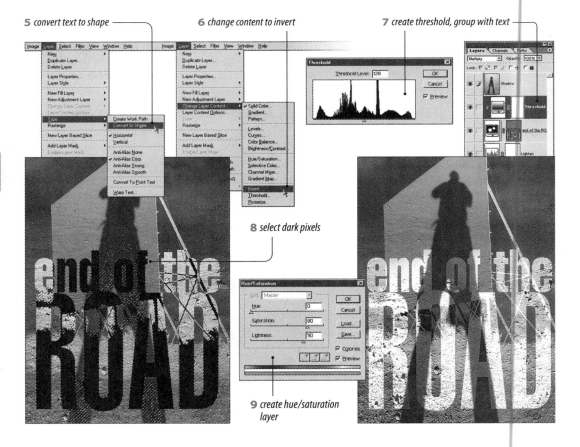

5 *convert text to shape*

6 *change content to invert*

7 *create threshold, group with text*

8 *select dark pixels*

9 *create hue/saturation layer*

chapter 14

Apply Filters & Effects

Every kitchen has a junk drawer. In Photoshop, that junk drawer is the **Filter** menu. This is not intended as a slur on the **Filter** commands—known simply as *filters*—many of which are excellent. But they are a hodgepodge. Of the nearly 100 filters included with Photoshop, a few are essential, two or three dozen are nice to have around, and the rest are highly amusing but rarely useful for day-to-day imaging.

Although filters vary dramatically in design and purpose, they share two traits in common. First, they are exclusively applicable to pixels. If you apply a filter when a shape or text layer is active, Photoshop warns you that doing so will convert the layer to pixels, a process called *rasterizing*. Second, filters are expandable. Companies such as Corel, Alien Skin, and Ulead sell collections of *plug-ins* that add commands to the **Filter** menu. Note, however, that I discuss only those filters that ship with Photoshop 6.

The Sharpen Filters

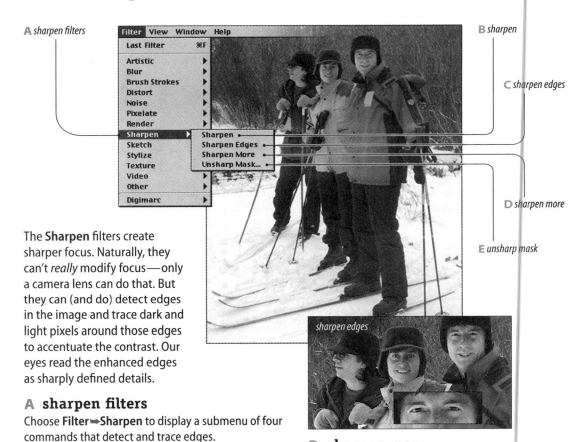

A *sharpen filters*

B *sharpen*

C *sharpen edges*

D *sharpen more*

E *unsharp mask*

The **Sharpen** filters create sharper focus. Naturally, they can't *really* modify focus—only a camera lens can do that. But they can (and do) detect edges in the image and trace dark and light pixels around those edges to accentuate the contrast. Our eyes read the enhanced edges as sharply defined details.

A sharpen filters

Choose **Filter➡Sharpen** to display a submenu of four commands that detect and trace edges.

B sharpen

This filter applies a wee bit of sharpening. The effect looks good on screen—making it suitable for Web work—but it won't make much difference in print.

C sharpen edges

All **Sharpen** filters sharpen edges. But **Sharpen Edges** enhances only the most prominent edges. It applies the enhancement of **Sharpen** (B) to fewer pixels.

D sharpen more

This filter applies three times as much edge enhancement as **Sharpen** (B). Be careful though. **Sharpen More** has a habit of drawing out jagged patterns in an image, producing an effect known as *oversharpening*.

E unsharp mask

This is the one filter that permits you to control the amount of sharpening you apply to an image. It does everything the other three filters do, and much more.

Sharpen Focus With Unsharp Mask

The strangely named **Unsharp Mask** enhances edges in a photograph by offsetting a blurred negative (the *"unsharp" mask*) over the original. In addition to being Photoshop's primary sharpening function, it's the one command I recommend you use on *every* image you edit.

1 get image
Open an image that's generally in focus but could use some extra crispness. Do *not* open a blurry image. Photoshop can enhance focus, but it can't invent focus out of thin air.

2 choose unsharp mask
Sadly, there's no shortcut for **Filter➞Sharpen➞ Unsharp Mask**. However, on the PC, you can press the key sequence **alt+T, S, enter, U**. Or assign an action, as in Make A Custom Shortcut on page 243.

3 set preview
Select the **Preview** check box to view the results of your settings in the image window. Then click in the image to set the area displayed in the dialog box. You can zoom and scroll either image or preview using the standard **spacebar** techniques (see pages 38 and 39).

4 specify amount
Use the **Amount** value to change the degree of sharpening. Higher values result in more enhancement. Values from 50% to 150% are most common.

5 set radius
The **Radius** value defines the thickness of the traced edge, in pixels. A thin edge, such as **0.5**, is ideal for Web work. For high-resolution printing, values of **0.8** to **2.0** generally work best.

> *tip* To enhance the contrast of an image without boosting the sharpness, combine a low **Amount**, (such as 30%) with a high **Radius** (say, 15 pixels).

6 set threshold
Raise this value to prevent low-contrast edges from being sharpened. For a better solution, see Sharpen An Old Photo on pages 216 through 218.

7 click OK
After applying **Unsharp Mask**, you can repeat it by pressing **ctrl+F** (**command-F** on the Mac).

> *tip* To reapply the filter with different settings, press **ctrl+alt+F** (**command-option-F** on the Mac).

1 *get image*

2 *choose unsharp mask*

3 *set preview*

4 *specify amount*

5 *set radius*

6 *set threshold*

7 *click OK*

🌀 **Sharpen An Old Photo...**

Unsharp Mask does a great job of enhancing clean, well-focused photographs captured using modern film or digital cameras. However, random *artifacts* such as film grain, dust, and scratches confuse **Unsharp Mask**. This is particularly a problem when sharpening old photographs.

1 get image
To demonstrate what I mean, open a vintage photo. Anything pre-1950 should do nicely.

2 choose unsharp mask
Don't even think about using one of the other **Sharpen** filters for this job.

3 enter 0 for threshold
Then enter an **Amount** of 250% and a **Radius** of 2.0 pixels to make the sharpening nice and obvious. The **Threshold** of 0 tells Photoshop to sharpen all pixels equally. The result is an image marked by sharp edges and even sharper film grain. Like turning up the treble on an AM radio, sharpening brings out the static.

4 raise threshold & amount
The purpose of **Threshold** is to circumvent the static. Still inside the **Unsharp Mask** dialog box, raise the **Threshold** to 25 and the **Amount** to 500%. This tells the filter to sharpen only those edges where neighboring colors differ by at least 25 brightness levels. More subtle edges are ignored. As shown below, this eliminates some grain, but by no means all. In fact, there's no way to avoid all the grain and keep the real edges. Instead, you get a pockmarked effect.

5 click cancel
If **Threshold** doesn't work, what does? The solution is to use some of Photoshop's other, more sensitive edge filters to create a custom *edge mask*.

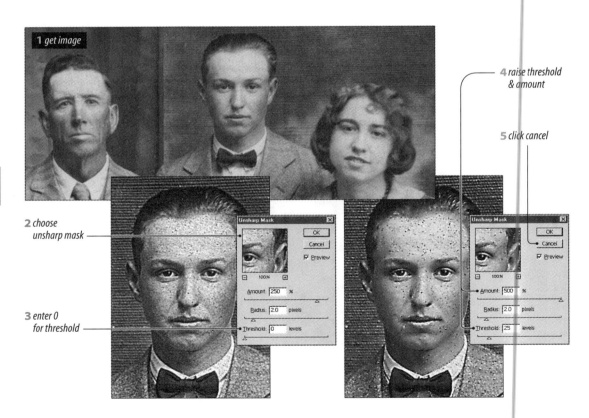

1 get image

2 choose unsharp mask

3 enter 0 for threshold

4 raise threshold & amount

5 click cancel

⑭ **Apply Filters & Effects:** Sharpen An Old Photo With An Edge Mask

...With An Edge Mask

6 duplicate channel

To begin the mask, go to the **Channels** palette. Then drag the **Green** or **Gray** channel onto the **New Channel** button at the bottom of the palette.

7 apply find edges filter

Choose **Filter→Stylize→Find Edges** to trace the edges in the new alpha channel.

8 choose invert

This makes the edges white so you can select them.

9 apply maximum filter

Choose **Filter→Other→Maximum**, raise the **Radius** to 6, and press **enter**. This expands the maximum brightness value, white, by 6 pixels in all directions.

10 apply median & gaussian blur

The bigger pixels are awfully jagged. To smooth them out, choose **Filter→Noise→Median** (see The Noise Filters, page 220). Enter the same **Radius** as before, 6, and press **enter**. Then repeat the process with **Filter→Blur→Gaussian Blur** (The Blur Filters, page 219).

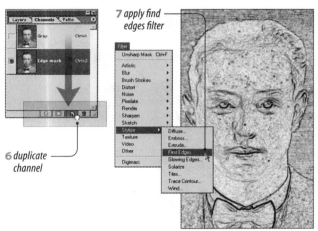

7 apply find edges filter

6 duplicate channel

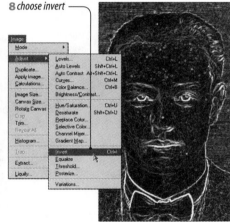

8 choose invert

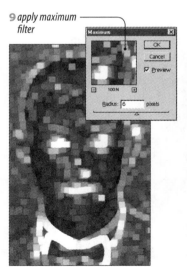

9 apply maximum filter

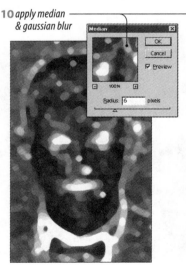

10 apply median & gaussian blur

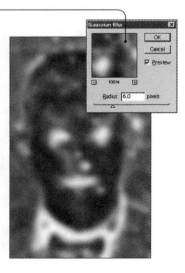

11 adjust levels

Use **Image➠Adjust➠Levels** to exaggerate the contrast of the mask. I set the blacks to **60** and the whites to **215**. This hides the grain and strengthens the edges.

12 switch to composite view

The mask is done; now to use it. Press **ctrl+~** (Win) or **command-~** (Mac) to switch to the grainy photo.

13 load selection

Press **ctrl** (Win) or **command** (Mac) and click the mask to convert it to a selection outline.

14 apply unsharp mask

Choose **Filter➠Sharpen➠Unsharp Mask**. Enter an **Amount** of 250%, a **Radius** of 2.0 pixels, and leave the **Threshold** set to 0, just as before (3).

15 retouch as needed

Thanks to the edge mask, Photoshop was able to sharpen the edges and leave the grain largely untouched. All that remained was for me to deselect the image and retouch it here and there with the rubber stamp tool (as in Retouch An Old Photograph on pages 101 and 102).

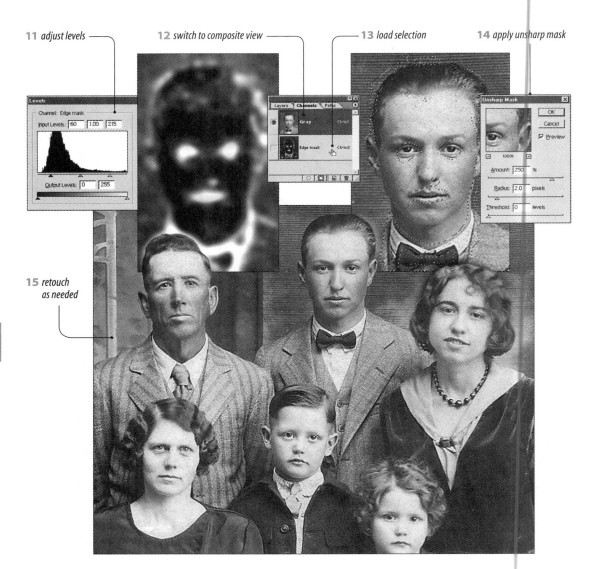

11 *adjust levels* — 12 *switch to composite view* — 13 *load selection* 14 *apply unsharp mask*

15 *retouch as needed*

The Blur Filters

A blur filters

B blur & blur more
C gaussian blur
D motion blur
E radial blur
F smart blur

The **Blur** filters soften the focus of an image by fading pixels into each other. Use them to smooth away artifacts, add soft glows, or blur the background behind an element. They also come in handy for creating soft transitions inside masks.

A blur filters

Choose **Filter➡Blur** to display six commands. To show this submenu on the PC, press **alt+T, B, enter.**

B blur & blur more

These filters apply the moderate blurs shown below. Both are based on the more capable **Gaussian Blur** (C).

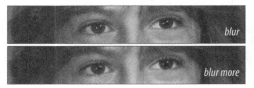

blur

blur more

C gaussian blur

Choose this filter to set the amount of blur you want to apply. The blur is measured as an ever-softening circle gently scrubbing through the image. Use the **Radius** value to specify the radius of that circle.

D motion blur

The **Motion Blur** filter applies a directional blur to an image to indicate movement. You specify the direction

and distance of the blur. As with **Gaussian Blur**, the effect previews in the full image window.

motion blur, 20°, 15 pixels

E radial blur

This filter can either spin an image around a center point or zoom it in a rush toward the viewer. Drag the **Blur Center** to position the effect. One of Photoshop's slowest filters, **Radial Blur** lacks a preview.

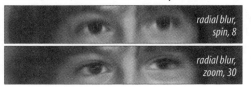

radial blur, spin, 8

radial blur, zoom, 30

F smart blur

The first of the 48 **Gallery Effects** filters sprinkled throughout the **Filter** menu (see The Effects Filters on page 229), **Smart Blur** offers a **Threshold** value so you can blur regions while maintaining sharp edges.

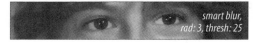

smart blur, rad: 3, thresh: 25

The Noise Filters

A *noise filters*

B *add noise*

C *despeckle*

D *dust & scratches*

E *median*

Noise is Photoshop's word for random pixels of colors that don't contribute to the quality or detail of the image, the visual equivalent of static. Noise can result from film grain, scanner dust, or poor lighting conditions. The **Noise** filters are designed not only to reduce noise, but to create it as well.

A noise filters
On the PC, press alt+T, N to display the **Filter➡Noise** submenu. (Because **Noise** is the only N word in the **Filter** menu, you don't have to press enter.)

B add noise
This filter adds noise, useful for matching edits to the original film grain. The **Amount** value defines the percentage by which random colors can vary from existing colors in the image. Select **Gaussian** to increase the contrast of the noise pixels; select **Monochromatic** to color the noise to match the image.

add noise, 6.5%, gaussian

C despeckle
Choose this filter to cover up single-pixel anomalies. It does a decent job of reversing noise created with the

Add Noise filter (B), but it rarely helps with natural noise, which is typically bigger than a single pixel.

D dust & scratches
Dust & Scratches averages the colors of pixels. Raise the **Radius** to average a larger area at a time; raise the **Threshold** to preserve low-contrast edges. While an interesting filter, it fairs poorly at its advertised purpose. **Threshold** in particular does a better job of preserving dust than eliminating it.

dust & scratches, radius: 4, threshold: 20

E median
Remove **Threshold** from **Dust & Scratches** (D) and you get **Median**. All it does is average pixels, great for bonding pixels in preparation for sharpening.

median, radius: 6

Descreen A Scanned Halftone

When you scan film, you scan a continuous-tone image. But when you scan something that's been commercially reproduced, you scan a series of colored *halftone dots* (as in Select The Ideal Resolution on page 25 of Chapter 2). The result is a visible pattern that interferes with sharpening and future printing. Fortunately, halftone dots are just another kind of noise to Photoshop, so you can eliminate them using **Median** and a few other techniques.

(Naturally, these steps assume you have the right to use whatever it is you're scanning. As a layman, my understanding is that reproducing printed material is a potential violation of copyright law. But I'm no lawyer; if in doubt, talk to someone who is.)

1 scan halftoned image
Position the page crooked on the scanner, so you have to rotate it in Photoshop (4). Then scan the image at 1200 to 1600 ppi, 9 to 12 times the typical halftone frequency of 133 lpi. If your scanner doesn't go that high, use the highest resolution you can.

2 open in photoshop
Some scanners let you scan directly into Photoshop via the **File→Import** submenu. If not, scan to the TIFF or JPEG format using the software that came with your scanner, and then open the image in Photoshop.

3 measure angle
Select the measure tool from the eyedropper flyout. Then drag along an edge to set the angle of rotation.

4 rotate canvas
Choose **Image→Rotate→Arbitrary** and click **OK** (**alt+I, E, A, enter** on the PC). Photoshop rotates the image according to the measure tool line (3). This interpolates the pixels, which blurs the halftone dots.

5 crop image
Use the crop tool to cut out the straightened image (see Crop Away Extraneous Details, page 29).

6 downsample image
By scanning at a high resolution (1), you gave yourself more pixels than you need. Choose **Image→Image**

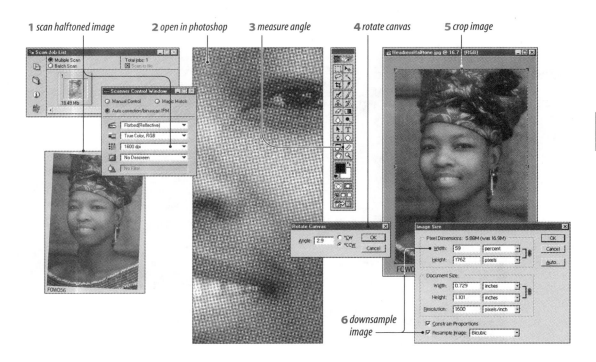

1 *scan halftoned image* **2** *open in photoshop* **3** *measure angle* **4** *rotate canvas* **5** *crop image*

6 *downsample image*

Size and turn on the **Resample Image** check box. Then set the **Width** option in the **Pixel Dimensions** area to **Percent**, enter 59% or some other prime number, and click **OK**. This forces a random downsampling, which maximizes the dot blurring.

7 switch to red channel

From here on out, it's a matter of applying filters to independent color channels. Assuming that you're editing an RGB image, press **ctrl+1** (Win) or **command-1** (Mac) to switch to the Red channel.

8 apply median filter

Choose **Filter➡Noise➡Median** to defeat the noise in the active channel. As a function of the way our eyes work, the Red channel contains the pivotal color information in an image. This means you can afford to gum it up a little, but not too much. A **Radius** value of 4 pixels generally works well. Then click **OK**.

9 repeat median in green...

Press **ctrl+2** (**command-2** on the Mac) to switch to the Green channel, which most closely resembles a grayscale composite of the overall image. Because this brightness information contributes so much to clarity and edge detail, you have to be very careful

with it. I recommend you apply **Median** with half the **Radius** of the Red channel, or in our case, 2 pixels.

10 ...and blue channels

Click **OK**, and then press **ctrl+3** (**command-3**) to switch to Blue. Human eyes are least sensitive to blue light, so you can get away with murder in this channel. Press **ctrl+alt+F** (**command-option-F**) to display the **Median** dialog box and enter three times the Green **Radius**, or 6 pixels. Then click **OK**.

11 switch to RGB view

Press **ctrl+~** (**command-~**) to edit all channels.

12 apply gaussian blur

The **Median** filter displaces edges in an image. The best way to merge these variously displaced edges is to blur them. Choose **Filter➡Blur➡Gaussian Blur** and enter the lowest **Radius** value you applied to any of the channels, or in our case, 2 pixels. Then click **OK**.

13 apply unsharp mask

After averaging and blurring the edges so fiercely, some equally fierce sharpening is in order. Choose **Filter➡Sharpen➡Unsharp Mask**, enter 500 for the **Amount**, 2.0 for the **Radius**, and click **OK**.

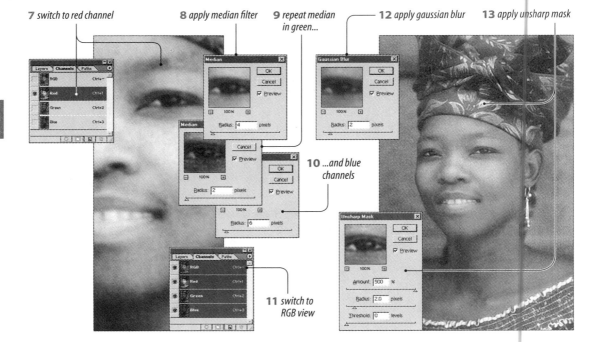

7 switch to red channel *8 apply median filter* *9 repeat median in green...* *12 apply gaussian blur* *13 apply unsharp mask*

10 ...and blue channels

11 switch to RGB view

IMPORTANT INFORMATION!
AFFIX SERIAL NUMBER
STICKER ON THE RETURN
PORTION OF THE
REGISTRATION CARD.

THIS TSID NUMBER WILL
BE REQUIRED WHEN
CONTACTING TECHNICAL
SUPPORT.

TSID:1000229300042
(1P) PRODUCT P/N: 1772900

(S) PRODUCT S/N: BC0C04200XJ

TSID:1000229300042
(1P) PRODUCT P/N: 1772900

(S) PRODUCT S/N: BC0C04200XJ

The Render Filters

A *render filters*
B *3D transform*
C *clouds & difference clouds*
D *lens flare*
E *lighting effects*
F *texture fill*

In the world of 3-D graphics, you *render* a final scene by projecting light onto it and generating a photo-realistic image. In this vein, the **Render** filters create 3-D effects, lighting effects, or a combination of the two. Half the filters (B, D, & E) work only in the RGB mode and need lots of RAM to complete successfully.

A render filters

Windows users can press **alt+T, R** to display the **Filter➟Render** submenu.

B 3D transform

This filter wraps an image around a cube, sphere, or cylinder. Draw the shape. Then use the trackball tool to rotate it in space. The filter does not apply any lighting. I used a layer effect to create the drop shadow on right.

C clouds & difference clouds

The **Clouds** filter creates a pattern of cloud-like noise in the foreground and background colors. **Difference Clouds** adds clouds with the **Difference** blend mode.

> *tip* For a nifty effect, choose **Difference Clouds**, and press **ctrl+F** (or **command-F**) multiple times.

D lens flare

This filter adds a flash that simulates light from a bright source reflecting off the camera lens.

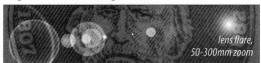

lens flare, 50-300mm zoom

E lighting effects

Lighting Effects shines lights onto the image. Select a preset from the **Style** pop-up menu. Then modify the light source in the **Preview** area on the left side of the dialog box. Drag from the light bulb icon to make a new light source. Use the **Texture Channel** option to create a textured lighting effect.

lighting effects, soft spotlight texture: red height: 30

F texture fill

Dating back to Photoshop's early years, this obsolete command loads a flat image stored in the PSD format and repeats it inside the active layer.

The Distort Filters

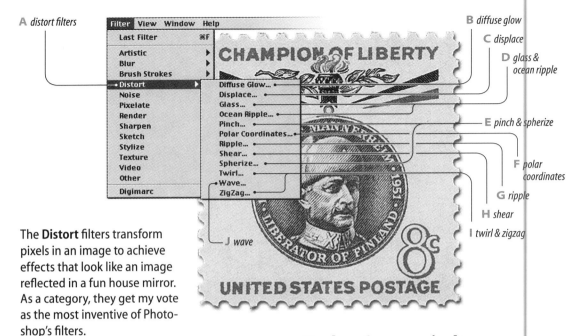

A *distort filters*

B *diffuse glow*

C *displace*

D *glass & ocean ripple*

E *pinch & spherize*

F *polar coordinates*

G *ripple*

H *shear*

I *twirl & zigzag*

J *wave*

The **Distort** filters transform pixels in an image to achieve effects that look like an image reflected in a fun house mirror. As a category, they get my vote as the most inventive of Photoshop's filters.

A   distort filters

Choose **Filter→Distort** to display a submenu of an even dozen filters. On the PC, press alt+T, D, enter.

B   diffuse glow

The first **Distort** filter is the least representative. Rather than distort the image, it shines a soft glow on the lightest pixels in the image.

C   displace

This remarkable filter creates custom distortions according to a separate *displacement map* (or *dmap*) stored on disk. The dmap is nothing more than a grayscale gradient or pattern saved as a PSD file. Choose **Displace** and open the dmap. As below, white in the dmap moves pixels up or left, black moves pixels down or right, and gray keeps pixels stationary.

displacement map

displace, horizontal: 100%, vertical: 0%

D   glass & ocean ripple

The **Glass** filter refracts colors in an image through a textured pattern. You can choose from a predefined pattern or load a PSD file. Based on a similar code, **Ocean Ripple** refracts colors through a water texture.

glass, tiny lens, distort: 3, smooth: 6

ocean ripple, size: 6, magnitude: 9

E   pinch & spherize

Similar in design, **Pinch** dents an image inward and **Spherize** pushes it out. Both filters accept negative **Amount** values; however, note that a negative of one is not the same as a positive of the other. **Pinch** pushes to a point, **Spherize** produces a more rounded effect.

pinch 50%

spherize 75%

The Liquify Command

K *liquify command*   **L** *liquify dialog box*

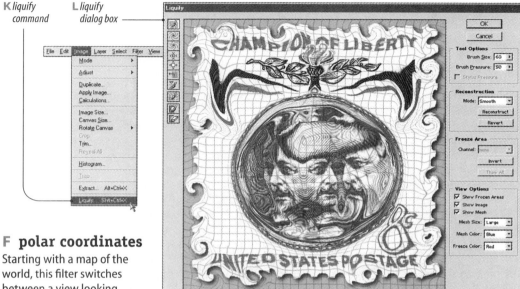

F polar coordinates

Starting with a map of the world, this filter switches between a view looking down from the North Pole and a rectangular projection. Below, I selected **Polar to Rectangular** to convert the postage stamp's circle of letters to a straight line.

polar coordinates: polar to rectangular

G ripple

This filter adds watery ripples of various sizes and intensities. Why two **Ripple** filters? This one dates back to Photoshop 1.0; **Ocean Ripple** (D) was added with the **Gallery Effects** filters (see page 229).

H shear

Use this filter to apply a horizontal wave to an image. Click on the line to add points, and then drag the points to make the waves.

> *tip* To add a vertical wave, choose **Image ➥ Rotate Canvas ➥ 90° CW**, and then apply **Shear**. When you're done, rotate the image back with **90° CCW**.

I twirl & zigzag

These filters work in circular patterns around the center of the layer or selection. **Twirl** wraps an image into a spiral; **Zigzag** creates concentric ripples.

twirl 48°   *zigzag, pond ripples, 40, 10*

J wave

This filter bends an image into a wave pattern. For the quickest results, reduce the **Number of Generators** to 1. Use the **Scale** values to define the amount of side-to-side and up-and-down wave. Then click **Randomize** a few times until you arrive at an effect you like.

K liquify command

Choose **Image ➥ Liquify** or press **ctrl+shift+X** (command-shift-X on the Mac) to access the one distortion filter not included in the **Filter ➥ Distort** submenu.

L liquify dialog box

Use any of the first seven tools to brush on various real-time distortions. The eighth tool (which you get by pressing E) restores original details. The freeze tool (press F) protects areas from distortion; the thaw tool (T) unprotects. Press **[** and **]** to change the brush size.

The Stylize Filters

A *stylize filters*

B *diffuse*

C *emboss*

D *extrude & tiles*

E *find edges & glowing edges*

F *solarize*

G *trace contour*

H *wind*

The **Stylize** filters create textural effects, either imbuing an image with surface texture or outlining the contours of the image.

A stylize filters

Stylize is the third **Filter** command that starts with an S, so its PC key equivalent is **alt+T, S, S, S, enter.**

B diffuse

Named for a *diffusion dither*, this filter randomizes the pixels around the edges of details in an image.

C emboss

Emboss lights an etched surface by tracing edges with black and white and converting non-edges to gray. The filter's primary use is generating textures.

emboss, angle: 60°; height: 3, amount: 150%

D extrude & tiles

The **Tiles** filter breaks an image into lots of little squares. **Extrude** breaks it into squares and projects those squares at the viewer. Extrude can also project dagger-like pyramids, as shown above at right.

extrude, pyramids, size: 10, depth: 30, level-based

E find edges & glowing edges

Find Edges traces the edges in the image with black and makes non-edges white. **Glowing Edges** inverts the colors, plus it permits you to expand and smooth the edges, similar to steps 7 through 10 in Sharpen An Old Photo With An Edge Mask (see page 217).

F solarize

This filter inverts the lightest colors, changing white to black while leaving gray and black pixels intact.

G trace contour

Use this filter to trace the boundary between dark and light pixels, converting the image into line art.

trace contour, level: 84, edge: upper

H wind

This filter blasts pixels either to the left or right. Apply **Wind** to a layer to make a motion trail, and then rotate the layer to the desired orientation.

The Pixelate Filters

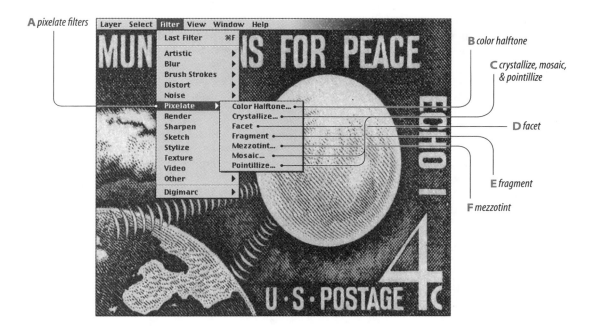

A *pixelate filters*

B *color halftone*

C *crystallize, mosaic, & pointillize*

D *facet*

E *fragment*

F *mezzotint*

The **Pixelate** filters generate natural patterns by gathering like-colored pixels into clusters. Without exception, they break down the detail in an image, making it very difficult to edit. These filters are best suited to backgrounds and support elements.

A pixelate filters

Windows users can press **alt+T, P** to display the **Filter➡Pixelate** submenu.

B color halftone

This filter converts an image into a pattern of large halftone dots. Photoshop calculates the dots independently in each color channel. So if you want to create CMYK dots, choose **Image➡Mode➡CMYK Color** before choosing the filter.

color halftone, max. radius: 8 pixels

C crystallize, mosaic, & pointillize

These filters create patterns according to a prescribed **Cell Size** value, where the *cell* is an individual polygon (**Crystallize**), square (**Mosaic**), or circle (**Pointillize**).

crystallize, cell size: 14 pixels
mosaic, cell size: 8 pixels
pointillize, cell size: 10 pixels

D facet

This filter congeals the edges in an image, as if you had chosen the **Median** and **Sharpen More** filters.

E fragment

Fragment creates four copies of an image and offsets them from each other at reduced opacities.

fragment

F mezzotint

This filter converts each channel of an image into one of ten black-and-white dot and line patterns.

mezzotint, type: long strokes

The Video & Other Filters

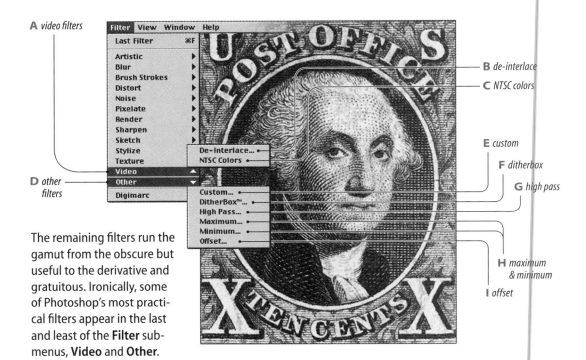

A *video filters*

B *de-interlace*

C *NTSC colors*

E *custom*

F *ditherbox*

G *high pass*

D *other filters*

H *maximum & minimum*

I *offset*

The remaining filters run the gamut from the obscure but useful to the derivative and gratuitous. Ironically, some of Photoshop's most practical filters appear in the last and least of the **Filter** submenus, **Video** and **Other**.

A video filters
Choose **Filter➠Video** (alt+T, V on the PC) to process still frames for export to or import from videotape.

B de-interlace
A frame of video is divided into two *fields*. One field conveys the even-numbered lines of screen data; the other conveys the odd lines. When you capture a still frame from videotape or DVD, the two fields are often out of sync, as below. **De-Interlace** averages the fields for a smoother image.

video frame prior to de-interlace

C NTSC colors
Before exporting an image for use in video, choose this filter to remap colors for optimum TV display.

D other filters
Filter➠Other offers an assortment of demanding but handy filters that don't quite belong in any other submenu. Windows users can press alt+T, O.

E custom
This filter lets you create custom effects by entering values into the central option boxes. For the best results, the sum of these values should always be 1.

custom:

F ditherbox
DitherBox simulates any color in the RGB gamut using only the 216 colors in the "Web-safe" palette.

G high pass
This filter makes non-edges gray, useful when making masks. Lower **Radius** values increase the effect.

H maximum & minimum
Maximum expands the maximum brightness value, white (see page 217). **Minimum** expands black.

I offset
This filter circulates pixels within a selection or layer, useful when working with repeating patterns.

The Effects Filters

Years ago, a company named **Silicon Beach** (the same folks who originally developed **Macromedia Flash**) created a series of Photoshop plug-ins called **Gallery Effects**. Adobe acquired them and now they ship with the program. This is significant because the **Effects** filters continue to work similarly. Each includes a preview inside the dialog box; they rely on vague, sometimes inconsistent numerical values; and none works in the CMYK mode. In addition to the **Smart Blur**, **Diffuse Glow**, **Glass**, **Ocean Ripple**, and **Glowing Edges** filters (see pages 219, 224, and 226), the 48 **Effects** filters include those in the following submenus:

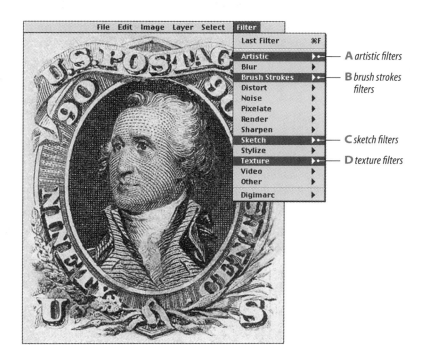

A *artistic filters*

B *brush strokes filters*

C *sketch filters*

D *texture filters*

A artistic filters

The 15 filters in the **Filter➞Artistic** submenu are meant to emulate traditional art techniques. The most successful are those that clump pixels together, like **Cutout** (below). Others, such as **Rough Pastels**, leave behind stray pixels that may not survive printing.

*cutout:
8, 2, 3*

*rough pastels:
8, 3, canvas*

B brush strokes filters

The eight **Brush Strokes** filters add brush and contour lines to an image. Note the similar use of diagonal strokes in the examples below.

*angled strokes:
75, 10, 5*

*ink outlines:
8, 20, 20*

C sketch filters

The 14 commands in the **Filter➞Sketch** submenu create grayscale effects and then colorize the darks and lights in the foreground and background colors. So if you like an effect but not the colors, choose **Edit➞Undo**, change the colors in the **Color** palette, and press **ctrl+F** (**command-F**) to reapply the filter.

*note paper:
26, 10, 12*

*reticulation:
36, 44, 8*

D texture filters

The **Texture** filters stamp the image onto a textured surface, as in the case of **Craquelure** below. Or they render the image in a textured medium, such as **Stained Glass** or **Patchwork** (also below).

*craquelure:
25, 5, 9*

*patchwork:
5, 14*

📄 Fade, Float, & Filter

By itself, a typical filter is moderately versatile. But when you throw in Photoshop's ability to mix an effect using **Fade** and **Blending Options**, you increase a filter's range of effects a thousandfold.

1 get image
Open a picture featuring friends or family. In these steps, you'll give your loved ones a soft glow.

2 apply median filter
Choose **Filter➡Noise➡Median**, enter a **Radius** value of **6** pixels, and click **OK**. This merges colors as if you had painted them with a 12 pixel-diameter brush.

3 choose fade command
Choose **Edit➡Fade Median** to mix the effect with the original. Change **Opacity** to 70% and **Mode** to **Darken**. Click **OK** to keep the darkest averaged colors.

4 float to new layer
Press **ctrl+A**, **ctrl+J** to float the image to a new layer. (On the Mac, press **command-A**, **command-J**.)

5 apply gaussian blur filter
Choose **Filter➡Blur➡Gaussian Blur**. Again, enter a **Radius** of 6 and click **OK**.

6 nudge layer up & to the left
Select the move tool (press **V**), and then press **shift-↑** and **shift-←** to move the layer 10 pixels up and left.

7 adjust blending options
Double-click the layer in the **Layers** palette. Change **Blend Mode** to **Screen** and **Opacity** to 80%. Press **alt** (Win) or **option** (Mac) and drag the black **Underlying Layer** triangle so the values read 30 and 140. This creates a glow effect only possible with layers.

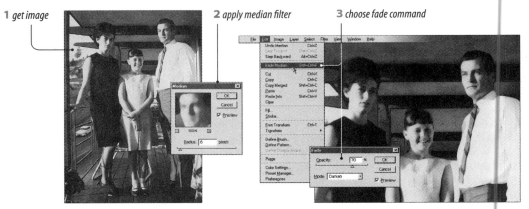

1 *get image* 2 *apply median filter* 3 *choose fade command*

4 *float to new layer* 5 *apply gaussian blur filter* 6 *nudge layer up & to the left* 7 *adjust blending options*

Work With History

Editing an image involves plenty of trial and error. Fortunately, Photoshop lets you undo multiple past operations, so almost no mistake is irreversible. But unlike most programs that offer multiple undos, Photoshop doesn't limit you to simple backstepping. Instead, it allows you to travel backward in time—often nonsequentially—to revisit any particular step in the progression of an image.

In addition to letting you undo errors with unparalleled selectivity, Photoshop's history functions offer scads of other practical and creative applications. You can take a picture of an image at a particular moment in time, view before and after versions of your edits, and paint back to a previous point in time to brush away mistakes or create impressionistic effects. You can even experiment with alternative realities and merge those realities with the present.

The History Palette

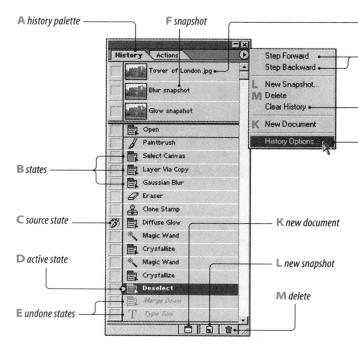

A *history palette*
F *snapshot*
G *opened state*
H *step forward/backward*
I *clear history*
J *history options*
K *new document*
L *new snapshot*
M *delete*
B *states*
C *source state*
D *active state*
E *undone states*

The **History** palette is Photoshop's central head-quarters for time travel. It records each significant action you perform on an image and adds it to a sequential list.

A history palette

Choose **Window→Show History**. Or press F9 to dis-play the **Actions** palette and then click the **History** panel tab. Either way, you get the **History** palette.

B states

Each item in the palette list represents a *state* of the image at a particular moment in time. Photoshop names each state according to the command, tool, or action involved in the operation. The icon to the left of the name serves as a further identifier.

> *tip* By default, the **History** palette tracks the last 20 operations. To change the number of states the palette list can hold, press **ctrl+K** (**command-K** on the Mac) and enter a value from 1 to 100 in the **History States** option box.

C source state

Click the box to the left of a state to select it as the *source state*. You can paint with the source state using the history brush (see The History Brush, page 234), art history brush (The Art History Brush, page 235), and eraser (The Eraser Tool, page 118). You can also use the **Fill** com-mand to fill a selection with the source state, as explained in Undo & Revert on the facing page.

D active state

Click a state to revert to that point in the history of your image. All of the operations performed after that state are immediately undone (E) and the image changes accordingly on screen. To redo all the oper-ations you just undid, choose **Edit→Undo State Change** or press **ctrl+Z** (**command-Z** on the Mac).

E undone states

States listed after the active state appear gray to indi-cate they've been undone. You can click an undone state to redo it. But if you perform a new operation, all undone states disappear from the palette list. Press **ctrl+Z** (**command-Z** on the Mac) to redisplay them. If you perform a second operation before pressing **ctrl+Z**, the once-grayed states are perma-nently deleted. So be careful.

> *tip* To prevent undone states from disappearing when you perform a new operation, choose the **History Options** command (J) and select the **Allow Non-Linear History** check box.

F snapshot

You can preserve an important state as a *snapshot* so it never falls off the palette list. Simply select the state and click the **New Snapshot** button (L).

G opened state

Photoshop automatically creates a snapshot of your image as it appears when first opened. To prevent this behavior, choose the **History Options** command (J) and turn off the first check box.

H step forward/backward

Use these two commands to step forward (down) or backward (up) through the list of states. Alternatively, press **ctrl+alt+Z** (**command-option-Z** on the Mac) or **ctrl+shift+Z** (**command-shift-Z** on the Mac) to move up or down the list, respectively. You can drag the right-pointing triangle next to the active state (D) up or down to move backward or forward more quickly.

> *tip* You can backstep through states even after saving, great for restoring an image after accidentally pressing **ctrl+S**.

I clear history

Photoshop can get sluggish as states accumulate. To clear the states without affecting the image, choose **Clear History** from the palette menu. If you change

your mind, press **ctrl+Z** (**command-z** on the Mac) to bring the states back.

J history options

Choose this command to display a dialog box that contains options for creating and saving snapshots and recording states out of order.

K new document

To save a state permanently (beyond the current session), click this button or choose **New Document**. Photoshop duplicates the state to a new window.

L new snapshot

Click this button to create a snapshot (F) of the active state. **Alt-click** (Win) or **option**-click (Mac) the button or choose the **New Snapshot** command to name a snapshot as you create it.

M delete

Drag a state to the trash can to delete it and subsequent states. If you turned on **Allow Non-Linear History** (J), clicking the **Delete** button deletes only the active state.

Undo & Revert

In addition to the capabilities of the **History** palette, Photoshop offers more traditional undo and reversion methods.

Undo/redo last operation

Choose **Edit➞Undo** to restore an image to the way it appeared before the last operation. You also can press **ctrl+Z** (Win) or **command-Z** (Mac). To redo what you just undid, press **ctrl+Z** again. Note that you cannot undo disk operations, such as saving. If you accidentally save an image, you can

restore it by backstepping through states in the **History** palette, as explained above (H).

Revert to image on disk

If you've made a mess of things and cleared the **History** palette (I), don't despair. You can reload the image from disk. Choose **File➞Revert** or press the F12 key.

> *tip* The **History** palette tracks the **Revert** command, so even reverting to the image saved on disk is undoable.

Revert a selection

Use the **Fill** command to revert a selected area to the way it looked at any prior state. Simply set the source state (C) in the **History** palette, choose **Edit➞Fill**, and then choose **History** from the **Use** pop-up menu in the **Fill** dialog box. Alternatively, you can skip the dialog box rigmarole and just press **ctrl+alt+backspace** (**command-option-delete** on the Mac) to fill a selection with the source state on the fly.

The History Brush

A *history brush tool* B *brush preview* C *brush picker* D *blend mode* E *opacity* F *brush dynamics*

Photoshop rounds out its history functions with two brush tools: the history brush (A) and the art history brush (G). Both enable you to paint into the past to achieve creative results.

A history brush tool

The history brush works much like the eraser does when the **Erase to History** option is turned on (The Eraser Tool, page 118). Drag with the tool to paint with the source state specified in the **History** palette (C on page 232). But unlike the eraser tool, the history brush offers 18 blend modes (D) that enable you to mix pixels from the source and target states to create interesting effects. Press the Y key to select the history brush from the keyboard.

> *tip* The history brush is a convenient tool for brushing away mistakes, but you can also use it to selectively merge different states, as I explain in Merge Alternative Snapshots on pages 236 through 238.

B brush preview

Click here to display the brush editor, which includes options for setting the size and shape of the brush. For more information on these options, see Brush Size & Shape on pages 96 and 97 of Chapter 7.

C brush picker

Click this down-pointing arrow to display a drop-down palette of brush presets, also explained in the Brush Size & Shape section of Chapter 7.

D blend mode

Choose an option from this pop-up menu to blend the pixels from the source state and active state of the image. See The Blend Modes on pages 137 through 139 of Chapter 10 for a complete rundown on how each mode works.

E opacity

Reduce the **Opacity** value to create translucent brush-strokes. You can press a number key to change the value from the keyboard.

The Art History Brush

G art history brush tool

F brush dynamics

Click this button to display options for varying the size and opacity of a brushstroke. You can choose to either fade it over a specified distance or link it to stylus pressure if you have a pressure-sensitive tablet.

G art history brush tool

Press shift-Y to switch to the art history brush, which enables you to paint with the source state to create impressionistic effects. The art history brush offers the same options as the history brush (A), except you have fewer blend modes (D) to choose from.

H style

The art history brush is equipped with four options beyond those of the history brush, starting with **Style**. Choose a setting from this pop-up menu to determine the basic shape of brushstrokes. Tighter and shorter shapes preserve more detail in the image; looser and bigger shapes produce less focused results. The **Dab** option sprays dots of color, handy for creating pointillistic effects.

I fidelity

The art history brush paints with colors lifted from the source state. Reduce the **Fidelity** value to allow brushstrokes to deviate from the source color. Lower values enable colors to vary from the source color more significantly.

J area

This option controls the area covered by each click or drag with the art history brush. Raise the value to lay down more brushstrokes over a larger area; lower the value to produce fewer strokes in a smaller area.

K spacing

The **Spacing** value limits where the art history brush can paint based on how much the colors in the image differ from the source state. Higher **Spacing** values restrict strokes to regions where colors differ significantly; lower values permit strokes in areas where color differences are less dramatic. Enter a value of 0 to permit the art history brush to paint anywhere inside the image.

Steps Merge Alternative Snapshots

Using the history brush and **History** palette, you can selectively merge any number of states to achieve effects that would otherwise require much more effort. The possibilities are nearly endless. The following steps present one example:

1 get image
Open an image you want to enhance with filters. I chose a runner in dire need of some speed.

2 apply filter
The filter you choose depends on your image and the effect you want to achieve. I chose **Filter➠Stylize➠ Wind** and selected **From the Left** to give my runner a stylized sense of forward motion. Then I pressed **ctrl+F** (**command-F** on the Mac) to apply a second pass of the **Wind** filter. As with any operation, Photoshop adds the filter as a state—or in my case, two states—in the **History** palette.

3 create & name snapshot
Alt-click (Win) or **option**-click (Mac) the little page button at the bottom of the **History** palette to display the **New Snapshot** dialog box. Enter a name for your snapshot and press **enter** (Win) or **return** (Mac). Be sure to use something descriptive, like the name of the filter you just applied, so you'll be able to identify it easily later.

> *tip* To avoid having to **alt**-click (or **option**-click) the little page button to display the **New Snapshot** dialog box, choose the **History Options** command from the **History** palette menu. Then select the **Show New Snapshot Dialog by Default** check box and click **OK**. From then on, a simple click of the button will invoke the dialog box.

4 allow non-linear history
By default, if you select the top snapshot item in the **History** palette and then perform a new operation (as you will in 5 and 6), Photoshop deletes any previous states from the palette. To prevent this from happening, choose **History Options** from the palette menu and turn on the **Allow Non-Linear History** check box. Then click **OK** to accept the new setting.

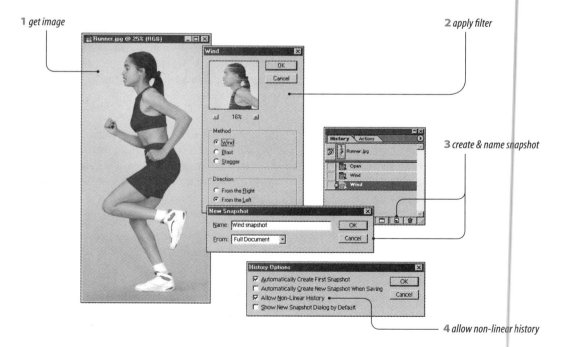

1 *get image*

2 *apply filter*

3 *create & name snapshot*

4 *allow non-linear history*

5 select top snapshot

You'll want to apply the next filter to the original image, so you can combine it with the first filter effect according to your tastes. Click the top snapshot item—the one that shares the same name as your image when you opened it—to revert the image to the way it appeared when first opened.

6 apply another filter

As in step 2, the filter you apply is up to you. I wanted to add to my motion effect, so I chose **Filter➡Blur➡Motion Blur** and entered an **Angle** value of 0° and a **Distance** of 30 pixels.

7 save as snapshot

Save the new filter state as a snapshot by **alt**-clicking (**option**-clicking on the Mac) the tiny page button and entering a name in the **New Snapshot** dialog box.

8 set target & source

It's now time to paint your snapshots back into the original image. Your first order of business is to select the very first snapshot in the **History** palette to make it the target state. Then click in the box to the left of the filter snapshot that you want to make the source state. I clicked next to the **Motion Blur snapshot** because I wanted to apply that effect first.

9 select history brush

Press the Y key to activate the history brush.

10 set brush options & paint

Click the brush preview (B on page 234) in the options bar to specify the brush size and shape. Then choose a blend mode from the **Mode** pop-up menu, enter a value in the **Opacity** option box, and paint inside the image. If you don't like the results, press **ctrl+Z** (command-Z on the Mac), change the **Mode** and **Opacity** settings, and try again.

I set the blend mode to **Normal** and the **Opacity** to 80% to paint in the **Motion Blur snapshot**. This results in a loss of image detail, which I'll selectively restore by painting with my **Wind snapshot**.

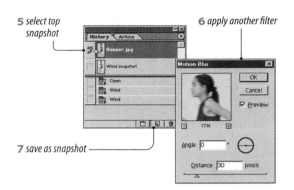

5 *select top snapshot*

6 *apply another filter*

7 *save as snapshot*

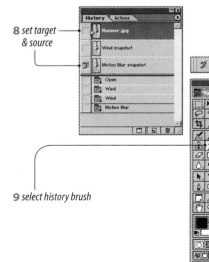

8 *set target & source*

9 *select history brush*

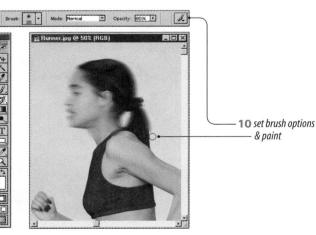

10 *set brush options & paint*

11 set new source

Now it's time to merge the second filter effect with the first. To do so, click to the left of the other snapshot in the **History** palette (in my case, the **Wind snapshot** item) to set it as the source for the history brush. Leave the target state, which should be the last **History Brush** item in the palette, as is.

12 adjust brush options

If you've switched away from the history brush, press the Y key to reactivate it. Then change the **Mode** and **Opacity** settings in the options bar to suit the effect you're trying to achieve. For example, I set the blend mode to **Lighten** and changed the **Opacity** value to 50% so I could paint in my **Wind** effect without obliterating the **Motion Blur**.

> *tip* Remember, you can change the **Opacity** value from the keyboard by pressing a number key. Press 1 for 10%, 2 for 20%, and so on.

13 paint & repeat

You can vary the **Opacity** value and blend mode as you work. For example, after painting one pass with

the **Wind snapshot** at 50% opacity, I raised the **Opacity** value to 70% and brushed over the runner's hair, shoulder, and lower-left arm to enhance the overall motion effect.

From here on, it's a matter of swapping back and forth between snapshots and painting with the history brush until you achieve the desired results. Remember, you can always backstep through previous states, so feel free to experiment.

14 choose save as

Choose **File➞Save As** to save the altered image under a new name or press **ctrl+S** (**command**-S on the Mac) to save over the original file on disk. The snapshots and other items in the **History** palette remain intact until you close the image, at which point they're gone for good.

> *tip* If you arrive at a state that you might want to revisit even after closing the image, select the state item and click the leftmost button at the bottom of the **History** palette. This opens the state in a new window, which you can then save as a separate image.

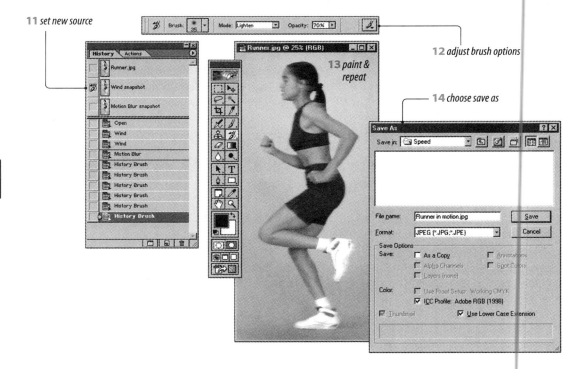

11 *set new source*

12 *adjust brush options*

13 *paint & repeat*

14 *choose save as*

16

Play & Record Actions

It's easy to love Photoshop, but it's difficult to know it. With a few hundred commands and far more options and settings, it can seem quite the unmanageable monster. Luckily, Photoshop ships with lots of predefined shortcuts to help you quickly apply desired effects and tame Photoshop's beastly side.

Of course, not every command includes a shortcut. That's why you can make your own with the **Actions** palette. An *action* consists of one or more *operations*, each of which is a record of a task you execute, such as choosing a command or specifying options in a dialog box. When you record an action, you can choose a unique keyboard equivalent to go with it, permitting you to design your own shortcuts. The number of operations in an action is limited only by the amount of memory in your system. This means that you can record a long list of operations that you plan to use over and over again.

The Actions Palette

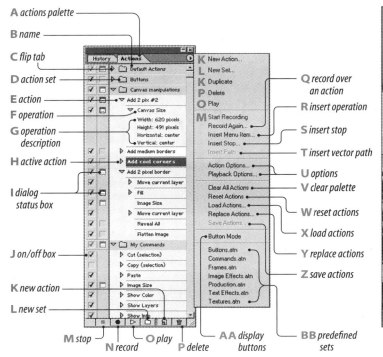

- **A** actions palette
- **B** name
- **C** flip tab
- **D** action set
- **E** action
- **F** operation
- **G** operation description
- **H** active action
- **I** dialog status box
- **J** on/off box
- **K** new action
- **L** new set
- **M** stop
- **N** record
- **O** play
- **P** delete
- **AA** display buttons
- **BB** predefined sets
- **K** New Action...
- **L** New Set...
- **K** Duplicate
- **P** Delete
- **O** Play
- **M** Start Recording
- Record Again...
- Insert Menu Item...
- Insert Stop...
- Insert Path
- Action Options...
- Playback Options...
- Clear All Actions
- Reset Actions...
- Load Actions...
- Replace Actions...
- Save Actions...
- Button Mode
- **Q** record over an action
- **R** insert operation
- **S** insert stop
- **T** insert vector path
- **U** options
- **V** clear palette
- **W** reset actions
- **X** load actions
- **Y** replace actions
- **Z** save actions

Before Photoshop can go into autopilot and execute your time-saving actions, you need to familiarize yourself with the nuts and bolts of the **Actions** palette. Prepare for takeoff.

A actions palette
Choose **Window➡Show Actions** or press the F9 key to display the **Actions** palette.

B name
To identify its contents, every set (D), action (E), and operation (F) has a name. Change the name of a set or action by double-clicking on it. Note that Photoshop names operations automatically.

C flip tab
Click the right-pointing triangle to the left of a palette item to display its contents. If a flip tab appears next to an operation (F), a specific description (G) of the operation's settings is available. Sets and actions always have flip tabs since they require content.

D action set
Sets are intended to conveniently group similar actions. They are also necessary for saving actions (Z).

E action
You record a series of operations as an action in order to apply the same steps to any image with a simple click of the **Play** button (O). By using actions for common tasks, you can automate parts of your everyday workflow. You can give an action any name you like (B) and even assign it a keyboard shortcut (U).

> *tip* If you want to add a shortcut to a command that doesn't have one, simply record an action that consists only of choosing the command and assign that action a unique shortcut. See Make A Custom Shortcut on page 243 for all the details.

F operation
Each significant operation you perform while recording an action (E) is saved as a separate item in the

Actions palette. I say "significant" because Photoshop can't record some operations, such as zooming, scrolling, and choosing commands under the **View** and **Window** menus, but in most cases you can manually insert them (R).

G operation description

A flip tab (C) next to an operation name indicates that the operation will implement specific settings upon playback. Click the tab to review a description of the settings, which helps you decide whether an operation's respective dialog box should display when the operation next activates (I). If an operation doesn't have a flip tab, such as **Reveal All**, it will execute the same way each time it plays.

> (tip) If an operation that would typically record with specific settings lacks a description, that means the operation was added via **Insert Menu Item** (R) and requires you to view its dialog box upon each play.

H active action

This is the action that's ready to play or accept modification via the palette menu commands. To make an action active, simply click it.

I dialog status box

When a tiny *dialog status box* appears to the left of an operation, it means that Photoshop will display the operation's dialog box to give you a chance to choose different settings. The settings you specify during a particular playback session have no impact on the settings recorded with the operation. If you turn off a status box by clicking it, Photoshop uses your recorded settings when it next applies the operation. Turn the status box next to an action on or off to activate or deactivate the status box for each operation the action contains. Similarly, the status box next to a set controls the status boxes of all the actions and operations within that set.

> (tip) A dimmed version of the dialog status box means that the operation was added using the **Insert Menu Item** (R) command. You have to view the operation's dialog box every time it plays.

J on/off box

A checked box indicates that an operation is on and will execute with its action. Click to uncheck an operation and turn it off, thus permitting you to customize the behavior of an action. You can also toggle the on/off state of a group of operations at the action (E) and set (D) levels.

K new action

Click this button or choose **New Action** from the palette menu to display the **New Action** dialog box, where you begin recording a new action. Name the action and choose the set in which you want to store it. Then assign a shortcut, consisting of a function key and up to two modifiers—**shift** and **ctrl** (Win) or **command** (Mac). You can also assign a color to the action, which comes into play when working in the button mode (AA). Click **Record** to start recording.

L new set

Click here or choose **New Set** from the palette menu to display the **New Set** dialog box, which lets you create and name a new set.

> (tip) To bypass the **New Action** or the **New Set** dialog box, alt-click (**option**-click on the Mac) the appropriate button. Photoshop creates a generically named action or set. In the case of an action, it assigns neither a shortcut nor a color.

M stop

Click here when you're done recording an action.

N record

To add operations to the end of an action, select the action and click this button. Photoshop records each operation you perform and tacks it on to the end of the action. When you're done, click the **Stop** button (M). To insert additional operations at a specific point in an action, select an operation (F) and click the **Record** button. Photoshop adds the new operations below the operation you selected.

Note that the **Record** button is active when you create a new action (K) because Photoshop starts recording automatically. Clicking the **Stop** button turns it off.

O play

Click this button or choose **Play** from the palette menu to execute the active action. To play an action from a specific operation on, select that operation and click **Play**.

> *tip* You can also play an action by pressing **ctrl** (Win) or **command** (Mac) and double-clicking it.

P delete

To delete an operation, action, or set, drag it to the trash can. Or select the item and **alt**-click (**option**-click on the Mac) the trash can.

Q record over an action

If you're unhappy with an action's settings but you want to retain its overall structure, choose **Record Again** to play the current action, pausing at every operation that includes a dialog box so you can record new settings. Any changes made to an operation during this play session become the default settings. To change the recorded settings of a single operation, either double-click the operation or select it and choose **Record Again**.

R insert operation

Some tasks you perform while creating an action will not record as operations. This means that you need to insert these operations manually after you finish the initial recording. To do so, choose **Insert Menu Item**, select the desired command, and click **OK**. Photoshop inserts the missing command in the action. Unfortunately, when you use **Insert Menu Item**, you can't set the options associated with the command.

S insert stop

A *stop* is an operation that performs no image-related function, but instead displays a message. Stops can serve to introduce a complicated action to a user or explain prep-work required for an action. Be sure to check the **Allow Continue** check box so that the user has the option to continue after viewing the stop's content. You can use the **Insert Stop** command to add a stop to an existing or currently recording action.

> *tip* If a stop's only purpose is to introduce an action, uncheck it (J) once you're familiar with the action so you don't have to view it every time.

T insert vector path

The only way to record the addition of a path (see The Paths Palette on page 76) is to draw the path and choose the **Insert Path** command. Note that Photoshop does not record other operations related to path construction or editing.

U options

To change the name of a set, choose **Set Options** or double-click the set. Choose **Action Options** or double-click an action to change its name, keyboard shortcut, or button color (AA). Use the **Playback Options** command to control how quickly an action plays. The default setting, **Accelerated**, plays actions at full speed. **Step by Step** allows just enough extra time to display each operation. **Pause For** slows the playback by delaying the execution of each operation a specified number of seconds.

V clear palette

Choose **Clear All Actions** to empty the palette of every single operation, action, and set.

W reset actions

Choose this command to remove all currently shown sets except **Default Actions**.

X load actions

To load a set stored on disk, choose this command.

Y replace actions

Choose this command to clear all active sets from the palette and replace them with the set of your choice.

Z save actions

Photoshop saves sets of actions at a time. When you choose this command, the **Photoshop Actions** folder is the default destination. Any set saved in that folder appears as a predefined set (BB) in the palette menu the next time you start Photoshop.

AA display buttons

Choose **Button Mode** to display each action as a button. In this mode, you can click a button to play its action, but you can't alter an action in any way.

BB predefined sets

Any set saved in the **Photoshop Actions** folder appears at the end of the menu. Choose a set from the list to make it available in the palette.

Make A Custom Shortcut

Photoshop ships with hundreds of predefined keyboard equivalents, but some extremely useful commands—including such stalwart workhorses as **Color Range**, **Unsharp Mask**, and **Gaussian Blur**—somehow never made the cut. Fortunately, creating a shortcut for a command is a simple task. All you need is an open image and these steps:

1 select set
Select the set in which you want to record the action. If you need to create a new set, click the **New Set** button, enter a name for the set, and click **OK**.

2 create action
Before you can begin recording, you need to create a new action. Click the tiny page at the bottom of the **Actions** palette or choose the **New Action** command. The **New Action** dialog box appears.

3 assign name & shortcut
Since you're creating an action based on a single command, just name the action after the command. Assign the action a keyboard shortcut by choosing a key from the **Function Key** pop-up menu. Add the **Shift** and **Control** (Win) or **Command** (Mac) modifiers as desired. If an F-key or modifier is dimmed, it's because it's already taken by another action.

When you're done, click **Record** to exit the **New Action** dialog box and begin recording.

4 choose command, enter settings
In the example below, I chose **Image⇒Canvas Size**. If the command you choose is associated with a dialog box, enter the desired settings and click **OK**. Many dialog boxes, including **Canvas Size**, require you to enter some kind of settings to record the operation.

> *tip* If Photoshop doesn't record your command as an operation, choose **Insert Menu Item** from the palette menu and then choose the command.

5 stop recording
Click the **Stop** button to end the action.

6 set dialog status box
If you want to use the operation with the settings you entered while recording (4), leave this box empty. If you prefer to customize the settings every time you apply the action, click the dialog status box to turn it on. Photoshop will display the dialog box each time you press the keyboard shortcut (3).

> *tip* To change the default settings for an operation, double-click it or choose **Record Again** from the palette menu and enter new settings.

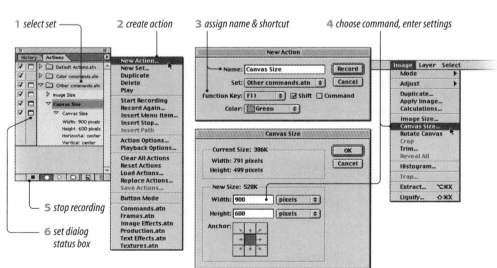

1 select set   2 create action   3 assign name & shortcut   4 choose command, enter settings

5 stop recording

6 set dialog status box

⏺steps Record A Multistep Action

A multistep action contains a series of commands and operations that you can apply to an image with a single click or keystroke. The following steps take you through one example that demonstrates the general process of recording a multistep action.

1 get image
For the purpose of this demonstration, open an image that you want to place on a painterly cloud background. I opted for a photograph of Big Ben.

2 select set
Select the set in which you want to record the action. If you like, click the **New Set** button to create and name a new set.

3 create action
Click the **New Action** button. When the dialog box appears, give the action a name, something descriptive so you can easily identify it later. Assign a function key shortcut and choose a color if you like. Then press **enter** (Win) or **return** (Mac) to begin recording.

4 remove background
The best way to create the clouds was to set them on an independent layer in back of Big Ben. So I

had to remove the existing background from the image. To make this as action-friendly as possible, I chose **Select➡Color Range**. I clicked in the background with the eyedropper tool. Then I increased the **Fuzziness** value until the background in the preview appeared white and clicked the **OK** button. Having selected the background, I still had to delete it. I double-clicked **Background** in the **Layers** palette and clicked **OK** to convert it to a floating layer. Then I pressed **backspace** (**delete** on the Mac) to clear the background, leaving only Big Ben.

5 render clouds on new layer
Ctrl-click (**command**-click on the Mac) the tiny page in the **Layers** palette to create a new layer behind the active one. Press **ctrl+D** (**command-D**) to deselect the image. Select the desired foreground and background colors for your clouds and choose **Filter➡Render➡Clouds**. Feel free to add a few applications of **Difference Clouds** to get the right effect.

6 duplicate original layer
Click the original layer or press **alt+]** (Win) or **option-]** (Mac) to select it. Then choose **Duplicate Layer** from the palette menu and give the new layer an appropriate name, such as **Applied Filters**. Click **OK**.

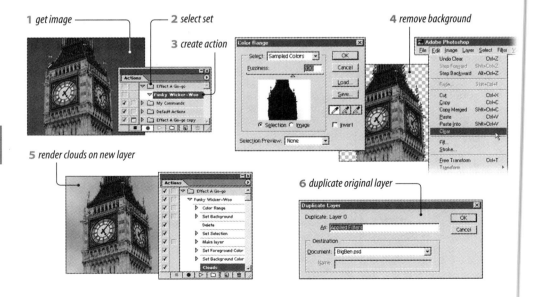

1 *get image* — 2 *select set* — 3 *create action* — 4 *remove background*

5 *render clouds on new layer* — 6 *duplicate original layer*

7 apply poster edges filter

Next, I applied **Filter➡Artistic➡ Poster Edges** to the duplicate layer. I adjusted the settings as shown below to create a painterly effect.

8 set layer blending options

Double-click the duplicate layer to display the **Layer Styles** dialog box. Here I chose the **Multiply** blend mode, set the **Opacity** to 75%, and dragged the black triangle under the **This Layer** slider to 36. This made the image look like a painted photograph.

9 apply accented edges

I wanted a bit more edge. So I chose **Filter➡Brush Strokes➡Accented Edges** and applied the settings below. This gave the edges a thick, inky look.

10 apply unsharp mask filter

As my final effect, I used **Filter➡Sharpen➡Unsharp Mask** to bring out the contrast in the image and give it a slightly otherworldly appearance.

11 click stop

Satisfied with the effect, I clicked the **Stop** button in the **Actions** palette. But you can record more filters if you like. Nothing says your effect has to look like mine.

12 clean up action

Look over the action and delete any unnecessary operations. For example, during my experimentations, I recorded extra colors for the **Clouds** filter and hid and displayed layers to check their impact. To remove these extraneous steps from the action, click and ctrl-click (**command**-click on the Mac) to select the offending operations, and then drag them onto the trash can at the bottom of the **Actions** palette.

13 test action

Open a new image. Then press **ctrl** (**command** on the Mac) and double-click the action to play it. Note how the action performs and how it might be improved.

14 adjust play options

Toggle each operation's on/off and dialog status boxes as needed. For example, I noticed that the first operation, **Color Range**, didn't select the test image's background to my satisfaction. So I forced the **Color Range** dialog box to display during future executions, allowing me to make a more precise selection. I also turned off the **Set Foreground Color** and **Set Background Color** operations so the action would skip them during playback. Finally, I inserted a stop to preface the action with a brief description.

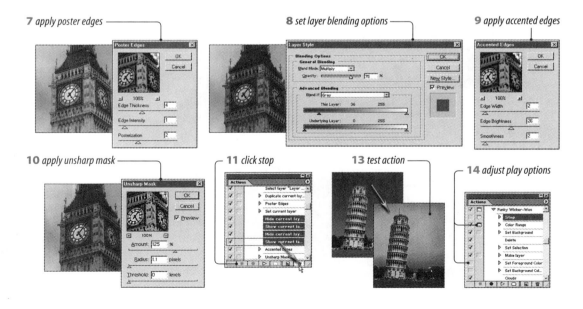

7 apply poster edges

8 set layer blending options

9 apply accented edges

10 apply unsharp mask

11 click stop

13 test action

14 adjust play options

steps Save An Action As A Droplet

A *droplet* is a special version of an action that you save as an independent file. It contains all the action's instructions, permitting you to use it on any machine that has Photoshop installed.

1 select action
Select the action that you want to save as a droplet.

2 choose create droplet
Choose **File➡Automate➡Create Droplet**. The **Create Droplet** dialog box appears.

3 set folder & name
Since a droplet is an external version of an action, you need to find a place to store it. Click the **Choose** button to display the standard **Save** dialog box. Select a destination for the droplet and give it a name. For convenience, you may want to save it in the same folder as the images for which the droplet is designed.

4 verify set & action
By default, the **Play** pop-up menus display the set and action you selected in step 1. If you have since changed your mind, adjust the options as necessary.

5 set play options
If your action contains operations that use the **Open** command, select **Override Action "Open" Commands** to make Photoshop ignore them in favor of the droplet's own opening functions. Select **Include All Subfolders** to make the droplet process all files inside a folder, even those buried several folders deep. Select **Suppress Color Profile Warnings** to disable any warnings related to color profiling. If in doubt, leave these three check boxes on.

6 select destination for images
Use the **Destination** pop-up menu to specify where you want to store your images after the droplet processes them. To save the files to a new location, choose **Folder**. Then click the **Choose** button and select a destination folder.

7 override save commands (optional)
If your action contains **Save** operations, select **Override Action "Save In" Commands**. This prevents the action from saving the images—possibly to a different folder than the one you specified (6)—before the droplet has finished processing them.

8 choose filename
A droplet can use up to six modifiers when naming a processed file, including the original filename, a progressive serial number, the current date, and the file extension. If you need to name the files so they comply with a foreign operating system, select the appropriate check box (**Windows, Mac OS,** or **Unix**). If in doubt, select them all.

9 set error handling
Photoshop may encounter errors while running a droplet. From the **Errors** pop-up menu, choose **Stop For Errors** to tell Photoshop to pause for every error. Or choose **Log Errors To File** to make Photoshop log errors in a text file on disk. Finally, click **OK** to save the droplet.

1 select action

2 choose create droplet

3 set folder & name

4 verify set & action

5 set play options

6 select destination for images

7 override save commands

8 choose filename

9 set error handling

Batch Process With A Droplet

Once you create a droplet (as in Save An Action As A Droplet on the facing page), you're just a drag and a drop away from automating images in Photoshop. A droplet lets you apply an action to a folder full of images in one fell swoop, called *batch processing*.

1 locate droplet

Open the folder that contains the droplet you want to use. If you've stored your images separately from the droplet, leave this folder open as you locate the images you plan to process (2).

2 locate image folder

Locate the folder of images you wish to process. Since you're going to drag the folder onto the droplet (3), you need to be sure that you can see both the droplet and the image folder simultaneously.

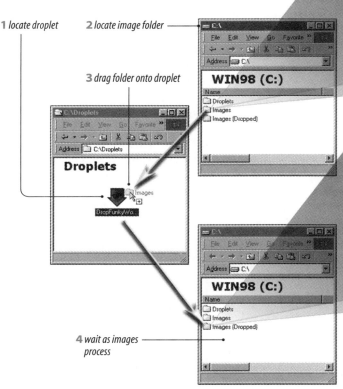

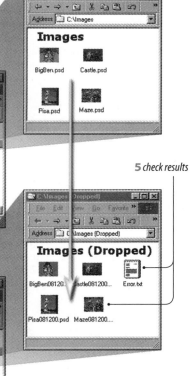

3 drag folder onto droplet

You can drag a single image or an entire folder of images onto a droplet. Provided that you set the droplet to recognize subfolders (as in step 5 on page 246), it will process all image files within the dragged folder without exception.

4 wait as images process

If Photoshop isn't currently running, it will launch automatically. Be patient. It may take awhile for the droplet to finish processing.

5 check results

After Photoshop has saved the images and deposited them into the destination folder (step 6 on the facing page), you should verify that all images have processed properly. If Photoshop encountered any problems, check the **Error.txt** document for details.

<img_1_icon> Batch Process Inside Photoshop

Droplets are great for applying actions to collections of images over and over again. But for one-time only batching, you don't need to bother. You can use the **Batch** command to process a folder of images without ever leaving Photoshop.

1 select action
Although not absolutely necessary, it helps to open the **Actions** palette and select the action that you want to use before choosing the **Batch** command.

2 choose batch command
Choose **File➔Automate➔Batch** to display the **Batch** dialog box, shown below.

3 confirm set and action
By default, the **Play** pop-up menus list the active set and action (1). Change the selections if desired.

4 specify source
Use the **Source** pop-up menu to specify the location of the images you want to batch. Select the **Opened Files** option if you want Photoshop to process only those files that are currently open. Select **Import** to process images acquired from a scanner or digital camera. Then use the **From** pop-up menu to select

from the import module that corresponds to the device. If you want to process a folder of images, select **Folder** and click the **Choose** button to identify the source folder.

5 set options
When **Folder** is your source, three check boxes appear below the **Choose** button. **Override Action "Open" Commands** suppress **Open** operations in the action; **Include All Subfolders** ensures that files within subfolders of the source folder are also processed; and **Suppress Color Profile Warnings** hides any pesky warnings related to color profiling.

6 choose destination
The **Destination** pop-up menu offers three post-processing choices. **None** leaves the images open inside Photoshop without saving them. The potentially dangerous **Save And Close** closes the files after saving over the originals. Unless the originals are safely backed up, I don't recommend it. Your best bet, **Folder**, gives you the option to specify where you want to save the processed images. Click the **Choose** button to select the destination folder. Turn on the **Override Action "Save In" Commands** check box to prevent the action from saving files before processing is complete.

7 choose filename
If you choose **Folder** as the **Destination** (6), you can select from six **File Naming** modifiers, including original filename, serial number or letter, current date, and extension. To force the modifiers to comply with the wide world of operating systems, select the appropriate **Compatibility** check boxes.

8 set error handling
You can make Photoshop stop for any errors that occur while processing (**Stop For Errors**) or simply report them to a text file that you can review later (**Log Errors To File**). When your settings are complete, click **OK** to begin processing.

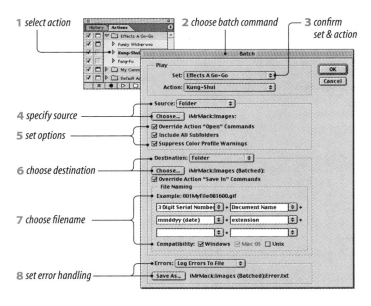

- 1 select action
- 2 choose batch command
- 3 confirm set & action
- 4 specify source
- 5 set options
- 6 choose destination
- 7 choose filename
- 8 set error handling

Print An Image

Printing an image can be a tricky endeavor, requiring you to wade through a multitude of options and undertake numerous preparations in order to achieve the desired results. The process can be arduous, intimidating, and more than a little confusing.

The ensuing pages whittle this complicated topic down to size, showing you all you need to know about Photoshop's most useful and essential printing-related features. You'll learn how to ensure accurate color when sending a photograph to your desktop printer, when to use the various Photoshop-specific print options, and how to convert an image to CMYK for professional-quality output. And that's just for starters. I also take you step by step through a few other important processes: adding colors to a gray-scale image, assigning a spot color to a CMYK image, and using clipping paths to mask portions of an image for import into a page-layout program.

ⓢⓣⓔⓟⓢ Print A Color Photograph

The following steps walk you through the process of printing a color photograph to a typical color inkjet printer, an **Epson Stylus Photo EX**. Although this device is fairly representative, the options available to your printer are certain to differ.

> 💬 **tip** The *printer driver* software included with an inkjet printer automatically converts images from RGB to CMYK. To avoid double-conversion, it's best to save yourself a step and leave your photograph in the RGB space before printing.

1 choose page setup

Choose **File→Page Setup** or press **ctrl+shift+P** (**command-shift-P** on the Mac) to display the **Page Setup** dialog box, which lets you specify the paper size, orientation, and other printer-specific options.

2 choose paper size & orientation

Use the **Paper Size** pop-up menu (**Size** on the PC) to select the size of the paper on which you plan to print. Then click the **Orientation** button that corresponds to the orientation of your photograph.

3 click OK

Or press **enter** (Win) or **return** (Mac) to save your settings and exit the **Page Setup** dialog box.

4 choose print options

Choose **File→Print Options** or press **ctrl+alt+P** (**command-option-P** on the Mac) to open the **Print Options** dialog box (The Print Options Command, page 252), which sets how the image fits on the page.

5 preview & scale image

The preview on the left shows the size and position of the image on the page. If the image exceeds the page boundaries, then portions of the photograph will be clipped when printed. A white area around the image means the image won't fill the page. To make the printed image larger or smaller, enter a value above or below 100%, respectively, in the **Scale** option box. You can also set a specific size using the **Height** and **Width** options. Or select **Scale to Fit Media** to make the image fill the page. Note that all these options affect the resolution of the image (as in Change The Print Size on page 25 of Chapter 2).

6 click print

This brings up the **Print** dialog box, which varies dramatically from printer to printer.

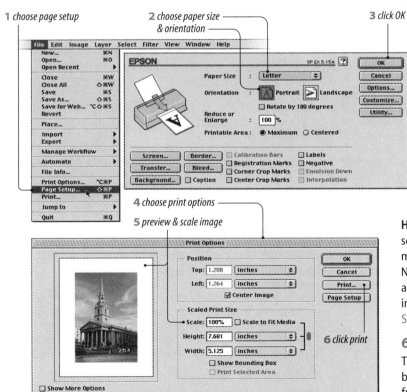

1 choose page setup
2 choose paper size & orientation
3 click OK
4 choose print options
5 preview & scale image
6 click print

7 click setup & properties (Win)

Next, you'll want to adjust the quality, media, and color settings, which are accessible from the **Print** dialog box on the Mac. On the PC, however, these options reside in the **Properties** dialog box, which you invoke by clicking **Setup** and then **Properties**.

8 click more settings

If this button appears dimmed, select the **Advanced** option to activate it.

9 adjust quality

Most inkjet printers let you adjust the print quality. Lower settings are fine for proofing, but be sure to use the highest quality setting for the final image.

10 choose media type

It's also best to use photo quality paper when printing final output. If you have it, let your printer know.

11 select CMS

Most likely, your printer's own color management system (CMS) is active by default. You may achieve more accurate colors by selecting an alternative CMS, such as Apple's **ColorSync** or Microsoft's **ICM**, or by adjusting color settings manually. For my Stylus Photo EX, I found **ColorSync** generally produces the best results. But your best bet is to experiment with the different options available to your printer.

12 click OK

Or press **return** (Mac) to save your settings and return to the **Print** dialog box. On the PC, you need to click **OK** twice to get back to the **Print** dialog box.

13 choose color profile

Choose **Printer Color Management** from this pop-up menu to print using the specified color settings (11).

> **tip** If the **Profile** pop-up menu does not appear, you can access it in the **Color Management** section of the **Print Options** dialog box, as explained on the next page.

14 click print (Mac) or OK (Win)

If you're unhappy with the results, adjust your print settings and try again.

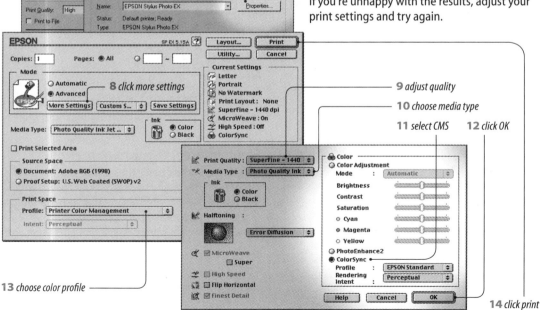

7 *click setup & properties*

8 *click more settings*

9 *adjust quality*

10 *choose media type*

11 *select CMS*   12 *click OK*

13 *choose color profile*

14 *click print*

The Print Options Command

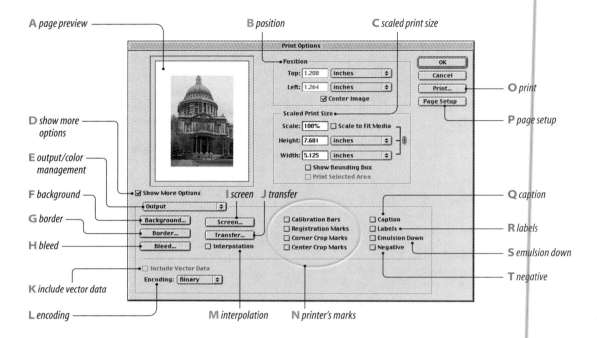

A *page preview*

B *position*

C *scaled print size*

O *print*

P *page setup*

D *show more options*

E *output/color management*

F *background*

I *screen* **J** *transfer*

Q *caption*

G *border*

R *labels*

H *bleed*

S *emulsion down*

T *negative*

K *include vector data*

L *encoding*

M *interpolation*   **N** *printer's marks*

Choose **File→Print Options** to display the **Print Options** dialog box, which contains a bevy of print settings to suit any model of printer.

A page preview
The page preview represents the image on the printable area of the page. The preview updates to reflect your changes to the dialog box settings.

B position
Enter values in the **Top** and **Left** option boxes to numerically position the image with respect to the top and left edges of the page. Use the pop-up menus to choose one of four different measurement units. Select the **Center Image** check box to center the image on the page.

C scaled print size
Use these options to specify the size of the image for the current print job; these settings do not affect the number of pixels in the image, but they do change the resolution (see Change The Print Size, page 25). The **Scale** option adjusts the image size by a specific

percentage. To numerically set the size, enter **Height** and **Width** values. Alternatively, you can select **Scale to Fit Media** to automatically scale the image to fill the page. Or select **Show Bounding Box** to manually resize the image by dragging handles in the preview window (A). If the image contains a selection made with the rectangular marquee tool, the **Print Selected Area** check box lets you print the selection only.

D show more options
Select this option to reveal more options (E through N, Q through T).

E output/color management
Choose **Output** to display the options shown above (F through N, Q through T). Choose **Color Management** to display options for setting the source and print spaces. If any options appear dimmed, don't fret; it merely means your printer doesn't support them.

F background
If you want a color to appear in the printable area around the image, click this button to display the **Color Picker** and then select a color.

G border

Click this button to add a black border around the perimeter of the image. Enter a border width in the dialog box that appears.

H bleed

A *bleed* allows an image to print off the edge of the page, useful for avoiding thin white gaps if paper shifts when printing. To create a bleed, click this button, enter a **Width** value, and click **OK**.

> *tip* If you're unsure how wide to make your bleed, 24 points (2 picas) will usually do the trick.

I screen

To represent images, printers organize pixels into tiny spots called *halftone cells*. The cells shrink or grow to reproduce light or dark shades of color, respectively. The cells combine to form a pattern called a *halftone screen*. Click the **Screen** button to display the **Halftone Screens** dialog box, which lets you change the size, shape, and angle of the individual halftone cells.

J transfer

If your output device prints too light or dark, you can compensate for the overlightening or overdarkening effect. Click this button to bring up the **Transfer Functions** dialog box, which enables you to adjust the way brightness values translate to printed shades.

K include vector data

If you're using a PostScript printer and the image contains vector-based shapes or type, select this check box to send all vector data to the printer. This means the objects will print at the full resolution of your printer, which is typically higher than the image resolution. If you deselect the check box, shapes and type print at the same resolution as the rest of the image.

> *tip* Including vector data increases the complexity of the file. That can slow printing, but the increase in quality is usually well worth it.

L encoding

Choose an option from this pop-up menu to specify the method of encoding used to send the file to a local (**ASCII**), network (**Binary**), or PostScript Level 2 or later (**JPEG**) printer.

M interpolation

Select this option to antialias a low-resolution image when printing to a PostScript Level 2 or later printer.

N printer's marks

Turn on **Calibration Bars** to print a 10-step grayscale gradation, which your commercial printer can use to ensure that shades are accurate. With color separations, Photoshop prints a gradient tint bar and a progressive color bar instead.

The **Registration Marks** option prints crosshairs and targets near the image's corners, necessary to ensure accurate registration when printing color separations.

The **Corner Crop Marks** and **Center Crop Marks** check boxes print hairline rules in the corners and center of the image, respectively, to indicate where the image should be trimmed.

O print

When you've finished specifying print options, click here to move on to the **Print** dialog box.

P page setup

Click this button to display the **Page Setup** dialog box, where you can specify the paper size, source, orientation, and other printer-specific options.

Q caption

If the image includes a caption (as in Add A Copyright & URL on page 52), turn on this check box to print it.

R lablels

Select this option to print the name of the image in 9-point Helvetica type.

S emulsion down

This option and the next (T) are useful only when printing film from an imagesetter. Turn on the check box to print an image on film with the *emulsion*, or photosensitive, side down.

T negative

Select this check box to print blacks as white and whites as black when printing film negatives.

steps Prepare A CMYK Image...

Before you import a color image into a page-layout program—such as **QuarkXPress** or **Adobe InDesign**—for professional output, you need to set the resolution and convert the RGB image to CMYK. The following steps show you how:

1 choose image size

Choose **Image➡Image Size** to bring up the **Image Size** dialog box.

2 deselect resample image

To avoid adversely affecting image quality when you change the resolution (3), turn this check box off.

3 set resolution

What **Resolution** value should you use? It depends on the output device and media on which your final

document will be printed. See the table in Select The Ideal Resolution on page 25 for some general suggestions or ask your commercial printer for specific recommendations. Remember, when the **Resample Image** check box is off, changing the resolution changes the print size as well. When in doubt, trust your eyes and go with what looks best on the page.

4 choose color settings

Choose **Edit➡Color Settings** or press **ctrl+shift+K** (Win) or **command-shift-K** (Mac) to display the **Color Settings** dialog box. This is where you specify the CMYK profile that will be assigned to the image.

Ask your print shop whether they have a Photoshop CMYK (**.api**) or ICC (**.icm**) profile for the device your document will be printed to. If they do, copy the file to the **Windows\System\Color** directory on the PC or

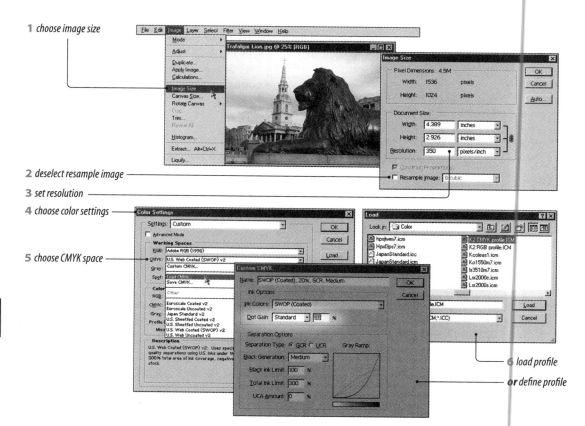

1 *choose image size*

2 *deselect resample image*

3 *set resolution*

4 *choose color settings*

5 *choose CMYK space*

6 *load profile*

or define profile

to the System Folder\Preferences\ColorSync Profiles folder on the Mac. If you use Windows, make sure the filename ends in the proper three-character extension (.api or .icm). Then proceed to step 5.

If your commercial printer doesn't have a profile, you'll need to define your own. For starters, ask for some sample output along with the CMYK image used to create it. Then open the CMYK image, choose **Image➥Mode➥Assign Profile**, and select **Don't Color Manage This Document**. Then click **OK**.

5 choose CMYK space

Back in the **Color Settings** dialog box, choose an option from the **CMYK** pop-up menu. If your print shop provided a profile, choose **Load CMYK** to display the **Load** dialog box, and move on to step 6.

If you need to create your own profile, make sure the **Preview** check box is selected, and choose **Custom CMYK** to display the **Custom CMYK** dialog box.

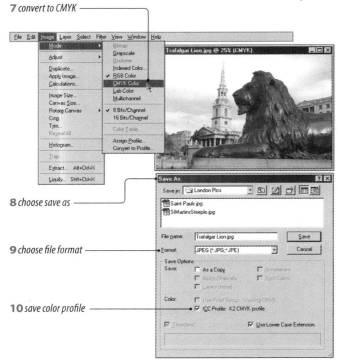

7 *convert to CMYK*

8 *choose save as*

9 *choose file format*

10 *save color profile*

6 load or define profile

If you chose **Load CMYK** in the preceding step, select the profile in the **Load** dialog box, and press **enter** (Win) or **return** (Mac) twice to close the **Load** and **Color Settings** dialog boxes, respectively. Then go directly to step 7.

If you chose **Custom CMYK**, some more work is required. First, compare the sample printed image that you got from your commercial print house to the original image on screen. If the printed image looks darker (as is likely) or lighter, select the **Dot Gain** value and raise or lower it slightly by pressing the ↑ or ↓ key, respectively. Then click **OK** and examine the effects of your changes to the image on screen.

If you can't achieve a decent match, choose **Curves** from the **Dot Gain** pop-up menu to display the **Dot Gain Curves** dialog box. Modify the display of each color channel by selecting its radio button and dragging the small point on the curve in the graph. Drag up to darken the display; drag down to lighten it.

When you're done, click **OK** to close each dialog box. Then return to the RGB image you intend to print.

7 convert to CMYK

Choose **Image➥Mode➥CMYK Color** to convert the image to CMYK using the profile you just specified (6).

8 choose save as

Choose **File➥Save As** or press **ctrl+shift+S** (Win) or **command-shift-S** (Mac) to display the **Save As** dialog box.

9 choose file format

To save the CMYK profile with the image, you need to select a format—such as TIFF, JPEG, or EPS—that supports profiles. TIFF is generally best.

10 save color profile

Make sure the **ICC Profile** (Win) or **Embed Color Profile** (Mac) check box is selected and then click **Save**.

The Duotone Command

A *duotone options* B *type* C *color swatch* D *color name* E *preview*

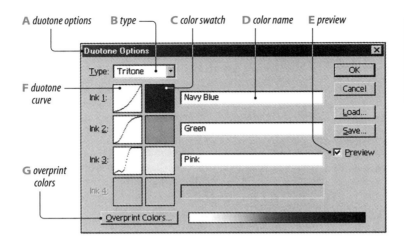

F *duotone curve*

G *overprint colors*

tip You can access the **Color Picker** from the **Custom Colors** dialog box, and vice versa, by clicking the **Picker** or **Custom** button, respectively.

A *duotone* is a grayscale image printed with two inks instead of one. By allowing additional shades for midtones, highlights, and shadows, a duotone increases the depth and clarity of an image.

A duotone options

Choose **Image▸Mode▸Duotone** to display the **Duotone Options** dialog box. Here, you can add up to three additional inks to convert a *monotone* grayscale image (one ink) to a duotone (two inks), *tritone* (three inks), or *quadtone* (four inks).

B type

By default, the **Type** pop-up menu is set to **Monotone** and the **Ink 2**, **Ink 3**, and **Ink 4** options appear dimmed to show that they're unavailable. Choose **Duotone** to activate **Ink 2**, **Tritone** to activate **Ink 2** and **Ink 3**, or **Quadtone** to activate all four inks.

C color swatch

To specify the color of an ink, click its color swatch to display the **Color Picker** (for **Ink 1**) or the **Custom Colors** dialog box (for all other inks). Use the **Color Picker** to define your own color; use the **Custom Colors** dialog box to choose from a wide variety of predefined colors. To ensure a uniform color range when the image prints, be sure to specify ink colors in descending order, from the darkest at the top to the lightest at the bottom.

D color name

After you specify an ink color, enter a name for it here. The name appears on the separation.

E preview

Turn on this check box so you can preview the effects of your changes in the image window.

F duotone curve

Click here to open the **Duotone Curve** dialog box, which lets you adjust how the associated ink is distributed across the image. The horizontal axis of the graph represents on-screen brightness values from light (at the left) to dark (at the right). The vertical axis represents the percentage of printed ink used. By default, inks are distributed evenly, and therefore blend evenly, as indicated by a diagonal line. Click in the graph to add a point to the line. Drag a point up to darken the output; drag down to lighten the output. Alternatively, you can enter percentage values in the option boxes to the right of the graph.

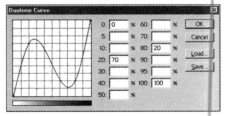

G overprint colors

You can also control how inks blend by clicking this button to display the **Overprint Colors** dialog box, which contains color swatches that show how each combination of colors will look on screen when mixed together. Click a color swatch to display the **Color Picker**, where you can modify the mixed color.

steps Create A Duotone

You can use the **Duotone** command to turn an ordinary grayscale image into a rich, sensous work of art.

1 get image
Open any image. If it's not already grayscale, choose **Image→Mode→Grayscale** to make it so.

2 choose duotone command
Choose **Image→Mode→Duotone** to bring up the **Duotone Options** dialog box. Make sure the **Preview** check box is selected.

3 select type
Choose **Duotone**, **Tritone,** or **Quadtone,** depending on whether you want to apply two, three, or four inks to your image. Keep in mind, more inks mean higher printing costs. For the purpose of my example, I figured the sky's the limit, so I chose **Quadtone**.

4 define & name colors
Click the color swatch for each ink and use the **Color Picker** or **Custom Colors** dialog box to select a color.

In the **Color Picker**, use the color slider to zero in on the color you're looking for and click in the color field on the left to select a color.

In the **Custom Colors** dialog box, choose a color family from the **Book** pop-up menu, drag the color slider to scroll through the list of available colors, and then click a color swatch to select it.

If you select a color in the **Custom Colors** dialog box, its name automatically appears in the **Duotone Options** dialog box. If you use the **Color Picker**, you need to name the color from the keyboard.

5 adjust curves
Click the curve box for each ink and use the controls in the **Duotone Curve** dialog box (F) to emphasize different inks in different areas of the image. In my quadtone, for example, **Dark Brown** is present only in the darkest portions of the image, **Orange** and **Light Blue** are stronger in lighter areas, and **Yellow** appears in the midtones.

6 click OK
After you've selected ink colors and adjusted how they blend, click **OK** to convert the image according to your specifications. If you change your mind and want to make further adjustments, choose the **Duotone** command (2) again and edit your settings.

7 save as EPS
If you plan to import the image into a page-layout program, save it as an EPS or PDF file. Other than the native Photoshop format, these are the only formats that support duotones.

1 *get image*

2 *choose duotone command*

3 *select type*

4 *define & name colors*

5 *adjust curves*

6 *click OK*

7 *save as EPS*

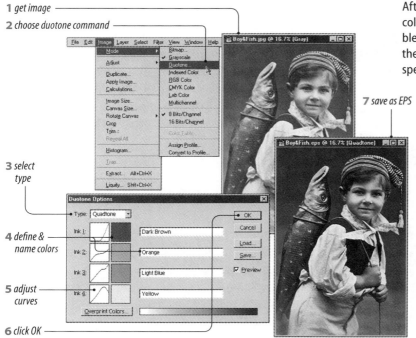

steps Add A Spot Color

Photoshop increases the number of printable colors available to you by letting you add premixed inks, called *spot colors*, to your images. Suppose you're working on a full-color advertisement for a client. The image is perfect, except the client's logo looks too dark and dull. The problem? The logo normally appears in a spot color, such as Pantone 340 green, and the CMYK equivalent just doesn't cut it. The solution? Assign the correct spot color to the logo.

1 get image
If the image is not already in the CMYK color space, choose **Image➡Mode➡CMYK Color** to convert it.

2 make selection
Use the **Color Range** command, marquee, lasso, or some other selection tool to select the element to

which you want to assign a spot color. I used the magic wand to select the **25¢** sign in my slot machine image.

3 create spot channel
Choose **Window➡Show Channels** to display the **Channels** palette. Then **ctrl**-click (Win) or **command**-click (Mac) the tiny page button at the bottom of the palette. The **New Spot Channel** dialog box appears.

4 click color swatch
This brings up the **Custom Colors** dialog box. (If the **Color Picker** appears instead, click the **Custom** button to switch to the **Custom Colors** dialog box.)

5 select spot color
Choose **Pantone Coated** or **Pantone Uncoated** from the **Book** pop-up menu, depending on whether you'll be printing your image on coated or uncoated paper.

1 *get image*

2 *make selection*

3 *create spot channel*

4 *click color swatch*

5 *select spot color*

6 *click OK*

If you're looking for a particular spot color, simply type its number to select it. For example, I typed 311 to select **Pantone 311 CVC** blue. Otherwise, use the color slider to scroll through the available colors. When you find one that suits you, click its swatch in the color list to select it.

6 click OK

Or press **enter** (Win) or **return** (Mac) twice to close the **Custom Colors** and **New Spot Channel** dialog boxes. Photoshop applies the spot color to the selection and adds a new spot channel item at the bottom of the **Channels** palette. Notice that Photoshop doesn't automatically erase, or *knock out*, the original CMYK color, so the two colors mix. To fix this, you need to knock out the CMYK color manually.

7 load selection

Ctrl-click (Win) or **command**-click (Mac) the spot channel item to redisplay your selection outline.

8 select composite

Click the **CMYK** item in the **Channels** palette to view the CMYK composite.

9 choose contract

Color separations can misalign during the commercial printing process, resulting in a slight white gap between the spot color and surrounding CMYK inks. To avoid this problem—called *misregistration*—you need to create a small overlap between the spot color and underlying CMYK color, a process known as *trapping*. To do so, choose **Select➝Modify➝Contract**, which brings up the **Contract Selection** dialog box.

10 enter amount

Enter a value of **1** or **2** pixels in the **Contract By** option box and click

OK. This contracts—or *chokes*—the selected area very slightly, preparing the way for a small overlap between the spot and CMYK colors.

11 fill with white

Now that you've established your trap, it's time to knock out the CMYK colors. Press the D key to make the background color white. Then press **ctrl+backspace** (Win) or **command-delete** (Mac). The spot color now appears all by its lonesome.

7 load selection

8 select composite

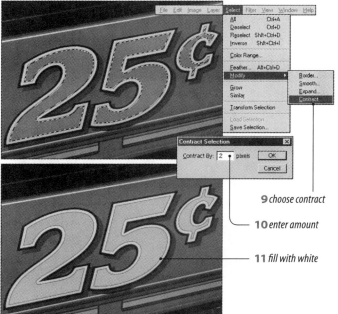

9 choose contract

10 enter amount

11 fill with white

ᶜˢᵗᵉᵖˢ Draw & Export A Clipping Path

To make portions of an image appear transparent when you import it into a page-layout program, create a *clipping path* and save it with the image file. Only the pixels that lie inside the clipping path will be visible when the final page is printed.

1 select pen tool
First, you need to draw a path, a job best tackled with the pen tool. Press P to select it.

2 draw path
Click and drag with the pen tool to draw one or more paths around the portions of the image that you want to remain visible. (For more information on using the pen tool, see The Pen Tools on pages 74 and 75.)

3 save path
Choose **Window→Show Paths** and double-click the **Work Path** item in the **Paths** palette. Then type a name for the path and click **OK**.

4 choose clipping path
Click the right-pointing arrow in the **Paths** palette and choose the **Clipping Path** command. The **Clipping Path** dialog box appears.

5 specify path
From the **Path** pop-up menu, choose the name of the path you just saved (3). Then press **enter** (Win) or **return** (Mac). This defines the path as a clipping path, which Photoshop indicates by displaying the item's name in outline type in the **Paths** palette.

6 choose save as
Choose **File→Save As** to display the **Save As** dialog box.

7 select format
Some layout programs—including **InDesign** and **QuarkXPress**—recognize clipping paths saved with a TIFF or JPEG image. But older programs require that clipping paths be saved in the EPS format. Therefore, to ensure maximum compatibility, choose **Photoshop EPS**.

An even better format—provided you'll be working in a layout program that supports it—is *Desktop Color Separation*, or DCS. A variation on the EPS format, DCS facilitates the printing of high-resolution color separations. If your image contains one or more spot colors, choose **Photoshop DCS 2.0**; otherwise, **Photoshop DCS 1.0** will do just as well.

8 click save
Or press **enter** (Win) or **return** (Mac) to save the image with the clipping path embedded and ready for import into your page-layout application.

1 select pen tool   *2 draw path*   *3 save path*

6 choose save as

7 select format

4 choose clipping path

5 specify path

8 click save

---

steps Create A Contact Sheet

To help you keep track of your images, Photoshop offers the **Contact Sheet II** command, an automated plug-in that lets you print a folder of images as thumbnails on a contact sheet.

1 choose contact sheet II
Choose **File➡Automate➡Contact Sheet II** to display the **Contact Sheet II** dialog box.

2 include all subfolders
If the folder with the images you want to print contains subfolders, turn on the **Include All Subdirectories** (Win) or **Include All Subfolders** (Mac) check box to include images within those subfolders on the contact sheet. If you don't want to include images within subfolders, make sure this option is off.

3 click choose
The **Browse For Folder** (Win) or **Select image directory** (Mac) dialog box appears.

4 locate & choose folder
Navigate to the folder containing the images you want to print on the contact sheet. Then select it and click the **Choose** button.

> *tip* Don't worry about how many images the folder contains. If there are more images than will fit on a single contact sheet, Photoshop will automatically create additional sheets to accommodate all the thumbnails.

5 enter size
Use the **Width** and **Height** options to specify the dimensions of the contact sheet. The default setting of 8 x 10 inches is generally fine.

6 set resolution
Keep in mind, higher resolution values mean larger file sizes. For example, a contact sheet with 30 image thumbnails at 300 ppi is likely to weigh in at 20MB or more. So you might want to go with the default resolution of 72 ppi or thereabouts, considering that the sheets are merely for reference.

7 choose color mode
Use the **Mode** pop-up menu to choose a color space. Again, since contact sheets are for cataloging images and aren't destined for professional output, **RGB Color** is perfectly acceptable.

1 *choose contact sheet II*   **2** *include all subfolders*   **3** *click choose*

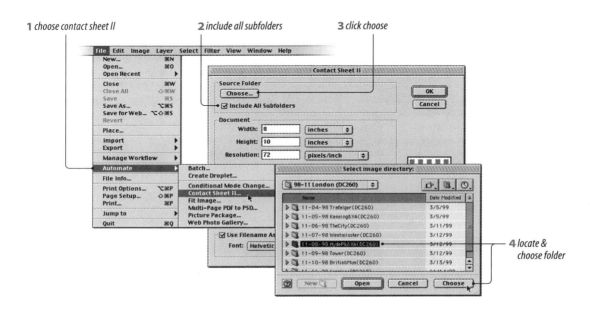

4 *locate & choose folder*

8 choose arrangement

By default, thumbnails are printed in order from left to right across the page. If you prefer to have them print from top to bottom, choose **down first** from the **Place** pop-up menu.

9 set columns & rows

Use the **Columns** and **Rows** option boxes to specify how many thumbnails will fit on a page. For example, the default settings of 5 columns and 6 rows print 30 thumbnails. (Remember, Photoshop will generate additional pages to accommodate excess images, so you don't have to fit all thumbnails on a single sheet.) Note that increasing the number of rows and columns decreases the size of the thumbnails. The page preview on the far right gives you a general idea of how changing the number of columns and rows affects the thumbnail size. For precise measurements, check the **Width** and **Height** values next to the **Columns** and **Rows** options.

10 enable caption

Select the **Use Filename As Caption** check box to label image thumbnails according to their filenames, extremely useful for matching thumbnails with their associated files on disk. Then choose one of five type-faces for the labels from the **Font** pop-up menu and enter a type size in the **Font Size** option box.

11 click OK

Or press **enter** (Win) or **return** (Mac). Photoshop creates a new contact sheet image and then opens, copies, and pastes each image from the specified folder (and subfolders, if applicable) into the contact sheet image. If Photoshop runs out of room in the contact sheet image, it creates a new one and continues. Depending on the number of images in the source folder, the process can take several minutes.

When the contact sheet is complete, save it to disk and print it as you would any image.

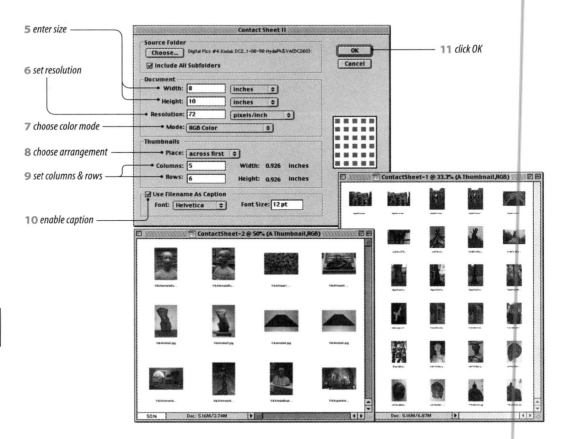

5 enter size

6 set resolution

7 choose color mode

8 choose arrangement

9 set columns & rows

10 enable caption

11 click OK

Save For The Web

When it comes to saving graphics for the Web, striking a balance between good image quality and small file size is easily the most important concern. Web pages that load slowly due to stunning but large graphics are likely to lose would-be viewers. Similarly, lightning-fast loading pages with poor-quality graphics aren't likely to see many return visitors.

Photoshop's solution is the **Save For Web** dialog box, which lets you track both image quality and file size when saving Web graphics. By tinkering with its numerous settings, you can reach the optimal accord. You can even use the **Save For Web** dialog box to generate Web pages based on your images.

Photoshop includes the most essential features found in its companion Web image editor, ImageReady. That means you can create small and speedy Web graphics without ever switching programs.

The Save For Web Command

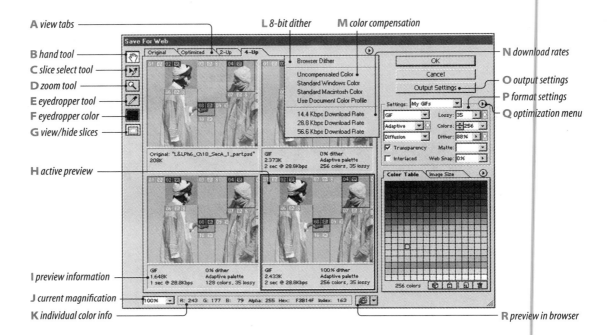

A view tabs
B hand tool
C slice select tool
D zoom tool
E eyedropper tool
F eyedropper color
G view/hide slices
H active preview
I preview information
J current magnification
K individual color info
L 8-bit dither
M color compensation
N download rates
O output settings
P format settings
Q optimization menu
R preview in browser

Choose **File→Save For Web** to display the **Save For Web** dialog box. One of Photoshop's most involved dialog boxes, it includes everything you need to optimize and save images for use on the Web.

A view tabs

The **Save For Web** dialog box gives you four ways to view your image. **Original** displays the image just as it appears in Photoshop. **Optimized** shows the effect of all your settings (P). **2-Up** lets you view the original and optimized images side-by-side. **4-Up** displays these same two image views, plus two additional previews that show the effects of settings that lie between those of the original and optimized versions. To switch between the different views, simply click the appropriate tab.

B hand tool

Drag with the hand tool to reposition an image within the **Save For Web** dialog box. When in the **2-Up** or **4-Up** view, the hand tool (as with all the tools) only works in the active preview (H). All of the other previews update to conform to the active view.

C slice select tool

To select an image slice that you created prior to opening the **Save For Web** dialog box, click with the slice select tool. **Shift**-click to select multiple slices. You can apply different settings to each slice and save slices in different file formats. For more information on creating slices, see The Slice Tools and Slice Options on pages 272 and 273.

> *tip* If an image contains slices, you must select a slice to activate the format settings (P) and display colors in the **Color Table** (S).

D zoom tool

Click with the zoom tool to increase the magnification of the active preview (H). **Alt**-click (**option**-click on the Mac) to decrease the view size. All of the other previews will change to match the magnification of the active preview.

E eyedropper tool

Click with the eyedropper to lift a color from the active image preview or from the **Color Table** (S).

F eyedropper color

This color swatch represents the last color you lifted with the eyedropper tool (E). This color is now ready to serve as the **Matte** color (see Save A Photograph In JPEG on pages 268 and 269).

G view/hide slices

Click this button to show or hide image slices.

H active preview

When in the **2-Up** or **4-Up** view, the active preview appears with a black outline. Only the active preview responds to tools and your changes to settings (P).

I preview information

The gray box below each preview displays that view's information, including the file format and its settings, the resulting file size, and the download time.

J current magnification

You can choose from nine preset levels of magnification or enter a percentage from 1 to **1600**. Choose **Fit on Screen** to display the entire image in each preview.

K individual color information

Hover the cursor over a color in the image or the **Color Table** (S) to view the color's red, green, and blue values, its RGB hexadecimal equivalent, and the gray-scale value of the transparency. For GIF and PNG-8 images, you also see the **Color Table** index number.

L 8-bit dither

Click the right-pointing arrowhead just above the view area to display a pop-up menu of preview options (L through N). Choose the first command, **Browser Dither**, to see how the image will look on an old-style 8-bit monitor.

M color compensation

These commands give you different ways to preview colors in the image. **Standard Windows Color** and **Standard Macintosh Color** show the image in the respective platform's standard colors. If the image includes a color profile, **Use Document Color Profile** displays the colors as they appear in Photoshop. The default, **Uncompensated Color**, leaves colors unchanged. These commands only change the image previews, leaving the **Color Table** unaffected.

N download rates

Photoshop estimates the download time of an image based on one of these settings. The program uses the same modem speed to calculate the download time for each preview.

JPEG, GIF, & PNG

Three file formats rule the world of Web graphics, and each has its strengths and weaknesses.

JPEG

Named for its designers, the *Joint Photographic Experts Group*, JPEG produces the smallest file sizes. It uses a *lossy* compression scheme, which means that details in the image are actually redrawn, sacrificing image quality to reduce file size. JPEG supports 24-bit color (over 1.6 million colors) but doesn't support transparencies. The format is best suited for continuous-tone photographic images with smooth color transitions, which suffer the least from JPEG compression.

GIF

GIF, or *Graphics Interchange Format*, employs the *lossless* LZW compression scheme, which takes advantage of areas of solid color in the image. Although it only supports 8-bit color (or just 256 colors), it does permit transparent pixels. GIF works well for images containing sharp details or high contrast. When using the **Save For Web** dialog box, Photoshop can further shrink GIF files by strategically rearranging pixels, a process akin to JPEG compression.

PNG

The PNG, or *Portable Network Graphics*, format was designed as a patent-free alternative to GIF. Photoshop supports two varieties of PNG—PNG-8 and PNG-24—allowing 8-bit color and 24-bit color, respectively. PNG-8 is similar to GIF but employs better compression. PNG-24 is far less efficient than JPEG but supports multiple levels of transparency. The biggest drawback to PNG is that many browsers don't support it.

The Color Table Panel

O output settings

Click this button to display the **Output Settings** dialog box, which contains a slew of options that affect the way Photoshop saves an image that includes slices. For more information, see Define & Export An HTML Page on pages 274 through 276.

P format settings

You can save a Web graphic in one of three formats: JPEG, GIF, or PNG. With each of these formats, you can specify settings that impact the image's appearance and size. A number of predefined format settings are accessible through the **Settings** pop-up menu. For more information, see Save A Photograph In JPEG on pages 268 and 269 and Save Artwork In GIF on pages 270 and 271.

Q optimization menu

This pop-up menu gives you access to four options that affect your settings (P). **Save Settings** lets you save a particular instance of settings so that you may easily return to it later. By default, Photoshop directs you to save in the **Optimized Settings** folder. Any settings saved in this folder will appear in the **Settings** pop-up menu. **Delete Settings** allows you to delete settings you previously saved.

Choose the **Optimize to File Size** command to display its like-named dialog box. Here you enter a target file size. Photoshop attempts to hit your target size by optimizing the image in the currently selected format (**Current Settings**) or in the most appropriate format (**Auto Select GIF/JPEG**). For an image containing slices, you can optimize just the active slice (**Current Slice**), optimize each slice separately to the target size (**Each Slice**), or optimize so that the total file size of all slices equals the target size (**Total of All Slices**).

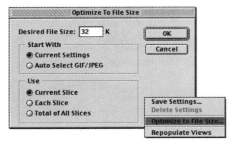

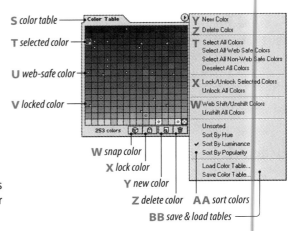

If you're working in the **4-Up** view, the **Optimization** menu's last command, **Repopulate Views**, generates new previews based on your settings.

R preview in browser

Click here to see your settings applied to the image in your default Web browser. Click the down-pointing arrowhead to preview the image in any other browser installed on your machine. The temporary Web page that Photoshop creates is governed by the options in the **Output Settings** dialog box (see Define & Export An HTML Page on pages 274 through 276).

S color table

Since GIF uses LZW compression, color management plays a big role in file size. Photoshop centralizes the GIF color needs in the **Color Table**. Double-click a color swatch to bring up the standard **Color Picker** dialog box so you can make adjustments to that color. Be forewarned, you cannot undo any actions you perform in the **Color Table**.

T selected color

Click a color in the **Color Table** to select it. This activates the controls at the bottom of the **Color Table** panel (W through Z).

> *tip* Ctrl-click (**command**-click on the Mac) to select a number of individual colors. **Shift**-click to select a series of contiguous colors.

The Image Size Panel

You can also use the pop-up menu commands to **Select All Colors**, **Select All Web Safe Colors**, and **Select All Non-Web Safe Colors**. If any colors are selected, you can choose to **Deselect All Colors**.

U web-safe color

Colors that are among the 216 Web-safe colors are marked with a center dot. For more information on working with Web-safe colors, read The Web-Safe Palette on page 271.

V locked color

A small square in the lower-right corner of a color swatch indicates that the color is locked (X).

W snap color

Click this button or choose **Web Shift/Unshift Colors** to convert each selected color to its nearest equivalent in the Web-safe palette. Click again to return a converted color to its original appearance. To return all colors to their initial composition, choose **Unshift All Colors** from the pop-up menu.

X lock color

To lock a selected color so it can't be changed, click this button or choose **Lock/Unlock Selected Colors**. Once locked, a color will remain part of the image as long as there are enough colors to support it. This means that even if the locked color would not normally appear as part of the palette you've chosen for the image, it will remain in the **Color Table**. To unlock one or more selected colors, click the lock button. To unlock all colors, choose **Unlock All Colors**. Surprisingly, you can delete a locked color or convert it to its Web-safe equivalent without unlocking it.

Y new color

If the eyedropper color (F) is not among those in the **Color Table**, click this button or choose **New Color** from the pop-up menu to add it. If the **Color Table** is full, Photoshop replaces the color that most closely matches the eyedropper color.

Z delete color

Click here or choose **Delete Color** to delete all selected colors.

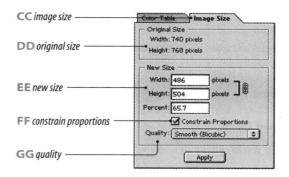

CC *image size*
DD *original size*
EE *new size*
FF *constrain proportions*
GG *quality*

AA sort color

Photoshop can organize the **Color Table** by grouping colors by similar hues (**Sort By Hue**), by similar shades (**Sort By Luminance**), or by how often a color appears in the image (**Sort By Popularity**).

BB save & load tables

Choose **Save Color Table** to save the current **Color Table** so that you can easily load it (**Load Color Table**) for use with another image or slice later.

CC image size

No matter which file format you choose, you can resize the image inside the **Save For Web** dialog box without affecting the original. Click the **Image Size** tab to display the panel normally hidden by the **Color Table**.

DD original size

Look here to see the dimensions of the original image.

EE new size

You can change the image's size by exact pixels or a specific percentage.

FF constrain proportions

Select this check box to maintain the proportions of the image when resizing. A chain icon indicates that proportions are locked.

GG quality

This pop-up menu offers two of the three interpolation methods available via the **Image Size** command. See Resample An Image on page 24 for more information about these options.

steps Save A Photograph In JPEG

Using the **Save For Web** dialog box to save a JPEG
file lets you see exactly how much image quality
you will have to sacrifice to save on file size.

1 get image
Open the image you want to export as a Web graphic.
The **Save For Web** command works best on full-color
RGB images.

2 choose save for web
Choose **File➟Save For Web** to display the **Save For
Web** dialog box. Alternatively, you can bring up the
dialog box by pressing **ctrl+alt+shift+S (command-
option-shift-S** on the Mac).

> *tip* Every time you use the **Save For Web** dialog
> box, Photoshop remembers your settings and
> stores them as the preferences for the dialog
> box. To clear these preferences and open the
> dialog box with its default settings, press and hold
> **ctrl+alt (command-option** on the Mac) while
> choosing **File➟Save For Web**. Click the **Yes** button
> when Photoshop asks you to confirm.

3 click desired view tab
To see the effect of your settings, you need to use the
Optimized, **2-Up**, or **4-Up** view. Side-by-side comparisons provide the best way to find the perfect balance between image quality and file size.

4 choose JPEG preset
JPEG Medium makes for a good starting point. Its
Quality setting of 30 provides a substantial reduction
in file size while preserving much of the image's detail.

5 adjust quality
Use the **Quality** option to adjust the amount of compression applied to the image. Lower values apply
more compression, resulting in smaller file sizes and
loss of image detail. If the appearance of the image
deteriorates too much, bump up the **Quality** value.

> *tip* Instead of typing a number directly into the
> **Quality** option box, you can select the value and
> press the ↑ or ↓ key to increase or decrease the
> value by 1. Or press **shift-↑** or **shift-↓** to increase or
> decrease the value by 10.

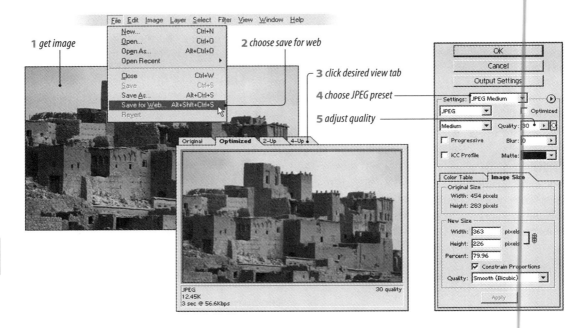

6 use mask channel (optional)

If your image contains a mask channel (see The Channels Palette on pages 125 and 126), you can use it to delineate areas of high and low image quality. Click the tiny button to the right of the **Quality** option to bring up the **Modify Quality Setting** dialog box. Select a mask channel from the **Channel** pop-up menu. A black-and-white thumbnail preview of the channel appears. Position the black and white tabs on the slider bar to set the image quality for the black and white areas of the channel. This lets you preserve the image detail of the white area and reduce the file size at the expense of the black area.

7 adjust blur (optional)

Since JPEG compression works better on soft transitions than hard edges, increasing the blurriness of the image can reduce the file size. But keep in mind, it also reduces the image detail.

> *tip* Use this option sparingly. A **Blur** value of more than 0.1 can easily cause more damage to the image and result in less of a reduction in file size than decreasing the **Quality** value by 10.

8 set matte color

Since JPEG doesn't support transparencies, Photoshop will fill any transparent pixels in the image with the color specified in the **Matte** pop-up menu.

9 adjust image size

In an attempt to further reduce the file size, you can reduce the physical dimensions of the image using the **Image Size** panel. For best results, select the **Constrain Proportions** check box and enter a value in the **Percent** option box.

> *tip* It can take Photoshop awhile to update the image to reflect your changes when in the **2-Up** or **4-Up** view. So it may be easier to adjust settings, especially changes you make to the image's size, while in the **Optimized** view, and then switch to the **2-Up** or **4-Up** view when you want to preview the results.

10 save best preview

When you're done experimenting with different optimization settings (by repeating steps 5 through 9 as necessary), select the image preview that looks the best and click **OK**.

6 *use mask channel*

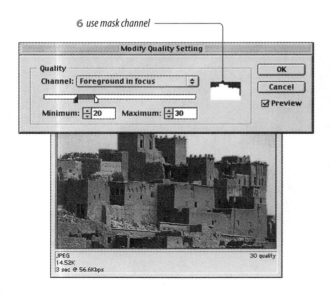

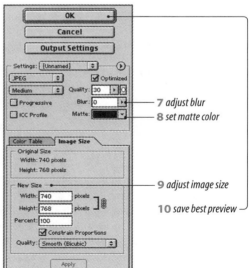

7 *adjust blur*
8 *set matte color*

9 *adjust image size*
10 *save best preview*

🔵steps Save Artwork In GIF

Unlike the standard **Save** command, the **Save For Web** dialog box lets you reduce the number of colors in an image, compare the results of different settings side-by-side, and save an image as a GIF file all in one convenient location.

1 get image
Open the image you want to save as a GIF. High-contrast images, such as line art or text, work best.

> *tip* When using the **Save For Web** dialog box, there's no need to reduce colors via the **Index Color** command before saving an image as a GIF. In fact, it's best to leave your original image in full-color RGB and handle all color management inside the **Save For Web** dialog box.

2 choose save for web
Choose **File➦Save For Web** or press **ctrl+alt+shift+S** (**command-option-shift-S** on the Mac) to display the **Save For Web** dialog box.

3 click 4-up view tab
The **4-Up** view lets you preview the effects of three different optimization settings alongside the original image, perfect for discerning subtle differences in color and image quality.

4 choose GIF preset
With the top-right preview selected (as it is by default when you first open the **Save For Web** dialog box), choose one of the seven GIF presets from the **Settings** pop-up menu. **GIF 128 No Dither** provides a good starting point, giving you ample colors with which to work (128 to be exact), as well as a rough idea of the upper file size boundary. You can work your way down from there.

> *tip* If **GIF 128 No Dither** isn't selected by default, choose **Repopulate Views** from the **Optimization** pop-up menu (Q, page 266). This refreshes the bottom two previews so they show the results of slightly different GIF optimization settings.

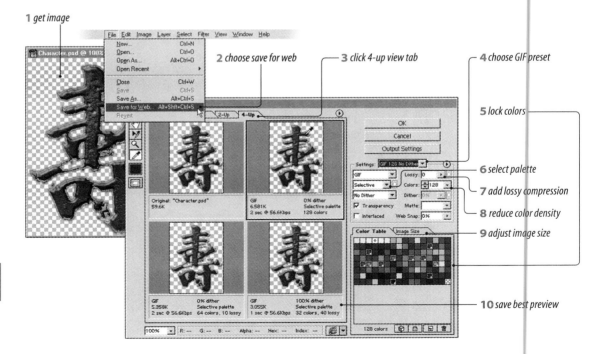

1 *get image*
2 *choose save for web*
3 *click 4-up view tab*
4 *choose GIF preset*
5 *lock colors*
6 *select palette*
7 *add lossy compression*
8 *reduce color density*
9 *adjust image size*
10 *save best preview*

270   🔵 **Save For The Web:** Save Artwork In GIF

5 lock colors

Click and **shift**-click with the eyedropper in the preview or in the **Color Table** to select the colors that you feel are important to retain in the image. Then click the **Lock** button at the bottom of the **Color Table** to lock the colors so they can't be changed.

6 select palette

With each of the bottom previews, experiment with different palettes from the **Palette** pop-up menu. Your options are **Adaptive**, **Perceptual**, **Selective**, and **Web**. Each time you choose a new palette, Photoshop repopulates the **Color Table**, leaving your locked colors (5) alone. **Adaptive** retains the most frequently used colors in your image. **Perceptual** keeps the colors that produce the best transitions. **Selective** tries to strike a balance between retaining the most popular colors and converting the others to their Web-safe counterparts. **Web** converts each unlocked color to its associated Web-safe color. For details on the Web palette, see The Web-Safe Palette below.

7 add lossy compression

While GIF relies on lossless compression, you can dramatically reduce file size by manually applying some lossy compression. Enter a value in the **Lossy** option box. Photoshop redistributes the image's pixels so they compress better. Continue to increase the value until just before it damages the quality of the image.

8 reduce color density

Again with each of the bottom previews, try reducing the number of colors to see whether you can eliminate a few without compromising the graphic's visual integrity. Fewer colors translate to a smaller file.

9 adjust image size (optional)

To further save on file size, you may want to reduce the physical dimensions of the image using the controls in the **Image Size** panel.

10 save best preview

When you arrive at the ideal optimization settings, select the best preview and click **OK**.

The Web-Safe Palette

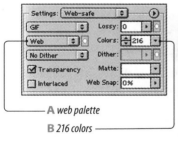

A web palette

B 216 colors

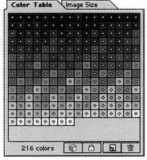

The so-called "Web-safe" palette is made up 216 colors whose R, G, and B values are each divisible by 51. This means that each color's RGB value is restricted to either 0, 51, 102, 153, 204, or 255 (00, 33, 66, 99, CC, or FF in hexadecimal code). Calculate all possible combinations, and you get 216 colors.

These are the same 216 colors that an 8-bit monitor can display. Although 8-bit monitors are no longer standard, some folks still use them. If this segment of the Web-viewing population is your primary concern, you need to use the Web-safe palette in the **Save For Web** dialog box to ensure that what you see on your screen is also what your guests see.

A web palette

To access the Web-safe palette, choose **Web** from the **Palette** pop-up menu. Don't worry if your image temporarily looks horrible.

B 216 colors

Enter 216 in the **Colors** option box, or choose **256** from the pop-up menu. Photoshop forces all 216 Web-safe colors into your image. All 216 colors appear in the **Color Table** as well, each marked with a center dot. From there, reduce the number of colors to see just how many your image really needs.

The Slice Tools

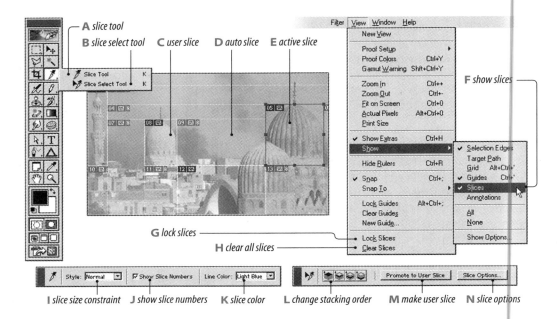

A *slice tool*
B *slice select tool* C *user slice* D *auto slice* E *active slice*

F *show slices*

G *lock slices*
H *clear all slices*

I *slice size constraint* J *show slice numbers* K *slice color* L *change stacking order* M *make user slice* N *slice options*

With the slice tool (A), Photoshop comes one step closer to being the perfect Web-page creation program. You can create a Web page as a single graphic and then cut it up into its components.

A slice tool
Press **K** to select the slice tool. Drag with the tool to create a user slice (C). Photoshop then divides the rest of the image into auto slices (D). **Shift**-drag to cut a square slice. **Alt**-drag (**option**-drag on the Mac) to create a slice centered around your starting point. **Shift+alt**-drag to draw a square slice from the center out. Press and hold **ctrl** (Win) or **command** (Mac) to temporarily switch to the slice select tool (B).

> *tip* Press the **spacebar** while dragging with the slice tool to move a slice that you're drawing. This is handy for relocating a poorly positioned slice.

B slice select tool
Press **shift-K** to select the slice select tool. Then click on a user slice (C) or auto slice (D) to select it. Press and hold **ctrl** (Win) or **command** (Mac) to temporarily switch to the slice tool (A).

C user slice
Dragging with the slice tool creates a solid bordered *user slice*. A user slice is an independent slice that you can manipulate when it's active (E). You can apply different optimization settings to each user slice in the **Save For Web** dialog box. See Define & Export An HTML Page on pages 274 through 276 for more information on working with user slices.

D auto slice
When you create a user slice (C), Photoshop dices up the remaining area with *auto slices*. An auto slice is dependent on the placement of user slices and cannot be directly manipulated. Instead, Photoshop redraws the borders of an auto slice to compensate for the changes you make to a user slice.

E active slice
Click a user slice with the slice select tool (B) to make it the active slice. You can then move the slice by dragging it with the slice select tool. To change the size and shape of an active slice, drag one of its eight handles. **Alt**-drag (Win) or **option**-drag (Mac) an active slice to duplicate it.

Slice Options

F show slices

Choose **View➞Show➞Slices** to display or hide slices. A check mark indicates slices are visible.

G lock slices

To lock all slices so that they can't be moved, choose **View➞Lock Slices**.

H clear all slices

Choose **View➞Clear Slices** to delete all slices. To delete a single user slice, select it and press **backspace** (Win) or **delete** (Mac).

I slice size constraint

In addition to normal slices, which can be any size, you can create slices of specific proportions. Choose **Constrained Aspect Ratio** from the **Style** pop-up menu to limit slices to the ratio you specify in the **Width** and **Height** option boxes in the options bar. Choose **Fixed Size** to make slices of these exact dimensions.

J show slice numbers

Photoshop assigns each slice a number so that you can easily keep track of it. To display the numbers, select the **Show Slice Numbers** check box.

K slice color

If the slice outlines are difficult to see against the image, choose a new color from this pop-up menu.

L change stacking order

If you create user slices that overlap, the more recently created slice is the top slice. Click the intersection of the overlapping slices to select the topmost slice. To change the stacking order of an overlapping slice, select the slice and click one of these buttons. The buttons (from left to right) move the active slices to the top, one step closer to the top, one step closer to the bottom, and to the bottom of the stack.

M make user slice

To convert an auto slice to a user slice, select it and click the **Promote to User Slice** button.

N slice options

Click the **Slice Options** button or double-click a slice to display the **Slice Options** dialog box, which lets

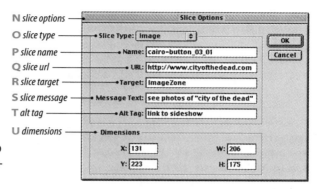

you add HTML data to an individual slice. When you create a Web page from the slice's parent image in the **Save For Web** dialog box, Photoshop records this data in the page. These options (O through U) require some knowledge of HTML.

O slice type

You can fill a slice with an image or with text. Choose **No Image** to bring up a text-entry box into which you can enter the HTML text and format tags.

P slice name

If you don't like the name that's automatically assigned to the slice, enter a new one here.

Q slice url

To make the slice act as a button, enter the URL you want the button to link to in the **URL** option box.

R slice target

Enter any necessary frame tag in this option box.

S slice message

Text entered in this option box appears in the browser's status bar when you hover your cursor over the slice.

T alt tag

In the **Alt Tag** option box, enter the text that you want to appear in the slice's HTML alt tag.

U slice dimensions

In the **X** and **Y** option boxes, enter the coordinates where the slice should appear. In the **W** and **H** option boxes, you can specify the slice's new dimensions.

⟨steps⟩ Define & Export An HTML Page

In addition to saving images, you can use the **Save For Web** dialog box to generate a Web page from an image. If your image contains slices, Photoshop can save each slice as an individual graphic file, and create the HTML code that's necessary to assemble the slices into a single Web page.

1 choose save for web

Choose **File➟Save For Web** or press **ctrl+alt+shift+S** (**command-option-shift-S** on the Mac) to open the **Save For Web** dialog box. We'll assume that your image and its slices are optimized to your specifications, but you can always make adjustments after you set the HTML options. For details on optimizing images, see Save A Photograph In JPEG on pages 268 and 269, and Save Artwork In GIF on pages 270 and 271.

2 click output settings

This displays the **Output Settings** dialog box, which lets you control how Photoshop formats the HTML it uses to construct the page, how it handles the page's background, and how files and slices are named.

3 choose HTML

The second pop-up menu in the **Output Settings** dialog box gives you access to four categories of

output settings, each with its own set of options. HTML is the default starting point.

> ⓘ **tip** The options discussed in steps 4 through 6 do not affect the appearance of your Web page. So if you're not familiar with HTML, don't even worry about them. Just go with the default HTML format settings and proceed to step 7.

4 specify HTML format

Use the **Tag Case** and **Attribs Case** pop-up menus to specify a capitalization scheme for HTML tags and attributes, respectively. For example, if you choose **BODY** and **rowspan**, Photoshop will write all HTML tags in uppercase and all the HTML attributes in lowercase. Using all uppercase generally makes code easier to read, but it's a matter of personal preference. Select **Always Quote Attributes** to ensure that Photoshop puts quotes around the different attributes' values. In the **Indent** pop-up menu, decide how you want Photoshop to handle indentations in the HTML code. In the **Line Endings** pop-up menu, choose which platform's end-of-line character you want at the end of each line of HTML code. They all work the same but may appear differently if you view the source HTML in a text editor.

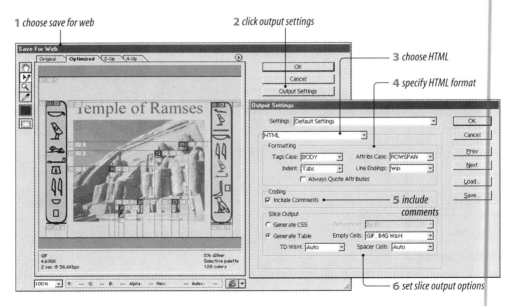

1 choose save for web

2 click output settings

3 choose HTML

4 specify HTML format

5 include comments

6 set slice output options

5 include comments

When the **Include Comments** option is selected, Photoshop will include helpful comments in the HTML code that explain which areas of the page were constructed in Photoshop-unique style.

6 set slice output options

Photoshop can use either *cascading style sheets* (CSS) or tables to display your image slices in the Web page. To use style sheets, select the **Generate CSS** radio button. Then use the **Referenced** pop-up menu to specify whether you want the style sheets to appear in each and every case that they're needed (**Inline**) or all together at the top of the page to be called as necessary later in the page, referenced by class (**By Class**) or by style ID (**By ID**). Note that Photoshop cannot generate external style sheets. To create an external CSS, you need to manually cut the style definitions from the page you create and paste them into a separate file, making sure to properly link the page to its style sheet.

Unless you're familiar with CSS and want to integrate this new page into a larger set of pages that are also dependent on CSS, select the **Generate Table** option. Then choose either **GIF, IMG W&H** or **GIF, TD W&H** from the **Empty Cells** pop-up menu to tell Photoshop how to handle the space between the slices. In either case, Photoshop will fill the empty table cell with a transparent 1-by-1 pixel image that it can stretch to fit the space as needed. Your choice determines whether height and width attribute tags are included within the **IMG** (image) or **TD** (table data) HTML tag. The **TD W&H** pop-up menu gives you control over how often

Photoshop includes height and width attribute tags within the table cells filled with your image slices. Use the **Spacer Cells** pop-up menu to specify when you want Photoshop to add a row and column of empty cells around the table to act as placement guides for the other cells in the table.

7 choose background

Choose **Background** from the pop-up menu directly below the **Settings** pop-up menu to display the next panel of options. Here you can choose a background for your Web page and specify how Photoshop handles the transparencies in the slices.

8 select background style

Select the **Image** radio button to fill the entire background region, including the transparent areas between your image slices, with the image of your choice (9). The image will automatically repeat over and over, tiling the entire background. To fill the background with a solid color instead, select the **Background** radio button.

9 choose image

If you selected the **Image** radio button (8), use the **Image** option box to specify the image you want to use to tile the background. You can also click the **Choose** button to locate the image file using the **Choose Background Image** dialog box.

10 choose background color

From the **Color** pop-up menu, choose a solid color for the page's background. If you've also selected an image for the background, the color you choose will appear while the image is loading in the browser window. It will also fill the transparencies in the background image.

11 choose saving files

Choose **Saving Files** from the pop-up menu directly below the **Settings** pop-up menu to move to the next panel of options. These settings let you construct a naming convention for all files, specify the filenames' platform compatibility, and choose from some additional options for the HTML related to the image files.

7 *choose background*   **8** *select background style*

Background
View As: Image   Background
Background
Image: Choose...
Color: Matte

9 *choose image*   **10** *choose background color*

12 set file naming convention

The first set of options on this panel lets you specify a naming convention for the user slices that you created with the slice tool (see The Slice Tools on page 272 and Slice Options on page 273). From the nine **File Naming** pop-up menus, you can choose naming elements such as the original document name, individual slice name, slice number, rollover state, rollover trigger name, and today's date. You can then separate these elements with an underscore, a hyphen, or a space. Note that Photoshop will ignore both the rollover state and rollover trigger name unless you previously constructed them in ImageReady.

13 set filename compatibility

Leave all three of these check boxes turned on to ensure that your filenames can be recognized on Windows, Mac OS, and UNIX systems.

14 set HTML options for images

If you opt to use an image to fill your Web page's background (9), select **Copy Background Image when Saving** to save a copy of the image in the same folder as all the other page elements.

> 🛈 It's a good idea to leave this option turned on. Otherwise, if you later move the image file from its original location, you'll break the link between the page and its background image, requiring you to manually fix the page's HTML code.

To save all the images Photoshop constructs from your slices in a separate subfolder or directory, select the **Put Images in Folder** check box and enter a name for the folder.

Select the **Include Copyright** check box to include the information you entered in the **Copyright & URL** panel of the **File Info** dialog box. For more information on adding copyright information to an image, see Add A Copyright & URL on page 52.

15 choose slices

Choose **Slices** from the pop-up menu directly below the **Settings** pop-up menu to display a panel of options that let you specify a naming convention for auto slices (D, page 272).

16 set slice naming convention

Just as the **File Naming** pop-up menus (12) in the **Saving Files** panel let you you specify a naming convention for the image's user slices, the **Default Slice Naming** pop-up menus let you set a naming scheme for the auto slices that Photoshop creates around your user slices. (Read The Slice Tools on page 272 for the lowdown on auto slices.) From these six pop-up menus, you can choose naming modifiers such as the original document name, the word "slice", the slice number, and today's date. Using the word "slice" as one of your naming modifiers makes it easy to differentiate the auto slices from your user slices.

17 click OK

This puts you back in the **Save For Web** dialog box. Click **OK** again to display the **Save Optimized As** dialog box. Make sure the **Save as type** pop-up menu (**Format** on the Mac) is set to **HTML and Images**. Then select a location for the Web page and click **Save**.

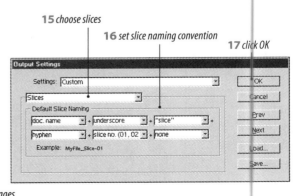

11 *choose saving files*   12 *set file naming convention*

13 *set filename compatibility*   14 *set HTML options for images*

15 *choose slices*

16 *set slice naming convention*

17 *click OK*

⟨steps⟩ Create A Web Photo Gallery

In addition to generating free-form Web pages, you can create Web photo galleries. This is where Photoshop takes a group of your images and generates a thumbnail preview of each. The thumbnails are then collected into a Web page where they serve as links. Click a thumbnail to view its full-sized parent image.

1 choose web photo gallery

Choose **File➧Automate➧Web Photo Gallery** to display the **Web Photo Gallery** dialog box.

2 choose layout style

The **Style** pop-up menu offers four page layout options. Choose **Simple** or **Table** to construct the page using tables. With the **Simple** style, the table consists of alternating rows of images and text. With the **Table** style, each image and its corresponding text are together in a single cell. With either of these layouts, when you click a thumbnail, its full-size image opens in a new page. To see both thumbnails and full-size images in the same window, choose **Horizontal Frame** or **Vertical Frame**. Each of these options generates one frame for the thumbnails and one frame for the full-size image, with both inside a parent frame page. With **Horizontal Frame**, Photoshop places the full-size image frame above

the thumbnail frame, where the thumbnails appear horizontally side by side. With **Vertical Frame**, the full-size image frame appears to the right of the thumbnail frame, where the thumbnails are stacked vertically one on top of the other.

3 choose gallery thumbnails

Here you determine the look of the Web photo gallery page. The **Options** pop-up menu includes four commands, each of which offers a number of unique options. The first set of options determines the appearance and layout of the thumbnails and their captions.

4 include caption

Select the **Use Filename** check box to use the image's name as the thumbnail's caption. Check **Use File Info Caption** to use the description you saved with the image (via the **File➧File Info** command) as the thumbnail's caption. You can then choose from one of four fonts and seven font sizes for the captions. Turn off both check boxes for no captions.

5 set thumbnail size

Choose one of the three presets in the **Size** pop-up menu to specify the width of each thumbnail. Or enter a custom width, measured in pixels, in the option box to the right of the **Size** pop-up menu.

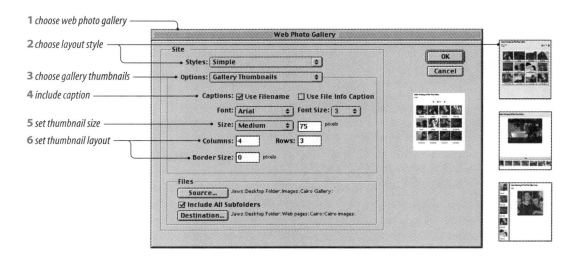

1 *choose web photo gallery*
2 *choose layout style*
3 *choose gallery thumbnails*
4 *include caption*
5 *set thumbnail size*
6 *set thumbnail layout*

6 set thumbnail layout
Specify the row and column configuration. To add a border around each thumbnail, enter a width value in the **Border Size** option box.

7 choose gallery images
From the **Options** pop-up menu, choose **Gallery Images** to display options that control the appearance of the images to which the thumbnails link.

8 add image border
Here you set the size of the images' borders.

9 set image size & quality
If you want Photoshop to resize your images, select **Resize Images** and specify the size and amount of JPEG compression. Turn the **Resize Images** check box off to use exact copies of your originals.

10 choose banner
From the **Options** pop-up menu, choose **Banner**. These options let you add page and image information to the top of the page.

11 name page
The name you give your page will appear in both the browser's title bar and in the header (or banner) area at the top of the page.

12 give photo credit & date page
Enter the photographer's name, if you like, and include a date to help chronicle the images.

13 choose banner font
Choose a font and type size for the banner elements.

14 choose custom colors
This panel lets you color the page's background and text links and choose a source and destination folder.

15 select page colors
Click the **Banner** and **Background** color swatches to select a background color for the header area and the rest of the page.

16 select text colors
Use the bottom four color swatches to select colors for normal text and links.

17 choose image source folder
Click the **Source** button to select the folder or directory that contains the images you want to use in your gallery. (Note that you cannot select individual images.) The **Include All Subdirectories** option (**Include All Subfolders** on the Mac) ensures that all images within any subfolders in the source folder are also included.

18 choose destination folder
Click the **Destination** button to specify where you want to save all the page components. Don't worry about creating new folders for the sake of organization; Photoshop handles this for you. It creates one subfolder for the images, one for the thumbnails, and one for all of the subordinate pages.

19 click OK
Then wait while Photoshop does its thing. When the process is complete, Photoshop displays the Web photo gallery in your default Web browser.

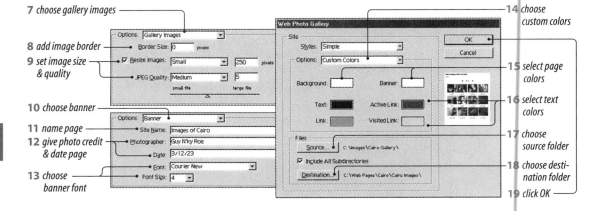

7 *choose gallery images*

8 *add image border*

9 *set image size & quality*

10 *choose banner*

11 *name page*

12 *give photo credit & date page*

13 *choose banner font*

14 *choose custom colors*

15 *select page colors*

16 *select text colors*

17 *choose source folder*

18 *choose destination folder*

19 *click OK*

If you've used a Windows or Macintosh system for any amount of time, you've probably come to love the convenience of keyboard shortcuts. For example, if a program lets you choose **File➡Print**, chances are good that it also lets you press **ctrl+P** (Win) or **command-P** (Mac) to perform the very same operation. And pressing keys is easier.

Photoshop is no stranger to shortcuts. In fact, it's one of the most shortcut-savvy programs on the market, going so far as to supply a wealth of functions that are accessible only from the keyboard.

You'll use some shortcuts so often that you'll want to assign them to memory. These include keys that select tools, display palettes, and choose common menu commands. But even after a decade of using Photoshop, I can't keep them all straight in my head. When memory fails, let this chapter be your guide.

Toolbox Shortcuts

The figure on right shows the keyboard shortcuts for every tool in Photoshop. The keystroke appears in blue. The ⇧ symbol indicates the **shift** key. For example, Ⓜ️ shows that you can switch from one marquee tool to the next by pressing **shift-M**. Or avoid **shift** by choosing **Edit➞Preferences➞General** and turning off **Use Shift Key for Tool Switch**. The ⟳ symbol, as in Ⓠ, denotes a key that cycles through settings without **shift**. Arranged in alphabetical order, the following list itemizes shortcuts and the tools they select:

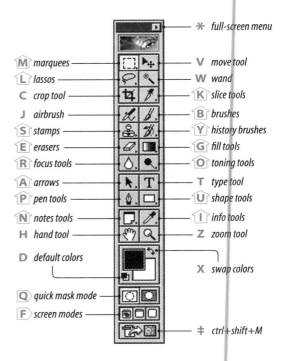

A arrows
Selects the black or white arrow tool. When a pen or shape tool is active, press **ctrl** (**command** on the Mac).

B brushes
Switches between the paintbrush and pencil tools.

C crop tool
Selects the crop tool.

D default colors
Makes the active colors black and white, respectively.

E erasers
Selects the standard, background, or magic eraser.

F screen modes
Cycles from one screen mode to the next (see ✳).

G fill tools
Switches between the gradient and paint bucket tool.

H hand tool
Or press the **spacebar** to get the hand tool temporarily.

I info tools
Selects the eyedropper, color sampler, or measure tool.

J airbrush
Selects the airbrush tool.

K slice tools
K and **ctrl** switch between the slice and slice select tools.

L lassos
Selects the standard, polygon, or magnetic lasso.

M marquees
Switches between the rectangular and oval marquees.

N notes tools
Switches between the notes and audio annotation tools.

O toning tools
Selects the dodge, burn, or sponge tool.

P pen tools
Switches between the standard and freeform pen tools.

Q quick mask mode
Enters and exits the quick mask mode.

R focus tools
Selects the blur, sharpen, or smudge tool.

S stamps
Switches between the clone and pattern stamp tools.

T type tool
Selects the type tool.

U shape tools
Cycles between the six shape tools.

V move tool
Or press **ctrl** to select the move tool when a tool other than the slice, arrow, pen, shape, or hand tool is active.

W wand
Selects the magic wand tool.

X swap colors
Swaps the foreground and background colors.

Y history brushes
Switches between the standard and art history brushes.

Z zoom tool
Or press **ctrl+spacebar** (**command-spacebar** on the Mac).

✳ full-screen menu (Windows)
When in the full-screen mode on the PC, click this arrowhead to access a full list of menu commands. On the Mac or PC, press **shift-F** to display the menu bar.

‡ ctrl+shift+M/command-shift-M
Launches the Web image editor, ImageReady.

Palette Shortcuts

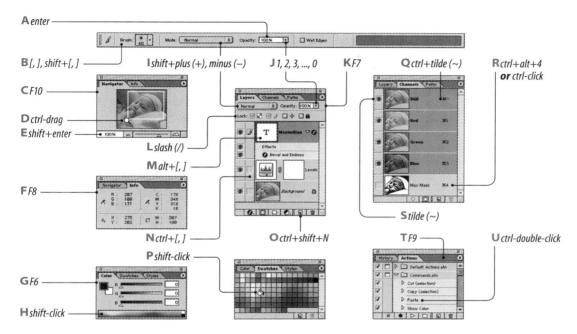

From the options bar to the **Actions** palette, Photoshop lets you display palettes from the keyboard. You can also use key and mouse tricks to activate functions inside the palettes.

A enter/return
Displays the options bar and highlights the first value. After entering a new value, press **enter** or **return** to apply it.

B [,], shift+[,]
Brackets change brush size; **shift** changes softness.

C F10
When **Commands.atn** is loaded (see page 283), displays **Navigator** palette.

D ctrl-drag/command-drag
Draws custom zoom boundary inside **Navigator** palette.

E shift+enter/shift-return
Applies value, but keeps value active for further editing.

F F8
Displays or hides **Info** palette.

G F6
Displays or hides **Color** palette.

H shift-click
Changes color model in bar at bottom of **Color** palette.

I shift+plus (+), minus (−)
Switches blend mode in options bar or **Layers** palette.

J 1, 2, 3, ..., 0
Changes **Opacity** value in options bar or **Layers** palette.

K F7
Displays or hides **Layers** palette.

L slash (/)
Locks or unlocks first available attribute of active layer.

M alt+[,]/option-[,]
Selects next layer down or up in stack.

N ctrl+[,]/command-[,]
Moves active layer backward or forward in stack.

O ctrl+shift+N/command-shift-N
Creates new layer. Add **alt** (**option**) to name automatically.

P shift-click
Replaces clicked color with current foreground color.

Q ctrl+tilde (~)/command-tilde (~)
Switches to full-color composite image.

R ctrl+alt+4/command-option-4
Converts alpha channel to selection outline.

S tilde (~)
When alpha channel is active, displays image with mask.

T F9
Displays or hides **Actions** palette.

U ctrl-/command-double-click
Plays double-clicked action.

Menu Command Shortcuts

The following table lists keyboard shortcuts for common menu commands. To save space, I don't document shortcuts for commands that are common to virtually every program on the planet, such as **ctrl+X**

for **Cut**, **ctrl+C** for **Copy**, **ctrl+V** for **Paste**, **ctrl+O** for **Open**, and **ctrl+S** for **Save**.

Most of the shortcuts listed here work with Photoshop exactly as it is when you first install it. The

menu command	windows shortcut	macintosh shortcut
actual pixels	ctrl+alt+0	command-option-0
auto contrast	ctrl+alt+shift+L	command-option-shift-L
auto levels	ctrl+shift+L	command-shift-L
bring layer forward/to front	ctrl+] / ctrl+shift+]	command-] / command-shift-]
clear	backspace	delete
close all	ctrl+shift+W	command-shift-W
color settings	ctrl+shift+K	command-shift-K
copy merged	ctrl+shift+C	command-shift-C
curves*	ctrl+M	command-M
desaturate	ctrl+shift+U	command-shift-U
deselect	ctrl+D	command-D
extract	ctrl+alt+X	command-option-X
fade last operation	ctrl+shift+F	command-shift-F
feather selection	ctrl+alt+D	command-option-D
fill	shift+backspace	shift-delete
fill from history	ctrl+alt+backspace	command-option-delete
filter, repeat last	ctrl+F	command-F
filter, repeat with new settings	ctrl+alt+F	command-option-F
fit image on screen	ctrl+0	command-0
flatten image†	F2	F2
flip horizontal/flip vertical†	shift+F6/shift+F7	shift-F6/shift-F7
free transform	ctrl+T	command-T
group with previous layer	ctrl+G	command-G
hue/saturation*	ctrl+U	command-U
image size†	F11	F11
inverse selection	ctrl+shift+I	command-shift-I
invert	ctrl+I	command-I
layer via copy/cut	ctrl+J/ctrl+shift+J	command-J/command-shift-J
levels*	ctrl+L	command-L
lock guides	ctrl+alt+semicolon (;)	command-option-semicolon (;)
merge down, linked, or set	ctrl+E	command-E
merge visible	ctrl+shift+E	command-shift-E
new image/with default settings	ctrl+N/ctrl+alt+N	command-N/command-option-N

exception is any shortcut marked with a dagger (†), which relies on a special action set that ships with Photoshop 6. Press **F9** to display the **Actions** palette, and choose **Commands.atn** from the palette menu.

An asterisk (∗) next to a command name indicates that you can press the **alt** or **option** key along with the keys listed to bring up the command's dialog box with the last-used settings still intact.

menu command	windows shortcut	macintosh shortcut
new layer	ctrl+shift+N	command-shift-N
new snapshot	shift+F11	shift-F11
page/print setup	ctrl+shift+P	command-shift-P
paste into	ctrl+shift+V	command-shift-V
path, show or hide	ctrl+shift+H	command-shift-H
preferences, general	ctrl+K	command-K
preferences, most recent panel	ctrl+alt+K	command-option-K
print options	ctrl+alt+P	command-option-P
proof colors	ctrl+Y	command-Y
purge all†	shift+F3	shift-F3
reselect	ctrl+shift+D	command-shift-D
revert†	F12	F12
rotate 90 degrees CW/CCW†	shift+F8/shift+F9	shift-F8/shift-F9
rotate 180 degrees†	shift+F10	shift-F10
rulers, show or hide	ctrl+R	command-R
save as	ctrl+shift+S	command-shift-S
save as a copy	ctrl+alt+S	command-option-S
save for web	ctrl+alt+shift+S	command-option-shift-S
select all	ctrl+A	command-A
select similar†	shift+F4	shift-F4
send layer backward/to back	ctrl+[/ctrl+shift+[	command-[/command-shift-[
show/hide extras	ctrl+H	command-H
show/hide grid	ctrl+alt+quote (')	command-option-quote (')
show/hide guides	ctrl+quote (')	command-quote (')
show/hide path	ctrl+shift+H	command-shift-H
snap to extras	ctrl+semicolon (;)	command-semicolon (;)
step backward	ctrl+alt+Z	command-option-Z
step forward	ctrl+shift+Z	command-shift-Z
transform again	ctrl+shift+T	command-shift-T
transform again with copy	ctrl+alt+shift+T	command-option-shift-T
undo/redo	ctrl+Z	command-Z
ungroup layers	ctrl+shift+G	command-shift-G
zoom in/out	ctrl+plus (+)/ctrl+minus (−)	command-plus (+)/minus (−)

Navigation & View Shortcuts

In the course of editing a piece of artwork, much of your time is spent just getting around the image window. You have to zoom in to check out a magnified cluster of pixels and then pop out to see how your edits fit into the larger image as a whole. Armed with these shortcuts, you'll fly around your image at the speed of thought. If you need more information, consult Chapter 3, Open, Navigate, Save.

Items marked with an asterisk (∗) assume default preference settings, which you can modify by choosing a command from the **Edit➧Preferences** submenu or by pressing **ctrl+K** (**command-K** on the Mac).

navigation or view task	windows shortcut	macintosh shortcut
scroll image with any tool	spacebar-drag	spacebar-drag
scroll up/down one screen	page up/down	page up/down
scroll left/right one screen	ctrl+page up/down	command-page up/down
scroll up/down a few pixels	shift+page up/down	shift-page up/down
scroll left/right a few pixels	ctrl+shift+page up/down	command-shift-page up/down
switch to upper-left corner	home	home
switch to lower-right corner	end	end
zoom in, change window size∗	ctrl+alt+plus (+)	command-plus (+)
zoom in, leave window unchanged∗	ctrl+plus (+)	command-option-plus (+)
zoom in at specific point	ctrl+spacebar-click	command-spacebar-click
zoom out, change window size∗	ctrl+alt+minus (–)	command-minus (–)
zoom out, leave window unchanged∗	ctrl+minus (–)	command-option-minus (–)
zoom out at specific point	alt+spacebar-click	option-spacebar-click
zoom to 100%	ctrl+alt+0	command-option-0
zoom to fit	ctrl+0	command-0
zoom to custom size	ctrl+spacebar-drag	command-spacebar-drag
apply zoom value, magnification box active	shift+enter	shift-return
display or hide rulers	ctrl+R	command-R
change unit of measure	right-click ruler	control-click ruler
reset ruler origin	double-click origin box	double-click origin box
display guides	ctrl+quote (')	command-quote (')
display grid	ctrl+alt+quote (')	command-option-quote (')
snap to guide or grid	ctrl+semicolon (;)	command-semicolon (;)
lock or unlock all guides	ctrl+alt+semicolon (;)	command-option-semicolon (;)
move guide	ctrl-drag guide	command-drag guide
snap guide to ruler tick marks	shift-drag guide	shift-drag guide
change guide color	ctrl-double-click guide	command-double-click guide
change guide orientation	ctrl+alt-drag guide	command-option-drag guide
fill screen with foreground window	F	F
fill screen with all windows	shift-click button in toolbox	shift-click button in toolbox
show menu bar in full-screen mode	shift+F	shift-F

Selection Shortcuts

Making and manipulating selections rank among Photoshop's most fundamental operations. In addition to the selection-related shortcuts that appear in Menu Command Shortcuts on pages 282 and 283—including **Select All**, **Deselect**, **Reselect**, and **Feather**—Photoshop offers a number of shortcuts dedicated to creating and manipulating selection outlines. Use the shortcuts in the following table to quickly move, combine, modify, and clone selections from the keyboard.

For complete information on working with marquees and selected pixels, read Chapter 5, Make Selections.

selection task	windows shortcut	macintosh shortcut
draw marquee from center outward	alt-drag	option-drag
constrain marquee to square or circle	shift-drag	shift-drag
move marquee as you draw it	spacebar-drag	spacebar-drag
add corner to straight-sided selection	alt-click with lasso tool	option-click with lasso tool
lock down point in magnetic selection	click with magnetic lasso tool	click with magnetic lasso tool
delete last point in magentic selection	backspace	delete
tighten or spread magnetic tool width	[or]	[or]
close lasso outline	enter or double-click	return or double-click
...with straight segment	alt+enter	option-return
cancel polygon or magnetic lasso outline	escape	escape
add to outline with selection tool	shift-drag/shift-click	shift-drag/shift-click
subtract from outline	alt-drag/alt-click	option-drag/option-click
retain intersection of outlines	shift+alt-drag/shift+alt-click	shift-option-drag/shift-option-click
select move tool	V or ctrl	V or command
move selection outline (selection tool)	drag	drag
move selected pixels (any tool)	ctrl-drag	command-drag
constrain movement	shift-drag	shift-drag
nudge outline in 1-/10-pixel increments	arrow/shift+arrow	arrow/shift-arrow
nudge pixels in 1-/10-pixel increments	ctrl+arrow/ctrl+shift+arrow	command-arrow/cmd-shift-arrow
clone selected pixels	ctrl+alt-drag	command-option-drag
nudge and clone	ctrl+alt+arrow	command-option-arrow
move outline to other image window	drag & drop	drag & drop
move selected pixels to other image	ctrl+drag & drop	command-drag & drop
paste image into selection	ctrl+shift+V	command-shift-V
paste image behind selection	ctrl+shift+alt+V	command-shift-option-V
change opacity of floating selection	ctrl+shift+F	command-shift-F
hide selection outline	ctrl+H	command-H
insert point into selected path (pen tool)	click segment	click segment
delete anchor point from selected path	click point	click point
convert anchor point in selected path	alt-click/alt-drag point	option-click/option-drag point
convert work path to selection outline	ctrl+enter	command-return

Fill, Paint, & Edit Shortcuts

When it comes to coloring, painting, and editing pixels in an image, Photoshop provides a bounty of keyboard tricks that can make your life much easier. The table below includes all the highlights. Commit these shortcuts to memory and you'll save yourself time, effort, and frustration.

Read Chapter 6, Apply Color & Gradients, for complete information on defining, applying, and editing colors. In particular, Backspace & Delete on page 85 contains additional details on applying fills from the keyboard. See Chapter 7, Paint & Retouch, for the lowdown on Photoshop's paint and edit tools.

fill, paint, or edit task	windows shortcut	macintosh shortcut
revert image with eraser tool	alt-drag	option-drag
specify area to clone with stamp tool	alt-click	option-click
sharpen with blur tool (& vice versa)	alt-drag	option-drag
darken with dodge/lighten with burn	alt-drag	option-drag
fingerpaint with smudge tool	alt-drag	option-drag
paint or edit in straight line	shift-click	shift-click
change opacity or pressure by 10%	1, 2, 3, ..., 0	1, 2, 3, ..., 0
change opacity or pressure by 1%	0-1, 0-2, 0-3, ..., 9-9	0-1, 0-2, 0-3, ..., 9-9
reduce or enlarge brush diameter	[or]	[or]
make brush softer or harder	shift+[or]	shift-[or]
cycle through brush modes	shift+plus (+) or minus (−)	shift-plus (+) or minus (−)
restore normal brush mode	shift+alt+N	shift-option-N
delete shape from brushes pop-up	alt-click brush shape	option-click brush shape
create new shape in brushes pop-up	click in empty area	click in empty area
lift foreground color with paint tool	alt-click	option-click
lift background color with eyedropper	alt-click	option-click
target color with eyedropper	shift-click	shift-click
delete color target	shift+alt-click	shift-option-click
display color palette	F6	F6
lift foreground color in colors palette	click color bar	click color bar
lift background color	alt-click color bar	option-click color bar
cycle through color bars	shift-click color bar	shift-click color bar
specify new color bar	right-click color bar	control-click color bar
delete swatch from swatches palette	ctrl-click swatch	command-click swatch
replace swatch with foreground color	shift-click swatch	shift-click swatch
fill with foreground color	alt+backspace	option-delete
...and preserve transparency	shift+alt+backspace	shift-option-delete
fill with background color	ctrl+backspace	command-delete
...and preserve transparency	shift+ctrl+backspace	shift-command-delete
fill selection with history source state	ctrl+alt+backspace	command-option-delete
display fill dialog box	shift+backspace	shift-delete

Layers & Channels Shortcuts

Layers and channels are easily a couple of Photoshop's most powerful and versatile features. Use these shortcuts to create, clone, move, modify, and select layers and channels. Read Chapter 8, Create & Modify Layers, and Chapter 10, Blend & Stylize Layers, for the full scoop on working with layers. In particular,

see Keyboard Tricks on page 139 for a complete list of blend mode shortcuts. Consult Chapter 9, Define Channels & Masks, for all your channel-related needs.

An asterisk (✳) indicates that you can add the **alt** (Win) or **option** (Mac) key to the shortcut to either display or bypass the **New Layer** dialog box.

layers or channels task	windows shortcut	macintosh shortcut
hide all layers but one (in layers palette)	alt-click eyeball	option-click eyeball
create new layer above current layer✳	ctrl+shift+N	command-shift-N
create new layer below current layer✳	ctrl-click new layer button	command-click new layer button
clone/cut selection to new layer✳	ctrl+J/ctrl+shift+J	command-J/command-shift-J
convert floating selection to layer✳	ctrl+shift+J	command-shift-J
duplicate layer to new layer	ctrl+A, ctrl+J	command-A, command-J
decend or ascend one layer	alt+[or]	option-[or]
select back or front layer	alt+shift+[or]	option-shift-[or]
activate layer containing image element	ctrl+alt-right-click element	cmd-option-control-click element
select from list of overlapping layers	ctrl-right-click element	command-control-click element
send layer backward or forward	ctrl+[or]	command-[or]
send layer to back or front of composition	ctrl+shift+[or]	command-shift-[or]
merge active layer with layer below	ctrl+E	command-E
clone contents of layer onto layer below	ctrl+alt+E	command-option-E
lock transparency of layer	slash (/)	slash (/)
move entire layer	ctrl-drag	command-drag
nudge layer in 1-/10-pixel increments	ctrl+arrow/ctrl+shift+arrow	command-arrow/cmd-shift-arrow
enter transformation mode	ctrl+T	command-T
switch between channels	ctr+1, 2, 3, ..., 9	command-1, 2, 3, ..., 9
create selection from channel	ctrl+alt+1, 2, 3, ..., 9	command-option-1, 2, 3, ..., 9
create selection from color image	ctrl+alt+tilde (~)	command-option-tilde (~)
activate or deactivate channel in palette	shift-click channel name	shift-click channel name
create alpha channel from selection✳	click save channel button	click save channel button
convert layer mask to selection outline	ctrl+alt+backslash (\)	command-option-backslash (\)
add mask to selection	ctrl+shift-click channel name	cmd-shift-click channel name
subtract mask from selection	ctrl+alt-click channel name	cmd-option-click channel name
retain intersection of mask and selection	ctrl+alt+shift-click channel	cmd-option-shift-click channel
switch focus to layer mask	ctrl+backslash (\)	command-backslash (\)
view layer mask as rubylith	backslash (\)	backslash (\)
toggle image visibility when editing mask	tilde (~)	tilde (~)
switch focus to image	ctrl+tilde (~)	command-tilde (~)

Shapes & Type Shortcuts

Shapes and type differ from other of Photoshop's layers in that they print at the maximum resolution of a PostScript-equipped printer. Yet despite their differences, both features conform to Adobe's core logic. Shapes sire from Photoshop's selections and paths (see Chapter 11). Text behaves like that in **Illustrator** or **InDesign** (Chapter 12). For example, when editing a type layer, ctrl+T and M (command-T and M) display the **Character** and **Paragraph** palettes, respectively.

Below, an asterisk (*) indicates that you can add the **alt** or **ctrl** key (**option** or **command** on the Mac) to increase the increment of the formatting adjustment.

shapes or type task	windows shortcut	macintosh shortcut
move shape as you draw it	spacebar-drag	spacebar-drag
constrain shape to square or circle	shift-drag	shift-drag
draw shape from center outward	alt-drag	option-drag
reduce sides in polygon by 1 or 10	[or shift+[	[or shift+[
increase sides in polygon by 1 or 10	] or shift+]	] or shift+]
reduce or increase line thickness	[or]	[or]
fill shape with image layer above it	ctrl+G	command-G
add clipping path to image layer	ctrl-click add mask button	command-click add mask button
hide shape outline	ctrl+shift+H	command-shift-H
activate/dismiss shape outline	enter	return
select arrow tool	A or ctrl	A or command
add selected outline to shape area	plus (+)	plus (+)
subtract selected outline from shape	minus (–)	minus (–)
select entire shape with white arrow	alt-click	option-click
move shape (shape or pen tool)	ctrl-drag	command-drag
clone shape (shape or pen tool)	ctrl+alt-drag	command-option-drag
create point/paragraph text (type tool)	click/drag	click/drag
commit/cancel text layer	ctrl+enter/esc	command-return/esc
select all text on layer	double-click T in palette	double-click T in palette
...when text layer is active	ctrl+A	command-A
rename text layer	alt-double-click layer name	option-double-click layer name
select word/paragraph with type tool	double-/triple-click	double-/triple-click
select word to left or right	ctrl+shift+← or →	command-shift-← or →
insert paragraph/line break	enter/shift+enter	return/shift-return
fill type with foreground color	alt+backspace	option-delete
decrease or increase type size by 2*	ctrl+shift+< or >	command-shift-< or >
tighten or expand leading by 2 pixels*	alt+↑ or ↓	option-↑ or ↓
kern together or apart by $^{20}/1000$ em*	alt+← or →	option-← or →
raise or lower baseline by 2*	shift+alt+↑ or ↓	shift-option-↑ or ↓
align paragraph left, center, or right	ctrl+shift+L, C, or R	command-shift-L, C, or R
justify paragraph/including last line	ctrl+shift+J/ctrl+shift+F	command-shift-J/command-shift-F

index

X

Look It Up & Learn

Sections @ A Glance

This unique index combines words and pictures to help you locate the exact topic you're looking for.

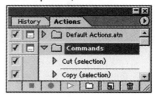

GO

3-D effects, 223

3D Transform filter, 223

90 degrees CCW command, 26

90 degrees CW command, 26

100% view, 40
   command-option-0 (Mac) keyboard shortcut, 40
   ctrl+alt+0 (Win) keyboard shortcut, 40

180 degrees command, 26

 A

A key (select the arrow tool), 77

actions, 239
   active, 241
   append operations to, 241
   as buttons, 242
   cancel, 12
   clean up, 245
   delete, 242

actions, *continued*
   flip tabs, 240
   group, 240
   keyboard shortcuts, 243
   load, 242
   names, 240
   record, 240–241
   record over, 242
   replace, 242
   reset, 242
   save, 242
   save as droplet, 246
   sets, 240
   test, 245

Actions palette, 240–242

empty, 242

Index

Index

 continued
(begins on page 289)

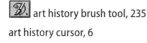 art history brush tool, 235

art history cursor, 6

artifacts, 216

Artistic filters, 229

aspect ratio, 63

 audio annotation tool, 50

audio icon, 51

Auto Contrast command, 208

Auto Levels command, 208

auto slices, 272–273

.axt file extension, 117

 B

B key (select the paintbrush tool), 92

background color
    default, 81
    fill with, 94
    paint, 93
    toolbox swatch, 81

background eraser cursor, 119

 background eraser tool, 119

Background layer, 104
    composition lacking, 131
    empty, 168

banding, 87

baseline, 59

baseline shift, 173

Batch dialog box, 248

batch processing, 247–248

Behind mode, 98
    shift+alt+Q (Win) keyboard
    shortcut, 98

bevel effects, 150

bevels, 150–151
    command-5 (Mac) keyboard
    shortcut, 150
    ctrl+5 (Win) keyboard shortcut, 150

black-and-white printing, 59

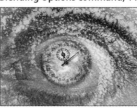 black arrow tool, 77

bleed, 253

blend
    brushstrokes, 99
    channels, 129
    clipping group in composition,
    143
    layers, 142–143
    layers in clipping group, 143
    multicolored layers, 140

blend modes
    adjustment layers, 210
    bevels, 151
    Color Overlay effect, 152
    glows, 148
    history brush, 234
    keyboard shortcuts, 139
    layer sets, 106

blend modes, *continued*
    layers, 136–139
    paint and edit, 98–99
    Satin effect, 152
    shapes, 161
    strokes, 154
    switch between, 99
    text, 177
    turn off, 98

blended colors, 99

Blending Options command, 142–144

blown highlights, 186

Blur filter, 219

blur filters, 219

Blur More filter, 219

 blur tool, 94

blurring bevels, 150

blurry brushes, 101

Border command, 68

borders, 33

bounding box
    layers, 107
    paths, 77
    text, 171

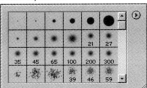
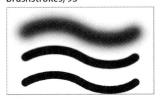

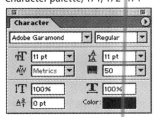

Index

 continued
(begins on page 292)

Choose Background Image dialog box, 275

cleanup tool, 121

clear
    all slices, 273
    history states, 233

Clear History command, 233

clicking, 7

clipped colors, 185

clipper, 134

clipping group, 131

command-G (Mac) keyboard shortcut, 167

ctrl+G (Win) keyboard shortcut, 167

clipping layers, 134

Clipping Path dialog box, 260

clipping paths, 77
    add to adjustment layer, 210
    add to layer, 168
    export, 260
    shapes, 159

clone, 71

images, 6
pixels, 94

clone cursor, 6

 clone stamp tool, 94

close button, 4

Clouds filter, 223

CMS (color management system), 251

CMYK (cyan, magenta, yellow, and black) color model, 82

CMYK dots, 227

CMYK images, 59
    brightness curve, 201
    channels, 125
    convert RGB images to, 254–255

CMYK profiles, 254-255

CMYK Sliders command, 80

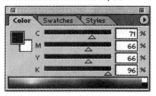

CMYK (cyan, magenta, yellow, and black) space, 59–60

CMYK values, 21

color bar, 80–81

Color Burn mode, 138

color casts, 184
    fix 186–189

color controls, 8

color correction, 183

Color Dodge mode, 138

Color Halftone filter, 227

color management policies, 59

Color mode
    change, 125
    layers, 139
    paint and edit, 99
    shift+alt+C (Win) keyboard shortcut, 139
    shift-option-C (Mac) keyboard shortcut, 139

color model, change, 80–81

Color Overlay effect, 152

Color palette, 80–81

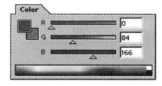

F6 keyboard shortcut, 80

color photographs, print, 250–251

Color Picker dialog box, 81

color profiles, 59

Color Range command, 116–117
    alt+S (Win) keyboard shortcut, 116

Color Range dialog box, 116–117

color sampler tool, 82

Color Settings dialog box, 58–59
    command-shift-K (Mac) keyboard shortcut, 254
    ctrl+shift+K (Win) keyboard shortcut, 254

color stops, 88

Color Table, 266

Index

 continued
(begins on page 292)

colorize
  images, 99
  layers or selections, 191

colors, 183
  adjust channels, 195
  adjust range of, 116–117

  adjustment layers, 209–210
  annotation icons, 51
  assign to layers, 106
  average pixels, 82
  background, 80
  base selection on, 117
  baseline, 59
  brightness, 186
  brightness levels, 80
  change vibrancy, 95
  channels, 125–126
  clipped, 185
  CMYK values, 21
  collect, 83
  Color Overlay effect, 152
  correct with layers, 211–212
  darken, 186
  dodge & burn range, 95
  drop shadow, 146
  equalize, 208
  foreground, 80
  gamma, 196
  glows, 148
  high-definition TV screen, 59

colors, *continued*
  histogram, 195
  hues, 190–191
  inner shadow, 146

  input levels, 201
  intensity, 95
  invert, 99
  layers, 112
  lift from images, 81
  lighten, 186, 201
  lightness, 190
  load settings, 185
  management, 58–59
  mix, 80
  organize, 83
  output levels, 201
  predefined range of, 116
  preserve darker or lighter, 99
  preset options, 58
  preview, 191
  primaries, 79
  range of, 191
  reduce number of, 208
  remap, 204
  remove prevalent, 184
  replace, 80
  RGB values, 21
  sample and erase, 119
  Satin effect, 152
  saturation, 185, 189–191
  save settings, 185
  set to black and white, 208
  settings, 58
  slices, 273
  strength of adjustment, 185
  temporarily mask, 144–145

colors, *continued*
  text, 171, 173
  thumbnail previews, 184
  transparent range of, 119
  unprintable, 185
  upset balance of, 197–198
  variations, 186
  visually adjust, 80
  Web-safe, 267
  Web-safe palette, 271

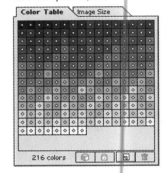

  working spaces, 58

ColorSync, 251

combine
  paths, 77
  shapes, 161

command key (Mac), 13

commands, 10–11
  custom keyboard shortcuts, 243
  keyboard shortcuts, 282–283

Commands.atn, 283

committing text, 171

common work path, 167

completing paths, 76–77

Index

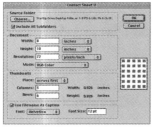

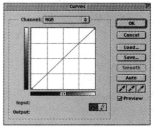

Index

Index

Index

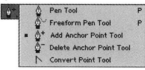

Index

 continued
(begins on page 298)

fractional widths, 174

Fragment filter, 227

Free Transform command, 108–111

Free Transform mode, 167
  command-T (Mac) keyboard
    shortcut, 109–110
  ctrl+T (Win) keyboard shortcut,
    109–110

freeform outlines, 74

 freeform pen tool, 74–75

freeform selection outline, 64

full-image preview, 16

full-screen view, 9

function keys, 12
  F1 for Help, 18
  F2 for Flatten Image command, 282
  F6 for Color palette, 80
  F7 for Layers palette, 104
  F8 for Info palette, 21
  F9 for Actions palette, 240
  F10 for Navigator palette, 281
  F11 for Image Size command, 282
  F12 for Revert command, 233

G

G key (select the gradient tool), 87

Gallery Effects filters, 229

gamma, 196

Gaussian Blur filter, 219

General panel, preferences, 53
  command-K (Mac) keyboard
    shortcut, 53
  ctrl+K (Win) keyboard shortcut, 53

geometric shapes, 158

GIF (Graphics Interchange Format)
  files, 265
  save, 270–271

Glass filter, 224

Glowing Edges filter, 226

glows, 148–149

glyphs, 175

go to ImageReady button, 9

Gradient command, 162

Gradient Editor dialog box, 88

Gradient Fill dialog box, 162

Gradient Map command, 204

Gradient Map dialog box, 204

gradient presets, 204

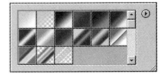

gradient thumbnail, 57

 gradient tool, 87

gradients, 79

gradients, *continued*
  design, 87–89
  dithering, 87, 204
  edit color stops, 88
  glows, 148–149
  layers, 153
  limit color range, 89
  midpoints, 88
  name, 89
  noise, 89
  orientation of color, 153
  preset, 87–88
  preset as channel-by-channel
    curve, 204
  printable CMYK colors, 89
  random levels of translucency, 89
  resize, 153
  reverse color order, 87
  reverse direction of, 204
  roughness, 89
  set angle, 153
  smoothness, 89
  styles, 87
  translucent areas, 87
  transparency stops, 88

grayscale images, 60
  colorize, 99
  convert layers or selections to, 191
  monotone, 256

Grayscale Slider command, 81

grayscale space, 59

group actions, 240

Group with Previous command, 134
  command-G (Mac) keyboard
    shortcut, 134
  ctrl+G (Win) keyboard shortcut, 134

Grow command, 67

H

H key (select the hand tool), 38

Index

 continued
(begins on page 300)

hair, select, 128–130

halftone cells, 59, 253

halftone dots, 221, 227

halftone screen, 253

Halftone Screens dialog box, 253

halftones, 25

    descreen scanned, 221–222

 hand tool, 38

hanging indent, 175

hard brushes, 101

Hard Light mode, 138

help document, 18

help.htm file, 18

Help menu, 11

    Contents (Win) command, 18

    Help Contents (Mac) command, 18

hide

    application window, 4.

    cropped areas, 28, 31

    images, 4

    layers, 104

    menu bars, 9

    options bar, 9

    paths, 77

    sampler targets, 82

    slices, 273

hide and show notes, 51

Hide Color Sampler command, 82

Hide Extras command, 68

    command-H (Mac) keyboard
        shortcut, 68

    ctrl+H (Win) keyboard shortcut, 68

Hide Others command, 5

hide/show item, 17

hide/show menu bar (shift-F)
    keyboard shortcut, 9

hide/show toolbox and palettes (tab)
    keyboard shortcut, 9

High Pass filter, 228

highlight text, 7

highlights

    create, 140

    lighten or darken, 186

histogram, Levels command, 195

Histogram window, 202

 history brush tool, 234

    blend modes, 234

    opacity, 234

    presets, 234

    size and opacity of brushstroke, 235

    size and shape, 234

    source, 238

History Options command, 233

History palette, 232–233

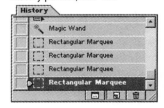

History palette, *continued*

    number of undos, 54

History palette menu, 236

history states, 232

    save as snapshot, 233

    step forward and backward
        through, 233

hold cursor, 7

"horned" lasso cursor, 64

hover mouse, 7

HSL (hue, saturation, and luminosity)
    color model, 13, 190

HTML colors, 81

HTML pages, define and export,
    274–276

Hue blend mode, 191

hue metrics, 191

Hue mode, 139

hues, 190–191

Hue/Saturation command, 190

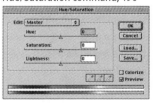

    command-U (Mac) keyboard
        shortcut, 190

    ctrl+U (Win) keyboard shortcut, 190

Hue/Saturation dialog box, 190–191

hyphenate text, 175

Hyphenation command, 175

Hyphenation dialog box, 175

I key (select the eyedropper tool), 81

Index

Index

Index

continued
(begins on page 304)

layers, *continued*
  move selections to, 114
  name, 104–105
  Opacity value, 136
  outer glow, 148
  overlapping shapes, 161

  paint behind pixels, 98
  paint inside and behind, 132
  reduce opacity, 136
  rename, 106
  repeating patterns, 153
  resize thumbnails, 106
  rotate or flip, 109
  save, 43
  selection outline from, 66
  shape, 105
  source state fills, 84
  styles, 146–154
  switch, 107
  temporarily mask colors, 144–145
  temporary strokes, 154
  text, 105
  thumbnails, 104
  trace boundaries, 90
  trace outline, 154
  transform, 107
  transformations, 108–111
  translucent, 106, 136

layers, *continued*
  transparency mask, 136
  update content, 162
  view content, 159
  view styles, 106

Layers palette, 104–106

  add folder to, 144
  adjustment layers, 209
  Background layer, 167
  Background option, 31
  blend modes, 137–139
  Channels tab, 125
  effects markers, 149
  F7 keyboard shortcut, 104
  layer content thumbnail, 166
  Lock box, 106
  New Layer button, 105
  Overlay item, 168
  Paths tab, 78

layer-specific masks, 131

leading, 173

Lens Flare filter, 223

Less Saturation thumbnail, 185

letter keys, 13

Levels command, 194
  command-L (Mac) keyboard
    shortcut, 195
  ctrl+L (Win) keyboard shortcut, 195
  incrementally undoing, 199

Levels dialog box, 194

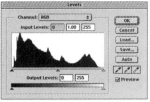

  Auto button, 197
  brightness levels black, 195
  Channel pop-up menu, 195
  gamma, 196
  histogram, 195
  increase contrast, 195
  Input Levels values, 197–198

ligatures, 173

Lighten mode
  layers, 138
  paint and edit, 99
  shift+alt+G (Win) keyboard
    shortcut, 139
  shift-option-G (Mac) keyboard
    shortcut, 139

lightening
  amount of, 99
  badly lit areas, 95
  blended colors, 99
  colors, 186

Lighter thumbnail, 186

lighting effects, 223

Lighting Effects filter, 223

lightness, 190

Index

Index

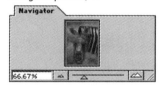

continued
(begins on page 307)

Index

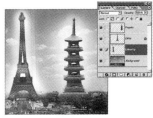

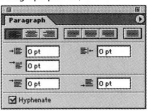

Index

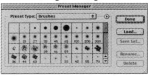

Index

 continued
(begins on page 309)

print, *continued*
 number of pixels, 23
 output and color management, 252
 page preview, 252
 per inch or centimeter, 23
 position, 252
 preview, 15
 printer's marks, 253
 quality, 251
 resize image, 25
 scale image, 250
 scaled print size, 252
 spot color, 258–259
 vector data, 253

Print dialog box, 250–251, 253

Print Options command, 252
 command-option-P (Mac)
  keyboard shortcut, 250
 ctrl+alt+P (Win) keyboard
  shortcut, 250

Print Options dialog box, 252–253

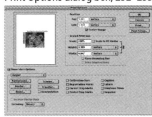

printer drivers, 250

printers
 CMS (color management
  system), 251
 compensate for, 253

printer's marks, 253

process-color keys, 59

Properties dialog box, 251

PSD files
 minimize size of, 54
 save, 45

Q key (switch to quick mask mode), 122

quadtone, 256

QuarkXPress, prepare images for, 21, 254–255

quick mask mode, 122
 refine selection with, 123–124

Quick Mask Options dialog box, 122

R key (select the blur tool), 95

Radial Blur filter, 219

radio buttons, 16

randomizing noise gradient, 89

rasterizing, 213
 type, 182

reapply filter, keyboard shortcut
 command-F (Mac), 215
 ctrl+F (Win), 215

reapply filter with different settings,
 keyboard shortcut
  command-option-F (Mac), 215
  ctrl+alt+F (Win) keyboard, 215

recent files, 54

recolor elements, 192–193

record
 actions, 240–241
 addition of paths, 242
 audio annotation, 51
 multistep actions, 244–245
 over actions, 242
 states out of order, 233

Record dialog box, 50–51

 rectangle tool, 158

rectangles, 158

 rectangular marquee tool, 62

red-eye, eliminate, 206–207

redisplay images, 4

reduce
 canvas, 32
 focus of images, 94
 number of colors, 208
 palettes, 17

registration marks, 253

relocate palettes, 17

remap colors, 204

Index

 continued
(begins on page 312)

remove
 color casts, 186
 prevalent color, 184
rename
 layers, 106e
 presets, 57
Render filters, 223
repeat transformations, 108
replace
 actions, 242
 image element with another, 72–73
 selection outline, 69
resample images, 23–24
Reselect command, 68
 command-shift-D (Mac) keyboard shortcut, 68
 ctrl+shift+D (Win) keyboard shortcut, 68
reselect pixels, 68
reset actions, 242
Reset Swatches command, 83
reshape paths, 161
resize, 32
 bevels, 150
 Color Overlay effect, 152
 glows, 149
 gradients, 153
 images, 22–23
 path thumbnails, 77
 Preset Manager dialog box, 57
 Satin effect, 152
 selection outline, 71
 Web graphics, 267
 windows, 5
 window with zoom tool, 39
resolution, 22, 25
restore button, 4

Restore command, 4
Restrict Selection button, 69
retouch photographs, 101–102
reverse
 brightness levels, 208

 direction of gradients, 204
 selected and deselected pixels, 117
revert selections, 233
revert settings to default, keyboard shortcut
 alt+escape (Win), 12
 option-escape (Mac), 12
RGB devices, 58
RGB images, 60
 brightness curve, 201
 channels, 125
 convert to CMYK images, 254–255
 display of, 58–59
 split, 126
RGB (red, green, and blue) color model, 82
RGB Sliders command, 80
RGB space, 60
RGB values, 21
right-angle rotations, 109
right-clicking, 7
Ripple filter, 225

roman hanging punctuation, 175
rotate
 crop boundary, 28
 images, 26
 layers, 108
 selection outline, 71
Rotate Canvas commands, 26
Rotate command, 108
rotate cursor, 28
Rough Pastels filter, 229

 rounded rectangle tool, 158
Rubber Band option, 75
 rubber stamp tool, 94
rubylith, 123
ruler guides, 21
rulers
 command-R (Mac) keyboard shortcut, 14
 ctrl+R (Win) keyboard shortcut, 14
 display, 20
 origin, 20
 ruler guide, 21
 shortcut menu, 20

S

S key (select the rubber stamp tool), 94
Sample Size pop-up menu, 82
sampler targets, 82
Satin effect, 152

continued
(begins on page 313)

Index

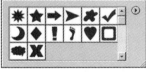

continued
(begins on page 313)

shapes, *continued*
 patterns, 162
 select path, 161
 solid color fill, 162, 166
 star, 164
 transformation handles, 161
 vector-based, 159

Sharpen Edges filter, 214

Sharpen filter, 214

sharpen images, 214–216

Sharpen More filter, 214

 sharpen tool, 95

Shear filter, 225

shift key, 12

shortcut menu key, 13

shortcut menus, 14

Show Color Samplers command, 82

Show Rulers command, 20
 command-R (Mac) keyboard
 shortcut, 20
 ctrl+R (Win) keyboard shortcut, 20

Show Status Bar command, 5, 15

shrink icon (Mac), 4

single column marquee tool, 62

single row marquee tool, 62

size box
 image window, 5
 palette, 17

Sketch filters, 229

Skew command, 108

skew images, 108–109

slant selection outline, 71

Slice Options dialog box, 273

slice select tool, 272
 in Save For Web dialog box, 264

slice tool, 272

slices, 273

slicing images, 272–273

Slide Show, keyboard shortcut
 control-tab (Mac), 9
 ctrl+tab (Win), 9

slider bar, 16

Small List command, 83

Small Thumbnails command, 83

Smart Blur filter, 219

smear pixels, 95

smooth point, 75

smudge tool, 95

snapshots
 name, 236
 preserve state as, 233

Soft Light mode, 138

soft strokes, 90

soft transitions, 117

soften focus, 219

software, 49

Solarize filter, 226

solid color fills, 162

source images, update, 54

source state, 232
 fill layer or selection with, 84
 paint, 234–235
 revert images to, 118

space after paragraphs, 175

space before paragraphs, 175

spacebar, 13

Spatter brushes, 100

Spherize filter, 224

Split Channels command, 126

split RGB images, 126

sponge tool, 95

spot color channel, 126

spot colors, 258–259
 dot gain, 59
 save, 44

Stained Glass filter, 229

standard image window, 9

Standard Macintosh Color command, 265

Standard Windows Color command, 265

star, 164

starfish, 164

Start➞Settings➞Control Panel
 command, 51

Index

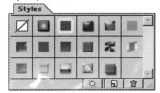
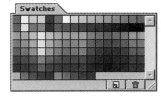

Index

 continued
(begins on page 317)

text, *continued*
  faux styles, 173
  fonts, 170
  formatting options, 172–175

  fractional widths, 174
  friendly effect, 181
  glyphs, 175
  highlight, 7
  horizontal distortion, 179
  horizontal scale, 173
  hyphenate, 175
  justification, 174, 175
  kerning, 172
  leading, 173
  ligatures, 173
  mystery effect, 181

  old style figures, 173
  prevent hyphenation, 174
  rotate, 173
  subscript, 173
  superscript, 173
  tracking, 173
  type size, 171–172
  type style, 170, 172
  vector-based, 169–170
  vertical distortion, 179
  vertical scale,173
  warp along curve, 178–179
text layers, 105, 171
text notes, 50

text-editing mode, 171
Texture Fill filter, 223
Texture filters, 229
texture map and bevels, 151
Threshold command, 208
thumbnails, 41
  arrange, 262
  folder of images as, 261–262
  layers, 104
  preview, 37
  resize for paths, 77
TIFF Options dialog box, 46
TIFF (tag image file format) files, 46
Tiles filter, 226

title bars, 2
tool tips, 5
toolbox, 8
  annotation, color, and navigation
    tools, 8
  arrow tool slot, 77
  buttons, 8
  color controls, 8
  full-screen view, 9
  go to ImageReady button, 9
  keyboard shortcuts, 280
  lasso tool slot, 64
  marquee tool slot, 62
  paint, edit, and fill tools, 8
  pen tool slot, 74
  quick mask mode, 9
  selection and crop tools, 8
  shape tool slot, 158
  swap foreground and background
    colors, 81

toolbox, *continued*
  tools, 8
  type and vector drawing tools, 8
tools, 8
  change behavior of, 9
  keyboard shortcuts, 5
  modify behavior of, 3
  restore default settings, 14, 54
  select, 8
  switch, 13
Total Training Web site, 8, 130
touch cursor, 7
touch up masks, 130
trace
  boundaries layers, 90
  images, 120
  outlines, 90
Trace Contour filter, 226

tracking, 173
Transfer Functions dialog box, 253
transform
  layers, 107

  selection outline, 70
Transform Again command, 108
  command-shift-T (Mac) keyboard
    shortcut, 108
  ctrl+shift+T (Win) keyboard
    shortcut, 108
transform boundary, 70

Index

Index

 continued
(begins on page 319)

vector-based text, 169–170

video filters, 228

View menu, 11

    Actual Pixels command, 40

    Fit on Screen command, 40

    Lock Slices command, 273

    New View command, 40, 102

    Print Size command, 40

    Show Rulers command, 20

    Zoom In command, 39

    Zoom Out command, 39

View➡Show submenu

    Notes command, 51

    Selection Edges command, 68, 207

    Show Extra Options command, 68

    Slices command, 273

views, 102

    keyboard shortcuts, 284

virtual memory, 55

voice messages, 50

W key (select the magic wand tool), 66

wait cursor, 7

warp orientation, 178–179

warp styles, 178

Warp Text dialog box, 178–179

Wave filter, 225

Web, save images for, 264–265

Web browsers and previewing Web
    graphics, 266

Web Color Sliders command, 81

Web graphics, 266–267

web offset printing, 59

Web Photo Gallery, 277–278

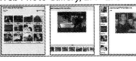

Web sites, connect to, 52

Web-safe color bar command, 81

Web-safe colors, 81, 267, 271

 white arrow tool, 77

white space, trim away from images, 34

Wind filter, 226, 236

Window menu, 11

    Show Actions command, 240

    Show Channels command, 125

    Show Character command, 172

    Show History command, 232

    Show Info command, 21

    Show Layers command, 104

    Show Navigator command, 41

    Show Paragraph command, 174

    Show Paths command, 76

    Show Styles command, 156

Windows, 1

    application title bar, 2

    arrow cursor, 6

    keyboard shortcuts, 12–13

    Open command, 36

    Photoshop desktop, 2

    record audio annotation, 51

    Save command, 42

    shortcut menu key, 13

Windows, *continued*

    taskbar, 4

windows

    resize, 5

    scroll, 4

    scroll images in, 7

    Start menu, 13

windows key (Win), 13

Windows\System\Color directory, 254

working spaces, 58

X key (swap foreground and
    background colors), 81

X option box, in Slice Options dialog
    box, 273

Y key (select the history brush tool), 234

Y option box, in Slice Options dialog
    box, 273

Z key (select the zoom tool), 39

Zigzag filter, 225

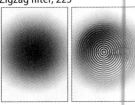

ZIP compression, 46

zoom icon (Mac), 4

zoom images, 39, 41

 zoom tool, 39

zoom value, 5